M000196917

HUGH JOHNSON'S POCKET ENCYCLOPEDIA OF WINE 1987

10TH ANNIVERSARY EDITION

Published by Simon & Schuster Inc.
Filmset by Vantage Photosetting Co. Ltd, Eastleigh and London
Printed in Hong Kong by Mandarin Offset International (H.K.) Ltd

**A Fireside Book
Published by Simon & Schuster, Inc.
New York**

KEY TO SYMBOLS

r.	red	
p.	rosé	(in brackets) means relatively unimportant
w.	white	
br.	brown	
sw.	sweet	
s/sw.	semi-sweet	
dr.	dry	
sp.	sparkling	

★	plain, everyday quality
★★	above average
★★★	well known, highly reputed
★★★★	grand, prestigious, expensive
☐	usually particularly good value in its class

83 84 etc.

    recommended years which may be currently available.

82' etc. Vintage regarded as particularly successful for the property in question.

80 etc. years in **bold** should be ready for drinking (the others should be kept). Where both reds and whites are indicated the red is intended unless otherwise stated.

    N.B. German vintages are codified by a different system. See note on p. 99.

D.Y.A. drink the youngest available

NV vintage not normally shown on label

Cross-references are in SMALL CAPS

See p. 5 for extra explanation

A quick-reference vintage chart for France and Germany appears on p. 191.

© 1977 Mitchell Beazley Publishers
Text © Hugh Johnson 1977, 1978, 1979, 1980, 1981, 1982, 1983, 1984, 1985, 1986
First edition published 1977
Revised editions published 1978, 1979, 1980, 1981, 1982, 1983, 1984, 1985, 1986
© 1986 Mitchell Beazley Publishers
A Fireside Book
Published by Simon & Schuster, Inc.
Simon & Schuster Building
1230 Avenue of the Americas
New York, New York 10020

ISBN 0-671-63328-7
Library of Congress Catalog Card Number 86–17698

The author and publishers will be grateful for any information which will assist them in keeping future editions up to date. Although all reasonable care has been taken in the preparation of this book, neither the publishers nor the author can accept any liability for any consequences arising from the use thereof, or from the information contained herein.

Editors Alison Franks, Kathie Gill
Production Androulla Pavlou
Senior Executive Editor Chris Foulkes
Senior Executive Art Editor Roger Walton
Filmsetting by Vantage Photosetting Co. Ltd. Eastleigh and London
Printed in Hong Kong by Mandarin Offset International (H.K.) Ltd.

Contents

Introduction

This is the tenth annual edition of what I suppose must have become the world's most-consulted wine reference book. These ten years have been the most tumultuous in wine's long history. The general trend has been steadily better quality from more and more proficient producers in more and more regions. Some of the exciting themes have been an astonishing run of good vintages in Bordeaux, the most imported wine region of all, the appearance of beautiful new wines from places where ten years ago there were none, and on the darker side some well-publicized (and in one case truly tragic) scandals.

I described this book in its original Introduction as an exercise in crowding angels on a pinhead, or students into a telephone box. That was in 1977, when I thought it was pretty ingenious to use symbols and a few abbreviations to make a pocketable encyclopedia. Looking back at the first edition I realize that I was hardly squeezing at all compared with later efforts. Experience has taught me how to get angels to stand on other angels' shoulders, how to pick pygmy students, starve them and then shove like a Tokyo train-filler.

This book is admittedly 48 pages longer than its prototype, but it contains at least twice as much information: on properties, appellations, brands, vintages, drinkability, values and the rest. If the grammar is sometimes so terse as to be nonexistent, it is at least consistent with my object: to waste no words, to be up-to-the-minute, to be as thorough and complete as possible — all in the cause of helping you get the most possible pleasure from wine.

The arrangement of the book is intended to be as helpful as possible when you are buying a bottle, whether you are on the nursery slopes or an old hand with a bad memory. You are faced with a list of wines or an array of bottles in a restaurant, wine merchant's or bottle store. Your mind goes blank. You fumble for your little book. All you need to establish is what country a wine comes from. Look up the principal words on the label in the appropriate country's section. You will find enough potted information to let you judge whether this is the wine you want.

Specifically, you will find information on the colour and type of wine, its status or prestige, whether it is usually particularly good value, which vintages are good and which are ready to drink — and often considerably more . . . about the quantity made, the grapes used, ownership and the rest. Hundreds of cross-references help you delve further.

How to read an entry

The top line of most entries consists of the following information in an abbreviated form.

1. Which part of the country in question the wine comes from. (References to the maps in this book.)
2. Whether it is red, rosé or white (or brown/amber), dry, sweet or sparkling, or several of these.
3. Its general standing as to quality: a necessarily rough and ready guide based principally on an ascending scale:

   ★ plain, everyday quality
   ★★ above average
   ★★★ well known, highly reputed
   ★★★★ grand, prestigious, expensive

So much is more or less objective. Additionally there is a subjective rating: a box round the stars of any wine which in my experience is usually particularly good (which means good value) within its price range. There are good everyday wines as well as good luxury wines. The box system helps you find them.

4. Vintage information: which were the more successful of the recent vintages which *may* still be available. And of these which are ready to drink this year, and which will probably improve with keeping. Your first choice for current drinking should be one of the vintage years printed in **bold** type. Buy light-type years for further maturing.

The German vintage information works on a different principle: see the Introduction to Germany, page 99.

Acknowledgements

This store of detailed recommendations comes partly from my own notes and partly from those of a great number of kind friends. Without the generous help and co-operation of every single member of the wine trade I have approached, I would not have attempted it. I particularly want to thank the following for giving me material help with research or in the areas of their special knowledge.

Rodrigo Alvarado	Miles Lambert-Gócs
Burton Anderson	Tim Marshall
Anthony Barton	Patrick Matthews
Jean-Claude Berrouet	Christian Moueix
Tim Bleach	David Peppercorn M.W.
Michael Broadbent M.W.	István Pusztai
Alain de Courseulles	Alain Querre
Len Evans	Jan and Maite Read
Dereck Foster	Belle Rhodes
Chris Foulkes	Dr. Bernard Rhodes
Francis Fouquet	Dr. Bruno Roncarati
Jean-Paul Gardère	Steven Spurrier
Rosemary George M.W.	Serena Sutcliffe M.W.
James Halliday	Hugh Suter M.W.
Robert Hart M.W.	Bob Thompson
Peter Hasslacher	Peter Vinding-Diers
Ian Jamieson M.W.	Manfred Völpel
Graham Knox	James Walker
Matt Kramer	David Wolfe
Tony Laithwaite	

Grape varieties

The most basic of all differences between wines stems from the grapes they are made of. Centuries of selection have resulted in each of the long-established wine-areas having its favourite single variety, or a group of varieties whose juice or wine is blended together. Red burgundy is made of one grape, the Pinot Noir; red Bordeaux of three or four: two kinds of Cabernet, Merlot, Malbec and sometimes others. The laws say which grapes must be used, so the labels assume it.

So in newer vineyards the choice of a grape is the planter's single must crucial decision. Where he is proud of it, and intends his wine to have the character of a particular grape, the variety is the first thing he puts on the label—hence the useful, originally Californian, term "varietal wine".

A knowledge of grape varieties, therefore, is the single most helpful piece of knowledge in finding wines you will like wherever they are grown. Learn to recognize the characters of the most important. At least seven—Cabernet, Pinot Noir, Riesling, Sauvignon Blanc, Chardonnay, Gewürztraminer and Muscat—have memorable tastes and smells distinct enough to form international categories of wine.

Further notes on grapes will be found on page 150 (for California) and in the sections on Germany, Italy, central and south-east Europe, South Africa, etc.

The following are the best and commonest wine grapes.

Grapes for white wine

Aligoté

Burgundy's second-rank white grape. Crisp (often sharp) wine, needs drinking young. Perfect for mixing with cassis (blackcurrant liqueur) to make a "Kir".

Blanc Fumé

Another name for SAUVIGNON BLANC, referring to the "smoky" smell of the wine, particularly on the upper Loire. Makes some of California's best whites.

Bual

Makes sweet Madeira wines.

Chardonnay

The white burgundy grape, one of the grapes of Champagne, and the best white grape of California and more recently Australia. Gives dry wine of rich complexity, especially when aged some months in new barrels. Italy, Spain, New Zealand, E. Europe all now make good Chardonnays.

Chasselas

A prolific and widely grown early-ripening grape with full flavour, also grown for eating. Best known as Fendant in Switzerland, Gutedel in Germany. Perhaps the same as Hungary's Leanyka and Romania's Feteasca.

Chenin Blanc

The leading white grape of the middle Loire (Vouvray, Layon, etc.). Wine can be dry or sweet (or very sweet), but always retains plenty of acidity—hence its popularity in California, where it can make fine wine, but is rarely so used. See also STEEN.

Clairette

A dull neutral grape widely used in the s. of France.

Fendant

See CHASSELAS

Folle Blanche

The third most widely grown grape of France, though nowhere making fine wine. High acid and little flavour makes it ideal for brandy. Known as Gros Plant in Brittany, Picpoul in the Midi. Perhaps at its best in California.

Furmint

A grape of great character: the trade mark of Hungary both in Tokay and as vivid vigorous table wine with an appley flavour. Called Sipon in Yugoslavia.

Gewürztraminer (or Traminer)

The most pungent wine grape, distinctively spicy to smell and taste, with flavours often identified as like rose petals or grapefruit. Wines are often rich and soft, even when fully dry. Best in Alsace; also good in Germany, eastern Europe, Australia, California, New Zealand.

Grüner Veltliner

An Austrian speciality. Round Vienna and in the Wachau and Weinviertel can be delicious: light but dry and lively. For drinking young.

Italian Riesling

Grown in n. Italy and all over central eastern Europe. Inferior to German or Rhine Riesling with lower acidity, but a fair all-round grape. Alias Wälschriesling, Olaszreisling (but no longer legally labelled "Riesling").

Kerner

The most successful of a wide range of recent German varieties, largely made by crossing Riesling and Sylvaner (but in this case Riesling and [red] Trollinger). Early-ripening, flowery wine with good acidity. Popular in RHEINPFALZ, RHEINHESSEN, etc.

Malvasia

Known as Malmsey in Madeira, Malvasia in Italy, Malvoisie in France. Alias Vermentino. Also grown in Greece, Spain, W. Australia, eastern Europe. Makes rich brown wines or soft whites with great potential, not often realized.

Müller-Thurgau

Dominant variety in Germany's Rheinhessen and Rheinpfalz; said to be a cross between Riesling and Sylvaner. Ripens early to make soft flowery wines to drink young. Makes good sweet wines but seldom excels. Grows well in Austria, England.

Muscadet

Makes light, very dry wines round Nantes in Brittany. They should not be sharp, but faintly salty, savoury and v. refreshing.

Muscat (many varieties)

Universally grown easily recognized pungent grape, mostly made into perfumed sweet wines, often fortified (as in France's VIN DOUX NATURELS). Muscat d'Alsace is unusual in being a dry wine.

Palomino

Alias Listan. Makes all the best sherry.

Pedro Ximénez

Said to have come to s. Spain from Germany. Makes very strong wine in Montilla and Malaga. Used in blending sherry. Also grown in Australia, California, South Africa.

Pinot Blanc

A close relation of CHARDONNAY without its strength of character. Grown in Champagne, Alsace (increasingly), n. Italy (good sparkling wine), s. Germany, eastern Europe, California. Called Weissburgunder in German.

Pinot Gris

Makes rather heavy, even "thick", full-bodied whites with a certain spicy style. Known as Tokay in Alsace, Tocai in n.e. Italy and Yugoslavia, Ruländer in Germany.

Pinot Noir

Superlative black grape (see under Grapes for red wine) used in Champagne and occasionally elsewhere (e.g. California) for making white wine, or a very pale pink "vin gris".

Riesling

Germany's finest grape, now planted round the world. Wine of brilliant sweet/acid balance, flowery in youth but maturing to subtle oily scents and flavours. Successful in Alsace (for dry wine), Austria, parts of eastern Europe, Australia, California, South Africa. Often called White, Johannisberg or Rhine Riesling.

Sauvignon Blanc

Very distinctive aromatic, herby and sometimes smoky scented wine, can be austere (on the upper Loire) or buxom (in Bordeaux, where it is combined with SEMILLON, and parts of California). Also called Fumé Blanc or vice versa.

Scheurebe

Spicy-flavoured German Riesling × Silvaner cross, very successful in Rheinpfalz, esp. for Ausleses.

Semillon

The grape contributing the lusciousness to great Sauternes; subject to "noble rot" in the right conditions. Makes soft dry wine of great potential. Traditionally called "Riesling" in parts of Australia.

Sercial

Makes the driest Madeira: where they claim it is really Riesling.

Seyval Blanc

French-made hybrid between French and American vines. Very hardy and attractively fruity. Popular and successful in the eastern States and England.

Steen South Africa's best white grape: lively fruity wine. Said to be the Chenin Blanc of the Loire.

Sylvaner (Silvaner)

Germany's workhorse grape: wine rarely better than pleasant except in Franconia. Good in the Italian Tyrol and useful in Alsace. Very good as "Johannisberg" in Switzerland.

Tokay

See PINOT GRIS. Also a table grape in California and a supposedly Hungarian grape in Australia.

Traminer

See GEWÜRZTRAMINER

Trebbiano

Important grape of central Italy, used in Orvieto, Chianti, Soave, etc. Also grown in s. France as Ugni Blanc, and Cognac as "St-Emilion". Normally rather thin, neutral wine.

Ugni Blanc

See TREBBIANO

Verdelho

Madeira grape making excellent medium-sweet wine.

Verdicchio

Gives its name to good dry wine in central Italy.

Vernaccia

Grape grown in central and s. Italy and Sardinia for strong lively wine inclining towards sherry.

Viognier

Rare but remarkable grape of the Rhône valley, grown at Condrieu to make very fine soft and fragrant wine.

Welschriesling (or Wälschriesling)

See ITALIAN RIESLING

Weissburgunder

See PINOT BLANC

Grapes for red wine

Barbera
> One of several standard grapes of Piemonte, giving dark, fruity, often sharp wine. High acidity makes it useful in California.

Brunello
> S. Tuscan form of SANGIOVESE, splendid at Montalcino.

Cabernet Franc
> The lesser of two sorts of Cabernet grown in Bordeaux; the Cabernet of the Loire making Chinon, etc., and rosé.

Cabernet Sauvignon
> Grape of great character; spicy, herby and tannic. The first grape of the Médoc, also makes the best Californian, Australian, South American and eastern European reds. Its red wine always needs ageing and usually blending. Makes v. aromatic rosé.

Carignan
> By far the commonest grape of France, covering hundreds of thousands of acres. Prolific with dull but harmless wine. Also common in North Africa, Spain and California.

Cinsaut
> Common bulk-producing grape of s. France; in S. Africa crossed with PINOT NOIR to make Pinotage.

Gamay
> The beaujolais grape: light very fragrant wines at their best quite young. Makes even lighter wine on the Loire and in Switzerland and Savoie. Known as Napa Gamay in California, Blaufränkisch in Germany.

Gamay Beaujolais
> Not Gamay but a variety of PINOT NOIR grown in California.

Grenache
> Useful grape for strong and fruity but pale wine: good rosé. Grown in s. France, Spain, California. Usually blended.

Grignolino
> Makes one of the good cheap table wines of Piemonte.

Malbec
> Minor in Bordeaux, important (as "Cot") in Cahors. Major quality grape of Argentina.

Merlot
> Adaptable grape making the great fragrant and rich wines of Pomerol and St-Emilion, an important element in Médoc reds, soft and strong in California, lighter but good in n. Italy, Italian Switzerland, Yugoslavia, Argentina, etc.

Nebbiolo (also called Spanna and Chiavennasca)
> Italy's best red grape, the grape of Barolo, Barbaresco, Gattinara and Valtellina. Intense, nobly fruity and perfumed wine but very tannic, taking years to mature.

Pinot Noir
> The glory of Burgundy's Côte d'Or, with scent, flavour, texture and body unmatched anywhere. Less happy elsewhere; makes light wines of no great distinction in Germany, Switzerland, Austria, Hungary. The great challenge to the winemakers of California and Australia. Shows great promise in Oregon.

Sangiovese
> The main red grape of Chianti and much of central Italy.

Spätburgunder
> German for PINOT NOIR.

Syrah (alias Shiraz)
> The best Rhône red grape, with heavy purple wine, which can mature superbly. Very important as "Shiraz" in Australia.

Tempranillo
> The characteristic fine Rioja grape, called Ull de Lebre in Catalonia, Cencibel in La Mancha.

Zinfandel
> Fruity adaptable grape peculiar to California. Also makes white.

Wine & Food

There are no rules or statutes about what wine goes with what food, but there is a vast body of accumulated experience which it is absurd to ignore.

This list of dishes and appropriate wines records many of the conventional combinations and suggests others that I personally have found good. But it is only a list of ideas intended to help you make quick decisions. Any of the groups of recommended wines could have been extended almost indefinitely, drawing on the whole world's wine list. In general I have stuck to the wines that are widely available, at the same time trying to ring the changes so that the same wines don't come up time and time again—as they tend to do in real life.

The stars refer to the rating system used throughout the book: see opposite Contents.

Before the Meal—Apéritifs

The traditional apéritif wines are either sparkling (epitomized by champagne) or fortified (epitomized by sherry). They are still the best, but eat almonds and avoid peanuts with them. The current fashion for a glass of white wine before eating calls for something light and stimulating, dry but not acid, with a degree of character, such as:

France:

> Alsace Edelzwicker, Riesling or Sylvaner; Chablis; Muscadet; Sauvignon de Touraine; Graves Blanc; Mâcon Blanc; Crépy; Bugey, Haut-Poitou.

Germany:

> Any Kabinett wine or QbA halbtrocken.

Italy:

> Soave; Orvieto Secco; Frascati; Pinot Bianco; Montecarlo; Vernaccia; Tocai; Lugano; Albana di Romagna.

Spain:

> Rioja Blanco Marqués de Caceres or Faustino V, or Albariño but fino sherry or Montilla is even better.

Portugal:

> Any vinho verde; Bucelas.

Eastern Europe:

> Leanyka, Welschriesling, Chardonnay.

U.S.A.:

> Californian "Chablis"; Chenin Blanc; Riesling; French Colombard; Fumé Blanc; Gewürztraminer, or a good "house blend"; Riesling or Semillon from the north-west.

Australia:

> Barossa or Coonawarra Riesling.

South Africa:

> Steen; Sauvignon Blanc; Riesling; Gewürztraminer.

England:

> English white.

References to these wines will be found in national A–Z sections.

First courses

Aïoli

> A thirst-quencher is needed with so much garlic. ★→★★ white Rhône, or Verdicchio, and mineral water.

Antipasto (see also Hors d'oeuvre)

> ★★ dry or medium white, preferably Italian (e.g. Soave) or light red, e.g. Valpolicella, Bardolino or young ★ Bordeaux.

Artichoke

    ★ red or rosé.

    vinaigrette ★ young red, e.g. Bordeaux, Côtes-du-Rhône.

    hollandaise ★ or ★★ full-bodied dry or medium white, e.g.
    Mâcon Blanc, Rheinpfalz, or a California "house blend".

Asparagus

    ★★→★★★ white burgundy or Chardonnay, or Corsican rosé.

Assiette anglaise (assorted cold meats)

    ★★ dry white, e.g. Chablis, Graves, Muscadet, Silvaner.

Avocado

    with prawns, crab, etc. ★★→★★★ dry to medium white, e.g.
    Rheingau or Rheinpfalz Kabinett, Graves, California or Aus-
    tralian Chardonnay or Sauvignon, Cape Steen, or dry rosé.

    vinaigrette ★ light red, or fino sherry.

Bisques

    ★★ dry white with plenty of body: Pinot Gris, Chardonnay. Fino
    sherry, or Montilla.

Bouillabaisse

    ★→★★ very dry white: Muscadet, Alsace Sylvaner, Entre-Deux-
    Mers, Pouilly Fumé, Cassis, Tuscan Trebbiano, Grechetto.

Caviare

    ★★★ champagne or iced vodka (or both).

Cheese fondue

    ★★ dry white: Fendant or Johannisberg du Valais, Grüner
    Veltliner.

Chicken Liver Pâté

    Appetizing dry white, e.g. ★★ white Bordeaux, or light fruity red;
    Beaujolais, Gamay de Touraine, young Chianti or Valpolicella.

Clams and Chowders

    ★★ big-scale white, not necessarily bone dry: e.g. Rhône, Pinot
    Gris, Dry Sauternes, Napa Chardonnay.

Consommé

    ★★→★★★ medium-dry sherry, dry Madeira, Marsala, Montilla.

Crudités

    ★→★★ light red or rosé, e.g. Côtes-du-Rhône, Beaujolais,
    Minervois, Chianti, Zinfandel.

Eggs (see also Soufflés)

    These present difficulties: they clash with most wines and spoil
    good ones. So ★→★★ of whatever is going.

Empanadas

    ★→★★ Chilean or Argentine Cabernet, Zinfandel.

Escargots

    ★★ red or white of some substance: e.g. Burgundy, Côtes-du-
    Rhône, Chardonnay, Shiraz, etc.

Foie gras

    ★★★→★★★★ white. In Bordeaux they drink Sauternes. Others
    prefer vintage champagne or a rich Gewürztraminer Vendange
    tardive.

Gazpacho

    Sangria (see Spain) is refreshing, but to avoid too much liquid
    intake dry Manzanilla or Montilla is better.

Grapefruit

    If you must start a meal with grapefruit try port, Madeira or
    sweet sherry with it.

Ham, raw

    See Prosciutto.

Herrings, raw or pickled

    Dutch gin or Scandinavian akvavit, and cold beer.

Hors d'oeuvres (see also Antipasto)

    ★→★★ clean fruity sharp white: Sancerre or any Sauvignon,
    Alsace Sylvaner, Muscadet, Cape Steen—or young light red
    Bordeaux, Rhône or equivalent.

Mackerel, smoked

    ★→★★★ full-bodied tasty white: e.g. Gewürztraminer, Tokay d'Alsace or Chablis Premier Cru. Or Manzanilla sherry.

Melon

    Needs a strong sweet wine: ★★ Port, Bual Madeira, Muscat, Oloroso sherry or Vin doux naturel.

Minestrone

    ★ red: Grignolino, Chianti, Zinfandel, Shiraz, etc.

Omelettes

    See observations under Eggs.

Onion/Leek tart

    ★→★★★ fruity dry white, e.g. Alsace Pinot Gris or Riesling. Mâcon-Villages of a good vintage, Jurançon, California or Australian Riesling.

Pasta

    ★→★★ red or white according to the sauce or trimmings, e.g.

    with seafood sauce (vongole, etc.) Verdicchio, Soave, Sauvignon.

    meat sauce Chianti, Montepulciano d'Abruzzo.

    tomato sauce Barbera or Sicilian red.

    cream sauce Orvieto, Frascati or Italian Chardonnay.

Pâté

    ★★ dry white: e.g. Mâcon-Villages, Graves, Fumé Blanc.

Peppers or aubergines (egg-plant), stuffed

    ★★ vigorous red: e.g. Chianti, Zinfandel.

Pizza

    Any ★★ dry Italian red or a ★★ Rioja, Australian Shiraz or California Zinfandel. Or Corbières or Roussillon.

Prawns or Shrimps

    ★★→★★★ dry white: burgundy or Bordeaux, Chardonnay or Riesling. ("Cocktail sauce" kills any wine.)

Prosciutto with melon

    ★★→★★★ full-bodied dry or medium white: e.g. Orvieto or Frascati, Pomino, Fendant, Grüner Veltliner, Alsace or California Gewürztraminer, Australian Riesling.

Quiches

    ★→★★ dry white with body (Alsace, Graves, Sauvignon) or young red according to the ingredients.

Ratatouille

    ★★ vigorous young red, e.g. Chianti, Zinfandel, Bulgarian or young red Bordeaux.

Salade niçoise

    ★★ very dry not too light or flowery white, e.g. white (or rosé) Rhône or Corsican, Catalan white, Dão California Sauvignon.

Salads

    As a first course: any dry and appetizing white wine. After a main course: no wine.

    N.B. Vinegar in salad dressings destroys the flavour of wine. If you want salad at a meal with fine wine, dress the salad with wine or a little lemon juice instead of vinegar.

Salami

    ★→★★ powerfully tasty red or rosé: e.g. Barbera, young Zinfandel, Tavel or Ajaccio rosé, young Bordeaux.

Salmon, smoked

    A dry but pungent white, e.g. fino sherry, Alsace Gewürztraminer, Chablis Grand Cru. Vernaccia di San Gimignano.

Soufflés

    As show dishes these deserve ★★→★★★ wines.

    Fish Dry white, e.g. burgundy, Bordeaux, Alsace, Chard, etc.

    Cheese Red burgundy or Bordeaux, Cabernet Sauvignon, etc.

Taramasalata

Calls for a rustic southern white of strong personality; not necessarily the Greek Retsina. Fino sherry works well.

Terrine

As for pâté, or the equivalent red; e.g. Beaune, Mercurey, Beaujolais-Villages, fairly young ★★ St-Emilion, California Cabernet or Zinfandel, Bulgarian or Chilean Cabernet, etc.

Trout, smoked

Sancerre, Pouilly Fumé, or California Fumé Blanc.

Fish

Abalone

★★→★★★ dry or medium white: e.g. Sauvignon Blanc, Chardonnay, Pinot Grigio, Muscadet sur Lie.

Bass, striped

Same wine as for sole.

Cod

A good neutral background for fine dry or medium whites, e.g. ★★→★★★ Chablis, Meursault, cru classé Graves, German Kabinett or dry Spätleses and their equivalents.

Coquilles St. Jacques

An inherently slightly sweet dish, best with medium-dry whites.

in cream sauces ★★★ German wines or a -Montrachet.

grilled or fried Hermitage Blanc, Gewürztraminer, California Chenin Blanc, Riesling or champagne.

Crab, cold, with salad

★★★ California or Rheinpfalz Riesling Kabinett or Spätlese.

Eel, jellied

NV champagne or a nice cup of tea.

smoked Either strong or sharp wine, e.g. fino sherry or Bourgogne Aligoté. Or schnapps.

Haddock

★★→★★★ dry white with a certain richness: e.g. Meursault, California or Australian Chardonnay.

Herrings

Need a white with some acidity to cut their richness. Burgundy Aligoté or Gros Plant from Brittany or dry Sauvignon Blanc.

Kippers: a good cup of tea, preferably Ceylon (milk, no sugar).

Lamproie à la Bordelaise

★★ young red Bordeaux, St-Emilion, Pomerol or Fronsac.

Lobster or Crab

salad ★★→★★★★ white. Non-vintage champagne, Alsace Riesling, Chablis Premier Cru, Condrieu.

richly sauced Vintage champagne, fine white burgundy, cru classé Graves, California or Australian Chardonnay, Rheinpfalz Spätlese, Hermitage Blanc.

Mackerel

★★ hard or sharp white: Sauvignon Blanc from Bergerac or Touraine, Gros Plant, vinho verde, white Rioja.

Mullet, red

★★ Mediterranean white, even Retsina, for the atmosphere.

Mussels

★→★★ Gros Plant, Muscadet, California "Chablis".

Oysters

★★→★★★ white. Champagne (non-vintage), Chablis or (better) Chablis Premier Cru, or Muscadet or Entre-Deux-Mers.

Salmon, fresh

★★★ fine white burgundy: Puligny- or Chassagne-Montrachet, Meursault, Corton-Charlemagne, Chablis Grand Cru, California, Idaho or Australian Chardonnay, or Rheingau Kabinett or Spätlese, California Riesling or equivalent.

Sardines, fresh grilled
> ★→★★ very dry white: e.g. vinho verde, Dão Muscadet.

Scallops
> See Coquilles St. Jacques.

Shad
> ★★→★★★ white Graves or Meursault or Hunter Semillon.

Shellfish (general)
> Dry white with plain boiled shellfish, richer wines with richer sauces.

Shrimps, potted
> Fino sherry, Chablis, Gavi or New York Chardonnay.

Skate with black butter
> ★★ white with some pungency (e.g. Alsace Pinot Gris) or a clean one like Muscadet.

Sole, Plaice, etc.
> **plain, grilled or fried** An ideal accompaniment for fine wines: ★ up to ★★★★ white burgundy, or its equivalent.
> **with sauce** Depending on the ingredients: sharp dry wine for tomato sauce, fairly sweet for Sole véronique, etc.

Sushi (and sashimi)
> Sparkling wines, incl. Californian, or Calif. or Australian Chardonnay or Sauvignon. Chablis Grand Cru.

Trout
> Delicate white wine, e.g. ★★★ Mosel.
> **Smoked**, a full-flavoured ★★→★★★ white: Gewürztraminer, Pinot Gris, Rhine Spätlese or Australian Hunter white.

Turbot
> Fine rich dry white, e.g. ★★★ Meursault or its California, Australian or New Zealand equivalent.

Meat, Poultry, etc.

Beef, boiled
> ★★ red: e.g. Cru Bourgeois Bordeaux (Bourg or Fronsac), Côtes-du-Rhône-Villages, Patrimonio, Australian Shiraz or Claret.

Beef, roast
> An ideal partner for fine red wine. ★★→★★★★ red of any kind.

Beef stew
> ★★→★★★ sturdy red, e.g. Pomerol or St-Emilion, Hermitage, Shiraz Calif. or Oregon Pinot Noir.

Beef Strogonoff
> ★★→★★★ suitably dramatic red: e.g. Barolo, Brunello, Valpolicella, Amarone, Hermitage, late-harvest Zinfandel.

Cassoulet
> ★★ red from s.w. France, e.g. Madiran, Cahors or Corbières, or Barbera or Zinfandel.

Chicken or Turkey, roast
> Virtually any wine, including your very best bottles of dry or medium white and fine old reds.

Chili con carne
> ★→★★ young red: e.g. Bull's Blood, Chianti, Mountain Red.

Chinese food
> **Canton** or **Peking style** ★★→★★★★ dry to medium-dry white: e.g. Yugoslav "Riesling", Mâcon-Villages, California Chardonnay. Or NV Champagne.
> **Szechuan style** Very cold beer.

Choucroute
> Lager.

Cold meats
> Generally taste better with full-flavoured white wine than red.

Confit d'Oie

★★→★★★ rather young and tannic red Bordeaux helps to cut the richness. Alsace Tokay or Gewürztraminer matches it.

Coq au Vin

★★→★★★★ red burgundy. In an ideal world one bottle of Chambertin in the dish, one on the table.

Corned beef hash

★★ Zinfandel, Chianti, Côtes-du-Rhône red.

Curry

★→★★ medium-sweet white, very cold: e.g. Orvieto abboccato, certain California Chenin Blancs, Yugoslav Traminer.

Duck or Goose

★★★ rather rich white, e.g. Rheinpfalz Spätlese or Alsace Réserve Exceptionelle, or ★★★ Bordeaux or burgundy.

Wild Duck ★★★ big-scale red: e.g. Hermitage, Châteauneuf-du-Pape, Calif. or S. African Cabernet, Australian Shiraz.

Frankfurters

★→★★ German or Austrian white, or Beaujolais. Or beer.

Game birds

Young birds plain roasted deserve the best red wine you can afford. With older birds in casseroles ★★→★★★ red, e.g. Gevrey-Chambertin, St-Emilion, Napa Cabernet.

Game pie

(Hot) ★★★ red wine. (Cold) Equivalent white.

Goulash

★★ strong young red: e.g. Zinfandel, Bulgarian Cabernet.

Grouse

See under Game birds

Ham

★★→★★★ fairly young red burgundy, e.g. Volnay, Savigny, Beaune, Corton, or a slightly sweet German white, e.g. a Rhine Spätlese, or a Tuscan red, or a lightish Cabernet.

Hamburger

★→★★ young red: e.g. Beaujolais, Corbières or Minervois, Chianti, Zinfandel.

Hare

Jugged hare calls for ★★→★★★ red with plenty of flavour: not-too-old burgundy or Bordeaux. The same for saddle.

Kebabs

★★ vigorous red: e.g. Greek Demestica, Turkish Buzbag, Bulgarian or Chilean Cabernet, Zinfandel.

Kidneys

★★→★★★ red: Pomerol or St-Emilion, Rhône, Barbaresco, Rioja, California, Spanish or Australian Cabernet.

Lamb cutlets or chops

As for roast lamb, but less grand.

Lamb, roast

One of the traditional and best partners for very good red Bordeaux—or its Cabernet equivalents from the New World.

Liver

★★→★★★ young red: Beaujolais-Villages, St-Joseph, Médoc, Italian Merlot, Zinfandel. Oregon, Pinot Noir.

Meatballs

★★→★★★ red: e.g. Mercurey, Madiran, Rubesco, Dão, Bairrada, Zinfandel or Cabernet.

Mixed Grill

A fairly light easily swallowable red; ★★ red Bordeaux from Bourg, Fronsac or Premières Côtes; Chianti; Bourgogne Passe-tout-grains.

Moussaka

★→★★ red or rosé: e.g. Chianti, Corbières, Côtes de Provence, Ajaccio, Calvi or Patrimonio, California Burgundy.

Oxtail

    ★★→★★★ rather rich red: e.g. St-Emilion or Pomerol, Burgundy, Barolo or Chianti Classico, Rioja Reserva, California Cabernet or a dry Riesling Spätlese.

Paella

    ★★ Young Spanish red, dry white or rosé, e.g. Penedés or Rioja or vinho verde.

Partridge, pheasant

    See under Game birds.

Pigeons or squabs

    ★★→★★★★ red Bordeaux, Chianti Classico, Californian or Australian Cabernet.

Pork, roast

    The sauce or stuffing has more flavour than the meat. Sharp apple sauce or pungent sage and onion need only a plain young wine. Pork without them, on the other hand, is a good, rich, neutral background to very good white or red wine.

Rabbit

    ★→★★★ young red: Italian for preference.

Ris de veau

    See Sweetbreads.

Sauerkraut

    See Choucroute.

Shepherd's Pie

    ★→★★ rough and ready red seems most appropriate, but no harm would come to a good one.

Steak and Kidney Pie or Pudding

    Red Rioja Reserva or mature ★★→★★★ Bordeaux.

Steaks

    Au poivre a fairly young ★★★ Rhône red or Cabernet.

    Tartare ★★ light young red: Bergerac, Valpolicella.

    Filet or Tournedos ★★★ red of any kind (but not old wines with Béarnaise sauce).

    T-bone ★★→★★★ reds of similar bone-structure: e.g. Barolo, Hermitage, Australian Cabernet or Shiraz.

    Fiorentina (bistecca) Chianti Classico Riserva.

    Ostrich South African Pinotage.

Stews and Casseroles

    A lusty full-flavoured red, e.g. young Côtes-du-Rhône, Corbières, Barbera, Shiraz, Zinfandel, etc.

Sweetbreads

    These tend to be a grand dish, suggesting a grand wine, e.g. ★★★ Rhine Riesling Kabinett or Spätlese, or well-matured Bordeaux or Burgundy, depending on the sauce.

Tongue

    Ideal for favourite unpretentious bottles of any red or white.

Tripe

    ★→★★ red: Corbières, Mâcon Rouge, etc., or rather sweet white, e.g. Liebfraumilch. Better: W. Australian "white Burgundy".

Veal, roast

    A good neutral background dish for any fine old red which may have faded, or a ★★★ German white.

Venison

    ★★★ big-scale red (Rhône, Bordeaux of a grand vintage) or rather rich white (Rheinpfalz Spätlese or Tokay d'Alsace).

Wiener Schnitzel

    ★★→★★★ light red from the Italian Tyrol (Alto Adige) or the Médoc: or Austrian Riesling, Grüner Veltliner or Gumpoldskirchener.

Cheese

Very strong cheese completely masks the flavour of wine. Only serve fine wine with mild cheeses in peak condition.

Bleu de Bresse, Dolcelatte, Gorgonzola

Need fairly emphatic accompaniment: young ★★ red wine (Barbera, Dolcetto, Moulin-à-Vent, etc.) or sweet white.

Cream cheeses: Brie, Camembert, Bel Paese, Edam, etc.

In their mild state marry with any good wine, red or white.

English cheeses

Can be either mild or strong and acidic. The latter need sweet or strong wine.

Cheddar, Cheshire, Wensleydale, Stilton, Gloucester, etc. If mild, claret. If strong, ruby, tawny or vintage-character (not vintage) port, old dry oloroso sherry, or a very big red: Hermitage, Châteauneuf-du-Pape, Barolo, etc.

Goat cheeses

★★→★★★ white wine of marked character, either dry (e.g. Sancerre) or sweet (e.g. Monbazillac, Sauternes).

Hard Cheese, Parmesan, Gruyère, Emmenthal

Full-bodied dry whites, e.g. Tokay d'Alsace or Vernaccia, or fino or amontillado sherry.

Roquefort, Danish Blue

Are so strong-flavoured that only the youngest, biggest or sweetest wines stand a chance. Old dry sherries have the horse-power.

Desserts

Apple pie, apple strudel

★★→★★★ sweet German, Austrian or Hungarian white.

Apples, Cox's Orange Pippins

Vintage port (55, 60, 63, 66, 70, 75).

Baked Alaska

Sweet champagne or Asti Spumante.

Cakes

Bual or Malmsey Madeira, Oloroso or cream sherry.

Cheesecake

★★→★★★ sweet white from Vouvray or Coteaux du Layon.

Chocolate cake, mousse, soufflés

Huxelrebe Auslese or California orange muscat.

Christmas pudding

Sweet champagne or Asti Spumante, or cream sherry.

Creams and Custards

★★→★★★ Sauternes, Monbazillac or similar golden white.

Crème brûlée

The most luxurious dish, demanding ★★★→★★★★ Sauternes or Rhine Beerenauslese, or the best Madeira or Tokay.

Crêpes Suzette

Sweet champagne or Asti Spumante.

Fruit flans (i.e. peach, raspberry)

★★★ Sauternes, Monbazillac or sweet Vouvray or Anjou.

Fruit, fresh

Sweet Coteaux du Layon white, light sweet muscat (e.g. California).

Fruit salads, orange salad

No wine.

Nuts

Oloroso sherry, Bual, Madeira, vintage or tawny port, Vinsanto.

Sorbets, ice-creams

No wine.

Stewed fruits, i.e. apricots, pears, etc.

      Sweet Muscatel: e.g. Muscat de Beaumes de Venise, Moscato di Pantelleria or from Tarragona.

Strawberries and cream

      ★★★ Sauternes or Vouvray Moelleux.

Wild strawberries Serve with ★★★ red Bordeaux poured over them and in your glass (no cream).

Summer Pudding

      Fairly young Sauternes of a good vintage (e.g. 75, 76, 79, 80).

Treacle Tart

      Too sweet for any wine but a treacly Malmsey Madeira.

Trifle

      No wine: should be sufficiently vibrant with sherry.

Sweet Soufflés

      Sweet Vouvray or Coteaux du Layon. Sweet Champagne.

Zabaglione

      Light gold Marsala.

Savoury

Cheese straws

      Admirable meal-ending with a final glass (or bottle) of a particularly good red wine.

Temperature

Temperature

No single aspect of serving wine makes or mars it so easily as getting the temperature right. White wines almost invariably taste dull and insipid served warm and red wines have disappointingly little scent or flavour served cold. The chart below gives an indication of what is generally found to be the best and most satisfactory temperature for serving each class of wine.

	°F	°C	
	68	20	
Room	66	19	
temperature	64	18	Best red wines
	63	17	especially Bordeaux
Red Burgundy	61	16	Chianti, Zinfandel
	59	15	Côtes-du-Rhône
Best white Burgundy	57	14	
Port Madeira	55	13	Ordinaires
	54	12	Lighter red wines
Ideal	Sherry	52	11	e.g. Beaujolais
cellar	Fino sherry	50	10	Rosés
Most dry white wines	48	9	Lambrusco
Champagne	46	8	
Domestic	45	7	
fridge	43	6	Most sweet white wines
	41	5	Sparkling wines
	39	4	
	37	3	
	35	2	
	33	1	
	32	0	

A little learning . . .

The last fifteen years have seen a revolution in wine technology. They have also heard a revolution in wine-talk—and the beginnings of a reaction. Attempts to express the characters of wine used to get no further than such vague terms as "fruity" and "full-bodied". Then came the demand for sterner, more scientific, stuff: the jargon of laboratory analysis. This hard-edge wine-talk is very briefly explained below.

The most frequent references are to the ripeness of grapes at picking; the resultant alcohol and sugar content of the wine; various measures of its acidity; the amount of sulphur dioxide used as a preservative, and the amount of "dry extract"—the sum of all the things that give wine its characteristic flavours.

Currently the fashion is for analogues with a quasi-poetic effect: "Scents of apricots, raspberries, leather; flavours of plum and truffle, shading to tar with a hint of fish-glue". Anybody can play. Few can play well.

The **sugar** in wine is mainly glucose and fructose, with traces of arabinose, xylose and other sugars that are not fermentable by yeast, but can be attacked by bacteria. Each country has its own system for measuring the sugar content or ripeness of grapes, known as the "**must-weight**". The chart below relates the three principal ones (German, French and American) to each other, to specific gravity, and to the potential alcohol of the wine if all the sugar is fermented.

Specific Gravity	°O °Oechsle	Baumé	Brix	% Potential Alcohol v/v
1.065	65	8.8	15.8	8.1
1.070	70	9.4	17.0	8.8
1.075	75	10.1	18.1	9.4
1.080	80	10.7	19.3	10.0
1.085	85	11.3	20.4	10.6
1.090	90	11.9	21.5	11.3
1.095	95	12.5	22.5	11.9
1.100	100	13.1	23.7	12.5
1.105	105	13.7	24.8	13.1
1.110	110	14.3	25.8	13.8
1.115	115	14.9	26.9	14.4
1.120	120	15.5	28.0	15.0

Residual sugar is the sugar left after fermentation has finished or been artificially stopped, measured in grammes per litre.

Alcohol content (mainly ethyl alcohol) is expressed as a percentage by volume of the total liquid.

Acidity is both fixed and volatile. **Fixed acidity** consists principally of tartaric, malic and citric acids which are all found in the grape, and lactic and succinic acids, which are produced during fermentation. **Volatile acidity** consists mainly of acetic acid, which is rapidly formed by bacteria in the presence of oxygen. A small amount of volatile acidity is inevitable and attractive. With a larger amount the wine becomes "pricked"—i.e. starts to turn to vinegar.

Total acidity is fixed and volatile acidity combined. As a rule of thumb for a well-balanced wine it should be in the region of 1 gramme/thousand for each 10°Oechsle (see above).

pH is a measure of the strength of the acidity, rather than its volume. The lower the figure the more acid. Wine normally ranges in pH from 2.8 to 3.8. Winemakers in hot climates can have problems getting the pH low enough. Lower pH gives better colour, helps prevent bacterial spoilage, allows more of the SO_2 to be free and active as a preservative.

Sulphur dioxide (SO_2) is added to prevent oxidation and other accidents in wine-making. Some of it combines with sugars, etc., and is known as "bound". Only the "**free SO_2**" that remains in the wine is effective as a preservative. **Total SO_2** is controlled by law according to the level of residual sugar: the more sugar the more SO_2 needed.

France

English Channel

• Le Havre

Normandy

• Brest

Brittany

Tours •

Loire Lo

Saumur •

R. Loire

• Nantes

Bay of Biscay

Cognac

Bordeaux •
Bordeaux
B'x

S.W. France

• Biarritz

Spain

France makes every kind of wine, and invented most of them.
Her wine trade, both exporting and importing, dwarfs that of
any other country. Tens of thousands of properties make wine
over a large part of France's surface. This is a guide to the best
known of them and to the system by which the rest can be
identified and to some extent evaluated.

All France's best wine regions have Appellations Contrôlées,
which may apply to a single small vineyard or a whole large
district: the system varies from region to region, with Burgundy
on the whole having the smallest and most precise appellations,
grouped into larger units by complicated formulae, and
Bordeaux having the widest and most general appellations, in
which it is the particular property (or "château") that matters.
In between lie an infinity of variations.

Belgium

W. Germany

Lille

Reims
Epernay
Paris
Champagne **Champ**

Strasbourg

Alsace **Al**

R. Seine

Chablis
Dijon
Burgundy
B'y

Jura

Switzerland

Upper Loire

Sancerre

Beaune

R. Saône

Central France

Mâcon

Geneva

Beaujolais

Savoie

Italy

Clermont-Ferrand

Lyons

Dordogne

R. Rhône

Grenoble

R. Dordogne

Rhône
Rh

Nice

R. Tarn

Avignon
Montpellier

Provence **Prov**

Marseille

R. Garonne

Toulouse

Midi

Mediterranean

Pyrenees **Pyr**

Perpignan

Abbreviations of regional names
shown in bold type are used in the
text.

An Appellation Contrôlée is a guarantee of origin and of
production method, of grape varieties and quantities produced,
but only partially one of quality. All "A.C." wines are tasted,
but many of shoddy quality get through the net.

Appellations therefore help to identify a wine and indicate
that it comes from a major area. They are the first thing to look
for on a label. But they do not guarantee high quality.

Wine regions without the overall quality and traditions
required for an appellation can be ranked as Vins Délimités de
Qualité Supérieure (VDQS), or (a new third rank created
largely to encourage the improvement of mediocre wines in the
south of France) Vins de Pays. VDQS wines are almost always
good value, on the Avis principle. Vins de Pays are worth trying,
at least for curiosity's sake. They include some brilliant
originals.

Recent vintages of the French classics

Red Burgundy

Côte d'Or Côte de Beaune reds generally mature sooner than the bigger wines of the Côte de Nuits. Earliest drinking dates are for lighter commune wines: Volnay, Beaune, etc. Latest for the biggest wines of Chambertin, Romanée, etc. Different growers make wines of different styles, for longer or shorter maturing, but even the best burgundies are much more attractive young than the equivalent red Bordeaux.

1985	Ripe, round and juicy. Concentrated wines will be splendid.
1984	Lacks natural ripeness; tends to be dry and/or watery but may gain weight.
1983	Powerful, vigorous, tannic and attractive vintage. The best will beat anything since 1978. Others can be flabby.
1982	Big vintage, pale but round. Best in Côte de Beaune. Be careful.
1981	A small crop, ripe but picked in rain. Good wines are improving.
1980	A late, wet year, but attractive wines from the best growers who avoided rot. Better in the Côte de Nuits. Keep the best another year or two.
1979	Big generally good ripe vintage with weak spots. S. Côte de Nuits suffered from hail. Already most wines are ageing.
1978	Poor summer saved by miraculous autumn. A small vintage of outstanding quality. The best will live 15 years.
1977	Very wet summer. Better wine than expected, but drink up.
1976	Hot summer, excellent vintage. As usual great variations, but the best (esp. Côte de Beaune) rich and long-lived—to 1990.
1975	Rot was rife, particularly in the Côte de Beaune. Mostly very poor.
1974	Another big wet vintage; even the best light and lean. Drink up.
1973	Light wines, but many fruity and delicate. Most are already too old.
1972	High acidity posed problems, but the wines are firm and full of character, ageing well. Few need keeping longer now.
1971	Very powerful and impressive wines, not as long-lasting as they first appeared. Most now ready. The best have 5 years ahead.

Older fine vintages: '69, '66, '64, '62, '61, '59 (all mature).

Beaujolais 1985 was a wonderful vintage, with Crus to keep. 1984 was fair, with some good Crus. 1983 was excellent. 1982 is now getting too old. Generally avoid older vintages except possibly 1976 Moulin à Vent.

White Burgundy

Côte de Beaune Well-made wines of good vintages with plenty of acidity as well as fruit will improve and gain depth and richness for some years—anything up to ten. Lesser wines from lighter years are ready for drinking after two or three years.

1985	Very ripe; many wines are too soft; be careful.
1984	Some well-balanced wines; most rather lean or hollow.
1983	Potent wines; some exaggerated, some faulty but the best splendid.
1982	Fat, tasty but delicate whites of low acidity, not for keeping.
1981	A sadly depleted crop with great promise. The best are excellent.
1980	A weak, but not bad, vintage. Drink soon.
1979	Big vintage. Overall good and useful, not great. Drink soon.
1978	Very good wines, firm and well-balanced. Keep the best.
1977	Rather light; some well-balanced and good. Drink up.
1976	Hot summer, rather heavy wines; good but not for keeping.
1975	Whites did much better than reds. Chablis best, but all now ready.
1974	All now need drinking.
1973	Very attractive, fruity, typical and plentiful. Drink up.
1972	High acidity, but plenty of character. All are now ready to drink.
1971	Great power and style, some almost too rich, but the best have good balance. Small crop. Generally ready.

The white wines of the Mâconnais (Pouilly-Fuissé, St Véran, Macon-Villages) follow a similar pattern, but do not last as long. They are more appreciated for their freshness than their richness.

Chablis Grand Cru Chablis of vintages with both strength and acidity can age superbly for up to ten years. Premier Crus proportionately less. Drink other Chablis young.

1985	Good but low-acid wines. Keep only Grands Crus.
1984	A small vintage. Most too feeble to last.
1983	Superb vintage if not over-strong. The best will improve for years.
1982	Charming light wines. Good value. Not to keep.
1981	Small, concentrated and fine harvest. Keeping well.
1980	More successful than the rest of Burgundy. Drink up.
1979	Very big crop. Good easy wines, not for storing.
1978	Excellent wines now passing their peak.

Red Bordeaux

Médoc/red Graves For some wines bottle-age is optional: for these it is indispensable. Minor châteaux from light vintages need only two or three years, but even modest wines of great years can improve for fifteen years or so, and the great châteaux of these years need double that time.

1985	Very good vintage, in a heatwave. Some great wines.
1984	Problematical. No Merlot but good ripe Cabernet. Generally overpriced.
1983	A classic vintage: abundant tannin with fruit to balance it.
1982	Made in a heatwave. Huge rich strong wines which promise fairly early maturing but a long life.
1981	Admirable despite rain. Not rich, but balanced and fine.
1980	Small, late harvest, ripe but rained-on. Many delicious light wines but few exciting ones. Drink now – '90.
1979	Abundant harvest of good average quality. Now – '95.
1978	A miracle vintage: magnificent long warm autumn saved the day. Some very good wines. Now – 2000.
1977	Pleasant light wine, many better than 1974. Now – '87.
1976	Excessively hot, dry summer; rain just before vintage. Generally very good, maturing rather quickly. Now – '95.
1975	A splendid summer and very fine vintage, with deep colour, high sugar content and tannin. For long keeping. "Petits Châteaux" are now ready.
1974	Oceans of disappointing light wines. Be very careful.
1973	A huge vintage, attractive young and still giving pleasure. Now or soon.
1972	High acidity from unripe grapes. Now.
1971	Small crop. Less fruity than '70 and less consistent. A few châteaux made outstanding wine. All are ready to drink.
1970	Abundance *and* uniform quality. Big fruity wines with elegance and attractive suppleness.
1969/68	Avoid them both.
1967	Never seductive, but characterful in its maturity. Drink soon.
1966	A very fine vintage with depth, fruit and tannin. Now.

Older fine vintages: '62, '61, '59, '55, '53, '52, '50, '49, '48, '47, '45, '29, '28.

St-Emilion/Pomerol

1985	One of the great years, with a long future.
1984	A sad story. Most of the crop wiped out in spring.
1983	Conditions were ideal. Some growers prefer this vintage to 1982.
1982	Enormously rich and concentrated wines, most excellent.
1981	A very good vintage, if not as great as it first seemed.
1980	A poor Merlot year; very variable quality. Choose carefully.
1979	A rival to '78; in most cases even better. Now – '95.
1978	Fine wines, but some lack flesh. Now – '92.
1977	Very wet summer. Mediocre with few exceptions.
1976	Very hot, dry summer and early vintage, but vintage rain made complications. Some excellent; the best great. Now – '95.
1975	Most St-Emilions good, the best superb. Frost in Pomerol cut crops and made splendid concentrated wine. Now – 2000.
1974	Vintage rain again. Disappointing light wines. Avoid.
1973	Good summer, big wet vintage. Pleasant wines. Drink up.
1972	Many unripe wines, but some are pleasant enough. Drink now, if at all.
1971	On the whole better than Médocs but generally now ready.
1970	Glorious weather and beautiful wines with great fruit and strength throughout the district. Very big crop. Now – '90s.
1969/68	avoid them both.
1967	Large and generally very good; better than Médoc. Now.

Older fine vintages: '66, '64, '61, '59, '53, '52, '49, '47, '45.

Ackerman-Laurance

The first champagne-method house of the Loire, at SAUMUR. Fine Crémant de Loire.

Ajaccio Corsica r. p. or w. dr. ┌─→★★┐ 83 84 85'

The capital of Corsica. A.C. for some v. good SCIACARELLO.

Aligoté

Second-rank burgundy white grape and its sharp wine, often agreeably fruity and with considerable local character when young. BOUZERON (A.C.) makes the best.

Aloxe-Corton B'y. r. or w. ★★★ 69 71 76 78 79 80 82 83 84 85

Northernmost village of CÔTE DE BEAUNE: best v'yds.: CORTON (red) and CORTON-CHARLEMAGNE (white). Village wines (called Aloxe-Corton) lighter but often good value.

Alsace Al. w. or (r.) ┌─★★┐ 76' 79 81 82 83' 84 85'

Aromatic, fruity dry white of Germanic character from French Rhineland. Normally sold by grape variety (RIESLING, GEWÜRZ-TRAMINER, etc.). Matures well up to 5, even 10, years.

Alsace Grand Cru ┌─★★★┐ 71 76 79 81 82 83' 84 85

Appellation restricted to the best named v'yds.

Alsace Grand Vin or Réserve

Wine with minimum 11° natural alcohol.

Amance, Marcel See MAUFOUX, PROSPER

Ampeau, Robert

Leading grower and specialist in MEURSAULT, POMMARD, etc.

Anjou Lo. (r.) p. or w. (sw. dr. or sp.) ★─→★★★ 76 78 79 81 82 83 84 85

Very various Loire wines, incl. good CABERNET rosé, luscious COTEAUX DU LAYON. Maturity depends on style.

Anjou-Côteaux de la Loire

A.C. for CHENIN BLANC whites, incl. the notable SAVENNIERES.

Appellation Contrôlée ("A.C." or "A.O.C.")

Government control of origin and production of all the best French wines (see France Introduction).

Apremont Savoie w. dr. ┌─★★┐ D.Y.A.

One of the best villages of SAVOIE for pale delicate whites.

Arbin Savoie r. ★★ Drink at 1–2 years

Deep-coloured lively red of Mondeuse grapes, like a good LOIRE Cabernet.

Arbois Jura r. p. or w. (dr. sp.) ★★ D.Y.A.

Various good and original light wines; speciality VIN JAUNE.

l'Ardèche, Coteaux de Central France r. (w. dr.) ┌─★→★★┐ D.Y.A.

Light country reds, the best made of SYRAH. A useful change from BEAUJOLAIS. Also remarkable CHARDONNAY from LOUIS LATOUR.

Armagnac

Region of s.w. France famous for its excellent brandy, a fiery spirit of rustic character. The red wine of the area is MADIRAN.

Auxey-Duresses B'y. r. or w. ┌─★★→★★★┐ 76 78 79 82 83 85

Second-rank (but v. pretty) CÔTE DE BEAUNE village: has affinities with VOLNAY and MEURSAULT. Best estates: Duc de Magenta, Prunier, Roy, HOSPICES DE BEAUNE Cuvée Boillot.

Avize Champ. ★★★★

One of the best white-grape villages of CHAMPAGNE.

Ay Champ. ★★★★

One of the best black-grape villages of CHAMPAGNE.

Ayala NV "Château d'Ay" 75 76 79 and Blanc de Blancs 79

Once-famous Ay-based old-style champagne concern.

Bandol Prov. r. p. or (w.) ★★★ 76 78 80 81 82 83 84 85

Little coastal region near Toulon with strong tasty reds from the Mourvèdre grape.

Banyuls Pyr. br. sw. ★★ NV

One of the best VIN DOUX NATURELS (fortified sweet red wines) of the s. of France. Not unlike port.

Barancourt Brut NV, Crémant Grand Cru NV, Crémant Grand Cru 76 78 79 80 81, Rosé NV

Grower at Bouzy making fine full-bodied champagnes.

Barsac B'x. w. sw. ★★→ ★★★ 70 71 75 76' 78 79' 80 81 82 83' 84 85

Neighbour of SAUTERNES with similar superb golden wines, often more racy and less rich. Top ch'x.: CLIMENS and COUTET.

Barton & Guestier

Bordeaux shipper since 18th century, now owned by Seagram's.

Bâtard-Montrachet B'y. w. dr. ★★★★ 71 73 76 78 81 82 83 84 85

Neighbour and almost equal of MONTRACHET, the top white burgundy. As rich in flavour as dry white wine can be.

Baumard, Domaine des

Leading grower of Anjou wine, especially SAVENNIERES and COTEAUX DU LAYON (Clos Ste Catherine).

Béarn s.w. France r. p. or w. dr. ★ D.Y.A.

Minor appellation of growing local (Basque country) interest, esp. wines from the coop. of Sallies de Béarn-Bellocq.

Beaujolais B'y. r. (p. w.) ★ D.Y.A.

The simple appellation of the big Beaujolais region: light short-lived fruity red.

Beaujolais de l'année

The Beaujolais of the latest vintage, until the next.

Beaujolais Primeur (or Nouveau)

The same made in a hurry (often only 4–5 days fermenting) for release at midnight on the third Wednesday in November. Best before Easter.

Beaujolais Supérieur B'y. r. (w.) ★ D.Y.A.

Beaujolais 1° of natural alcohol stronger than the 9° minimum. Since sugar is almost always added this means little.

Beaujolais-Villages B'y. r. ★★ 83 84 85

Wine from the better (northern) half of Beaujolais, stronger and tastier than plain Beaujolais. The 9 (easily) best "villages" are the "crus": FLEURIE, BROUILLY, etc. Of the 30 others the best lie around Beaujeu. The crus cannot be released "en primeur" before December 15th. They are best kept longer.

Beaumes de Venise Rh. (r. p.) br. sw. ★★★ NV

Sometimes France's best dessert MUSCAT, from the s. Côtes-du-Rhône; can be high-flavoured, subtle, lingering. The red and rosé from the cooperative are also good.

Beaune B'y. r. or (w. dr.) ★★★ 71 76 78' 79 80 82 83' 84 85

Middle-rank classic burgundy. Négociants' "CLOS" wines (usually "Premier Cru") are often best. "Beaune du Château" is a (good) brand of BOUCHARD PÈRE. V'yds incl.: Grèves, Bressandes, Teurons, Marconnets, Fèves.

Bégadan

Leading village of the n. MEDOC, with commendable coop.

Bellet Prov. p. r. w. dr. ★★★

Highly fashionable, much above average, local wine from near Nice. Tiny production. Very expensive.

Bergerac Dordogne r. or w. sw. or dr. ★★ 82 83 84 (w.) 85

Light-weight, often tasty, Bordeaux-style. Drink young, the white very young.

Besserat de Bellefon Cuvée Blanc de Blancs, NV, Rosé 79, Crémant Blanc Rosé 79, Brut Intégral 79

Rising champagne house for fine light wines, esp. CRÉMANT.

Beyer, Leon

Ancient ALSACE family wine business at Eguisheim making forceful dry wines that age well.

Bichot, Maison Albert

BEAUNE-based grower and merchant. V'yds in CHAMBERTIN, CLOS DE VOUGEOT, RICHEBOURG, etc., and Domaine Long-Depaquit in CHABLIS. Said to be the biggest B'y exporter.

Blagny B'y. r. or w. dr. |★★→★★★| 73 76 78 81 w. 82 83 84 (w.) 85
Hamlet between MEURSAULT and PULIGNY-MONTRACHET; affinities with both and VOLNAY for reds. Ages well.

Blanc de Blancs
Any white wine made from (only) white grapes, esp. CHAMPAGNE, which is usually made of black and white.

Blanc de Noirs White wine made from black grapes.

Blanck, Marcel
High-quality Alsace grower at Kientzheim.

Blanquette de Limoux Midi w. dr. sp. |★★| normally NV
Good cheap sparkler from near Carcassonne made by a version of the MÉTHODE CHAMPENOISE. Very dry and clean.

Blaye B'x. r. or w. dr. ★→★★ 79 81 82 83 85
Your average Bordeaux from e. of the Gironde. PREMIÈRES CÔTES DE BLAYE are better.

Boisset, Jean Claude
Dynamic Burgundy merchant/grower at NUITS ST GEORGES.

Bollinger NV "Special Cuvée 69 70 73 75 76 79 Année Rare 73, Rosé 81
Top champagne house, at AY. Dry full-flavoured style. Luxury wines "R.D." 73 75; Grande Année "79; rosé 81 and "Vieilles Vignes Françaises" 69 70 75 79 80 from ungrafted vines.

Bommes
Village of SAUTERNES. Best ch'x.: LATOUR-BLANCHE, LAFAURIE-PEYRAGUEY, etc.

Bonneau du Martray, Domaine
Major producer (with 22 acres) of CORTON-CHARLEMAGNE of the highest quality; also red CORTON.

Bonnes Mares B'y. r. |★★★★| 66 69 71 76 78' 79 80 82 83' 85
37-acre Grand Cru between CHAMBOLLE-MUSIGNY and MOREY-SAINT-DENIS. Sometimes better than CHAMBERTIN.

Bonnezeaux Lo. w. sw. |★★★| 76 78 81 82 83 84 85
Unusual fruity/acidic wine from CHENIN BLANC grapes, the best of COTEAUX DU LAYON.

Bordeaux B'x. r. or (p.) or w. ★ 81 82 83 85 (for ch'x. see p. 54)
Basic catch-all appellation for low-strength Bordeaux wine.

Bordeaux Supérieur ★→★★
Ditto, with slightly more alcohol.

Bordeaux Côtes–de-Francs B'x. r. or w. dr. |★| 81 82 83 85
Fringe Bordeaux from east of ST-EMILION. Light wines.

Borie-Manoux
Bordeaux shippers and château-owners, owned by the Castéja family. Ch'x. incl. BATAILLEY, HAUT BAGES-MONPELOU, DOMAINE DE L'EGLISE, TROTTEVIEILLE, BEAU-SITE.

Bouchard Aîné
Famous and long-established burgundy shipper and grower with 62 acres in Beaune, Mercurey, etc.

Bouchard Père et Fils
Important burgundy shipper (est. 1731) and grower with 209 acres of excellent v'yds., mainly in the CÔTE DE BEAUNE, and cellars at the Château de Beaune.

Bourg B'x. r. or (w. dr.) ★★ 78 79 81 82 83 85
Meaty, un-fancy claret from e. of the Gironde. CÔTES DE BOURG are better.

Bourgogne B'y. r. (p.) or w. dr. ★★ 83 85
Catch-all appellation for burgundy, but with theoretically higher standards than basic BORDEAUX. Light but often good flavour. BEAUJOLAIS crus can be sold as Bourgogne.

Bourgogne Grand Ordinaire B'y. r. or (w.) • D.Y.A.
The lowest burgundy appellation for Gamay wines. Rare.

Bourgogne Passe-tout-grains B'y. r. or (p.) |★| Age 1–2 years
Often enjoyable junior burgundy. ⅓ PINOT NOIR and ⅔ GAMAY grapes mixed in the vat. Not as "heady" as BEAUJOLAIS.

Bourgueil Lo. r. ∗∗∗ 76 81 82 83′ 84 85
> Normally delicate fruity CABERNET red from Touraine, the best from St. Nicolas de Bourgueil. Rich in exceptional years.

Bouvet-Ladubay
> Major producer of sparkling SAUMUR, controlled by TAITTINGER. Excellent CREMANT de Loire.

Bouzeron
> Village of the CÔTE CHALONNAISE distinguished for the only single-village appellation ALIGOTÉ.

Bouzy Rouge Champ. r. ∗∗∗ 79 81 82 83 85
> Still red wine from famous black-grape CHAMPAGNE village.

Brédif, Marc
> One of the most important growers and traders of VOUVRAY.

Brouilly B'y. r. ∗∗∗ 85
> One of the 9 best CRUS of BEAUJOLAIS: fruity, round, refreshing. One year in bottle is enough.

Brut Term for the driest wines of CHAMPAGNE until recently, when some completely unsugared wines have become available as "Brut Intégrale", "Brut non-dosé", "Brut zéro" etc.

Bugey Savoie w. dr. or sp. ∗→∗∗ D.Y.A.
> District with a variety of light sparkling, still or half-sparkling wines. Grapes incl. Roussette (or Roussanne) and v.g. CHARD.

Buzet s.w. France, r. or w. dr. ∗∗ 78 79 81 82 83 85
> Good light wines from just s.e. of Bordeaux. Promising area with well-run cooperative. Best wine: Cuvée Napoleon.

Cabernet See Grapes for red wine

Cabernet d'Anjou Lo. p. ∗→∗∗ D.Y.A.
> Delicate, often rather sweet, grapy rosé.

Cahors s.w. France r. ∗→ ∗∗ 75 76 78 79 80 81 82 83 85
> Traditionally hard "black" wine, now made more like Bordeaux but can be full-bodied and increasingly distinct. Top growers: Jouffreau, Vigouroux, Ch. de Caix.

Cairanne Rh. r. p. or w. dr. ∗∗ 80 81 82 83 84 85
> Village of CÔTES-DU-RHÔNE-VILLAGES. Good solid wines.

Calvet Once-great wine business in Bordeaux and Burgundy.

Canard-Duchêne NV Brut, rosé and Charles VII.
> NV, Vintage Charles VII and (sometimes) Coteaux Champenois. High quality champagne house owned (since 1978) by Veuve Clicquot.

Canon-Fronsac B'x. r. ∗∗ 70 75 78 79 81 82 83′
> Attractive solid reds from small area w. of POMEROL. Ch'x. include Canon, Canon-Moueix, Canon de Brem, Coustolle, Junayme, Mazeris-Bellevue, Moulin-Pey-Labrie, Toumalin, Vraye-Canon-Boyer. See also FRONSAC.

Cantenac B'x. r. ∗∗∗
> Village of the HAUT-MÉDOC entitled to the Appellation MARGAUX. Top ch'x. include PALMER, BRANE-CANTENAC, etc.

Cap Corse Corsica w. dr. br; ∗∗→∗∗∗
> The n. cape of the island. Splendid muscat and rare dry Vermentino white.

Caramany Pyr. r. (w. dr.) ∗ 81 82 83 84 85
> New appellation for part of CÔTES DE ROUSSILLON-VILLAGES.

Cassis Prov. (r. p.) w. dr. ∗∗ D.Y.A.
> Seaside village e. of Marseille known for its lively dry white, exceptional for Provence (e.g. Domaine du Paternel). Not to be confused with cassis, a blackcurrant liqueur made in Dijon.

Cave Cellar, or any wine establishment.

Cave coopérative
> Wine-growers' cooperative winery. Originally in many cases viticultural dustbins, almost all are now well run, well equipped and making some of the best wine of their areas.

Cépage Variety of vine, e.g. CHARDONNAY, MERLOT.

Cérons B'x. w. dr. or sw. ★★ 79 80 81 83 84 85

Neighbour of SAUTERNES with some good sweet-wine ch'x.

Chablis B'y. w. dr. ★★ 84 85

Distinctive full-flavoured greeny gold wine. Made only of CHARDONNAY in n. Burgundy.

Chablis Grand Cru B'y. w. dr. ★★★★ 78 81 82 83 84 85

Strong, subtle and altogether splendid. One of the great white burgundies. There are seven v'yds: Blanchots, Bougros, Clos, Grenouilles, Preuses, Valmur, Vaudésir. See also MOUTONNE.

Chablis Premier Cru B'y. w. dr. ★★★ 81 82 83 84 85

Second-rank but often excellent and more typical of Chablis than Grands Crus. Best v'yds incl.: Côte de Lechet, Fourchaume, Mont de Milieu, Montmains, Vaillons – 1,500 acres in all.

Chai Building for storing and maturing wine, esp. in Bordeaux.

Chambertin B'y. r. ★★★★ 69 71 76 78 79 80 82 83 84 85

32-acre Grand Cru giving the meatiest, most enduring and often the best red burgundy, 15 growers, incl. BOUCHARD PÈRE, Camus, Damay, Tortochot, Rebourseau, ROUSSEAU, Trapet.

Chambertin-Clos-de-Bèze B'y. r. ★★★★ 76 78 79 80 81 82 83 84 85

37-acre neighbour of CHAMBERTIN. Similarly splendid wine. Ten growers incl. CLAIR-DAU, DROUHIN, Damoy, ROUSSEAU.

Chambolle-Musigny B'y. r. (w.) ★★★ 76 78 80 82 83 84 85

420-acre CÔTE DE NUITS village with fabulously fragrant, complex wine. Best v'yds.: MUSIGNY, part of BONNES-MARES, Les Amoureuses, Les Charmes. Best growers incl.: DE VOGÜÉ, DROUHIN, FAIVELEY, Roumier, Mugnier, Hudelot-Noëllat.

Champagne

Sparkling wine from 60,000 acres 90 miles e. of Paris, made by the MÉTHODE CHAMPENOISE. Wines from elsewhere, however good, cannot be Champagne. (See also names of brands.)

Champagne, Grande The appellation of the best area of COGNAC.

Champigny See Saumur

Chanson Père et Fils

Growers (with 110 acres) and traders in fine wine at BEAUNE. Reds can be pale but generally last well.

Chante-Alouette

A famous brand of white HERMITAGE from CHAPOUTIER.

Chantovent Major brand of VIN DE TABLE, largely from MINERVOIS.

Chapelle-Chambertin B'y. r. ★★★ 76 78 79 80 82 83' 85

13-acre neighbour of CHAMBERTIN. Wine not so meaty.

Chapoutier

Long-established firm of growers and traders of Rhône wines.

Chardonnay See Grapes for white wine

Charmes-Chambertin B'y. r. ★★★ 71 76 78 79 80 82 83' 85

76-acre neighbour of CHAMBERTIN. Growers incl. Bachelet, Castagnier, Roty, ROUSSEAU.

Chassagne-Montrachet B'y. r. or w. dr. ★★★→★★★★ 76 78 80r. 81w. 82 83 84 85

750-acre CÔTE DE BEAUNE village with superlative rich dry whites and sterling hefty reds. Best v'yds.: MONTRACHET, BÂTARD-MONTRACHET, CRIOTS-BÂTARD-MONTRACHET, Ruchottes, Caillerets, Boudriottes (r. w.), Morgeot (r., w.), CLOS-ST-JEAN (r.). Growers incl. RAMONET-PRUDHON, Morey MAGENTA, DELAGRANGE-BACHELET, Gagnard-Delagrange, Niellon.

Chasseloir, Domaine du

The HQ of the firm of Chéreau-Carré, makers of several excellent domaine MUSCADETS.

Château

An estate, big or small, good or indifferent, particularly in Bordeaux. In Burgundy the term "domaine" is used. For all Bordeaux ch'x see pp. 54–72.

Château-Chalon Jura w. dr. ★★★
> Unique strong dry yellow wine, almost like sherry. Ready to drink when bottled (at about 6 years).

Château Corton-Grancey B'y. r. ★★★ 76 78 79 82 83 85
> Famous estate at ALOXE-CORTON, the property of Louis LATOUR. Impressive wine.

Château d'Arlay
> Major JURA estate; 160 acres in skilful hands.

Château de Beaucastel Rh. r. ★★★ 76 78' 79 80 81 83 84 85
> One of the biggest (173 acres) and best-run estates of CHÂTEAU-NEUF-DU-PAPE.

Château de la Chaize B'y. r. ★★★ 83 85
> The best known estate of BROUILLY, with 200 acres.

Château de la Maltroye B'y. r. w. dr. ★★★
> Sometimes excellent 32-acre estate at CHASSAGNE-MONTRA-CHET.

Château de Meursault B'y. r. w. ★★★
> 100-acre estate owned by PATRIARCHE with good v'yds in Meursault, VOLNAY, POMMARD, BEAUNE. Splendid cellars open to the public for tasting.

Château de Panisseau Dordogne w. dr. ★★ D.Y.A.
> Leading estate of BERGERAC: good dry SAUVIGNON BLANC.

Château de Selle Prov. r. p. or w. dr. ★★
> Estate near Cotignac, Var. Well-known and typical wines.

Château des Fines Roches Rh. r. ★★★ 78 79 80 81 83 84 85
> Large (112 acres) and distinguished estate in CHÂTEAUNEUF-DU-PAPE. Strong old-style wine.

Burgundy boasts one of the world's most famous and certainly its most beautiful hospital, the Hospices de Beaune, founded in 1443 by Nicolas Rolin, Chancellor to the Duke of Burgundy, and his wife Guigone de Salins. The hospital he built and endowed with vineyards for its income still operates in the same building and still thrives, tending the sick of Beaune without charge, on the sale of its wine. Many growers since have bequeathed their land to the Hospices. Today it owns 125 acres of prime land in Beaune, Pommard, Volnay, Meursault, Corton and Mazis-Chambertin. The wine is sold by auction every year on the third Sunday in November.

Château du Nozet Lo. w. dr. ★★★ 84 85
> Biggest and best-known estate of Pouilly (FUMÉ) sur Loire.

Château Fortia Rh. r. ★★★ 78 79 80 81 83 84 85
> First-class property in CHÂTEAUNEUF-DU-PAPE. Traditional methods. The owner's father, Baron Le Roy, also fathered the APPELLATION CONTRÔLLÉE system.

Château-Grillet Rh. w. dr. ★★★★ 81 82 83 84 85
> 3½-acre v'yd. with one of France's smallest appellations. Intense, fragrant, expensive. Drink fairly young.

Château-Gris B'y. r. ★★★ 76 78 82 83 85
> Well-known estate at NUITS-ST-GEORGES, linked with BICHOT.

Châteaumeillant Lo. r. p. or w. dr. ★ D.Y.A.
> Small VDQS area near SANCERRE. Light GAMAY and PINOT NOIR.

Châteauneuf-du-Pape Rh. r. (w. dr.) ★★★ 78 79 80 82 83 84 85
> 7,500 acres near Avignon. Best estate ("domaine") wines are dark, strong, long-lived. Others may be light and/or disappointing. The white is heavy: most now made to D.Y.A.

Château Rayas Rh. r. (w. dr.) ★★★ 78 80 81 83 84 85
> Famous old-style property in CHÂTEAUNEUF-DU-PAPE.

Château Simone Prov. r. p. or w. dr. ★★ D.Y.A.
> Well-known property in Palette; the only one in this appellation near Aix-en-Provence.

Château Vignelaure Prov. r. ★★★ 75 76 77 78 79 80 81 82 83 84 85
135-acre Provençal estate near Aix making good Bordeaux-style wine with CABERNET, Syrah and Grenache grapes.

Chatillon-en-Diois Rh. r. p. or w. dr. ★ D.Y.A.
Small VDQS e. of the Rhône near Die. Good GAMAY reds; white (some Aligoté) mostly made into CLAIRETTE DE DIE.

Chave, Gérard
To many the top grower of HERMITAGE, red and white.

Chavignol
Village of SANCERRE with famous v'yd., Les Monts Damnés.

Chénas B'y. r. ★★★ 83 84 85
Good Beaujolais cru, neighbour to MOULIN-À-VENT and JULIENAS. One of the weightier Beaujolais.

Chenin Blanc
See Grapes for white wine

Chevalier-Montrachet B'y. w. dr. ★★★★ 71 78 79 81 82 83 84 85
17-acre neighbour of MONTRACHET with similar luxurious wine, perhaps a little less powerful. Includes Les Demoiselles. Growers incl. BOUCHARD PÈRE, LEFLAIVE, Niellon.

Cheverny Lo. r. p. or w. dr. ★→★★ D.Y.A.
Light sharpish Loire country wine from near Chambord.

Chignin Savoie w. dr. ★ D.Y.A.
Light soft white of Jacquère grapes.

Chinon Lo. r. ★★★ 76 81 82 83' 84 85
Delicate fruity CABERNET from TOURAINE. Drink cool when young. Good vintages age like Bordeaux.

Chiroubles B'y. r. ★★★ 85
Good but tiny Beaujolais cru next to FLEURIE; freshly fruity silky wine for early drinking.

Chorey-lès-Beaune B'y. r. ★★ 80 82 83 85
Minor appellation on flat land n. of BEAUNE notable for one fine grower: TOLLOT-BEAUT.

Chusclan Rh. r. p. or w. dr. ★ 80 81 83 84 85
Village of CÔTE-DU-RHÔNE-VILLAGES. Good middle-weight wines from the cooperative.

Cissac HAUT-MÉDOC village just w. of PAUILLAC.

Clair-Daü
First-class 100-acre burgundy estate of the northern CÔTE DE NUITS, with cellars at MARSANNAY. Merged in 1986 with DROUHIN.

Clairet Very light red wine, almost rosé.

Clairette
Mediocre white grape of the s. of France. Gives neutral wine.

Clairette de Bellegarde Midi w. dr. ★ D.Y.A.
Plain neutral white from near Nîmes.

Clairette de Die Rh. w. dr. or s./sw. sp. ★★ NV
Popular dry or semi-sweet rather MUSCAT-flavoured sparkling wine from the e. Rhône, or straight dry CLAIRETTE white, surprisingly ageing well 3–4 years.

Clairette du Languedoc Midi w. dr. ★ D.Y.A.
Plain neutral white from near Montpellier.

La Clape Midi r. p. or w. dr. ★→★★
Full-bodied VDQS wines from near Narbonne. The red gains character after 2–3 years, the white even longer. V.g. rosé.

Claret Traditional English term for red BORDEAUX.

Climat
Burgundian word for individual named v'yd., e.g. Beaune Grèves, Chambolle-Musigny les Amoureuses.

Clos
A term carrying some prestige, reserved for distinct, usually walled, v'yds., often in one ownership. Frequently in Burgundy and Alsace. Les Clos in Chablis's Grandest Cru.

Clos-de-Bèze

See Chambertin-Clos-de-Bèze.

Clos de la Roche B'y. r. ★★★ **71 76** 78 **79 80 82** 83' 84 85

38-acre Grand Cru at MOREY-ST-DENIS. Powerful complex wine like CHAMBERTIN. Producers incl. BOUCHARD PÈRE, Ponsot, DUJAC, ROUSSEAU, Rémy, Castagnier.

Clos des Lambrays B'y. r. ★★★ **71 76** 78 83 85

15-acre Grand Cru v'yd. at MOREY-ST-DENIS. Changed hands in 1979 after a shaky period. Young vines need time.

Clos des Mouches B'y. r. or w. dr. ★★★

Splendid Premier Cru v'yd. of BEAUNE owned by DROUHIN.

Clos de Tart B'y. r. ★★★ **71 76** 78 **79 80 82** 83' 84 85

18-acre Grand Cru at MOREY-ST-DENIS owned by MOMMESSIN. Relatively delicate wines, recently much improved.

Clos de Vougeot B'y. r. ★★★ **71 76** 78 80 82 83 84 85

124-acre CÔTE-DE-NUITS Grand Cru with many owners. Variable, sometimes sublime. Maturity depends on the grower's technique and his position on the hillside.

Clos du Chêne Marchand

Well-known v'yd. at Bué, SANCERRE.

Clos du Roi B'y. r. ★★★

Part of the Grand Cru CORTON; also a Premier Cru of BEAUNE.

Clos St Denis B'y. r. ★★★ **76** 78 **79 80 82** 83' 84 85

16-acre Grand Cru at MOREY-ST-DENIS. Splendid sturdy wine.

Clos St Jacques B'y. r. ★★★ **71 76** 78 **79 80 82** 83' 84 85

17-acre Premier Cru of GEVREY-CHAMBERTIN. Excellent powerful velvety wine, often better (and dearer) than some of the CHAMBERTIN Grands Crus. Main grower: ROUSSEAU.

The Confrèrie des Chevaliers du Tastevin is Burgundy's wine fraternity and the most famous of its kind in the world. It was founded in 1933 by a group of Burgundian patriots, headed by Camille Rodier and Georges Faiveley, to rescue their beloved Burgundy from a period of slump and despair by promoting its inimitable products. Today it regularly holds banquets with elaborate and sprightly ceremonial for 600 guests at its headquarters, the old château in the Clos de Vougeot. The Confrèrie has branches in many countries and members among lovers of wine all over the world.

Clos St Jean B'y. r. ★★★ **76** 78 **79 80 82** 83' 84 85

36-acre Premier Cru of CHASSAGNE-MONTRACHET. Very good red, more solid than subtle.

Coche-Dury

Highly fashionable grower of a tiny quantity of oak-scented MEURSAULT.

Cognac Town and region of western France and its brandy.

Collioure Pyr. r. ★ **80 81 82 83** 84 85

Strong dry RANCIO red from BANYULS area. Small production.

Condrieu Rh. w. dr. ★★★★ D.Y.A.

Outstanding soft fragrant white of great character (and price) from the Viognier grape. The leading grower is Vernay. Ch.-GRILLET is similar.

Corbières Midi r. or (p.) or (w.) ★ **83 84** 85

Good vigorous cheap VDQS reds, steadily improving and often a bargain. Will soon graduate to APPELLATION CONTRÔLÉE

Cordier, Ets D.

Important Bordeaux shipper and château-owner, including Ch'x. GRUAUD-LAROSE, TALBOT, CANTEMERLE, MEYNEY.

Cornas Rh. r. ★★ **78 79 80 82** 83 84 85

Expanding 300-acre district s. of HERMITAGE. Typical sturdy Rhône wine of good quality from the SYRAH grape.

Corse   Corsica. Strong wines of all colours. Better appellations include PATRIMONIO, Sartene, AJACCIO, CAP CORSE.

Corton   B'y. r.   ★★★★   71 76′ 78′ 80 82 83′ 84 85
The only Grand Cru red of the CÔTE DE BEAUNE. 200 acres in ALOXE-CORTON incl. les Bressandes and le CLOS DU ROI. Rich powerful wines should be long-lived.

Corton-Charlemagne   B'y. w. dr. ★★★★ 78 79 80 81 82 83 84 85
The white section (one-third) of CORTON. Rich spicy lingering wine. Behaves like a red wine and ages magnificently.

Coste, Pierre   Influential wine-broker and maker of LANGON.

Costières du Gard   Midi r. p. or w. dr. ★→★★ D.Y.A.
VDQS of moderate (improving) quality from the Rhône delta.

Coteaux Champenois   Champ. r. (p.) or w. dr. ★★★
The appellation for non-sparkling champagne. Vintages follow those for Champagne.

Coteaux d'Aix-en-Provence   Prov r. p. or w. dr. ★→★★
Agreeable country wines tending to improve. Ch. VIGNELAURE is the leading property. Also Ch. de Calissanne.

Coteaux d'Ancenis   r. p. w. dr. ★ D.Y.A.
Light Cabernet and Gamay reds and pinks; sharpish whites from MUSCADET country.

Coteaux de la Loire   Lo. w. dr. sw.   ★★→★★★   78 79 81 82 83 84 85
Forceful and fragrant CHENIN BLANC whites from Anjou. The best are in SAVENNIERES. Excellent as an apéritif.

Coteaux de l'Aubance   Lo. p. or w. dr./sw. ★★ D.Y.A.
Light and typical minor Anjou wines. The best are MOELLEUX.

Coteaux de Pierrevert   Rh. r. p. or w. dr. or sp.   ★   D.Y.A.
Minor southern VDQS from nr. Manosque. Well-made coop wine mostly rosé, with fresh whites.

Coteaux de Saumur   Lo. w. dr./sw.   ★★   D.Y.A.
Pleasant dry or sweetish fruity CHENIN BLANC.

Coteaux des Baux-en-Provence   Prov. r. p. or w. dr. ★→★★ NV
A twin to COTEAUX D'AIX, sharing the same VDQS.

Coteaux du Giennois   r. w. dr. ★
Minor Loire area n. of SANCERRE. Light GAMAY and PINOT NOIR, SAUVIGNON and CHENIN BLANC.

Coteaux du Languedoc   Midi r. p. or w. dr.   ★→★★   D.Y.A.
Scattered better-than-ordinary Midi areas with VDQS status. The best (e.g. Faugères, St Saturnin, LA CLAPE, ST CHINIAN, Quatourze, St-Georges-d'Orques, Cabrières) age for 1 yr or two.

Coteaux du Layon   Lo. w. s./sw. or sw.   ★★   78 81 82 83 84 85
District centred on Rochefort, s. of Angers, making sweet CHENIN BLANC wines above the general Anjou standard. "C. du L-Chaume" is a higher appellation.

Coteaux du Loir   Lo. r. p. or w. dr./sw. ★★ 78 82 83 84 85
Small region n.. of Tours. Occasionally excellent wines. Best v'yd.: JASNIERES. The Loir is a tributary of the Loire.

Coteaux du Tricastin   Rh. r. p. or w. dr. ★★ D.Y.A.
Fringe CÔTES-DU-RHÔNE of increasing quality from s. of Valence. Pierre Labeye is the chief producer.

Coteaux du Vendomois   Lo. r. p. or w. dr. ★ D.Y.A.
Fringe Loire from n. of Blois. Mainly GAMAY.

Côte(s)
Means hillside; generally a superior vineyard to those on the plain. Many appellations start with either Côtes or Coteaux, which means the same thing. In ST-EMILION it distinguishes the valley slopes from the higher plateau.

Côte Chalonnaise   B'y. r. w. dr. sp.   ★★→★★★
Lesser-known v'yd. area between BEAUNE and MÂCON. See Mercurey, Givry, Rully, Montagny.

Côte de Beaune B'y. r. or w. dr. ★★→★★★★
Used geographically: the southern half of the CÔTE D'OR. Applies as an appellation only to parts of BEAUNE.

Côte de Beaune-Villages B'y. r. or w. dr. ★★ 78 80 83 85
Regional appellation for secondary wines of the classic area. They cannot be labelled "Côte de Beaune" without either "Villages" or the village name.

Côte de Brouilly B'y. r. ★★★ 83 85
Fruity, rich, vigorous Beaujolais cru. One of the best. Leading estate: Ch. Thivin.

Côte de Nuits B'y. r. or (w. dr.) ★★→★★★★
The northern half of the CÔTE D'OR. Nearly all red wine.

Côte de Nuits-Villages B'y. r. (w.) ★★ 78 80 83 85
A junior appellation, rarely seen but worth investigating.

Côte d'Or
Département name applied to the central and principal Burgundy v'yd. slopes, consisting of the CÔTE DE BEAUNE and CÔTE DE NUITS. The name is not used on labels.

Côte Rôtie Rh. r. ★★★ 71 76 78 79 80 82 83' 84 85
Potentially the finest Rhône red, from just s. of Vienne; achieves complex delicacy with age. Recent enlarged production has compromised quality. Top growers include JABOULET, CHAPOUTIER, VIDAL-FLEURY, Jasmin, Guigal.

Côtes d'Auvergne Central France r. p. or (w. dr.) ★ D.Y.A.
Flourishing small VDQS area near Clermont-Ferrand. Red (at best) like light BEAUJOLAIS. Chanturgues is the best known.

Côtes de Blaye B'x. w. dr. ★ D.Y.A.
Run-of-the-mill Bordeaux white from BLAYE.

Côtes de Bordeaux Saint-Macaire B'x. w. dr./sw. ★ D.Y.A.
Run-of-the-mill Bordeaux white from east of Sauternes.

Côtes de Bourg B'x. r. ★→★★ 78 79 81 82 83 85
Appellation used for many of the better reds of BOURG. Ch'x incl. de Barbe, La Barde, du Bousquet, La Croix de Millorit, de la Grave, Grand-Jour, Font Guilhem, Guerry, Rousset, Lalibarde, Lamothe, Mendoce, Falfas, Peychaud, de Thau.

Côtes de Castillon B'x. r. ★→★★ 78 79 81 82 83 85
Flourishing region just e. of St. Emilion. Similar wines, though a touch lighter. Ch'x incl. Belcier, Fonds-Rhondes, Haut-Tuquet, Lardit, PITRAY, Ste Colombe.

Côtes de Duras Dordogne r. or w. dr. ★ 82 83 85
Neighbour to BERGERAC. Similar light wines; the white best.

Côtes de Francs
See Bordeaux—Côtes de Francs.

Côtes de Fronsac See FRONSAC.

Côtes de Jura Jura r. p. or w. dr. (sp.) ★ D.Y.A.
Various light tints and tastes. ARBOIS is theoretically better.

Côtes de Montravel Dordogne w. dr./sw. ★ NV
Part of BERGERAC; trad. medium-sw. wine, now often dry.

Côtes de Provence Prov. r. p. or w. dr. ★→★★ NV
The wine of Provence; often with more alcohol than character. Standards have recently been improving. The best properties have the right to say "Cru Classé".

Côtes de Roussillon Pyr. r. p. or w. dr. ★→★★ 81 82 83 84 85
Country wine of e. Pyrenees. The hefty reds are best and can be very tasty. Some whites are sharp VINS VERTS.

Côtes de Roussillon-Villages Pyr. r. ★★ 81 82 83 84 85
The best reds of the region, incl. CARAMANY and LATOUR DE FRANCE.

Côtes de Saint-Mont s.w. France r. w. dr. p. ★
Promising VDQS from the Gers, not unlike MADIRAN.

Côtes de Toul E. France r. p. or w. dr. ★ D.Y.A.
Very light wines from Lorraine; mainly VIN GRIS (rosé).

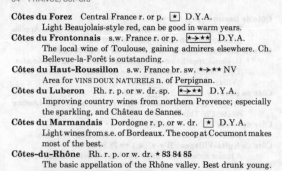

Côtes du Forez Central France r. or p. ★ D.Y.A.
Light Beaujolais-style red, can be good in warm years.

Côtes du Frontonnais s.w. France r. or p. ★→★★ D.Y.A.
The local wine of Toulouse, gaining admirers elsewhere. Ch. Bellevue-la-Forêt is outstanding.

Côtes du Haut-Roussillon s.w. France br. sw. ★→★★ NV
Area for VINS DOUX NATURELS n. of Perpignan.

Côtes du Luberon Rh. r. p. or w. dr. sp. ★→★★ D.Y.A.
Improving country wines from northern Provence; especially the sparkling, and Château de Sannes.

Côtes du Marmandais Dordogne r. p. or w. dr. ★ D.Y.A.
Light wines from s.e. of Bordeaux. The coop at Cocumont makes most of it.

Côtes-du-Rhône Rh. r. p. or w. dr. ★ 83 84 85
The basic appellation of the Rhône valley. Best drunk young. Wide variations of quality due to grape ripeness, therefore rising with degree of alcohol. See CÔTES-DU-RHÔNE-VILLAGES.

Côtes-du-Rhône-Villages Rh. r. p. or w. dr. ★→★★ 80 83 84 85
The wine of the 17 best villages of the southern Rhône. Substantial and on the whole reliable, sometimes delicious.

Côtes du Ventoux Prov. r. (w. dr.) ★★ 83 84 85
Booming appellation for tasty reds between the Rhône and Provence.

Côtes du Vivarais Prov. r. p. or w. dr. ★ NV
Pleasant country wines from s. Massif Centrale. Like light CÔTES-DU-RHÔNE.

Côtes Roannaises Central France r. ★ D.Y.A.
Minor GAMAY region high up the Loire.

Coulée de Serrant Lo. w. dr./sw. ★★★ 76 78 79 81 82 83 84 85
10-acre v'yd. on n. bank of Loire at SAVENNIERES, Anjou. Intense strong fruity/sharp wine, ages well.

Crémant
In Champagne means "Creaming"—i.e. half-sparkling. Since 1975 an appellation for high-quality champagne-method sparkling wines from Alsace, the Loire and Bourgogne—often a notable bargain.

Crémant de Loire w. dr. sp. ★★ NV
High-quality sparkling wine from ANJOU and TOURAINE.

Crépy Savoie w. dr. ★★ D.Y.A.
Light, Swiss-style white from s. shore of Lake Geneva. "Crépitant" has been coined for its faint fizz.

Criots-Bâtard-Montrachet B'y. w. ★★★ 76 78 79 81 82 83 84 85
4-acre neighbour to BÂTARD-MONTRACHET. Similar wine.

Crozes-Hermitage Rh. r. or (w. dr.) ★★ 78 80 82 83 84 85
Larger and less distinguished neighbour to HERMITAGE. Robust and often excellent reds, but choose carefully.

Cru "Growth", as in "first-growth"—meaning vineyard.

Cru Bourgeois
General term for MÉDOC châteaux below CRU CLASSÉ.

Cru Bourgeois Supérieur (Cru Grand Bourgeois)
Official rank one better than the last. Aged in barrels.

Cru Classé
Classed growth. One of the first five official quality classes of the Médoc, classified in 1855. Also any classed growth of another district (e.g. Graves, St-Emilion, Sauternes).

Cru Grand Bourgeois Exceptionnel
Official rank above CRU BOURGEOIS SUPÉRIEUR, immediately below CRU CLASSÉ. Several fine châteaux are unofficially Exceptionnel.

Cruse et Fils Frères
Long-established Bordeaux shipper famous for fine wine. Owner of Ch. D'ISSAN.

Cubzac, St.-André-de B'x. r. or w. dr. ★ 82 83 85
Town 15 miles n.e. of Bordeaux, centre of the minor Cubzaguais region. Sound reds have the appellation Bordeaux. Estates include: Ch. du Bouilh, Ch. de Terrefort-Quancard, Ch. Timberlay, Domaine de Beychevelle.

Cussac Village just s. of ST. JULIEN. Appellation Haut-Médoc.

Cuve Close
Short-cut method of making sparkling wine in a tank. The sparkle dies away in the glass much quicker than with MÉTHODE CHAMPENOISE wine.

Cuvée
The quality of wine produced in a "cuve" or vat. Also a word of many uses, incl. "blend". In Burgundy interchangeable with "Cru". Often just refers to a "lot" of wine.

d'Angerville, Marquis
Famous burgundy grower with immaculate estate in VOLNAY.

Daumas Gassac, Mas de Midi r. ★★★ 81 82 83 84 85
The outstanding estate of the Midi, producing huge Bordeaux-like wines on volcanic soil. Alarming quality.

Degré alcoolique
Degrees of alcohol, i.e. percent by volume.

De Ladoucette
Leading producer of POUILLY-FUMÉ, based at Ch. DE NOZET. Luxury brand "Baron de L.".

Delagrange-Bachelet
One of the leading proprietors in CHASSAGNE-MONTRACHET.

Delas Frères
Long-established firm of Rhône-wine specialists at Tournon, v'yds. at CÔTE RÔTIE, HERMITAGE, CORNAS etc. Owned by DEUTZ.

Delorme, André
Leading merchants and growers of the CÔTE CHALONNAISE. Specialists in sparkling wine and excellent RULLY.

De Luze, A. et Fils
Bordeaux shipper and owners of Ch'x. CANTENAC-BROWN and PAVEIL DE LUZE; owned by Rémy-Martin of Cognac.

Demi-Sec "Half-dry": in practice more than half-sweet.

Depagneux, Jacques de Cie
Well-regarded merchants of BEAUJOLAIS.

Deutz & Geldermann NV and 71 73 75 76 78 79 81 82, Rosé 82, Blanc de Blancs 78 79 81 82
One of the best of the smaller champagne houses. Full-flavoured wines. Luxury brand: Cuvée William Deutz (75 79).

Domaine
Property, particularly in Burgundy.

Domaine de Belair
An attractive light-weight branded red Bordeaux. D.Y.A.

Domaine de l'Eglantière
Important CHABLIS estate. See DURUP.

Domaine du Vieux Télégraphe Rh. r. w. dr. ★★★ 76 78 79 81 83 84 85
A leader in modern high-quality CHÂTEAUNEUF-DU-PAPE for long ageing.

Dom Pérignon 70 71 73 75 76 78 80 and Rosé 75 78
Luxury brand of MOËT ET CHANDON named after the legendary blind inventor of champagne.

Dopff "au Moulin"
Ancient family wine-house at Riquewihr, Alsace. Best wines: Riesling Schoenenbourg, Gewürztraminer Eichberg. Pioneers of sparkling wine in Alsace.

Dopff & Irion
Another excellent Riquewihr (ALSACE) business. Best wines include Muscat les Amandiers, Riesling de Riquewihr.

Doudet-Naudin

Burgundy merchant and grower at Savigny-lès-Beaune. V'yds. incl. BEAUNE CLOS DU ROI. Dark, heavy wines.

Dourthe Frères

Well-reputed Bordeaux merchant representing a wide range of ch'x., mainly good Crus Bourgeois, incl. Ch'x. MAUCAILLOU, TRONQUOY-LALANDE, BELGRAVE. "Beau-Mayne" is their reliable branded Bordeaux.

Doux Sweet.

Drouhin, J. et Cie

Prestigious Burgundy grower (130 acres) and merchant. Offices in BEAUNE, v'yds. in BEAUNE, MUSIGNY, CLOS DE VOUGEOT, CHABLIS, etc. Drouhin also owns Jaffelin et Cie. See also CLAIR DAU.

Duboeuf, Georges

Top-class BEAUJOLAIS merchant at Romanèche-Thorin. The leader of the region.

Duclot, Ets

Bordeaux merchant specializing in the top growths. Controlled by MOUEIX.

Dufouleur Frères

Growers and merchants of toothsome burgundy at NUITS-ST-GEORGES and MERCUREY.

Dujac, Domaine

Perfectionist burgundian grower at MOREY-ST-DENIS with v'yds in that village, ECHÉZEAUX, BONNES-MARES, GEVREY-CHAMBERTIN, etc.

Durup, Jean

One of the biggest Chablis growers with 140 acres, including the DOMAINE DE L'EGLANTIERE and Ch. de Maligny.

Echézeaux B'y. r. ★★★ 76 78′ 79 80 82 83′ 84 85

74-acre Grand Cru between VOSNE-ROMANÉE and CLOS DE VOUGEOT. Can be superlative fragrant burgundy without great weight e.g. from Mugneret, Gouroux, DOM DE LA ROMANÉE-CONTI, Jacqueline Jayer.

Edelzwicker Alsace w. ★ D.Y.A.

Light white from mixture of grapes, often fruity and good.

Entre-Deux-Mers B'x. w. dr. ★ D.Y.A.

Standard dry white Bordeaux from between the Garonne and Dordogne rivers. Often a good buy, ezp. "La Gamage", Ch. ST. BONNET.

Les Epenots B'y. r. ★★★

Famous Premier Cru v'yd. of POMMARD. Also spelt Epeneaux for the 12-acre Clos des Epeneaux owned by Comte Armand.

Eschenauer, Louis

Famous Bordeaux merchants, owners of Ch'x. RAUSAN-SEGLA and SMITH-HAUT-LAFITTE, DE LAMOUROUX and LA GARDE in GRAVES. Controlled by John Holt, part of the Lonrho group.

l'Etoile Jura w. dr./sw/sp. ★★

Sub-region of the Jura known for stylish whites, incl. VIN JAUNE like CHÂTEAU-CHALON and good sparkling.

Faiveley, J.

Family-owned growers (with 182 acres) and merchants at NUITS-ST-GEORGES, with v'yds. in CHAMBERTIN-CLOS-DE-BÈZE, CHAMBOLLE-MUSIGNY, CORTON, NUITS, MERCUREY (150 acres). Consistent high quality recently.

Faller, Théo

Top ALSACE grower at the Domain Weinbach, Kaysersberg.

Faugères Midi r. (p. or w. dr.) ★ 82 83 84 85

Isolated village of the COTEAUX DU LANGUEDOC making above-average wine. Became Appellation Contrôlée in 1982.

Fèvre, William
Conservative Chablis grower with the biggest Grand Cru holding (40 acres). His label is Domaine de la Maladière.

Fitou Midi r. ★★ 80 81 82 83 84 85
Superior CORBIÈRES red; powerful and ages well.

Fixin B'y. r. ★★ 76 78 80 82 83' 84 85
A worthy and under-valued neighbour to GEVREY-CHAMBERTIN. Often splendid reds. Best v'yds.: Clos du Chapitre, Les Hervelets, Clos Napoléon.

Fleurie B'y. r. ★★★ 83 84 85
The epitome of a Beaujolais cru: fruity, scented, silky, racy.

Frais Fresh or cool.

Frappé Ice-cold.

Froid Cold.

Fronsac B'x. r. ★→★★ 75 78 79 80 81 82 83 85
Pretty hilly area of good reds just w. of St-Emilion. Ch'x incl. Dalem, La Dauphine, Mayne-Vieil, la Rivière, de Carles, La Valade, Villars. See also CANON-FRONSAC.

Frontignan Midi br. sw. ★ NV
Strong sweet and liquorous muscat wine.

Gagnard-Delagrange, Jacques
Estimable small (13-acre) grower of CHASSAGNE-MONTRACHET, including some LE MONTRACHET.

Gaillac s.w. France r. p. or w. dr./sw. or sp. ★ NV
Ancient area showing signs of new life after generations of dullness. Slightly fizzy "Perlé" is good value.

Gallaire ★★ D.Y.A.
Very attractive fruity young Bordeaux from SICHEL.

Gamay
See Grapes for red wine

Geisweiler et Fils
One of the bigger merchant-houses of Burgundy, Cellars and 50 acres of v'yds. at NUITS-ST-GEORGES. Also 150 acres at Bevy in the HAUTES CÔTES DE NUITS and 30 in the CÔTE CHALONNAISE.

Gevrey-Chambertin B'y. r. ★★★ 76 78 79 80 82 83 85
The village containing the great CHAMBERTIN and many other noble v'yds. as well as some more commonplace.

Gewürztraminer
The speciality grape of ALSACE: perfumed and spicy, whether dry or sweet.

Gigondas Rh. r. or p. ★★ 78 80 81 83 84 85
Worthy neighbour to CHÂTEAUNEUF-DU-PAPE. Strong, full-bodied, sometimes peppery wine.

Gilbey, S.A.
British firm long-established as Bordeaux merchants at Ch. LOUDENNE in the MÉDOC. Now owned by International Distillers and Vintners.

Gisselbrecht, Louis
High-quality Alsace shippers at Dambach-la-Ville.

Givry B'y. r. or w. dr. ★★ 83 84 85
Underrated village of the CÔTE CHALONNAISE: light but tasty and typical burgundy.

Gosset NV, 73 75 76 78 79 80 81 "Grande Réserve"
Small, very old champagne house at Ay. Fine full wines. Now linked with Philiponnat.

Gouges, Henri
Worthy burgundy grower of NUITS-ST-GEORGES. Good reds and very rare white "La Perrière".

Goulaine, Château de
The ceremonial showplace of MUSCADET; a noble family estate and its appropriate wine.

Goulet, Georges NV, rosé **76 79**, Crémant Blanc de Blancs **79** and **71 73 75 76 79** 81

High-quality Reims champagne house. Abel Lepitre is a cheaper range. Luxury brand: Cuvée du Centenaire **74 76 79**.

Goût

Taste, e.g. "goût anglais"—as the English like it (i.e. dry).

Grand Cru

One of the top Burgundy v'yds. with its own Appellation Contrôlée. Similar in Alsace but more vague elsewhere. In ST-EMILION the third rank of château, numbering about 200.

Grand Roussillon Midi br. sw. ★★ NV

Broad appellation for muscat and other sweet fortified wines ("Vins Doux Naturels") of eastern Pyrenees.

Grands-Echézeaux B'y. r. ★★★★ **69 71 76 78 79 80 82 83 84 85**

Superlative 22-acre Grand Cru next to CLOS DE VOUGEOT.

Gratien, Alfred and Gratien & Meyer

Excellent smaller champagne house (fine, very dry, long-lasting wine **73 76 79**) and its counterpart at SAUMUR on the Loire.

Graves B'x. r. or w. ★-▶★★★★

Large region s. of Bordeaux city. Its best wines are red, but the name is used chiefly for its dry or medium whites.

Graves-Léognan

New APPELLATION CONTRÔLÉE for part of northern Graves.

Graves de Vayres B'x r. or w. ★

Part of ENTRE-DEUX-MERS; of no special character.

Les Gravières B'y. r. ★★★

Famous Premier Cru v'yd. of SANTENAY. Incl. Clos des Tavannes.

Griotte-Chambertin B'y. r. ★★★ **69 71 76 78' 79 80 82 83' 84 85**

14-acre Grand Cru adjoining CHAMBERTIN. Similar wine, but less masculine and more "tender". Growers incl. DROUHIN.

Gros Plant du Pays Nantais Lo. w. ⬛ D.Y.A.

Junior cousin of MUSCADET, sharper and lighter; made of the COGNAC grape also known as Folle Blanche, Ugni Blanc etc.

Haut-Benauge B'x. w. dr. ★ D.Y.A.

Appellation for a limited area within ENTRE-DEUX-MERS.

Hautes-Côtes de Beaune B'y. r. or w. dr. ★★ 78 81w. 83 85

Appellation for a dozen villages in the hills behind the CÔTE DE BEAUNE. Light wines, worth investigating.

Hautes-Côtes de Nuits B'y. r. or w. dr. ★★ 78 80 83 85

The same for the CÔTE DE NUITS. An area on the way up.

Haut-Médoc B'x. r. ★★-▶★★★ **66 70 71 75 76 78 79 80** 81 82 83 84 85

Big appellation including all the best areas of the Médoc. Most wines have château names: those without should still be above average.

Haut-Montravel Dordogne w. sw. ★ **81 82 83** 85

Medium-sweet BERGERAC.

Haut Poitou

Up-and-coming VDQS area south of ANJOU. Cooperative makes good whites, incl. CHARDONNAY and SAUVIGNON BLANC.

Heidsieck, Charles NV, rosé **81** and **73 75 76 79** 81

Major champagne house of Reims, family-owned, now merged with Henriot, controlled by Remy Martin; also Trouillard and de Venoge, Luxury brands: Cuvée Champagne Charlie **79**.

Heidsieck, Monopole NV, rosé and **73 75 76 79** 82

Important champagne merchant and grower of Reims now owned by MUMM. Luxury brand: Diamant Bleu (**76 79**).

Henriot NV, Blanc de Blancs Crémant Brut Souverain NV; Brut Rosé 81; Cuvée Baccarat 79; and 79

Old family champagne house now linked with CHARLES HEID-SIECK. Very dry style. Luxury brand: Réserve Baron Philippe de Rothschild.

Hérault Midi

The biggest v'yd. *département* in France with 400,000 hectares of vines. Chiefly vin ordinaire.

Hermitage Rh. r. or w. dr. ★★★ 71 72 76 78' 79 80 82 83' 84 85

The "manliest" wine of France. Dark, powerful and profound. Needs long ageing. The white is heady and golden; now usually made for early drinking, though it used to last many years. Top growers: CHAVE, JABOULET, CHAPOUTIER, Guigal.

Hospices de Beaune

Hospital in BEAUNE, with excellent v'yds. in MEURSAULT, POMMARD, VOLNAY, BEAUNE, CORTON, etc. See panel on page 29.

Huet, Gaston

Top VOUVRAY grower and mayor of the commune.

Hugel Père et Fils

The best-known ALSACE growers and merchants. Founded at Riquewihr in 1639 and still in the family. Best wines: Cuvées Exceptionnelles, Selections de Grains Nobles.

Imperiale

Bordeaux bottle holding 8½ normal bottles (5 litres).

Irancy B'y. r. or (p.) ★★ 78 82 83 85

Good light red made near CHABLIS of Pinot Noir and "César". The best vintages are long-lived and mature well. To watch.

Irouléguy s.w. France r.p. (or w. dr.) ★★ D.Y.A.

Agreeable local wine of the Basque country.

l'Isle de Beauté Name given to VINS DU PAYS from CORSICA.

Jaboulet, Paul

Old family firm at Tain, leading growers of HERMITAGE (esp. "La Chapelle" ★★★★) and merchants in other Rhône wines.

Jaboulet-Vercherre et Cie

Well-known Burgundy merchant-house with v'yds. (34 acres) in POMMARD, etc., and cellars in Beaune. Middling wines.

Jadot, Louis

Much-respected top-quality Burgundy merchant-house with v'yds (50 acres) in BEAUNE, CORTON, etc.

Jaffelin see Drouhin.

Jardin de la France

Name given to VINS DU PAYS of the LOIRE.

Jasnières Lo. (r.) (p.) or w. dr. ★★★ 71 76 78 79 80 82 83 84 85

Rare VOUVRAY-like wine of n. Touraine.

Jeroboam

In Bordeaux a 6-bottle bottle, or triple magnum; in Champagne a double magnum.

Juliénas B'y. r. ★★★ 85

Leading cru of Beaujolais: vigorous fruity wine.

Jura See Côtes de Jura

Jurançon s.w. France w. sw. or dr. ★★ 78 79 81 82 83 84 85

Unusual high-flavoured and long-lived speciality of Pau in the Pyrenean foothills. Ages well for several years. Top growers: Barrère, Chigné, Guirouilh, Lamouroux.

Kressman, E.S. & Cie

Family-owned Bordeaux merchants and owners of Ch. LATOUR-MARTILLAC in GRAVES. "Monopole Rouge" is very good.

Kriter

Popular low-price sparkling wine processed in Burgundy by PATRIARCHE.

Krug "Grande Cuvée" (NV), 64 66 69 71 73 76 79, Rosé and Clos du Mesnil 79

Small but very prestigious champagne house known for full-bodied very dry wine of the highest quality.

Kuentz-Bas

High-quality ALSACE grower and merchant at Husseren-les-Châteaux.

Labarde
Village just s. of MARGAUX and included in that appellation. Best ch.: GISCOURS.

Labouré-Gontard
Producer of high-quality Crémant de Bourgogne at NUITS.

Labouré-Roi
Good little merchant at NUITS-ST-GEORGES, esp. for MEURSAULT.

Lafon, Domaine des Comtes
31-acre top-quality Burgundy estate in VOLNAY, MEURSAULT and LE MONTRACHET. Excellent '83s.

Lalande de Pomerol B'x. r. ★★ 75 76 78 79 81 82 83
Neighbour to POMEROL. Wines similar but considerably less fine. Top ch'x, Les Annereaux, Les Hauts-Conseillants, Les Hauts-Tuileries, Moncets, Tournefeuille, Belair, Siaurac.

Langlois–Château
Producer of sparkling SAUMUR, controlled by BOLLINGER.

Langon The principal town of the s. GRAVES/SAUTERNES district.

Lanson Père et Fils Black Label NV, rosé NV, and 71 75 76 79
Important growers and merchants of Champagne, cellars at Reims. Luxury brand: Noble Cuvée. Black Label has improved recently.

Laroche, Domaine
Important (160 acres) grower and merchant of CHABLIS, incl. Domaine La Jouchère. Labels incl. Bacheroy-Josselin. Also owns the Chateau de PULIGNY-MONTRACHET.

Latour, Louis
Top Burgundy merchant and grower with v'yds. (120 acres) in CORTON, BEAUNE, etc. Among the best, esp. for white wines.

Latour de France r. (w. dr.) ★→★★ 80 81 82 83 84 85
New appellation in CÔTES DE ROUSSILLON-VILLAGES.

Latricières–Chambertin B'y. r. ★★★ 71 76 78 79 80 82 83' 84 85
17-acre Grand Cru neighbour of CHAMBERTIN. Similar wine, but lighter and "prettier".

Laudun Rh. r. p. or w. dr. ★
Village of CÔTES-DU-RHÔNE-VILLAGES. Attractive wines from the cooperative incl. fresh whites.

Laugel, Michel
One of the biggest ALSACE merchant-houses, at Marlenheim.

Laurent–Perrier NV, rosé brut and 71 73 75 78 79
Highly successful young champagne house at Tours-sur-Marne. Luxury brand: Cuvée Grande Siècle. Ultra Brut is just that.

Leflaive, Domaine
Much sought-after top-quality white burgundy grower at PULIGNY-MONTRACHET. Best v'yd.: Clavoillons.

Léognan B'x.
Leading village of the GRAVES. Best ch'x.: DOMAINE DE CHEVALIER, MALARTIC-LAGRAVIÈRE and HAUT-BAILLY.

Leroy
Important burgundy merchants at AUXEY-DURESSES with superb stocks of old wines. Part-owners and distributors of the DOMAINE DE LA ROMANÉE-CONTI.

Lichine, Alexis et Cie
Post-war Bordeaux merchants, proprietors of Ch. LASCOMBES.

Lie, sur
"On the lees." Muscadet is often so bottled (or so its makers say), for maximum freshness.

Limoux Pyr. r. or w. dr. ★★ D.Y.A.
The non-sparkling version of BLANQUETTE DE LIMOUX and a remarkable claret-like red: Anne des Joyeuses.

Lirac Rh. r. p. or (w. dr.) ★★ 81 83 84 85
Neighbouring village to TAVEL. Similar wine; the red becoming more important than the rosé, esp. Ch. de Segriés.

Listel Midi r. p. w. dr. `*→**` D.Y.A.
  Vast estate on the sandy beaches of the Golfe du Lion. Owned by the giant Salins du Midi, making very pleasant light "vins des sables". Domaine du Bosquet is a fruity red.

Listrac B'x. r. `**→` `***`
  Village of HAUT-MÉDOC next to MOULIS. Best ch'x.: FOURCAS-HOSTEN, FOURCAS-DUPRÉ, CLARKE.

Loire
  The major river of n.w. France. See under wine and regional names.

Loron et Fils
  Big-scale burgundy grower and merchant, specialist in BEAUJOLAIS and sound *vins de table*.

Loupiac B'x. w. sw. `**` 76 79 80 81 83 84 85
  Neighbour to SAUTERNES with similar but less good wine. Top ch'x: Loupiac-Gaudiet, de Ricaud.

Ludon
  HAUT-MÉDOC village s. of MARGAUX. Best ch.: LA LAGUNE.

Lugny ("Macon-Lugny") B'y. r. w. dr. sp. `**` 83 84 85
  Village next to VIRÉ with active and good cooperative. Wine of Les Genevrières v'yd. is sold by LOUIS LATOUR.

Burgundy: a grower's own label

MISE EN BOUTEILLES AU DOMAINE	Domaine is the burgundy equivalent of château.
NUITS ST GEORGES	The Appellation Contrôlée is Nuits St Georges.
LES PRULIERS	The individual v'yd. in Nuits is called Les Pruliers.
APPELLATION CONTRÔLÉE DOMAINE HENRI GOUGES A NUITS ST GEORGES, CÔTE D'OR	The name and address of the grower/producer. (The word propriétaire is often also used.)

A merchant's label

SANTENAY	The village.
LES GRAVIERES	The vineyard.
APPELLATION CONTRÔLÉE PROSPER MAUFOUX NEGOCIANT À SANTENAY	The wine qualifies for the Appellation Santenay. Prosper Maufoux is a Négociant, or merchant, who bought the wine from the grower to mature, bottle and sell.

Lupé-Cholet et Cie
  Merchants and growers at NUITS-ST-GEORGES controlled by BICHOT. Best estate wines: Château Gris and Clos de Lupé.

Lussac-Saint-Emilion B'x. r. `**` 78 79 81 82 83 85
  North-eastern neighbour to ST-EMILION. Often good value. Co-operative makes "Roc de Lussac".

Macau
  HAUT-MÉDOC village s. of MARGAUX. Best ch.: CANTEMERLE.

macération carbonique
  Traditional Beaujolais technique of fermentation with whole bunches of unbroken grapes in an atmosphere saturated with carbon dioxide. Fermentation inside each grape eventually bursts it, giving vivid and very fruity mild wine for quick consumption. Now much used in the Midi and elsewhere.

Machard de Gramont
  Burgundy family estate: cellars in NUITS and v'yds. in NUITS, SAVIGNY, BEAUNE, POMMARD. Extremely well-made reds.

Mâcon B'y. r. (p.) or w. dr. ★★ 84 85

Southern district of sound, usually unremarkable, reds and tasty dry (CHARDONNAY) whites. Wine with a village name (e.g. Mâcon-Prissé) is better. POUILLY-FUISSÉ is best appellation of the region. See also Mâcon-Villages.

Mâcon-Lugny See Lugny

Mâcon Supérieur

The same but slightly stronger from riper grapes.

Mâcon-Villages B'y. w. dr. ⸍★★⸍ 84 85

Increasingly well-made and typical white burgundies. Mâcon-Prissé, MÂCON-VIRÉ, MÂCON-LUGNY are examples.

Mâcon-Viré See Mâcon-Villages and Viré

Madiran s.w. France r. ⸍★★⸍ 75 76 78 79 81 82 83 84 85

Dark vigorous fragrant red from ARMAGNAC. Worth ageing. Top growers: Peyros, Laplace, Barréjat.

Magenta, Duc de

Burgundy estate (30 acres) based at CHASSAGNE-MONTRACHET.

Magnum A double bottle (1.5 litres).

Mähler-Besse

First-class Dutch wine-merchants in Bordeaux, with a majority share in Ch. PALMER. Brands incl. Cheval Noir.

Maire, Henri

The biggest grower and merchant of JURA wines.

Marc

Grape skins after pressing; also the strong-smelling brandy made from them. (cf. Italian "Grappa").

Marcillac s.w. France r.p. ⸍★⸍ D.Y.A.

Good rustic VDQS from the coop.

Margaux B'x. r. ★★→★★★★ 66 70 71 73 75 77 78 79 80 81 82 83' 84 85

Village of the HAUT-MÉDOC making the most "elegant" red Bordeaux. The name includes CANTENAC and several other villages as well. Top ch'x. include MARGAUX, LASCOMBES, etc.

Margnat Major producer of everyday VIN DE TABLE.

Marque déposée Trade mark.

Marsannay B'y. (r.) or p. ★★★ 78 80 83 85 (rosé D.Y.A.)

Village near Dijon with excellent light red and delicate PINOT NOIR rosé, perhaps the best rosé in France.

Maufoux, Prosper

Family firm of burgundy merchants at SANTENAY. Reliable wines with good keeping qualities. Alias Marcel Amance.

Maury Pyr. r. sw. ★→★★ NV

Red VIN DOUX NATUREL from ROUSSILLON.

Mazis (or Mazy) Chambertin B'y. r. ★★★ 71 76 78 79 80 82 83 85

30-acre Grand Cru neighbour of CHAMBERTIN. Lighter wine.

Médoc B'x. r. ★★ 75 76 78 79 81 82 83 84 85

Appellation for reds of the less good (n.) part of Bordeaux's biggest and best district. HAUT-MÉDOC is better.

Meffre, Gabriel

The biggest southern Rhône estate, based at GIGONDAS. Includes Ch. de Vaudieu, CHÂTEAUNEUF-DU-PAPE.

Ménétou-Salon Lo. r. p. or w. dr. ★★ D.Y.A.

Attractive light wines from w. of SANCERRE. SAUVIGNON white; PINOT NOIR red.

Mercier et Cie NV, Extra Rich and Rosé 80 81 and 73 75 78 80 81

One of the biggest champagne houses, at Epernay. Controlled by MOËT & CHANDON.

Mercurey B'y. r. or w. dr. ★★ 78 82 83 84 85

Leading red-wine village of the CÔTE CHALONNAISE. Good middle-rank burgundy.

Métaireau, Louis

The ring-leader of a group of top Muscadet growers. Expensive well-finished wines.

méthode champenoise
> The traditional laborious method of putting the bubbles in champagne by refermenting the wine in its bottle.

Meursault B'y. (r.) w. dr. ★★★ 78 81 82 83 84 85
> CÔTE DE BEAUNE village with some of the world's greatest whites: rich, smooth, savoury, dry but mellow. Best v'yds. incl. Perrières, Genevrières, Charmes. Top growers incl: AMPEAU, COCHE-DURY, Delagrange, LAFON, LATOUR, MAGENTA, CH. DE MEURSAULT, P. Morey, G. ROULOT.

Meursault-Blagny See Blagny

Midi General term for the south of France, where standards have risen consistently in recent years.

Minervois Midi r. or (p.) (w.) or br. sw. ★→★★ 83 84 85
> Hilly VDQS area with some of the best wines of the Midi: lively and full of flavour. Also sweet MUSCAT de St. Jean de M.

mise en bouteilles au château, au domaine
> Bottled at the château, at the property or estate. N.B. dans nos caves (in our cellars) or dans la région de production (in the area of production) are often used but mean little.

Moelleux Mellow. Used of the sweet wines of VOUVRAY, etc.

Moët & Chandon NV, rosé 81, Dry Imperial 71 73 75 76 78 80 81
> The biggest champagne merchant and grower, with cellars in Epernay and sparkling wine branches in Argentina, Brazil and California. Luxury brand: DOM PÉRIGNON.

Moillard
> Big firm of growers and merchants in NUITS-ST-GEORGES, recently revitalized and making fine CÔTE DE NUITS wines.

Mommessin, J. Major Beaujolais merchant. Owner of CLOS DE TART.

Monbazillac Dordogne w. sw. ★★ 71 75 76 78 79 80 81 83 85
> Golden SAUTERNES-style wine from BERGERAC. Ages well. Ch. Monbazillac is best known.

Mondeuse Savoie r. ★★ D.Y.A.
> Red grape of SAVOIE. Good, vigorous, deep-coloured wine.

Monopole Vineyard in single ownership.

Montagne-Saint-Emilion B'x. r. ★★ 75 76 78 79 81 82 83 85
> North-east neighbour of ST-EMILION with similar wines, becoming more important with each year. Top ch'x: Calon, St-André-Corbin, Vieux-Ch-St-André, Roudier, Teyssier, des Tours.

Montagny B'y. w. dr. ★★ →★★★ 78 81 82 83 84 85
> CÔTE CHALONNAISE village between MÂCON and MEURSAULT, both geographically and gastronomically.

Montée de Tonnerre B'y. w. dr. ★★★
> Famous and excellent PREMIER CRU of CHABLIS.

Monthelie B'y. r. ★★★ 76 78 79 80 82 83
> Little-known neighbour and almost equal of VOLNAY. Excellent fragrant reds. Best estate: Château de Monthélie.

Montlouis Lo. w. sw./dr. ★★ 75 76 78 81 82 83′ 84
> Neighbour of VOUVRAY. Similar sweet or dry long-lived wine.

Montrachet B'y. w. dr. ★★★★ 69 71 73 75 76 78 79 80 81 82 83 84 85
> 19-acre Grand Cru v'yd. in both PULIGNY and CHASSAGNE-MONTRACHET. Potentially the greatest white burgundy: strong, perfumed, intense, dry yet luscious. (The "ts" are silent.)

Montravel See Côtes de Montravel

Mont-Redon, Domaine de Rh. r. (w. dr.) ★★★ 78 79 80 81 83 84 85
> Outstanding 235-acre estate in CHÂTEAUNEUF-DU-PAPE. Relatively early-maturing wines.

Moreau et Fils
> CHABLIS merchant and grower with 175 acres. Also major table-wine producer. Best wine: Clos des Hospices.

Morey-Saint-Denis B'y. r. ★★★ 69 71 76 78 79 80 82 83 84 85
> Small village with four Grands Crus between GEVREY-CHAMBER-TIN and CHAMBOLLE-MUSIGNY. Glorious wine, often overlooked.

Morgon B'y. r. ✶✶✶ 78 82 83 84 85

The "firmest" cru of BEAUJOLAIS, needing time to develop its rich and savoury flavour.

Moueix, J-P et Cie

The leading proprietor and merchant of St-Emilion and Pomerol. Ch'x. incl. MAGDELAINE, LAFLEUR-PETRUS, and part of PETRUS. Now also has a venture in California, see DOMINUS.

Moulin-à-Vent B'y. r. ✶✶✶ 82 83 84 85

The "biggest" and best wine of Beaujolais; powerful and long-lived, eventually tasting more like CÔTE D'OR wine.

Moulis B'x. r. ✶✶→✶✶✶

Village of the HAUT-MÉDOC with its own appellation and several Crus Exceptionnels: CHASSE-SPLEEN, POUJEAUX-THEIL, MAUCAILLOU, etc. Wines are growing steadily finer.

Mousseux Sparkling.

Mouton Cadet

Best-selling brand of blended red and white Bordeaux.

Moutonne

CHABLIS GRAND CRU honoris causa, owned by BICHOT.

Mumm, G. H. & Cie NV "Cordon Rouge", rosé 79, Crémant de Cramant (NV) and **69 71 73 75 76 79** 82

Major champagne grower and merchant owned by Seagram's. Luxury brand: Président René Lalou (79). The Cramant is superb.

Muscadet Lo. w. dr. ✶✶ D.Y.A.

Popular, good-value, often delicious dry wine from round Nantes in s. Brittany. Should never be sharp. Perfect with fish.

Muscadet de Sèvre-et-Maine

Wine from the central and usually best part of the area.

Muscat

Distinctively perfumed grape and its (usually sweet) wine, made dry in Alsace.

Muscat de Beaumes de Venise

One of the best French muscats (see Beaumes de Venise).

Muscat de Frontignan Midi br. sw. ✶✶ D.Y.A.

Sweet Midi muscat.

Muscat de Lunel Midi br. sw. ✶✶ NV

Ditto. A small area but good.

Muscat de Mireval Midi br. sw. ✶✶ NV

Ditto, from near Montpellier.

Muscat de Rivesaltes Midi br. sw. ✶ NV

Sweet muscat from a big zone near Perpignan.

Musigny B'y. r. (w. dr.) ✶✶✶✶ 69 71 76 78 79 80 82 83 84 85

25-acre Grand Cru in CHAMBOLLE-MUSIGNY. Often the best, if not the most powerful, of all red burgundies (and a little white). Best growers: DE VOGÜÉ, DROUHIN, Mugnier.

Nature Natural or unprocessed, esp. of still champagne.

Néac B'x. r. ✶✶

Village n. of POMEROL. Wines sold as LALANDE-DE-POMEROL.

Négociant-éléveur

Merchant who "brings up" (i.e. matures) the wine.

Nicolas, Ets.

Paris-based wholesale and retail wine merchants controlled by Rémy-Martin. One of the biggest in France and one of the best.

Nuits-St-Georges r. ✶✶→✶✶✶ 69 71 73 76 78' 79 80 82 83' 84 85

Important wine-town: wines of all qualities, typically sturdy and full-flavoured. Name can be shortened to "Nuits". Best v'yds. incl. Les St-Georges, Vaucrains, Les Pruliers, Clos des Corvées, Les Cailles, etc.

Oisly et Thesée, Vignerons de

A go-ahead cooperative in eastern TOURAINE (Loire), experimenting successfully with superior grapes.

Ordinaire Commonplace, everyday: not necessarily pejorative.

Ott, Domaine
>Important producer of high-quality PROVENCE wines.

Pacherenc-du-Vic-Bilh S.W. France w. sw. ★NV
>Rare minor speciality of the ARMAGNAC region.

Paillard, Bruno
>Small but prestigious young Champagne house with excellent silky vintage and NV wines.

Palette Prov. r. p. or w. dr. ★★
>Near Aix-en-Provence. Aromatic reds and good rosés.

Parigot-Richard
>Producer of high-quality CRÉMANT DE BOURGOGNE at SAVIGNY-LES-BEAUNE.

Pasquier-Desvignes
>Very old firm of Beaujolais merchants at St Lager, BROUILLY.

Patriarche
>One of the bigger firms of burgundy merchants. Cellars in Beaune; also owns Ch. DE MEURSAULT (100 acres), KRITER, etc.

Patrimonio Corsica r.w. dr. p ★★→★★★
>Wide range from dramatic chalk hills in n. Corsica. Full-bouqueted reds, crisp whites and fine V.D.N. Top grower: Gentile.

Pauillac B'x. r. ★★→★★★★ 66 70 71 73 75 76 78 **79** 81 82 83 84 85
>The only village in Bordeaux (HAUT-MÉDOC) with three first-growths (Ch'x. LAFITE, LATOUR, MOUTON-ROTHSCHILD) and many other fine ones, famous for high flavour but very various in style.

Pécharmant Dordogne r. ★★ **79 81 82 83** 85
>Slightly better-than-typical light BERGERAC red. Top estate: Ch. de Tiregand.

Pelure d'oignon
>"Onion skin"—tawny tint of certain rosés.

Perlant or Perlé Very slightly sparkling.

Pernand-Vergelesses B'y. r. or (w. dr.) ★★★ 76 78 **80** 81 82 83 85
>Village next to ALOXE-CORTON containing part of the great CORTON and CORTON-CHARLEMAGNE v'yds. and one other top v'yd.: Ile des Vergelesses.

Perrier, Joseph NV, rosé and **71** 73 75 76 79
>Family-run champagne house with considerable v'yds. at Chalon-s-Marne. Consistent light and fruity style.

Perrier-Jouet NV, Blason de France NV, **71** 73 75 76
>Excellent champagne-growers and makers at Epernay now linked with MUMM. Luxury brand: Belle Epoque 79 (in a painted bottle). Also Belle Epoque Rosé **79**.

Pétillant Slightly sparkling.

Petit Chablis B'y. w. dr. ★★ 83 85
>Wine from fourth-rank CHABLIS v'yds. Lacks great character but can be good value.

Piat Père et Fils
>Important growers and merchants of Beaujolais and Mâcon wines at MÂCON, now controlled by Grand Metropolitan Ltd. V'yds. in MOULIN-À-VENT, also CLOS DE VOUGEOT. BEAUJOLAIS, MÂCON-VIRÉ in special Piat bottles are good value.

Pic, Albert
>Well-reputed CHABLIS producer, now controlled by DE LADOU-CETTE.

Picpoul-de-Pinet Midi w. dr. ★ NV
>Rather dull very dry southern white, best cold on the spot.

Pineau de Charente
>Strong sweet apéritif made of white grape juice and Cognac.

Pinot See Grapes for white wine

Piper-Heidsieck NV, rosé **79**, Vintage **71 73 75 76**, Rare **76**, Brut Sauvage **79**

Champagne-makers of old repute at Reims. Luxury brand: Florens Louis.

Pol Roger NV, rosé **75 79**, Blanc de Blancs NV and **71 73 75 76 79**

Excellent champagne house at Epernay. Particularly good non-vintage White Foil. Luxury cuvée: "Sir Winston Churchill".

Pomerol B'x. r. ★★→★★★★ **70 71 75 76 78 79** 81 82 83 85

The next village to ST-EMILION: similar but more "fleshy" wines, maturing sooner, reliable and delicious. Top ch. PETRUS, LA FLEUR-PETRUS, VIEUX-CH-CERTAN, LATOUR À POMEROL, etc..

Pommard B'y. r. ★★★ **69 71 76** 78 **79 80 82** 83 84 85

The biggest and best-known village in Burgundy. No superlative wines, but many warmly appealing ones. Best v'yds.: Rugiens, EPENOTS and HOSPICES DE BEAUNE cuvées.

Pommery & Greno NV, NV rosé and **71 73 75 76 78 79** 80

Very big growers and merchants of champagne at Reims, revitalized by new owners after a dreary patch.

Pouilly-Fuissé B'y. w. dr. ★★→★★★ 81 83 84 85

The best white of the MÂCON area. At its best (e.g. Ch. Fuissé) excellent, but almost always over-priced.

Pouilly-Fumé Lo. w. dr. ★★→★★★ **82 83 84 85**

Smoky-fragrant, fruity, often sharp pale white from the upper Loire, next to SANCERRE. Grapes must be SAUVIGNON BLANC. Good vintages improve for 2–3 yrs.

Pouilly-Loché B'y. w. dr. ★★

Neighbour of POUILLY-FUISSÉ. Similar wine but little of it.

"Noble rot" (in French *pourriture noble*, in German *Edelfäule*, in Latin *Botrytis cinerea*) *is a form of mould that attacks the skins of ripe grapes in certain vineyards in warm and misty autumn weather.*

Its effect, instead of rotting the grapes, is to wither them. The skin grows soft and flaccid, the juice evaporates through it, and what is left is a super-sweet concentration of everything in the grape except its water content.

The world's best sweet table wines are all made of nobly rotten grapes. They occur in good vintages in Sauternes, the Rhine, the Mosel (where wine made from them is called Trockenbeerenauslese), in Tokaji in Hungary, in Burgenland in Austria, and occasionally elsewhere—California included. The danger is rain on the pulpy grapes when they are already far gone in noble rot. All too often, particularly in Sauternes, the grower's hopes are dashed by a break in the weather.

Pouilly-Sur-Loire Lo. w. dr. ★ D.Y.A.

Inferior wine from the same v'yds. as POUILLY-FUMÉ, but different grapes (CHASSELAS).

Pouilly-Vinzelles B'y. w. dr. ★★

Neighbour of POUILLY-FUISSÉ. Similar wine, worth looking for.

Pousse d'Or, Domaine de la

32-acre estate in POMMARD, SANTENAY, and (esp.) VOLNAY where its "monopoles", "Bousse d'Or" and "60 Ouvrées" are justly famous.

Preiss Zimmer, Jean

Old-established Alsace wine-merchants at Riquewihr.

Premières Côtes de Blaye B'x. r. w. dr. ★→★★ **78** 81 82 83 85

Restricted appellation for better reds of BLAYE. Ch'x. include Barbé, Charron, Bourdieu, l'Escadre, Segonzac, Le Menaudat.

Premier Cru

First-growth in Bordeaux (see page 54), but the second rank of v'yds. (after Grand Cru) in Burgundy.

Premières Côtes de Bordeaux B'x. r. (p.) or w. dr. or sw. ★→★★

Large area east of GRAVES: a good bet for quality and value, though never brilliant. Ch'x incl. Laffitte (sic), Gardera, Fayau, Haut-Brignon, REYNON, Tanesse.

Prieur, Domaine Jacques
> 35-acre estate all in top Burgundy sites, incl. Premier Cru MEURSAULT, BEAUNE, VOLNAY, and PULIGNY- and CHEVALIER-MONTRACHET.

Primeur
> Early wine (like early vegetables); esp. of BEAUJOLAIS.

Prissé See Mâcon-Villages

Propriétaire-récoltant
> Owner–manager.

Provence See Côtes de Provence

Puisseguin-Saint-Emilion B'x. r. ★★ 75 78 79 81 82 83 85
> Eastern neighbour of ST-EMILION; wines similar—not so fine but often good value. Ch'x incl. Laurets, Guibeau, Puisseguin, Soleil, Teyssier. Also "Roc de Puisseguin" from coop.

Puligny-Montrachet B'y. w. dr. (r.) ★★★ 71 76 78 79 81 82 83 84 85
> Bigger neighbour of CHASSAGNE-MONTRACHET with equally glorious rich dry whites. Best v'yds.: MONTRACHET, CHEVALIER-MONTRACHET, BATÂRD-MONTRACHET, Bienvenue-Bâtard-Montrachet, Les Combettes, Clavoillon, Pucelles, Champ-Canet, etc. Top growers incl: AMPEAU, BOUCHARD PÈRE, Chartron, LEFLAIVE, SAUZET.

Quarts de Chaume Lo. w. sw. ★★★ 75 76 78 82 83 84 85
> Famous 120-acre plot in COTEAUX DU LAYON, Anjou. CHENIN BLANC grapes. Long-lasting, intense, rich golden wine.

Quatourze Midi r. (p.) or w. dr. ★ 83 84 85
> Minor VDQS area near Narbonne.

Quincy Lo. w. dr. ★★ 83 84 85
> Small area making very dry SANCERRE-style wine of SAUVIGNON BLANC.

Ramonet-Prudhon
> One of the leading proprietors in CHASSAGNE-MONTRACHET with 34 acres. Sometimes excellent whites, and red Clos St-Jean.

Rancio
> Term for the tang of wood-aged fortified wine, esp. BANYULS and other VINS DOUX NATURELS. A fault in table wines.

Rasteau Rh. (r. p. w. dr.) or br. sw. ★★ NV
> Village of s. Rhône valley. Very sound reds. Good strong sweet dessert wine is the local speciality.

Ratafia de Champagne
> Sweet apéritif made in Champagne of ⅔ grape juice and ⅓ brandy.

Récolte Crop or vintage.

Reine Pédauque, La
> Burgundy growers and merchants at ALOXE-CORTON.

Remoissenet Père et Fils
> Fine Burgundy merchants (esp. for white wines) with a tiny estate at BEAUNE.

Rémy Pannier Important Loire-wine merchants at Saumur.

Reuilly Lo. (r.p.) w. dr. ★★ 83 84 85
> Neighbour of QUINCY with similar wine; also good PINOT GRIS.

Riceys, Rosé des
> Minute appellation in southern CHAMPAGNE for a notable PINOT NOIR rosé. Principal producer: A. Bonnet.

Richebourg B'y. r. ★★★★ 66 69 70 71 73 76 77 78 79 80 81 82 83 84 85
> 19-acre Grand Cru in VOSNE-ROMANÉE. Powerful, perfumed, fabulously expensive wine, among Burgundy's best.

Riesling See Grapes for white wine

Rivesaltes Midi r.w. dr. br. sw. ★★ NV
> Fortified sweet wine, some muscat-flavoured, from e. Pyrenees. An ancient tradition still very much alive, if struggling.

La Roche-aux-Moines Lo. w. dr./sw. ★★★ 71 75 76 78 79 81 82 83
> 60-acre v'yd. in Savennières, Anjou. Intense strong fruity/sharp wine ages well.

Rodet, Antonin
  Substantial Burgundy merchant and a well-known grower of MERCUREY (Ch. de Chamirey).

Roederer, Louis   Brut Premier NV, Rosé 75 and **69 70 71 73 74 75 77 78 79**
  One of the best champagne-growers and merchants at Reims. Excellent non-vintage wine. Luxury brand: Cristal Brut 79 (in white glass bottles).

La Romanée   B'y. r. **★★★★ 69 71 73 76** 78 **79 80 82** 83 84 85
  2-acre Grand Cru in VOSNE-ROMANÉE just uphill from ROMANÉE-CONTI, owned by M. l'Abbé Liger-Belair, distributed by BOUCHARD PÈRE. France's smallest A.C.

Romanée-Conti   B'y. r. **★★★★ 66 71 73** 76 77 78 **79 80 81 82** 83 84 85
  4½-acre Grand Cru in VOSNE-ROMANÉE. The most celebrated and expensive red wine in the world. Sometimes the best.

Romanée-Conti, Domaine de la
  The grandest estate of Burgundy, owning the whole of ROMANÉE-CONTI and LA TÂCHE and major parts of RICHEBOURG, GRANDS ECHÉZEAUX, ECHÉZEAUX and ROMANÉE-ST-VIVANT (under Marey-Monge label). Also a very small part of LE MONTRACHET.

Romanée-St-Vivant   B'y. r. **★★★★ 71 76** 78 **79** 80 **82** 83 84 85
  23-acre Grand Cru in VOSNE-ROMANÉE. Similar to ROMANÉE-CONTI but usually lighter.

Ropiteau
  Burgundy wine-growers and merchants at MEURSAULT. Specialists in Meursault and CÔTE DE BEAUNE wines.

Rosé d'Anjou   Lo. p. **★** D.Y.A.
  Pale, slightly sweet, rosé. Cabernet d'Anjou should be better.

Rosé de Loire   Lo. p. dr. **★→★★** D.Y.A.
  Appellation for dry Loire rosé (Anjou is sweet).

Roty, Joseph   Small grower of classic GEVREY-CHAMBERTIN.

Rousseau, Domaine A.
  Major burgundy grower famous for CHAMBERTIN, etc. of highest quality. But avoid his '82s.

Roussette de Savoie   Savoie w. dr.   **★★**   D.Y.A.
  The tastiest of the fresh whites from s. of Geneva.

Roussillon
  See Côtes du Roussillon. "Grands Roussillons" are VINS DOUX NATURELS.

Ruchottes-Chambertin   B'y. r. **★★★ 71 73 76** 78 **79 80 82** 83 84 85
  7½-acre Grand Cru neighbour of CHAMBERTIN. Similar splendid long-lasting wine.

Ruinart Père et Fils   NV, vintage rosé and Blanc de Blancs **76 79**
  The oldest champagne house, now belonging to Moët-Hennessy. Luxury brand: Dom Ruinart, Blanc de Blancs.

Rully   B'y. r. or w. dr. or (sp.)   **★★**   **83 84** w. **85**
  Village of the CÔTE CHALONNAISE famous for sparkling burgundy. Still reds and white light but tasty and good value.

Sablant   Lo. w. dr. sp. **★★** NV
  Brand name for high-quality CRÉMANT DE LOIRE.

Saint-Amour   B'y. r. **★★ 83 84 85**
  Northernmost cru of BEAUJOLAIS: light, fruity, irresistible.

Saint-Aubin   B'y. (r.) or w. dr.   **★★**   **78 80 81 82 83** 85
  Little-known neighbour of CHASSAGNE-MONTRACHET, up a side-valley. Not top-rank, but typical and good value. Also sold as CÔTE-DE-BEAUNE-VILLAGES.

Saint Bris   B'y. w. dr.   **★**   D.Y.A.
  Village w. of CHABLIS known for its fruity ALIGOTÉ, making good sparkling burgundy, but chiefly for SAUVIGNON de ST BRIS.

Saint Chinian   Midi r.   **★→★★**   81 82 83 84
  Hilly area of growing reputation in the COTEAUX DU LANGUEDOC. Appellation Contrôlée since 1982. Tasty reds.

Sainte Croix–du–Mont B'x. w. sw. **⋆⋆** 67 71 75 76 79 80 81 83 84
Neighbour to SAUTERNES with similar golden wine. No superlatives but well worth trying esp. Ch. Loubens. V. reasonably priced.

Sainte-Foy-Bordeaux B'x.
Part of ENTRE-DEUX-MERS, more akin to BERGERAC.

Saint-Emilion B'x. r. **⋆⋆→⋆⋆⋆⋆** 70 71 73 75 76 78 79 80 81 82 83 85
The biggest (13,000 acres) top-quality Bordeaux district; solid, rich, tasty wines from hundreds of ch'x., incl. CHEVAL-BLANC, AUSONE, CANON, MAGDELAINE, FIGEAC, etc.

Saint-Estèphe B'x. r. **⋆⋆** →⋆⋆⋆⋆ 75 76 78 79 80 81 82 83 84 85
Northern village of HAUT-MÉDOC. Solid, satisfying, occasionally superlative wines. Top ch'x.: CALON-SÉGUR, COS D'ESTOURNEL, MONTROSE, etc., and many notable CRUS BOURGEOIS.

St-Gall
Brand-name used by the very good champagne-growers' Co-operative at AVIZE, Union-Champagne.

Saint-Georges-Saint-Emilion
Part of MONTAGNE-ST-EMILION. Best ch'x.: ST-GEORGES, Belair-Montaiguillon, Marquis-St-Georges, Tour-du-Pas-St-Georges.

Saint-Joseph Rh. r. (p. or w. dr.) **⋆⋆** 76 78 79 80 82 83
Northern Rhône appellation of second rank but reasonable price. Substantial wine often better than CROZES-HERMITAGE.

Saint-Julien B'x. r. **⋆⋆⋆→⋆⋆⋆⋆** 70 71 75 76 78 79 80 81 82 83 84 85
Mid-Médoc village with a dozen of Bordeaux's best ch'x., incl. three LÉOVILLES, BEYCHEVELLE, DUCRU-BEAUCAILLOU, GRUAUD-LAROSE, etc. The epitome of well-balanced red wine.

Saint-Laurent
Village next to SAINT-JULIEN. Appellation Haut-Médoc.

Saint-Nicolas-de-Bourgueil Lo. r. **⋆⋆** 81 82 83 84 85
The next village to BOURGUEIL: the same light but lively and fruity CABERNET red.

Saint-Péray Rh. w. dr. or sp. **⋆⋆** NV
Rather heavy white from the n. Rhône, much of it made sparkling. A curiosity worth investigating.

Saint Pourçain Central France r. p. or w. dr **⋆** D.Y.A.
The agreeable local wine of Vichy, rather chic in Paris. Made from GAMAY and/or PINOT NOIR, the white from Tressalier, CHARDONNAY or SAUVIGNON BLANC.

Saint Romain B'y. r. w. dr. **⋆⋆**
Overlooked village just behind the CÔTE DE BEAUNE. Value, esp. for young whites. Top grower: Thévenin.

Saint-Sauveur HAUT-MÉDOC village just w. of PAUILLAC.

Saint-Seurin-de-Cadourne
HAUT-MÉDOC village just n. of SAINT-ESTÈPHE.

Saint-Véran B'y. w. dr. **⋆⋆** 83 84 85
Next-door appellation to POUILLY-FUISSÉ. Similar but better value: dry white of real character from the best slopes of MÂCON-VILLAGES.

Salins du Midi, Domaine Viticole See Listel

Salon 61 64 66 69 71 73 76
The original Blanc de Blancs champagne, from Le Mesnil. Fine very dry wine with extraordinary keeping qualities.

Sancerre Lo. (r. p.) or w. dr. **⋆⋆⋆** 84 85
Very fragrant and fresh SAUVIGNON white almost indistinguishable from POUILLY-FUMÉ, its neighbour over the Loire. Drink young. Also light PINOT NOIR red (best drunk at 2–3 yrs) and a little rosé.

Santenay B'y. r. or (w. dr.) **⋆⋆⋆** 69 71 73 76 78 79 80 82 83 84 85
Very worthy, rarely rapturous, sturdy reds from the s. of the CÔTE DE BEAUNE. Best v'yds.: Les Gravières, Clos de Tavannes, La Comme. Top grower: DOM. DE LA POUSSE D'OR.

Saumur Lo. r. p. or w. dr. and sp. ★→ ★★

Big versatile district in ANJOU, with fresh fruity whites, good-value champagne-method sparklers, pale rosés and increasingly good CABERNET reds, the best from Saumur-Champigny, esp. Ch. de Chaintres.

Sauternes B'x.w. sw. ★★ →★★★★ 67 71 75 76 78 79 80 81 82 83' 84

District of 5 villages (incl. BARSAC) making France's best sweet wine: strong (14% + alcohol) luscious and golden, demanding ,to be aged. Top ch'x.: D'YQUEM, SUDUIRAUT, COUTET, CLIMENS, GUIRAUD, etc. Also a few heavy dry wines which cannot be sold as Sauternes.

Sauvignon Blanc See Grapes for white wine

Sauvignon-de-St-Bris B'y. w. dr. ★★ D.Y.A.

A baby VDQS cousin of SANCERRE from near CHABLIS.

Sauvion et Fils

Ambitious and well-run Muscadet house, based at the Ch. de Cléray. Top wine: Cardinal Richard.

Sauzet, Etienne

White burgundy estate at PULIGNY-MONTRACHET. Recent quality patchy.

Savennières Lo. w. dr./sw. ★★★ 75 76 78 81 82 83 84 85

Small ANJOU district of pungent, traditionally long-lived whites, incl. COULÉE DE SERRANT, LA ROCHE AUX MOINES, Clos du Papillon. Recent wines show less character.

Savigny-lès-Beaune B'y. r. or (w. dr.) ★★★ 76 78 80 82 83 85

Important village next to BEAUNE, with similar well-balanced middle-weight wines, often deliciously delicate and fruity. Best v'yds.: Marconnets, Dominode, Serpentières, Vergelesses, les Guettes. Top growers incl: Bize, Girard-Vollot, TOLLOT-BEAUT.

Savoie E. France r. or w. dr. or sp. ★★ D.Y.A.

Alpine area with light dry wines like some Swiss wine or minor Loires. CRÉPY, SEYSSEL and APREMONT are best known whites, ROUSSETTE is often more interesting. Also MONDEUSE red.

Schlumberger et Cie

Alsace growers and merchants of luscious, potent wines at Guebwiller.

Schröder & Schyler

Old family firm of Bordeaux merchants, owners of CH. KIRWAN.

Sciacarello

Red grape at the heart of Corsica's best red and rosé wines, e.g. AJACCIO, Sartène.

Sec

Literally means dry, though champagne so-called is medium-sweet (and better at breakfast and tea-time than Brut).

Selection de Grains Nobles

Description coined by HUGEL for Alsace equivalent to German BEERENAUSLESE. "Grains nobles" are individual grapes with "noble rot" (see page 46).

Sèvre-et-Maine

The *département* containing the central and best v'yds. of MUSCADET.

Seyssel Savoie w. dr. or sp. ★★ NV

Delicate pale dry white making admirable sparkling wine.

Sichel & Co.

Famous Bordeaux (and Burgundy and Germany) merchants. In Bordeaux owners of Ch. D'ANGLUDET and part-owners of Ch. PALMER.

Soussans

Village just n. of MARGAUX, sharing its appellation.

Sylvaner

See Grapes for white wine

Syrah See Grapes for red wine

La Tâche B'y. r. ★★★★ 62 69 70 71 73 76 78 79 80 81 82 83 84 85
15-acre Grand Cru of VOSNE-ROMANÉE and one of the best v'yds.
on earth: dark, perfumed and luxurious wine. Owned by the
DOMAINE DE LA ROMANÉE-CONTI.

Taittinger NV, Collection Brut Reserve 78 and Brut 74 75 76 78 79 80.
Fashionable champagne growers and merchants of Reims.
Luxury brand: Comtes de Champagne 76 79 (also rosé 79).

Tastevin, Confrérie des Chevaliers du
Burgundy's colourful and successful promotion society. Wine
carrying their Tastevinage label has been approved by them and
will usually be of a fair standard. A tastevin is the traditional
shallow silver wine-tasting cup of Burgundy. See panel, page 31.

Tavel Rh. p. ★★★ D.Y.A.
France's most famous, though not her best, rosé, strong and dry,
starting vivid pink and fading to orange. Avoid orange bottles.

Tête de Cuvée
Archaic term vaguely used of the best wines of an appellation.

Thénard, Domaine
The major grower of GIVRY, but best known for his substantial
portion (4.5 acres) of LE MONTRACHET.

Thevenet, Jean
A master maker of white Mâcon-Clessé (Domaine de la Bon
Gran) at Quintaine-Clessé, near LUGNY.

Thorin, J.
Grower and major merchant of BEAUJOLAIS, at Pontanevaux,
owner of the Château des Jacques, MOULIN À VENT.

Thouarsais, Vin de Lo. r. ★ D.Y.A.
Light GAMAY VDQS area south of Saumur.

Tokay d'Alsace See Pinot Gris under Grapes for white wine

Tollot-Beaut
Stylish burgundy grower with some 50 acres in the CÔTE DE
BEAUNE, incl. CORTON, BEAUNE, Grèves, SAVIGNY (Les Champs
Chevrey) and at Chorey-lès-Beaune where he is based.

Tortochot, Domaine
25-acre estate based at GEVREY-CHAMBERTIN. Classic wines.

Touraine Lo. r. p. w. dr./sw./sp. ★→★★★
Big mid-Loire province with immense range of wines, incl. dry
white SAUVIGNON, dry and sweet CHENIN BLANC (e.g. Vouvray),
red CHINON and BOURGUEIL, light red CABERNETS, GAMAYS and
rosés. Cabernets, Sauvignons and Gamays of good years are
bargains. Amboise, Azay-le-Rideau and Mesland are sub-
sections of the appellation.

Trimbach, F. E.
Distinguished ALSACE grower and merchant at Ribeauvillé. Best
wines (incl. the austere Riesling Clos Ste. Hune) mature
magnificently.

Tursan s.w. France r. p. w. dr. ★
Emerging VDQS in the Landes. Sound reds.

Unidor
The union of cooperatives of the Dordogne, producing good
BERGERAC and MONBAZILLAC.

Vacqueyras Rh. r. ★★ 78 79 80 82 83 84 85
Prominent village of s. CÔTES-DU-RHÔNE, neighbour to GIGON-
DAS; comparable with CHÂTEAUNEUF-DU-PAPE but less heavy
and more "elegant".

Valençay Lo. w. dr. ★ D.Y.A.
Neighbour of CHEVERNY: similar pleasant sharpish wine.

Varichon & Clerc
Principal makers and shippers of SAVOIE sparkling wines.

Varoilles, Domaine des
Excellent burgundy estate of 30 acres, principally in GEVREY-
CHAMBERTIN. Wines with great keeping qualities.

Vaudésir B'y. w. dr. ★★★★ 78 81 83 84 85

Arguably the best of the 7 Grands Crus of CHABLIS (but then so are the others).

VDQS Vin Délimité de Qualité Supérieure (see p. 21).

Vendange Vintage.

Vendange tardive

Late vintage. In ALSACE equivalent to German AUSLESE.

Veuve Clicquot NV ("Yellow label"), NV Demi-Sec (White Label) and 73 75 76 78 79 and rosé

Historic champagne house of the highest standing. Cellars at Reims. Luxury brand: La Grande Dame 79.

Vidal-Fleury, J.

Long-established shippers and growers of top Rhône wines.

Vieilles Vignes

"Old vines" — therefore the best wine. Used for such wine by BOLLINGER, DE VOGÜÉ and others.

Viénot, Charles

Grower and merchant of good burgundy, at NUITS-ST-GEORGES. 70 acres in Nuits, CORTON, RICHEBOURG, etc., now owned by BOISSET.

Vignoble Area of vineyards.

Vin de garde

Wine that will improve with keeping. The serious stuff.

Vin de l'année

This year's wine. See Beaujolais.

Vin de paille

Wine from grapes dried on straw mats, consequently very sweet, like Italian passito. Especially in the JURA.

Vin de Pays

The junior rank of country wines (see Introduction). Over 100 are now in theory operational. Don't turn up your nose.

Vin de Table

Standard everyday table wine, not subject to particular regulations about grapes and origin. Choose the previous entry.

Vin Doux Naturel ("VDN")

Sweet wine fortified with wine alcohol, so the sweetness is "natural", not the strength. The most distinguished product of ROUSSILLON. A vin doux liquoreux is several degrees stronger.

Vin Gris

"Grey" wine is very pale pink, made of red grapes pressed before fermentation begins, unlike rosé, which ferments briefly before pressing. Oeil de Perdrix means much the same.

Vin Jaune Jura w. dr. ★★★

Speciality of ARBOIS: odd yellow wine like fino sherry. Ready when bottled. The best is CHÂTEAU CHÂLON.

Vin nouveau See Beaujolais Nouveau

Vin vert

A very light, acidic, refreshing white wine, a speciality of ROUSSILLON and v. necessary in summer in those parts.

Vinsobres Rh. r. (p. or w. dr.) ★★ 78 80 81 83 84 85

Contradictory name of good s. Rhône village. Strong substantial reds which mature well.

Viré B'y. w. dr. ★★ 84 85

One of the best white-wine villages of Mâcon. Good coop and excellent Ch. de Viré.

Visan Rh. r. p. or w. dr. ★★ 78 80 81 83 84 85

One of the better s. Rhône villages. Reds better than white.

Viticulteur Wine-grower.

Vogüé, Comte Georges de

First-class 30-acre burgundy domaine at CHAMBOLLE-MUSIGNY. At best the ultimate MUSIGNY and BONNES MARES.

Volnay B'y. r. ★★★ **69 71 76 78 79 80 81** 82 83 84 85

Village between POMMARD and MEURSAULT: the best reds of the CÔTE DE BEAUNE, not strong or heavy but fragrant and silky. Best v'yds.: Caillerets, Clos des Ducs, Champans, Clos des Chênes, etc. Best growers: POUSSE D'OR, d'ANGERVILLE.

Volnay-Santenots B'y. r. ★★★

Excellent red wine from MEURSAULT is sold under this name. Indistinguishable from VOLNAY.

Vosne-Romanée B'y. r. ★★★→★★★★ **69 71 76 78 79 80 81** 82 83 84 85

The village containing Burgundy's grandest Crus (ROMANÉE-CONTI, LA TÂCHE, etc.). There are (or rather should be) no common wines in Vosne.

Vougeot See Clos de Vougeot

Vouvray Lo. w. dr./sw./sp. ★★→★★★★ **69 71 76 78 79 82** 83 84 85

Small district of TOURAINE with very variable wines, at their best intensely sweet and almost immortal. Good dry sparkling.

"Y" (Pronounced ygrec) 78 79 80 84

Brand name of powerful dry wine of great character, occasionally made at Ch. D'YQUEM.

Zind-Humbrecht

64-acre Alsace estate in Wintzenheim, Turckheim and Thann. First-rate individual v'yd wines (esp. Clos St. Urbain Riesling).

THE COLOUR OF AGE

One very easy way of gauging the maturity of a red wine without opening the bottle is simply to hold the neck of the bottle up to a bright light. If the colour of the wine in the neck is deep red the wine is almost certainly still young and vigorous. If it appears a light orange colour, the wine is fully mature and should be drunk. If possible, compare a very fine Bordeaux and a simple one at, say, ten years old to see the difference: the better wine will look much darker.

Châteaux of Bordeaux

Some 350 of the best-known châteaux are listed below in alphabetical order.

The vintage information has been entirely revised for the 1987 edition in consultation with château proprietors, brokers and the many friends who have contributed their notes, as in previous editions, to supplement my own.

The vintages marked with an accent "(*)" are judged to epitomize the qualities of the château in question. Whether they are mature yet or will improve with keeping is indicated, as elsewhere in the book, by the style of type.

This information is complete up to the 1984 vintage (the most recent to be bottled), which was made in difficult conditions, culminating with a hurricane in October. Problems started with poor flowering which virtually eliminated the Merlot crop. The Merlot capital, Pomerol, suffered very severely and St-Emilion was badly affected.

In contrast the Medoc and Graves made a vintage of character (what vintage is not?), on the lean side but more substantial in most cases than the light (and attractive) 1980s. There are outstanding successes and it seems few major disappointments. In Bordeaux the making of a wine is only the preface to its history: in 20 years some '84s may be better wines than the much-vaunted '82s.

1985 red Bordeaux was made in ideal conditions in a late-September heatwave. Comment on individual '85s must wait until they are bottled, but it is already clear that the vintage is a challenge both to the super-ripe '82s and the excellent, classic-style '83s. There is interesting drinking ahead.

General information on the style of each vintage will be found on the vintage charts on pages 22 and 23. Further detail on each village or appellation will be found in the A – Z of France.

L'Abbé-Gorsse-de-Gorsse Margaux. r. ** 81 82 83 84
25-acre property. Sound, but not as memorable as its name.

d'Agassac Ludon, Haut-Médoc r. ⌈**⌉ 75' 76 78 79 80 81 82' 83 84
14th-century moated fort with 86 acres. Same owners as Ch'x CALON-SÉGUR and DU TERTRE and a growing reputation.

Andron-Blanquet St-Est. r. ** 82 83
Sister-château to COS LABORY. Can be a big rustic character.

L'Angélus St-Em. r. ** 70' 75' 76 78 79' 80 81' 82 83
Well-situated classed-growth of 60 acres on the St-Emilion Côtes w. of the town. More steady than exciting, but worth watching.

d'Angludet Cant-Mar. r. ⌈**⌉ 66 70' 75 76' 78' 79 80 81' 82 83' 84
75-acre British-owned Cru Exceptionnel of classed-growth quality. Lively fragrant Margaux of great style.

D'Arche Sauternes w. sw. ** 71 78 79 80 81 82 83'
Substantial second-rank classed-growth of 88 acres rejuvenated since 1980. Ch. d'Arche-Lafaurie was its second label until '81.

d'Arcins Central Médoc r. **
185-acre property of the Castel family (cf. Castelvin); sister-château to neighbouring Barreyres (160 acres). That's a lot of wine.

l'Arrosée St-Em. r. ⌈**⌉ 78 79 81 82 83
Substantial 24-acre Côtes property. Serious wine with "stuffing", despite its name (which means watered).

Ausone St-Em. r. **** 70 71' 75' 76' 78 79' 80 81' 82' 83'
Celebrated first-growth with 17 acres in a commanding position on the Côtes and famous rock-hewn cellars under the vineyard. Impresses more and more with each vintage. See also Ch. Belair.

Bahans-Haut-Brion Gr. r. *** NV
The second-quality wine of Ch. HAUT-BRION.

Balestard-la-Tonnelle St-Em. r. ⌈**⌉ 70' 75' 76' 78 79 81 82 83
Historic 25-acre classed-growth on the plateau near the town. Mentioned by the 15th-century poet Villon and still in the same family (which also owns Ch. CAP-DE-MOURLIN).

de Barbe Côtes de Bourg r. (w.) ⌈**⌉ 75 78 79' 81 82' 83
The biggest (148 acres) and best-known ch. of the right bank of the Gironde. Good tasty, accessible largely Merlot red.

Baret Graves r. and w. dr. ** 76 78 81w. 82 83
Little estate of good quality, better known for its white wine.

Bastor-Lamontagne Sauternes w. sw. ⌈**⌉ 76 79 80 82 83
Large "bourgeois" Preignac property making excellent rich wines.

Batailley Pauillac r. ⌈***⌉ 61 70 75' 76 78' 79' 80 81 82' 83 84
The bigger of the famous pair of fifth-growths (with HAUT-BATAILLEY) on the borders of Pauillac and St-Julien. 110 acres. Fine, firm strong-flavoured wine. Sold by Borie-Manoux.

Beaumont Cussac, Haut-Médoc r. ⌈**⌉ 75 76 78' 79 80 81 82 83 84
Considerable Cru Bourgeois, well-known in France for full-flavoured, consistently attractive wines. In new hands since '79. Second label: Ch. Moulin d'Arvigny.

Beauregard Pomerol r. ⌈***⌉ 70 71 75' 76 78' 79 81 82' 83
32-acre v'yd. with pretty 17th-century ch. near LA CON-SEILLANTE. Well-made delicate "round" wines.

Beau Séjour-Bécot St-Em. r. *** 75' 76' 78 79 80 81 82 83'
Half of the old Beau Séjour Premier Grand Cru estate on the w. slope of the Côtes. Easy, tasty wines. 16 acres. Controversially demoted in class in '85. The Bécots also own CH. GRAND PONTET.

Beauséjour-Duffau-Lagarosse St-Em. r. *** 70 75 76 78 79 80 81 82 83
The other half of the above, 11 acres in old family hands, making well-structured (not heavy) wine for long maturing.

Beau-Site St-Est. r. ★★ **70′ 75′ 76 78′ 79 80** 81 82 83 84
55-acre Cru Bourgeois Exceptionnel in same hands as Ch'x BATAILLEY, TROTTEVIELLE, etc. Regular quality and substance typical of St-Estèphe.

Belair St-Em. r. ★★★ **70 71 75′ 76′ 78 79′ 80 82′ 83′**
Sister-ch. and neighbour of AUSONE with 32.5 acres on the Côtes. A very high standard in recent vintages (esp. '85). Makes a NV, "Roc-Blanquant", in magnums only.

de Bel-Air Lalande de Pomerol r. ★★ **75′ 76 78 79 80** 81 82′ 83
The best-known estate of this village just n. of Pomerol, with very similar wine. 25 acres.

Bel Air-Marquis d'Aligre Sou-Mar. r. ★★ **70′ 75′ 76 78′ 79′ 80** 81 82′ 83
Cru Exceptionnel with 42 acres of old vines, now on fine form.

Belgrave St-Lau. r. ★★ 81 82 83
Obscure fifth-growth in St-Julien's back-country. 107 acres. Acquired by DOURTHE in 1979. To watch.

Bel-Orme-Tronquoy-de-Lalande St-Seurin-de-Cadourne (Haut-Médoc) r. ★★ **70′ 71 75′ 76 78′ 79′** 81 82′ 83 84
Reputable 60-acre Cru Bourgeois n. of St-Estèphe. Old v'yd. producing tannic wines. Same owner as Ch. RAUZAN-GASSIES.

Berliquet St-Em. r. ★★ 78 79 80 81 82 83
Tiny Grand Cru Classé recently v. well run (by the coop).

Beychevelle St-Jul. r. ★★★ **61 66 70′ 75′ 78 79 80** 81 82′ 83 84
170-acre fourth-growth with the Médoc's finest mansion. Wine of more elegance than power, recently uneven.

Bonnet Entre-Deux-Mers r. & w. dr. ★★
Big-scale producer of some of the Best Entre-Deux-Mers.

Bon-Pasteur Pom. r. ★★ **70 75 76 78 79 80** 81 82 83
Excellent very small property on the St-Emilion boundary. Concentrated, sometimes creamy, wines.

Le Bourdieu Vertheuil (Haut-Médoc) r. ★★ **75′ 76 78′ 79 80** 81 82 83
Cru Bourgeois with sister ch. Victoria (134 acres in all) known for well-made St-Estèphe-style wines.

A Bordeaux label

CHATEAU LANGOA-
BARTON

GRAND CRU CLASSE

APPELLATION ST-JULIEN
CONTROLEE

MIS EN BOUTEILLES AU
CHATEAU

1 A château is an estate, not necessarily with a mansion or a big expanse of vineyard.
2 Reference to the local classification. It varies from one part of Bordeaux to another.
3 The Appellation Contrôlée: look up St-Julien in the France A–Z.
4 "Bottled at the château"—now the normal practice with classed-growth wines.

Bourgneuf-Vayron Pomerol r. ★★ → ★★★ **75′ 76 78 79 81 82 83** 84
22-acre v'yd. on chalky clay soil making fairly rich wines with good typically plummy Pomerol perfume.

Bouscaut Graves r. w. dr. ★★★ **70′ 75′ 76 78′ 79 80** 81 82′ 83
Classed-growth at Cadaujac bought in 1980 by Lucien Lurton, owner of Ch. BRANE-CANTENAC, etc. 75 acres red (largely Merlot); 15 acres white. Never yet brilliant.

du Bousquet Côtes de Bourg r. ★★ **75′ 76 78 79 80** 81 82 83
Reliable estate with 148 acres making attractive solid wine.

Boyd-Cantenac Margaux r. ★★★ **70′ 75′ 76′ 78′ 79 80** 81 82′ 83′ 84
44-acre third-growth regularly producing attractive wine; tending to improve. See also Ch. POUGET.

Branaire-Ducru St-Jul. r. ★★★ 70′ 75′ 76 78 79′ 80 81 82′ 83 84
Fourth-growth of 118 acres producing notably spicy and flavoury wine: attractive and reliable.

Brane-Cantenac Cant-Mar. r. ★★★ 71 75′ 76 78′ 79 80 81 82′ 83
Big (211 acres) well-run second-growth. Fragrant, gamey wines occasionally sl. coarse. Same owners as Ch'x DURFORT-VIVENS, VILLEGEORGE, CLIMENS, BOUSCAUT, etc.

du Breuil Cissac, Haut-Médoc r. ★★ 70′ 75′ 76 78 79 81 82 83
57-acre v'yd. with a 10th-century castle producing full-bodied, sometimes stylish wine. Also nuts and melons.

Brillette Moulis, Haut-Médoc r. ★★ 75 78 79 80 81′ 82 83 84
70-acre v'yd. Reliable and attractive with growing ambitions.

La Cabanne Pomerol r. ★★★ 70′ 71 75′ 76 78′ 79 81 82′ 83
Highly-regarded 25-acre property near the great Ch. TROTANOY. Recently modernized.

Cadet Piola St-Em. r. ★★ 70′ 71 73 75′ 76 78 79 80 81 82 83
Reliable little property (17 acres) on the plateau just n. of the town of St-Emilion. Ch. Faurie de Souchard has the same enthusiastic owner; slightly less fine wine.

Caillou 'Sauternes w. sw. ★★ 83
Well-run second-rank 37-acre vineyard for easy, fruity wine.

Calon-Ségur St-Est. r. ★★★ 70 75 76 78′ 79′ 80 81 82′ 83 84
Big (123-acre) third-growth of great reputation. A great classic for big hearty wines, steadily fine through the '70s.

Cambon-la-Pelouse Haut-Médoc r. ★★ 81 82 83
Huge (145-acre) accessible Cru Bourgeois. A sure bet for fresh typical Médoc.

Camensac St-Lau. r. ★★ 70′ 75′ 76 78′ 79 80 81 82′ 83
149-acre fifth-growth, replanted in the '60s with new equipment and the same expert direction as LAROSE-TRINTAUDON. Good vigorous but scarcely classic wines.

Canon St-Em. r. ★★★ 66 70 71 75′ 76 78 79′ 80 81 82′ 83′ 84
Famous first-classed-growth with 44+ acres on the plateau w. of the town. Conservative methods; very impressive wine.

Canon-la-Gaffelière St-Em. r. ★★ 70 71 75 76 78 79 81 82′
45-acre classed-growth on the lower slopes of the Côtes in German ownership. Reliable lightish wines.

Canon-Moueix Fronsac r. ★★★ 83
Revolutionary new Canon Fronsac made like a luxury Pomerol.

Cantemerle Macau r. ★★★ 61 66 70′ 71 75′ 76 78′ 79 81 82 83′ 84
Superb estate at the extreme s. of the Médoc, with a romantic ch. in a wood and 150 acres of vines. Officially fifth-growth: potentially nearer second. Problems hampered quality in late '70s. A new broom (CORDIER) in 1981 is fulfilling potential.

Cantenac-Brown Cant-Mar. r. ★★ 61 70 75 76 78 79 80 81 82 83 84
Formerly old-fashioned 77-acre third-growth, not until recently exciting, but very promising '82 and '83. Big wines.

Capbern-Gasqueton St-Est. r. ★★ 75 76 78 79 80 81 82 83 84
Good 85-acre Cru Bourgeois; same owner as Ch. CALON-SÉGUR.

Cap de Mourlin St-Em. r. ★★ 70′ 71 75′ 78 79′ 81 82′ 83
Well-known 63-acre property of the Cap de Mourlin family, owners of Ch. BALESTARD. Classic St-Emilion.

Carbonnieux Graves r. and w. dr. ★★★ (r.) 75′ 76 78′ 79 80 81 82 83
Historic estate at Léognan making good fairly light wines by modern methods. The white is the better, up to 4–5 years.

La Cardonne Blaignan (Médoc) r. ★★ 78 79 80 81′ 82′ 83 84
Large (200+ acres) Cru Bourgeois in the n. Médoc bought in 1973 by the Rothschilds of Ch. LAFITE. A safe bet.

Les Carmes-Haut-Brion Graves r. ★★ 75 76 78 79 80 81′ 82′ 83
Small neighbour of HAUT-BRION with high bourgeois standards, distributed by Chantecaille.

Caronne-Ste-Gemme St-Lau.(Haut-Médoc)r.**→***70 75'76 78
79 **80** 81 82' 83 84
    Cru Bourgeois of 100 acres. Steady quality repays patience.

Chambert-Marbuzet St-Est. r. |**★★**| 78 79 80 81 82 83 84
    Tiny (20-acre) sister-ch. of HAUTE MARBUZET. Very good fruity
wine matures quite fast.

du Castéra Médoc r. |**★★**| 70 75 78 79 81 82 83 84
    Historic property at St-Germain in the n. Médoc. Recent
investment; to watch for tasty but not tannic wine.

Certan de May Pomerol r. |**★★★**| 70 71 73 75' 76 78 79 81 82' 83
    Neighbour of VIEUX-CHÂTEAU-CERTAN. Tiny property with full-
bodied rich and tannic wine, recently flying high.

Certan-Giraud Pomerol r. ★★★ 71 75 76 78 79 81 82' 83'
    Small (17-acre) property next to the great Ch. PETRUS.

Chantegrive Graves r. w. dr. |**★★**|
    150-acre estate half white, half red; useful modern Graves. Other
labels incl. Mayne-Levéque.

Chasse-Spleen Moulis r. |**★★★**| 70' 71 75' 76 78' 79 80 81' 82' 83' 84
    127-acre Cru Exceptionnel of classed-growth quality. Consisten-
tly good, sometimes outstanding, long-maturing wine.

Cheval Blanc St-Em. r. ★★★★ 66 70' 75' 76 78 79 80 81' 82' 83'
    This and AUSONE are the "first-growths" of St-Em. Rich, full-
blooded, intensely vigorous and perfumed, from 86 acres on the
border of Pomerol.

Chicane Graves r. |**★★**|
    Satisfying and reliable product of the Langon merchant Pierre
Coste. Domaine de Gaillat is another. Drink at 2–6 years.

Cissac Cissac r. |**★★**| 66 70' 71 75' 76 78' 79 80 81 82' 83 84
    A pillar of the bourgeoisie. 80-acre Grand Bourgeois Exception-
nel with a steady record for tasty long-lived wine.

Citran Avensan, Haut-Médoc r. ★★ 70' 75 76 78' 79 81 82 83
    Grand Bourgeois Exceptionnel of 178 acres. Stylish wine.

Clarke Listrac, Haut-Médoc r. (p.) |**★★**| 78 79 80 81 82 83 84
    Huge (350-acre) Cru Bourgeois Rothschild development, incl.
elaborate visitor facilities. Ch'x. Malmaison and Peyrelebade
are second labels.

Clerc-Milon Pauillac r. ★★★ 70' 75' 76 78' 79 80 81 82' 83
    Forgotten little fifth-growth bought by Baron Philippe de
Rothschild in 1970. Now 73 acres. Very decent, but not
thrilling.

Climens Sauternes w. sw. |**★★★**| 71' 75' 76' 78' 79 80 81 82 83' 84
    Famous 74-acre classed-growth at Barsac making some of the
best and most stylish sweet wine in the world for a good 10 years'
maturing. Same owner as Ch. BRANE-CANTENAC, etc.

Clinet Pomerol r. ★★ 70 71 75' 76 78 79 80 81 83
    15-acre property in central Pomerol making tannic "Pauillac-
style" wine. Some fatness would help.

Clos l'Eglise Pomerol r. |**★★★**| 71 75 76 78 79' 80 81 82' 83
    14-acre v'yd in one of the best sites in Pomerol. Excellent wine
without great muscle or flesh. The same family owns CH. PLINCE.

Clos Fourtet St-Em. r. |**★★★**| 70 75 76 78 79 80 81 82' 83
    Well-known 42-acre first-growth on the plateau with cellars
almost in the town. Back on top form after a middling patch.
Same owners as CLIMENS, BRANE-CANTENAC, etc.

Clos Haut-Peyraguey Sauternes w. sw. |**★★**| 78 79 80 81 82 83
    Tiny production of good medium-rich wine. The v.g. Cru
Bourgeois Ch. Haut- Bommes is in the same hands.

Clos des Jacobins St-Em. r. |**★★**| 75' 76 78 79 80 81 82' 83'
    Well-known and well-run little (18-acre) classed-growth owned
by the shipper CORDIER. Wines of increasing depth.

Clos l'Oratoire St-Em. r. ★★ 78 79 80 81 82 83
    Richly typical Grand Cru. See also Ch. PEYREAU.

Clos René Pomerol r. ★★★ 70 71′ 75 76 78 79 80 81 82′ 83
Leading ch. on the w. of Pomerol. 38 acres making powerful wine;
eventually delicate. Also sold as Ch. Moulinet-Lasserre.

La Closerie-Grand-Poujeaux Moulis (Haut-Médoc) r. ★★
Small but respected traditional middle-Médoc. To keep.

La Clotte St-Em. r. ★★ 70 71′ 75′ 76′ 78 79 81 82 83
Tiny Côtes Grand Cru with marvellously scented "supple" wine.

Colombier-Monpelou Pauillac r. ★★
Reliable small Cru Bourgeois to watch.

La Conseillante Pomerol r. ★★★ 70′ 71′ 75′ 76 77 78 79 80 81′ 82′ 83
29-acre classed-growth on the plateau between PETRUS and
CHEVAL BLANC. Some of the noblest and most fragrant Pomerol,
worthy of its superb position.

Corbin (Giraud) St-Em. r. ★★ 75 76 78 79 81 82′ 83′
28-acre classed-growth in n. St-Emilion where a cluster of
Corbins occupy the edge of the plateau. Can be very rich.

Corbin-Michotte St-Em. r. ★★ 70 71 75 76 78 79 81 82 83
Well-run small property; "generous" Pomerol-like wine.

Cos-d'Estournel St-Est. r. ★★★★ 61 66 70 71 73 74 75′ 76′ 77 78′ 79 80 81′ 82′ 83 84
140-acre second-growth with eccentric chinoiserie building
overlooking Ch. LAFITE. Always full-flavoured, often magnificent, wine. Now regularly one of the best in the Médoc.

Cos Labory St-Est. r. ★★ 70′ 75′ 76 78′ 79′ 80 81′ 82′ 83 84
Little-known fifth-growth neighbour of COS D'ESTOURNEL with
37 acres. Blunt fruity wines mature early. To watch.

Coufran St-Seurin-de-Cadourne (Haut-Médoc) r. ★★ 78′ 79 80 81 82′ 83′
Coufran and Ch. VERDIGNAN, on the northern-most hillock of
the Haut-Médoc, are under the same ownership. Coufran has
mainly Merlot vines; soft lightish wine. 148 acres.

Couhins Graves (r.) w. dr. ★★ 81 82 83′ 84
17-acre v'yd. at Villenave-d'Ornon run by the State. Fine white
(and a little red) for drinking young. Couhins-Lurton is part of
the v'yd. making v.g. all-Sauvignon white.

La Couronne Pauillac r. ★★ 75 76 78 79 81′ 82′ 83
Excellent (very) small Cru Exceptionnel made at Ch. HAUT-
BATAILLEY.

Coutet Sauternes w. sw. ★★★ 70′ 71′ 73 75′ 76 79 81 82 83′
Traditional rival to Ch. CLIMENS; 91 acres in Barsac. Often
slightly less rich; at its best equally fine but recently less reliable.
"Cuvée Madame" is a selection of the very best (71 75 76).

Couvent des Jacobins St-Em. r. ★★ 75 76 78 79′ 80 81 82′ 83
Well-known vineyard of 17 acres adjacent to the town of St-
Emilion on the east. Among the best of its kind.

Le Crock St-Est. r. ★★ 79 80 81 82 83
Well-situated Cru Bourgeois of 74 acres in the same family as
Ch. LÉOVILLE-POYFERRÉ. Among the excellent C.B's of the
commune.

La Croix Pomerol r. ★★ 70′ 71′ 75′ 76 78 79′ 81 82′ 83
Well-reputed property of 32 acres. Appealing plummy Pomerol
with a spine; matures well. Also La C.-St-Georges, La C.-
Toulifaut and Clos des Litanies.

La Croix de Gay Pomerol r. ★★★ 70′ 71′ 75′ 76′ 78 79 81 82′ 83
30 acres in the best part of the commune. Recently on form. Has
underground cellars, rare in Pomerol.

Croizet-Bages Pauillac r. ★★ 70′ 71′ 75′ 76 78′ 79′ 80 81 82′ 83 84
52-acre fifth-growth (lacking a ch.) with the same owners as
Château RAUZAN-GASSIES. Sound sturdy wines with growing
finesse.

Croque-Michotte St-Em. r. ★★ 70 75 76 78 79 81 82′ 83
30-acre Pomerol-style classed-growth on the Pomerol border.

Curé-Bon-la-Madeleine St-Em. r. ★★★70′71′7576′78 79 80 81 82′ 83
  Small (11-acre) property among the best of the Côtes; between
  AUSONE and CANON. Managed by MOUEIX.

Dassault St-Em. r. ★★ 78 79 **80** 81 82 83
  Notably consistent middle-weight Grand Cru. 58 acres.

Dauzac Lab-Mar. r. ★★ →★★★ **70** 75 76 78 79′ **80** 81 82′ 83 84
  Substantial fifth-growth near the river s. of Margaux. In new
  hands and much improved since '79. 120 acres.

Desmirail Mar. r. ★★→ ★★★ 81 82 83′
  Third-growth, now 45 acres. A long-defunct name recently
  revived by the owner of BRANE-CANTENAC. Gentle, fragrant
  wines.

Dillon Haut-Médoc r. (w. dr.) ★★ **70** 75′ **76** 78′ **79**′ 81 82 83
  Local wine college of Blanquefort, just n. of Bordeaux. 85 acres.
  Dry white: Ch. Lucas (D.Y.A.)

Doisy-Daëne Barsac w. sw. and dr. ★★★ **75 76**′ **78 79 80** 81 82 83′
  Forward-looking 34-acre estate making crisp dry white (incl.
  Riesling grapes) as well as notably fine sweet Barsac.

Doisy-Dubroca Barsac w. sw. ★★ **71**′ 75′ **76** 78′ 79 80 81 83
  Tiny (8½-acre) Barsac classed-growth allied to Ch. CLIMENS.

---

*Why do the Châteaux of Bordeaux have such a large section of this book devoted
to them? The reason is simple: collectively they form by far the largest supply of
high-quality wine on earth.*

  *A single typical Médoc château with 150 acres (some have far more) makes
approximately 26,000 dozen bottles of identifiable wine a year — the production
of two or three Californian "boutique" wineries. The tendency over the last two
decades has been for the better-known châteaux to buy more land. Many classed-
growths have expanded by as much as 10 times since they were classified in 1855.*

Doisy-Védrines Sauternes w. sw. ★★★ **71** 75′ **76**′ **78 79** 80 81 82′ 83′
  50-acre classed-growth at Barsac, near CLIMENS and COUTET.
  Deliciously sturdy rich wines designed for a long life.

Domaine de Chevalier Graves r. and w. dr. ★★★★ (r.)**61** 64 66 **70**′ 71 73
  75′ **76 77** 78′ 79′ **80** 81′ 82′ 83 84
  Superb small estate of 36 acres at Léognan. The red is stern at
  first, richly subtle with age. The white is delicate but matures to
  rich flavours. (w. **75 76**′ **78 79**′ **80** 81 **82** 83′ 84). Changed hands
  (but not management) in 1983.

Domaine de l'Eglise Pomerol r. ★★ **70** 71 75 76 78 79′ 81 **82**′ 83
  Small property: fragrant wine distributed by BORIE-MANOUX.

Domaine la Grave Graves r. w. dr. ★★ **80** 81 82 83 (w. 83) 84 85
  Innovative little estate at Portets. Lively medal-winning reds
  made for a long life. Oak-aged delicious whites.

Domaine de Toutigeac Entre-Deux-Mers r. (w. dr.) ★
  Enormous producer of useful Bordeaux at Targon.

La Dominique St-Em. r. ★★★ **70** 71′ 73 75 76 78 79 80 81 82′ 83
  Fine 40-acre classed-growth next door to Ch. CHEVAL BLANC,
  making wine almost as arresting.

Ducru-Beaucaillou St-Jul. r. ★★★ **61** 66 **70**′ 71 74 75′ **76 77** 78′ 79
  80 81 82′ 83′
  Outstanding second-growth; 120 acres overlooking the river.
  The owner, M. Borie, makes classical "cedar-pencil" claret.

Duhart-Milon-Rothschild Pauillac r. ★★★ **70**′ 71 75′ **76**′ **77** 78 79′
  80 81 82′ 83
  Fourth-growth neighbour of LAFITE under the same management. Maturing vines show very fine quality. 110 acres.

Durfort-Vivens Margaux r. ★★★ **70** 71 75′ **76** 78′ 79′ **80** 81 82′ 83
  Relatively small (49-acre) second-growth owned by M. Lurton
  of BRANE-CANTENAC. Recent wines (except '84) have real finesse.

Dutruch–Grand–Poujeaux Moulis r. ★★ **70 73′** 75 76 78′ 79 **80** 81 82′ 83 84
One of the leaders of MOULIS; full-bodied, rich and tannic wines.

L'Eglise–Clinet Pomerol r. ★★★ **70 71** 75 76 78 79 80 81 **82′** 83
11 acres. Highly ranked; full, fleshy wine. Changed hands in '82.

L'Enclos Pomerol r. ★★ **70 71 75 76 78 79 80** 81 82′ 83
Respected 26-acre property on the w. side of Pomerol, near CLOS-RENÉ. Big, well-made, long-flavoured wine.

L'Evangile Pomerol r. ★★★ **70′ 71′** 73 75′ 76 78 79 80 81 **82′** 83′
33 acres between PETRUS and CHEVAL BLANC. Impressive wines. In the same area and class as LA CONSEILLANTE.

Fargues Sauternes w. sw. ★★★ 70′ 71′ **75′ 76′** 78 79 **80** 81 83
25-acre v'yd. in same ownership as Ch. YQUEM. Fruity and extremely elegant but much lighter wines.

Ferrière Margaux r. ★★ **66 70 75** 78 79 81 82 83
Phantom third-growth of only 10+ acres. The wine is made at Ch. LASCOMBES.

Feytit–Clinet Pomerol r. ★★ **70′ 71′** 75′ **76 78** 79 80 81 82′ 83
Little property next to LATOUR-POMEROL. Has made some fine big strong wines. Managed by J-P MOUEIX.

Fieuzal Graves r. and (w. dr.) ★★★ **70′** 75′ **76** 78′ 79 80 81′ 82′ 83
56-acre classed-growth at Léognan. Finely made memorable wines.

Figeac St-Em. r. ★★★ **61 70′ 71 75 76 77 78** 79 80 81 82′ 83
Famous first-growth neighbour of CHEVAL BLANC. Superb 98-acre v'yd. gives one of Bordeaux's most attractive rich but elegant wines, maturing fairly quickly.

Filhot Sauternes w. sw. and dr. ★★★ **71′ 75 76′ 78 79′ 80** 81 82′ 83
Second-rank classed-growth with splendid ch., 148-acre v'yd. Good sw. wines for fairly early drinking, a little dry and r.

La Fleur St-Em. r. ★★ **70 75 76 78** 79 80 81 82′ 83
Very small Côtes estate producing luxurious wines.

La Fleur–Petrus Pomerol r. ★★★ **70 71′ 73** 75′ **76′** 78 79 80 81 **82′** 83′
18-acre v'yd. flanking PETRUS and under the same MOUEIX management. Exceedingly fine plummy wines; Pomerol at its best.

Fombrauge St-Em. r. ★★ **70′ 71 75′ 76 77 78′** 79 80 81 82′ 83
Major property of St-Christophe-des-Bardes, e. of St-Emilion with 120 acres. Reliable St-Emilion making great efforts.

Fonbadet Pauillac r. ★★ **70** 75 78 79 **80** 81′ 82 83 84
Flourishing Cru Bourgeois of high repute with 38 acres next door to Ch. PONTET-CANET. The Peyronies own several small Pauillac crus incl. La Tour du Roc-Milon.

Fonplégade St-Em. r. ★★ **71 73 75 76 78** 79 80 81 82′ 83
42-acre v'yd. on the Côtes w. of St. Emilion in another branch of the MOUEIX family. Sturdy and worthy wines.

Fonréaud Listrac r. ★★ **70′ 75′ 76 78′ 79 80** 81 82′ 83
One of the bigger (96 acres) and better Crus Bourgeois of its area, selling mainly in France and at the door.

Fonroque St-Em. r. ★★★ **67 70 71′ 73** 75′ **76′ 78** 79 80 81 82′ 83
48 acres on the plateau n. of St-Emilion, MOUEIX property. Big dark wine that needs time.

Les Forts de Latour Pauillac r. ★★★ 66 70 71 73 74 75 76 77 78
The second wine of Ch. Latour; well worthy of its big brother. Unique in being bottle-aged at least three years before release. Fetches the price of a second-growth Château.

Fourcas–Dupré Listrac r. ★★ **70′ 71 75 76** 78′ **79 80** 81 82′ 83′ 84
A top-class 100-acre Cru Bourgeois Exceptionnel making consistent and elegant wine. To follow.

Fourcas–Hosten Listrac r. ★★→★★★ **70** 75 **76** 78′ **79 80** 81 82′ 83 84
96-acre Cru Bourgeois currently considered the best of its commune. Firm wine with a long life.

Franc-Mayne St-Em. r. ★★ 70 71 73 75 **76 78 79 80 81** 82' 83
Small well-regarded v'yd. on the Côtes w. of St-Emilion.

La Gaffelière St-Em. r. ★★★ 61 66 70 71 75' **76** 78 79 80 81 82' 83'
55-acre first-growth at the foot of the Côtes below Ch. BEL-AIR.
Its great years are wonderful; lesser years not thrilling.

La Garde Graves r. (w. dr.) ⌈★★⌉ 70' 75' 76' **78 79 80** 81 82' 83 84
Substantial ESCHENAUER property making reliably sound red.

Le Gay Pomerol r. ★★★ 70 71 74 75' **76'** 78 79 81 **82'** 83'
Well-known 14-acre v'yd. on the northern edge of Pomerol. Same
owner as Ch. LAFLEUR. MOUEIX management. Splendid wine.

Gazin Pomerol r. ★★★ 70' 71' 75' **76** 78 79 81 82 83
Large property (for Pomerol) with 56 acres. Not quite as splendid as its position next to PETRUS.

Gilette Sauternes w. sw. ★★★ 49 55 59
Extraordinary small Preignac château which stores its rich wines
in cask to a great age.

Giscours Lab-Mar. r. ⌈★★★⌉ 66 70 71' 75' **76** 78' 79' **80** 81' 82' 83 84
Splendid 182-acre third-growth s. of CANTENAC. Dynamically
run and making excellent vigorous wine for long maturing.

du Glana St-Jul. r. ★★ 66 70' 75' 78 79 81 82' 83
Big Cru Bourgeois in centre of St-Julien. Undemanding quality.

Gloria St-Jul. r. ⌈★★★⌉ 66 67 70' 71 73 75' **76 78'** 79' **80** 81 82' 83 84
Outstanding Cru Bourgeois making wine of vigour and finesse,
among good classed-growths in quality. 110 acres. The owner,
Henri Martin, bought Ch. ST-PIERRE in 1982.

Grand-Barrail-Lamarzelle-Figeac St-Em. r. ⌈★★⌉ 70 71 73 75 76
78 79 81 82' 83
Substantial property near FIGEAC, incl. Ch. La Marzelle. Well-
reputed and popular.

Grand-Corbin-Despagne St-Em. r. ★★ 70 71 75 78 79 81 82' 83
One of the biggest and best Grands Crus on the CORBIN plateau.

Grand-Pontet St-Em. r. ★★ 75 76 78 79 81 82' 83
Widely distributed 35-acre neighbour of Ch. BEAU SÉJOUR-
BÉCOT, in the same hands since 1980. "Supple", smooth wine.

Grand-Puy-Ducasse Pauillac r. ⌈★★★⌉ 70 75 76 78 79 80 81 82' 83 84
Well-known little fifth-growth bought in '71, renovated and
enlarged to 90 acres under expert management. A best buy.

Grand-Puy-Lacoste Pauillac r. ⌈★★★⌉ 70' 71 73 75 76 78' 79' 80 81'
82' 83 84
Leading fifth-growth famous for excellent full-bodied vigorous
Pauillac. 110 acres among the "Bages" ch'x. s. of the town,
bought in 1978 by M. Borie of DUCRU-BEAUCAILLOU.

La Grave Trigant de Boisset Pom. r. ⌈★★★⌉ 75' 76' 78 79 80 81 82' 83
Verdant ch. with small but first-class v'yd. owned by Christian
MOUEIX. Firm, beautifully structured Pomerol improves each
year.

Gressier Grand Poujeaux Moulis r. ⌈★★★⌉ 66 70 71 73 75' **76** 78 79'
80 81 82 83' 84
Good Cru Bourgeois. Fine firm wine with a good track record.

Greysac Médoc r. ★★ 70' 75' **76 78 79' 80** 81' 82 83
Elegant 140-acre property well-known in the U.S.A.

Gruaud-Larose St-Jul. r. ⌈★★★⌉ 70' 71 73 75' **76** 78' 79 80 81 82' 83 84
One of the biggest and best-known second-growths. 189 acres
making smooth rich stylish claret. Owned by CORDIER. The
excellent second wine is called Sarget de Gruaud-Larose.

Guiraud Sauternes (r.) w. sw. (dr.) ⌈★★★⌉ 70' 76 78' 79' 80 81' 82 83'
Newly restored classed-growth of top quality. 250 + acres. At
best excellent sweet wine of great finesse and a small amount of
red and dry white. The '83 should be superb in time.

La Gurgue Margaux r. ★★ 81 82 83 84
Small well-placed property with fine typical Margaux recently
bought by owners of Ch. CHASSE-SPLEEN. To watch.

Hanteillan Cissac r. ★★ 75 76 79' 80 81 82' 83 84
Large (200 + acres) v'yd. renovated and enlarged since 1973.
Admirable bourgeois wine. Ch. Larrivaux-Hanteillan is second
quality.

Haut-Bages-Averous Pauillac r. ★★ 81 82 83
The second wine of Ch. LYNCH BAGES. Delicious easy drinking.

Haut-Bages-Libéral Pauillac r. ★★ 75 76 78 80 81 82' 83 84
Lesser-known fifth-growth of 64 acres now in same stable as
CHASSE-SPLEEN. The auguries are good.

Haut-Bages-Monpelou Pauillac r. ★★ 75' 76 78 79 80 81 82' 83
25-acre Cru Bourgeois stable-mate of CH. BATAILLEY on former
DUHART-MILON land. Good-value Pauillac.

Haut-Bailly Graves r. ★★★ 70' 75 78 79' 80 81' 82 83 84
60-acre estate at Léognan famous for ripe, round, sometimes
"feminine" red Graves, esp. since new regime (1979).

Haut-Batailley Pauillac r. ★★★ 70' 75' 76 78' 79 80 81 82' 83 84
The smaller section of the fifth-growth Batailley estate: 49 acres.
In a much gentler vein than its sister Ch. GRAND-PUY-LACOSTE.

Haut-Brignon 1ères Côtes r. & w. dr. ★
Big producer of standard wines at Cénac, owned by a major
Champagne coop.

Haut-Brion Pessac, Graves r. (w.) ★★★★ 61 62 64 66 67 70' 71 75' 76 78'
79 80 81' 82' 83 84
The oldest great ch. of Bordeaux and the only non-Médoc first-
growth of 1855. 108 acres. Reds of singular balance, particularly
good since 1975. A little full dry white in 76 78 79 81 83 84. See also
BAHANS-HAUT-BRION.

Haut-Marbuzet St-Estèphe r. ★★ 70' 75' 76 78' 79 80 81 82' 83 84
One of the best of many good St-Estèphe Crus Bourgeois. 100
acres. Ch'x Tour de Marbuzet, Chambert-Marbuzet, MacCar-
thy-Moula in same hands. New oak gives Haut-Marbuzet classic
style.

Haut-Pontet St-Em. r. ★★ 70 71 73 75 78 79 81 82' 83
12-acre v'yd. of the Côtes well deserving its Grand Cru status.

Haut-Quercus St-Em. r. ★★
Oak-aged coop wine to a very high standard.

Haut-Sarpe St-Em. r. ★★ 78 79 81 82 83'
Small Grand Cru Classé; same owner as Ch. LA CROIX. To follow.

Hortevie St-Jul. r. ★★ 81 82 83 84
Of the few St. Julien Crus Bourgeois. This tiny v'yd. and its sister
TERREY-GROS-CAILLOU are shining examples.

Houissant St-Estèphe r. ★★ 78 79 80 81 82 83 84
Typical robust well-balanced St-Estèphe Cru Bourgeois Exceptionnel, also called Ch. Leyssac; well known in Denmark.

d'Issan Cant-Mar. r. ★★★ 70 71 73' 75' 76' 78 79' 80 81 82' 83' 84
Beautifully restored moated ch. with 75-acre third-growth v'yd.
well known for fragrant, virile but gentle wine.

Kirwan Cant-Mar. r. ★★★ 70' 75' 76 78 79' 80 81 82' 83 84
Well-run 86-acre third-growth owned by SCHRÖDER & SCHYLER.
New planting of '60s now mature and results tasting v. good.

Labégorce Margaux r. ★★ 70' 73 75' 76 78' 79 80 81 82' 83 84
Substantial 69-acre property north of Margaux with long-lived
wines of true Margaux quality.

Labégorce-Zédé Margaux r. ★★ 70' 75' 76 78 79 80 81' 82' 83' 84
Outstanding Cru Bourgeois on the road n. from Margaux. 62
acres. Typical delicate fragrant Margaux, truly classic since '81.
The same family as VIEUX-CHÂTEAU-CERTAN.

Lacoste-Borie
The second wine of Ch. GRAND-PUY-LACOSTE.

Lafaurie-Peyraguey Sauternes w. sw. ★★★ 75' 76' 78' 79 80 81 83'
Fine classed-growth of only 49 acres at Bommes, belonging to
CORDIER. After a lean patch good, rich and racy wines.

Lafite-Rothschild   Pauillac r.   ★★★★   **61** 70′ 75′ **76**′ 78 79′ **80** 81′ 82′ 83 84

First-growth of fabulous style and perfume in its great vintages, which keep for decades. Off-form for several years but resplendent since '76. 225 acres.

Lafleur   Pomerol r.   ★★★ **66 67** 70′ **71**′ **73** 75′ **76** 78 79 **80** 81 **82**′ 83

Property of 12 acres just n. of PETRUS. Excellent wine of the finer, less "fleshy" kind. Same owner as LE GAY. MOUEIX direction.

Lafleur-Gazin   Pomerol r.   ★★   **70 71**′ 75′ **76** 78 **79** 81 **82**′ 83

Distinguished small MOUEIX estate on the n.e. border of Pomerol.

Lafon-Rochet   St-Est. r.   ★★ 70′ **71** 75′ **76** 78 **79** 81 82 83

Fourth-growth neighbour of Ch. COS D'ESTOURNEL, restored in the '60s. 110 acres. Rather hard dark full-bodied St-Estèphe. Same owner as Ch. PONTET-CANET.

Lagrange   Pomerol r.   ★★★ 70′ **71**′ 75′ **76** 78 79 **80** 81 **82**′ 83

20-acre v'yd. in the centre of Pomerol run by the ubiquitous house of MOUEIX. Maturing vines are giving deeper flavour.

"BREATHING IS FOR PEOPLE"

Fierce arguments take place between wine-lovers over whether it is a good or a bad thing to decant wine from its bottle into a carafe. The argument in favour is that it allows the wine to "breathe" and its bouquet to expand: against, that its precious breath is dissipated — or at the least that it makes no difference.

Two additional practical reasons in favour concern old wine which has deposited dregs, which can be left in the bottle by careful decanting, and young wine being consumed before it is fully developed: thorough aeration helps to create the illusion of maturity. An aesthetic one is that decanters are handsome on the table.

Decanting is done by pouring the wine into another container very steadily until any sediment reaches the shoulder of the bottle. To see the sediment clearly hold the bottle's neck over a light-bulb or a candle.

Lagrange   St-Jul. r.   ★★★ **66** 70′ 75′ 78 79′ 81 82 83

Run-down third-growth inland from St-Julien. Bought by Suntory in 1982. 123 + acres, being extensively restored. To watch. Second label: Les Fiefs de Lagrange.

La Lagune   Ludon r.   ★★★   **66** 70′ **71 73**′ 75′ **76**′ 78′ 79 **80** 81 82′ 83 84

Well-run ultra-modern 160-acre third-growth in the extreme s. of the Médoc. Attractively rich and fleshy wines; brilliant quality.

Lalande-Borie   St-Jul. r.   ★★   78 79 81 82 83

A baby brother of the great DUCRU-BEAUCAILLOU created from part of the former v'yd. of Ch. LAGRANGE.

Lamarque   Lamarque (Haut-Médoc) r.   ★★ 75′ **76** 78 79 **80** 81′ 82 83′

Splendid medieval fortress of the central Médoc with 113 acres giving admirable wine of high "Bourgeois" standard.

Lanessan   Cussac (Haut-Médoc) r.   ★★   70′ 75′ **76** 78′ 79 **80** 81 82′ 83

Distinguished 108-acre Cru Bourgeois Exceptionnel just s. of St-Julien. Same owner as PICHON-LONGUEVILLE-BARON.

Langoa-Barton   St-Jul. r.   ★★★   70′ **71** 75′ **76** 78′ 79 **80** 81 82 83′ 84

Fine 18th-century ch. housing the wine of third-growth Langoa (49 acres) as well as second-growth LÉOVILLE-BARTON. The wines are similar: Langoa slightly less potent.

Larcis-Ducasse   St-Em. r.   ★★★ 70′ **71**′ 75′ **76** 78 **79 80** 81 82 83

The top property of St-Laurent, eastern neighbour of St-Emilion, on the Côtes next to Ch. PAVIE. 24 acres. Coasting?

Larmande   St-Em. r.   ★★   75 76 78 79 80 81 82 83

Substantial property related to CAP-DE-MOURLIN. Replanted and now making rich, strikingly scented wine.

Laroque St-Em. r. ★★ 70′ 75′ 76′ 78 79 80 81 82′ 83
Important 108-acre v'yd. with an impressive mansion on the St-Emilion côtes in St. Christophe.

Larose-Trintaudon St-Lau. (Haut-Médoc) r. ★★ 70 75′ 76 78 79 80 81 82 83 84
The biggest v'yd. in the Médoc: 388 acres. Modern methods make reliable fruity and charming Cru Bourgeois wine.

Laroze St-Em. r. ★★ 70 71′ 75′ 76 78′ 79 80 81 82 83
Big v'yd. (70 acres) on the w. Côtes. Relatively light wines from sandy soil; soon enjoyable. Sometimes excellent.

Larrivet-Haut-Brion Graves r. (w.) ★★ 70′ 75′ 76 79′ 80 81 82′ 83
Little property at Léognan with perfectionist standards.

Lascombes Margaux r. (p.) ★★★ 61 66 70′ 75′ 76 78 79 81 82 83 84
240-acre second-growth owned by the British brewers Bass-Charrington and lavishly restored. After a poor patch, signs of new vigour and skill.

Latour Pauillac r. ★★★★ 61 62 64 66 67 70′ 71 73 74 75′ 76′ 77 78′ 79′ 80 81′ 82′ 83 84
First-growth. The most consistent great wine in Bordeaux, in France and probably the world: rich, intense and almost immortal in great years, almost always classical and pleasing even in bad ones. British-owned. 150 acres. Second wine LES FORTS DE LATOUR.

Latour à Pomerol Pomerol r. ★★★★ 70′ 71′ 75′ 76′ 78 79′ 80 81 82′ 83
Top growth of 19 acres under MOUEIX management. Pomerol of great power and perfume, yet also ravishing finesse.

Laujac Médoc r. ★★ 75′ 78 81 82 83
Cru Bourgeois in the n. Médoc owned by the CRUSE family. Well known but scarcely outstanding. 62 acres.

des Laurets St-Em. r. ★★ 70′ 75′ 76 78 79 81 82 83
Major property of Puisseguin and Montagne-St-Emilion (to the e.) with 160 acres on the Côtes. Sterling wine.

Laville-Haut-Brion Graves w. dr. ★★★★ 71 75 76 78 79 81 82 83′ 84
A tiny production of one of the very best white Graves for long maturing, made at Ch. LA MISSION-HAUT-BRION.

Léoville-Barton St-Jul. r. ★★★ 61 66 67 70′ 71 74 75′ 76 78′ 79 80 81 82′ 83 84
90-acre portion of the great second-growth Léoville v'yd. in the Anglo-Irish hands of the Barton family for over 150 years. Glorious classical claret, made by traditional methods at the Bartons' third-growth Ch. LANGOA.

Léoville-Las Cases St-Jul. r. ★★★★ 61 64 66 67 70′ 71 73 75′ 76 77 78′ 79 80 81 82′ 83 84
The largest portion of the old Léoville estate, 210 acres, with one of the highest reputations in Bordeaux. Elegant, complex, powerful but never heavy wines. Second label: Clos du Marquis.

Léoville-Poyferré St-Jul. r. ★★★ 70′ 73 75′ 76 78′ 79 80 81 82′ 83 84
For years the least outstanding of the Léovilles; since 1980 again living up to the great name. '82 is a triumph and '83 splendid. 156 acres. Second label: Ch. Moulin-Riche.

Lestage Listrac r. ★★ 75′ 76 78′ 79 80 81 82′ 83
130-acre Cru Bourgeois in same hands as Ch. FONRÉAUD. Light, quite stylish wine.

Liot Barsac w. sw. ★★ 70′ 71 75′ 76 78 79′ 80 81 83
Consistent fairly light golden wines from 94 acres.

Liversan St-Sau. (Haut-Médoc) r. ★★ 70′ 75′ 76 78 79 80 81 82′ 83 84
116-acre Grand Cru Bourgeois inland from Pauillac. Change of regime in 1984 should maintain high standards. Ch. Fonpiqueyre is the same wine in certain markets.

Livran Médoc r. ★★ 75 76′ 78′ 79 81 82′ 83
Big Cru Bourgeois at St-Germain in the n. Médoc. Consistent round wines (half Merlot).

Loudenne St-Yzans (Médoc) r. ★★★ (r.) 75′ 78′ 79 80 81 82′ 83 84
Beautiful riverside ch. owned by Gilbeys since 1875. Well-made Cru Bourgeois red and a very agreeable dry white from 120 acres. The white is best young.

Loupiac-Gaudiet Loupiac w. sw. ★★
Reliable source of good-value almost-Sauternes, just across the river Garonne.

La Louvière Graves r. and w. dr. ★★ (r.) 75 78 79 80 81 82′ 83 84
Noble 135-acre estate at Léognan. Excellent white for drinking fresh or maturing, and red recently of classed-growth standard.

de Lussac St-Em. r. ★★ 75′ 78′ 79 81 82 83
One of the best estates in Lussac-St-Emilion (to the n.e.).

Lynch-Bages Pauillac r. ★★★ 61 66 70 75′ 76 77 78′ 79 80 81 82′ 83′ 84
One of the biggest and best fifth-growths, closer to second- in quality. 200 acres making rich robust wine: delicious; occasionally great, with recent vintages esp. notable.

Lynch-Moussas Pauillac r. ★★ 71′ 75′ 76 78 79 80 81 82′ 83 84
Fifth-growth restored by the director of Ch. BATAILLEY since 1969. Now 60+ acres and new equipment are making serious wine, gaining depth as the young vines age.

du Lyonnat Lussac-St-Em. r. ★★
120-acre estate with well-distributed reliable wine.

Remember that vintage years generally ready for drinking in 1987 are printed in **bold type**. *Those in light type will benefit from being kept. For an indication of how long they will improve consult the vintage charts on pages 22 and 23.*

Magdelaine St-Em. r. ★★★ 67 70′ 71′ 73 75′ 76 78 79 80 81 82′ 83
Leading first-growth of the Côtes, 26 acres next to AUSONE owned by J-P MOUEIX. Beautifully balanced wine. On top form.

Magence Graves r. w. dr. ★★ (r.) 75 78 79′ 81 82 83 84 (w.) D.Y.A.
Go-ahead 45-acre property at St Pierre de Mons, in the s. of the Graves, well known for distinctly SAUVIGNON-flavoured very dry white and fruity red for early drinking.

Malartic-Lagravière Graves r. and (w. dr.) ★★★ (r.) 70′ 75′ 76′ 78 79 80 81 82′ 83 (w.) 75 76 79 80 81′ 82 83 84
Well-known Léognan classed-growth of 34 acres making well-structured red for long maturing and a very little excellent fruity SAUVIGNON white, hard to resist young.

Malescasse Lamarque (Haut-Médoc) r. ★★ 75 78 79′ 80 81 82 83
Renovated Cru Bourgeois with 100 acres in a good situation owned by M. Tesseron of Ch. LAFON-ROCHET.

Malescot St-Exupéry Margaux r. ★★★ 61 66 70′ 71 75′ 76 77 78′ 79′ 80 81 82′ 83′ 84
Third-growth of 84 acres allied until 1979 with Ch. MARQUIS-D'ALESME. Long-maturing, eventually classically fragrant and stylish Margaux.

de Malle Sauternes r. w. sw./dr. ★★★ (w. sw.) 70 71 75 76 78 79 80 81′ 82 83
Famous and beautiful ch. at Preignac. 55 acres. Good sweet and dry whites and red (Graves) Ch. de Cardaillan.

Maquin-St-Georges St-Em. r. ★★ 78 79 81 82 83
Steady producer of delicious "satellite" St-Em. at St-Georges.

de Marbuzet St-Est. r. ★★ 73 75 76 78 79 81 82 83 84
The second label of Ch. COS D'ESTOURNEL. (The actual ch. overlooks the river from the hill n. of Cos.)

Margaux Margaux r. (w. dr.) ★★★★**61** **66'** **70'** **71** 75' **76** 78' **79** 80 80 81' 82' 83' 84

First-growth, the most delicate and finely perfumed of all in its best vintages. New owners since '77 have revolutionized quality. Noble ch. and estate with 209 acres of vines. "Pavillon Rouge" (**79' 80** 81 82' 83') is the second wine. "Pavillon Blanc" is the best white (Sauvignon) wine of the Médoc, for 3–4 years ageing.

Marquis-d'Alesme Margaux r. ★★ **70' 71'** 75' **78** 79 **80** 81 82 83 84

Tiny (17-acre) third-growth, formerly made with Ch. MALES-COT; independent since '79. Finer than its reputation.

Marquis-de-Terme Margaux r. ★★★ 66 **70'** 75' **76** 78' **79** 80 81' 82 83

Renovated fourth-growth of 84 acres. Fragrant, fairly lean wines. Sells principally in France.

Martinens Margaux r. ★★ 75 76 78' 79' 80 81 82 83 84

75-acre Cru Bourgeois at Cantenac, recently much improved.

Maucaillou Moulis r. ★★ **70' 71** 75' **76'** 78 79 80 81 82 83 84

130-acre Cru Bourgeois with v. high standards, property of DOURTHE family. Full, fruity. "Franc Caillou" is second wine.

Meyney St-Est. r.★★→★★★ **70'** 75' 78' **79** 80 81 82' 83 84

Big (125-acre) riverside property next door to Ch. MONTROSE, one of many steady Crus Bourgeois in St-Estèphe. Owned by CORDIER. Second label: Prieur de Meyney.

Millet Graves r. w. dr. ★★ 78 79 81 82 83

160-acre estate at Portets; useful Graves.

La Mission-Haut-Brion Graves r. ★★★★ 61 64 66 71' 75' 76 77 78' 79 80 81 82' 83 84

Neighbour and long-time rival to Château. HAUT-BRION, since 1984 in the same hands. Serious and grand old-style claret for long maturing. 30 acres. Ch. Latour-H-B is its second-quality wine.

Monbousquet St-Em. r. ★★ 75 76 78' 79' 80 81 82 83

Fine 70-acre estate in the Dordogne valley below St-Emilion. Attractive early-maturing wine from deep gravel soil.

Montrose St-Est. r. ★★★ 61 66 70' 73 75' 76 78 79' 80 81 82' 83 84

158-acre family-run second-growth well known for deeply coloured, forceful, old-style claret. Recent vintages seem lighter.

Moulin-à-Vent Moulis r. ★★ **70' 71** 75' **76** 78' 79 80 81 82' 83 84

60-acre property now in the forefront of this up-and-coming appellation. Lively, forceful wine.

Moulin des Carruades

The second-quality wine of Ch. LAFITE.

Moulin du Cadet St-Em. r. ★★ 71' 73 75' **76' 78** 79 80 81 82' 83

First-class little vineyard on the Côtes managed by J. P. MOUEIX.

Moulinet Pomerol r. ★★★ 70 71 75 76 78 79 81 82 83

One of Pomerol's bigger estates; 43 acres on lightish soil.

Mouton-Baronne-Philippe Pauillac r. ★★★ **70'** 75' **76** 78' **79** 80 81 82' 83 84

Substantial fifth-growth with the enormous advantage of belonging to Baron Philippe de Rothschild, 125 acres making much gentler, less rich and tannic wine than Mouton.

Mouton-Rothschild Pauillac r. ★★★★ 61 66 67 **70' 71** 73 75' **76** 78' 79 80 81 82' 83 84

Officially a first-growth since 1973, though for 20 years worthy of the title. 175 acres (87% CABERNET SAUVIGNON) making wine of majestic richness (82 is Imperial). Also the world's greatest museum of works of art relating to wine.

Nairac Sauternes w. sw. ★★ 73 75 76 78 79 80 81 82 83

Barsac classed-growth with perfectionist owner. Fascinating wines to lay down.

Nenin Pomerol r. ★★★ 66 67 **70' 71'** 75' **76** 78 81 83

Well-known 66-acre estate; currently below par.

Olivier   Graves r. and w. dr. ★★★ (r.) **75' 76 78** 79' **80** 81 82 83 84
90-acre classed-growth, surrounding a moated castle at Léognan.
9,000 cases r., 12,000 w., both being upgraded from good to fine.

Les Ormes-de-Pez   St-Est. r.   **★★**   **70'** 75' **76** 78' 79 **80** 81' 82' 83' 84
Outstanding 72-acre Cru Bourgeois managed by Ch. LYNCH
BAGES. Increasingly notable full-flavoured St-Estèphe.

Les Ormes Sorbet   Medoc r.   **★★**   78 79 81 82 83
Emerging smaller producer of good solid red at Couquèques.

Palmer   Cant-Mar. r. ★★★★ **61 66 70** 71' 75' **76** 78' 79 **80** 81' 82 83' 84
The star ch. of CANTENAC; a third-growth often on a level just
below the first-growths. Wine of power, flesh and delicacy. 110
acres with Dutch, British and French owners.

Pape-Clément   Graves r. and w. dr. ★★★ **66 70 71 73** 75' **76** 78' 79' **80** 81
82' 83 84
Ancient v'yd. at Pessac, with record of seductive, scented reds,
but recent vintages less even.

Patache d'Aux   Bégadan (Médoc) r. ★★ **70** 75' **76'** 78 **79** **80** 81 82' 83'
90-acre Cru Bourgeois of the n. Médoc. Fragrant, lightish wine.

Paveil-de Luze   Margaux r.   **★★**   **70** ' 75' **76'** 78 **79 80** 81 82' 83 84
Old family estate at Soussans. Small but highly regarded.

Pavie   St-Em. r. ★★★ **64' 66 67 70** 71' 75' **76** 78' 79' **80** 81 82' 83'
Splendidly sited first-growth of 87 acres on the slope of the Côtes.
Typically rich and tasty St-Em., but lately less than brilliant.
The family owns the smaller Ch'x Pavie-Decesse and La
Clusière.

Pavie-Macquin   St-Em. r.   **★★**   75 76 78 79 81 82 83
Reliable small Côtes v'yd. e. of St-Emilion.

Pedesclaux   Pauillac r. ★★ **70'** 71 75' **76** 78 79 **80** 81 82' 83
50-acre fifth-growth on the level of a good Cru Bourgeois. Solid
strong wines loved by Belgians. Grand-Duroc-Milon and
Bellerose are second labels.

Petit-Village   Pomerol r. ★★★ **67 70** 71' 75' **76'** 78 **79 80** 81 82' 83
One of the best-known little properties: 26 acres next to VIEUX-
CH.-CERTAN, same owner as Ch. COS D'ESTOURNEL. Powerful
plummy wine.

Petrus   Pomerol r. ★★★★ **61 62 64 66 67 70' 71' 73** 75' **76'** 78 79' **80** 81 82' 83
The great name of Pomerol. 28 acres of gravelly clay giving the
world's most massively rich and concentrated wine. 95% Merlot
vines. Each vintage adds lustre. The price, too, is legendary.

Peyrabon   St. Sauveur r.   **★★**   75 76 78 79 **80** 81 82 83 84
Serious 82-acre Cru Bourgeois popular in the Low Countries.

Peyreau   St-Em. r. ★★
Sister-ch. of CLOS L'ORATOIRE.

de Pez   St-Est. r.   **★★★**   66 67 **70'** 71' 73 75' **76** 78' 79 **80** 81 82' 83 84
Outstanding Cru Bourgeois of 60 acres. As reliable as any of the
classed growths of the village. Needs very long storage.

Phélan-Ségur   St-Est. r.   **★★**   66 **70' 71** 75' **76'** 78 **79 80** 81 82' 83 84
Big and important Cru Bourgeois (125 acres) with some fine old
vintages. New owners in 1985.

Pichon-Longueville-Baron   Pauillac r.   **★★★**   66 **70'** 71 73 75 76 78'
79' **80** 81 82' 83 84
77-acre second-growth usually making fine sturdy Pauillac,
recently on cracking form.

Pichon-Longueville, Comtesse de Lalande   Pauillac r. ★★★★ **61 64
66 70' 71 73** 75' **76 77** 78' 79' **80** 81' 82' 83 84
Second-growth neighbour to Ch. LATOUR. 148 acres. Consistently among the very top performers; classic long-lived wine.

Pique-Caillou   Graves r.   **★★**
Little-known 40-acre neighbour of HAUT-BRION in the Bordeaux
suburbs. Worth watching.

Pindefleurs   St-Em. r. ★★ 75 76 78 79 81 82' 83
Up and coming 20-acre v'yd. on the St-Emilion plateau.

de Pitray Castillon r. ★★ 75 76' 78 79 80 81 82' 83
Substantial (62 acre) v'yd. on the Côtes de Castillon e. of St-Emilion. Good light wines.

Plince Pomerol r. ★★ 75 76 78 79 80 81 82 83
Reputable 20-acre property near Libourne. Attractive, perhaps rather simple wine from sandy soil.

La Pointe Pomerol r. ★★★ 70' 71' 75' 76 78 79 81 82 83'
Prominent 63-acre estate recently lacking true Pomerol flesh. Ch. LA SERRE is in the same hands.

Pontet-Canet Pauillac r. ★★★ 70 71 75' 76 78' 79' 80 81' 82' 83'
One of the biggest classed-growths. 182 acres, neighbour to MOUTON, potentially better than its official rank of fifth-growth, but dragged its feet for years. Current owners (same as LAFON-ROCHET) are trying hard. 2nd label: Les Hauts de Pontet.

Potensac Potensac (Médoc) r. ★★ 70 75' 76 78' 79 80 81 82' 83 84
The best-known Cru Bourgeois of the n. Médoc. The neighbouring Ch'x. Lassalle and Gallais-Bellevue belong to the same family, the Delons, owners of Ch. LÉOVILLE–LASCASES. The class shows.

Pouget Margaux ★★ 70' 75 76 78 79 80 81 82' 83
19-acre v'yd. attached to Ch. BOYD-CANTENAC. In 1983 separate chais were built. Similar, rather lighter, wines.

Poujeaux (Theil) Moulis r. ★★ 70' 71 75' 76 79' 80 81 82 83 84
Family-run Cru Exceptionnel of 120 acres selling its powerful, concentrated wine largely direct to an appreciative French public. 2nd label: La Salle de Poujeaux. Also Ch. Arnauld (83').

Prieuré-Lichine Cant-Mar.r. ★★★ 70 71 75 76 78' 79' 80 81 82' 83' 84
143-acre fourth-growth brought to the fore by Alexis Lichine since 1952. Excellent full-bodied and fragrant Margaux.

Puy-Blanquet St-Em. r. ★★ 71' 75' 76 78 79 81 82' 83
The major property of St-Etienne-de-Lisse, e. of St-Emilion, with over 50 acres. Typical full St-Em., if below the top class.

Puy-Razac St-Em. r. ★★ 75 76 78 79 80 81' 82' 83
Small property at the foot of the Côtes near Ch. PAVIE.

Rabaud-Promis Sauternes w. sw. ★★ 71 75 76 78 79 81 83
74-acre classed-growth at Bommes. Little seen outside France.

Rahoul Graves r. and w. dr. ★★ (r.) 78' 79 80 81 82 83 (w.) 81 82' 83 84
37-acre v'yd. at Portets making particularly good wine from maturing vines; 80% red. White is oaky for ageing. Same winemaker as DOMAINE LA GRAVE.

Ramage-la-Batisse Haut-Médoc r. ★★ 75' 76 78 79 80 81 82 83'
Outstanding Cru Bourgeois of 130 acres at St-Sauveur, west of Pauillac. Increasingly attractive since '80.

Rausan-Ségla Margaux r. ★★★ 61 70' 71' 75' 76 78 79 80 81 82' 83 84
94-acre second-growth; famous for its fragrance; a great Médoc name, but recently well below par. Owned by ESCHENAUER.

Rauzan-Gassies Margaux r. ★★★ 61 66 75' 76 78' 79' 80 81 82 83
74-acre second-growth neighbour of the last with little excitement to report for two decades, now seemingly perking up.

Raymond-Lafon Sauternes w. sw. ★★ 75 76 78 79 80' 81' 82 83'
Serious Sauternes estate run by the manager of Ch. d'YQUEM. Splendid wines for long ageing. Among the top Sauternes today.

de Rayne-Vigneau Sauternes w. sw. ★★★ 67 71' 76' 78 81 83
164-acre classed-growth at Bommes. Standard sweet wine and a little dry, "Raynesec". New equipment in 1980.

Respide Graves (r.) w. dr. ★★ 78 79 81 82 83 84
One of the better white-wine ch'x. of s. Graves, at St Pierre de Mons. Full-flavoured wines.

Reynon 1ères Côtes de Bordeaux r. and w. dr. ★★
100 acres producing extraordinary dry white from very old Sauvignon vines ("Vieilles Vignes": 80 81 83' 84). Also D.Y.A. white and serious red (79 81 82 83).

Reysson Vertheuil Haut-Médoc r. ★★ 81 82' 83
Recently replanted, up-and-coming 120-acre Cru Bourgeois with the same owners as Ch. CHASSE-SPLEEN.

Ricaud Loupiac w. sw. (or dr.) or r. ☐★★☐ 81 82 83
Substantial grower of Sauternes-like dessert wine, just across the river. New owners are working hard.

Rieussec Sauternes w. sw. ☐★★★☐ 70 71' 75' 76' 78 79 80 81' 82 83
Worthy neighbour of Ch. D'YQUEM with 136 acres in Fargues, bought in 1984 by the (Lafite) Rothschilds. Not the sweetest; can be exquisitely fine. Also a dry wine: "R".

Ripeau St-Em. r. ★★ 75 78 79 81 82 83
Increasingly high-performance Grand Cru in the centre of the plateau.

La Rivière Fronsac r. ★★
The biggest and most impressive Fronsac property. Tannic wines.

de Rochemorin Graves r. (w. dr.) 81 82 83
An important restoration at Martillac by the owner of ch. LA LOUVIÈRE. 135 acres of new vines promise great things.

Romer du Hayot Sauternes w. sw. ☐★★☐
A minor classed growth with a growing reputation.

Roquetaillade-la-Grange Graves r. w. dr. ★★
Substantial estate establishing a name for fine red (s.) Graves.

Roudier Montagne-St-Em. r. ☐★★☐
75-acre "satellite" St-Em. with the flavour of the real thing. Sister-ch. of BALESTARD.

Rouget Pomerol r. ★★ 70 71 75' 76' 78 79 81 82' 83
Attractive old estate with rising standards on the n. edge of Pomerol. Good vintages need 10 years + .

Royal St-Emilion
Brand name of the important and dynamic growers' cooperative. See also HAUT QUERCUS.

St-André Corbin St-Emilion r. ☐★★☐ 66 71 75' 76' 78 79' 81 82' 83
Considerable 54-acre property in Montagne-St-Emilion with a long record of above-average wines.

St. Bonnet Médoc r. ★★
Big n. Médoc estate at St Christoly. V. flavoury wine.

St-Estèphe, Marquis de St-Est. r. ☐★☐
The growers' co-operative; over 200 members. Good value.

St-Georges St-Geo., St-Em. r. ★★ 70 75 76 78 79 80 81 82 83
Noble 18th-century ch. overlooking the St-Emilion plateau from the hill to the n. 125 acres; good wine sold direct to the public.

Saint-Pierre St-Jul. r. ★★★ 70' 71 75' 76 78' 79 80 81' 82' 83'
Small (50-acre) fourth-growth many years in Belgian ownership; bought in 1982 by Henri Martin of Ch. GLORIA. A name to watch.

St-Pierre Graves (r.) r. ☐★★☐ 78 79 81 83 84
Estate at St Pierre de Mons making classic Graves of notable character and flavour.

de Sales Pomerol r. ★★★ 66 67 70' 71 75' 76' 78' 79 80 81 82' 83
The biggest v'yd. of Pomerol (116 acres), attached to the grandest château. Not poetry but excellent prose. Second labels: Ch. Chantalouette and Ch. du Delias.

Sénéjac Haut-Médoc r. (w. dr.) ★★ 70' 75 76' 78 79 80 81 82' 83'
43-acre Cru Bourgeois in s. Médoc run with increasing skill.

La Serre St-Em. r. ★★ 70 75' 78 79 80 81 82 83
Well-run small Grand Cru with same owner as LA POINTE.

Sigalas-Rabaud Sauternes w. sw. ☐★★★☐ 71' 75' 76' 78 79 81 82 83'
The lesser part of the former Rabaud estate: 34 acres in Bommes, making first-class sweet wine.

Siran Lab-Mar. r. ★★★ 61 66 70 71' 75' 78' 79 80 81' 82' 83
74-acre Cru Bourgeois of Cru Classé quality. Elegant, long-lived wines (and Bordeaux's first anti-nuclear cellar).

Smith-Haut-Lafitte Graves r. and (w. dr.) ★★★ (r.) 75' 76 78 79 80 81 82' 83 84 (w.) D.Y.A.

Run-down old classed-growth at Martillac restored by ESCHEN-AUER in the '60s and '70s. 122 acres (14 of white). The white wine is light and fruity; the red dry. Recent efforts should improve it.

Sociando-Mallet Haut-Medóc r. ★★ 70 75 78 79 81 82 83 84

Splendid Cru Grand Bourgeois at St-Seurin in the n. 65 acres. Dark dense wine for the patient.

Soutard St-Em. r. ★★ 66 70' 71 75' 76 78' 79 80 81 82' 83

Reliable 48-acre classed-growth n. of the town. Some vintages have been a bit "butch". A keeper.

Suduiraut Sauternes w. sw. ★★★ 67 70 76' 78 79 80 81 82 83

One of the best Sauternes: of glorious creamy richness. Over 173 acres of the top class, under capable new management.

Taillefer Pomerol r. ★★ 67 70 73 75 76 78 79 81 82' 83

24-acre property on the edge of Pomerol owned by another branch of the MOUEIX family. Give it time.

Talbot St-Jul. r. (w.) ★★★ 66 70' 71 75' 76 77 78' 79 80 81 82' 83 84

Important 240-acre fourth-growth, sister-ch. to GRUAUD-LAROSE, wine similarly attractive rich, satisfying. (V.g.) second label: Connétable Talbot. A little white is called "Caillou Blanc".

Tayac Sou-Mar. r. ★★

Margaux's biggest Cru Bourgeois. Reliable if not noteworthy wine.

Terrefort-Quancard Bordeaux r. w. dr. ★★ 78 79 80 81 82 83

Huge producer of good value wines at St-André-de-Cubzac. Rocky sub-soil contributes to surprising quality.

du Tertre Ar-Mar. r. ★★★ 66 70' 71 73 75 76 78 79' 80 81 82' 83

Fifth-growth, isolated s. of Margaux; restored to excellence by the owner of CALON-SEGUR. Fragrant and long-lived.

Tertre-Daugay St-Em. r. ★★★ 78 79 81 82' 83

Small Grand Cru in a spectacular situation on the brow of the Côtes. Restored to excellence since '78 by the owner of LA GAFFELIÈRE.

Timberlay Bordeaux r. (w. dr.) ★ 78 79 81 82 83 84

The biggest property of Cubzac; 185 acres. Pleasant light wines.

Toumilon Graves r. w. dr ★★

Notable little ch. in St. Pierre de Mons. Fresh and charming r. and w.

La Tour-Blanche Sauternes w. sw. (r.) ★★★ 75' 76 78 79 81' 83'

Top-rank 57-acre estate at Bommes with a state wine-growing school. Not among the leaders for a long time. But '83 is v.g.

La Tour-Carnet St-Lau. r. ★★ 70' 75' 76 78 79 80 81 82' 83 84

Fourth-growth reborn from total neglect in the '60s. Medieval tower with 79 acres just w. of St-Julien. Lightish, pretty wine.

La Tour de By Bégadan (Médoc) r. ★★ 75' 76 78' 79' 80 81 82' 83

Very well-run 144-acre Cru Bourgeois in the n. Médoc increasing its reputation for sturdy, impressive yet appealing wine.

La Tour-de-Mons Sou-Mar. r. ★★★ 70' 71' 73 75' 78 79 80 81 82' 83

Distinguished Cru Bourgeois of 75 acres, three centuries in the same family. Sometimes excellent claret with a long life.

La Tour-du-Pin-Figeac St-Em. r. ★★

24-acre Grand Cru worthy of restoration.

La Tour-du-Pin-Figeac-Moueix St-Em. r. ★★★ 76 78 79 81 82 83

Another 20-acre section of the same old property, owned by a branch of the famous MOUEIX family. Looking very good.

La Tour-Figeac St-Em. r. ★★ 70 75 78 79 80 81 82' 83

34-acre Grand Cru between Ch. FIGEAC and Pomerol, now showing the form that such a site suggests.

La Tour-Haut-Brion Graves r. ★★★ 70 75 76 78 79 80 81 82' 83

The second label of Ch. LA MISSION-HAUT-BRION. A plainer, harder, smaller-scale wine with the same fine pedigree.

La Tour-Martillac Graves r. and w. dr. ★★ (r.) 75' 78 **79 80** 81 82' 83 84
Small but serious property at Martillac. 10 acres of white grapes; 37 of black. Quantity is sacrificed for quality. The owner, Jean Kressmann, is resurrecting the neighbouring Ch. Lespault.

La Tour St-Bonnet Médoc r. ★★ 70' 75' 76 78' 79 80 81 82' 83
Consistently well-made and typical n. Médoc from St-Christoly. 100 acres.

La Tour du Haut Moulin Cussac (Haut-Médoc) r. ★★ 78 79 81 82 83
Little-known 70-acre property; concentrated wines to age.

Tournefeuille Lalande de Pomerol r. ★★ 71' 74 75' 76' 78 79 81' 82' 83
The star of Néac, overlooking Pomerol from the n. A small property (43 acres), but excellent long-lived wine.

des Tours Montagne-St-Em. r. ★★ 78 79 81 82 83
Spectacular ch. with modern 170-acre v'yd. Sound, easy wine.

Tronquoy-Lalande St-Est. r. ★★ 70 71 75 76 78 79 80 81 82' 83
40-acre Cru Bourgeois making typical high-coloured St-Estèphe needing long ageing. Distributed by DOURTHE.

Troplong-Mondot St-Em. r. ★★ 70' 71' 75' 76 78 79 81 82' 83
One of the bigger Grand Crus of St-Emilion. 70 + acres well sited on the Côtes above Ch. PAVIE. To watch.

Trotanoy Pomerol r. ★★★★ 61 70 71' 73 75' 76' 78 79 80 81 82' 83
Perhaps the 2nd Pomerol after PETRUS, from the same stable. Only 27 acres but a glorious fleshy perfumed wine ('71 is famous).

Trottevieille St-Em. r. ★★★ 70 71 75' 76 78 79' 80 81 82' 83
Grand Cru of 18 acres on the Côtes e. of the town, inexplicably-dragging its feet. Same owners as BATAILLEY.

Le Tuquet Graves r. and w. dr. ★★ 76 78 79 81 82 83
Big estate at Beautiran. Light fruity wines; the white better.

Verdignan Médoc r. ★★ 75 76 78 79 80 81 82
Substantial Grand Bourgeois sister property to Ch. COUFRAN. More Cabernet than Coufran: Jack Sprat and his wife.

Vieux-Château-Certan Pomerol r. ★★★ 76 78 79 80 81 82' 83 84
Traditionally rated close to PETRUS in quality, but totally different in style, with almost Médoc build. 34 acres, Belgian owned.

Vieux-Château-Landon Médoc r. ★★ 81 82 83
Up-to-date grower of vigorous wine worth keeping 3–4 years.

Vieux-Château-St-André St-Emilion r. ★★ 75' 76' 78 79' 81 82' 83
Small v'yd. in Montagne-St-Emilion owned by the leading wine-maker of Libourne. To follow.

Villegeorge Avensan r. ★★ 73' 75' 76 78' 79 80 81 82' 83
24-acre Cru Exceptionnel to the n. of Margaux with the same owner as Ch. BRANE-CANTENAC. Excellent full-bodied wine.

Villemaurine St-Em. r. ★★ 70' 71 75' 76 77 78 79' 80 81 82' 83
Good Grand Cru well sited on the Côtes by the town. Firm wine with a high proportion of Cabernet.

Vraye-Croix-de-Gay Pomerol r. ★★★ 70' 71' 75' 76 78 79 81 82' 83
Very small ideally situated v'yd. in the best part of Pomerol.

Yon-Figeac St-Em. r. ★★ 79 81 82 83
52-acre Grand Cru to follow for savoury and scented wine.

d'Yquem Sauternes w. sw. (dr.) ★★★★ 71' 73 75' 76' 77 78 79 80 81
The world's most famous sweet-wine estate. 250 acres making only 500 bottles per acre of very strong, intense, luscious wine kept 4 years in barrel. Most vintages need a decade of maturity. Also dry "Ygrec" in 78 79 80 84.

More Bordeaux châteaux are listed under Canon-Fronsac, Côtes de Bourg, Cubzac, Fronsac, Côtes-de-Castillon, Lalande de Pomerol, Loupiac, Ste-Croix-du-Mont, Premières Côtes de Blaye, Premières Côtes de Bordeaux.

Switzerland

Switzerland has some of the world's most efficient and productive vineyards. Costs are high and nothing less is viable. All the most important are lined along the south-facing slopes of the upper Rhône valley and Lake Geneva, respectively the Valais and the Vaud. For other areas see map. Wines are known both by place-names, grape-names, and legally controlled type-names. All three, with those of leading growers and merchants, appear in the following list. On the whole, D.Y.A.

Aigle Vaud w. dr. ★★
Principal town of CHABLAIS, between L. Geneva and the VALAIS. Dry whites of appropriately transitional style: at best strong and well balanced.

Amigne
Traditional white grape of the VALAIS. Heavy but tasty wine, usually made dry.

Arvine Another old VALAIS white grape, similar to the last; perhaps better. Makes good dessert wine. Petite Arvine is similar.

Auvernier Neuchâtel r. p. w. dr. (sp.) ★★
Village s. of NEUCHÂTEL known for PINOT NOIR, CHASSELAS and OEIL DE PERDRIX.

Blauburgunder
One of the names given to the form of PINOT NOIR grown in German Switzerland.

Bonvin Old-established growers and merchants at SION.

Chablais Vaud (r.) w. dr. ★★
The district between Montreux on L. Geneva and Martigny where the Rhône leaves the VALAIS. Good DORIN wines. Best villages: AIGLE, YVORNE, Bex.

Chasselas
The principal white grape of Switzerland, neutral in flavour but taking local character. Known as FENDANT in VALAIS, DORIN in VAUD and PERLAN round Geneva.

Clevner (or Klevner)
Another name for BLAUBURGUNDER.

Completer
Rare Grisons (see map) grape giving liquorous wine.

Cortaillod Neuchâtel r. (p. w.) ★★
Village near NEUCHÂTEL specializing in light PINOT NOIR reds.

Côte, La
The n. shore of L. Geneva from Geneva to Lausanne. Pleasant DORIN and SALVAGNIN. Best villages incl. Féchy and Rolle.

Dézaley Vaud w. dr. ★★★

Best-known village of LAVAUX, between Lausanne and Montreux. Steep s. slopes to the lake make fine fruity DORIN. Dézaley-Marsens is equally good.

Dôle Valais r. ★★

Term for red VALAIS wine of PINOT NOIR or GAMAY or both grapes, reaching a statutory level of strength and quality.

Dorin Vaud w. dr. ★★★

The name for CHASSELAS wine in the VAUD, the equivalent of FENDANT from the VALAIS.

Epesses Vaud w. dr. and r. ★★

Well-known lakeside village of LAVAUX. Good dry DORIN.

Ermitage

VALAIS name for white wine from MARSANNE grapes. Rich, concentrated and heavy; usually dry.

Fendant Valais w. dr. ★→★★★

The name for CHASSELAS wine in the VALAIS, where it reaches its ripest, strongest and smoothest. SION is the centre.

Flétri Withered grapes for making sweet wine, often MALVOISIE.

Gamay The Beaujolais grape; grown in W. Switzerland

Glacier, Vin du

Almost legendary long-matured white stored at high altitudes. Virtually extinct today.

Goron

Red VALAIS wine that fails to reach the DÔLE standard.

Hammel Major merchant and grower of La Côte at Rolle.

Herrschaft Grisons r. (w. sw.) ★→★★★

District near the border of Austria and Liechtenstein. Small amount of light PINOT NOIR reds and a few sweet whites.

Humagne

Old VALAIS grape. Some red Humagne is sold: decent country wine. The strong white is a local speciality.

Johannisberg

The Valais name for SYLVANER, which can make excellent stiff, dense and high-flavoured dry wine here, comparable to Frankenwein (see Germany).

Lavaux Vaud r. w. dr. ★→★★★

The n. shore of L. Geneva between Lausanne and Montreux. The e. half of the VAUD. Best villages incl. DÉZALEY, EPESSES, Villette, Lutry, ST-SAPHORIN.

Légèrement doux

Most Swiss wines are dry. Any with measurable sugar must be labelled thus or as "avec sucre résiduel".

Malvoisie

VALAIS name for PINOT GRIS. Makes some wonderful late-picked sweet wines.

Mandement Geneva r. (p.) w. dr. ★

Wine district just w. of Geneva, (see Vin-Union-Genève). Very light reds, chiefly GAMAY, and whites (PERLAN).

Marsanne

The white grape of Hermitage on the French Rhône, used in the VALAIS to make ERMITAGE.

Merlot Bordeaux red grape (see Grapes for red wine) used to make the better wine of Italian Switzerland (TICINO). See also Viti.

Mont d'Or, Domaine du Valais w. dr. sw. ★★★★

The best wine estate of Switzerland: 60 acres of steep hillside near SION. Good FENDANT, JOHANNISBERG, AMIGNE, etc., and real Riesling. Very rich concentrated wines.

Neuchâtel Neuchâtel r. p. w. dr. sp. ★→★★★

City and the wine from the n. shore of its lake. Pleasant light PINOT NOIR and attractive sometimes sparkling CHASSELAS.

Nostrano
> Word meaning "ours" applied to the lesser red wine of the TICINO, made from a mixture of native and Italian grapes, in contrast to MERLOT from Bordeaux.

Oeil de Perdrix
> Pale rosé of PINOT NOIR.

Orsat   Important and popular wine firm at Martigny, VALAIS.

Perlan   Geneva w. dr. ★
> The MANDEMENT name for the ubiquitous CHASSELAS, here at its palest, driest and least impressive.

Premier Cru
> Any wine from the maker's own estate can call itself this.

Provins   The excellent central cooperative of the VALAIS.

Rèze   The grape, now rare, used for VIN DU GLACIER.

Riesling-Sylvaner
> Swiss name for MÜLLER-THURGAU, common in E. Switzerland, where it was first bred.

Rivaz   Vaud r. w. dr. ★★
> Well-known village of LAVAUX.

St-Saphorin   Vaud w. dr. ★★
> One of the principal villages of LAVAUX: wines drier and more austere than DÉZALEY or EPESSES.

Salvagnin   Vaud r. ★→★★
> Red VAUD made to a tested quality: the equivalent of DÔLE.

Savagnin   Swiss name for the TRAMINER, called Païen in the VALAIS.

Schafiser   Bern (r.) w. dr. ★→★★
> The n. shore of L. Bienne (Bielersee) is well known for light CHASSELAS sold as either Schafiser or Twanner.

Schenk, S.A.
> The biggest Swiss wine firm, based at Rolle in the VAUD, with 570 acres as well as other world-wide interests.

Sion   Valais w. dr. ★→★★★
> Centre of the VALAIS wine region, famous for its FENDANT.

Sierre
> Important centre for some of the best VALAIS wines.

Spätburgunder
> PINOT NOIR: by far the commonest grape of German Switzerland, making very light wines.

Testuz, V. and P.
> Well-known growers and merchants at Dézaley, LAVAUX.

Ticino
> Italian-speaking s. Switzerland. See Merlot, Viti, Nostrano.

Twanner   See Schafiser

Valais
> The Rhône valley between Brig and Martigny. Its n. side is an admirable dry sunny and sheltered v'yd., planted mainly to the CHASSELAS grape, which here makes its best wine.

Vaud   The region of L. Geneva. Its n. shore is Switzerland's biggest v'yd. and in places as good as any. DORIN and SALVAGNIN are the main wines.

Vétroz   Valais (r.) w. dr. ★★
> Village near SION in the best part of the VALAIS.

Vevey
> Town near Montreux with a famous wine festival once every 30-odd years. The last was in 1977.

Vin-Union-Genève
> Big growers' cooperative at Satigny in the MANDEMENT. Light reds and white PERLAN are Geneva's local wine.

Viti   Ticino r. ★★
> Legal designation of better-quality TICINO red, made of MERLOT and with at least 12% alcohol.

Yvorne   Village near AIGLE with some of the best CHABLAIS v'yds.

Italy

In 1986 the increasingly good name of Italian wine was tragically damaged by a small handful of producers who were criminal and stupid enough to turn their product into deadly poison by adding methyl alcohol. It is a tragedy that the vast majority of highly conscientious and skilled producers should suffer from the actions of such enemies of wine. It is a double tragedy if consumers take fright and avoid the truly excellent wines now being made in almost all regions by highly qualified and imaginative winemakers.

Italy's wine industry today ranks with the greatest in the world. It does, however, have problems with its wine law, the DOC system, which is losing touch with the fast-moving realities of the modern wine world. A Denominazione di Origine Controllata (DOC) is defined in terms of tradition first, potential quality only second, and actual tested quality scarcely at all.

In these circumstances it is the maker's name that matters most. Many of the best makers are turning their backs on regulations which they consider run counter to the best modern practice. In their place they are putting internal quality controls at much higher levels than the law could apply overall.

Meanwhile the DOC system remains, for all its faults, the only general key to the Italian wine maze. It is the approximate equivalent of France's Appellations Contrôlées, built up over the last 25 years. Most of Italy's worthwhile wines have defined areas and standards under the system. A few, like Chianti Classico, it must be said, had them long before. An increasing number, however, have not – and DOCs have been granted to many areas of only local interest: so the mere existence of a DOC proves little. The entries in this book ignore a score of unimportant DOCs and include considerably more non-DOCs. They also include a large number of grape-name entries.

Italian wines are named in a variety of ways: some geographical like French wines, some historical, some folk-lorical, and many of the best from their grapes. These include old "native" grapes such as Barbera and Sangiovese and more and more imported "international" grapes from France and Germany. Many of the DOCs, particularly in the north-east, are area names applying to widely different wines from more than a dozen different varieties. No overall comment on the quality of such a diversity is really possible, except to say that general standards are rising steadily and a growing number of producers are emerging as outstanding by international standards.

The map is the key to the province
names used for locating each
entry.
Abbreviations of province names
shown in bold type are used in the
text.

Abboccato   Semi-sweet.

Aglianico del Vulture   Bas. DOC r. (s/sw. sp.)   ⟨★★★⟩   75 77 78 79 81
83 85

>   Among the best wines of s. Italy. Ages well to rich aromas. Called
>   Vecchio after 3 yrs., Riserva after 5 yrs.

Alba   Major wine-centre of PIEMONTE.

Albana di Romagna   Em-Ro. DOC w. dr. s/sw. (sp.) ★★ 85

>   Produced for several centuries in Romagna from Albana grapes.
>   Cold fermentation now robs it of much character. Fattoria
>   PARADISO makes some of the best.

Alcamo   Sic. DOC w. dr.   ⟨★⟩

>   Soft neutral whites from w. Sicily. Rapitalà is the best brand.

Aleatico   Red, slightly muscat-flavoured grape, chiefly of the south.

Aleatico di Gradoli   Lat. DOC r. sw. or f. ★★

>   Aromatic, fruity; alcohol 17.5%. Made near Viterbo.

Aleatico di Puglia   Apu. DOC r. sw. or f. ★★

>   Aleatico grapes make good dessert wine over a large area. Two
>   distinct types have 15% or 18.5% alcohol.

Alezio   Apu. DOC r. p. dr. ★★ 83 85

>   Recent Salento DOC for powerful Negro Amaro wines.

Allegrini

>   High-quality producer of Veronese wines, incl. VALPOLICELLA.

Alto Adige   Tr-Aad. DOC r. p. w. dr. sw. sp. ★★ → ★★★

>   A DOC covering some 17 different wines, usually named after
>   their grape varieties, in 33 villages round Bolzano.

Amabile   Semi-sweet, but usually sweeter than ABBOCCATO.

Amaro

>   Bitter. When prominent on a label the contents is a "bitters", not
>   a wine.

Amarone   See Recioto.

Antinori

>   A long-established Tuscan house of the highest repute producing
>   first-rate CHIANTI and ORVIETO, now also distinguished for
>   pioneering new styles: e.g. TIGNANELLO.

Artimino

>   Ancient hill-town and distinguished wine-estate west of
>   Florence, best known for its CHIANTI plus CABERNET: DOC
>   CARMIGNANO.

Assisi   Umbr. r. (w.dr.)   ⟨★★⟩

>   Rosso di Assisi is a very attractive new red *vino di tàvola*. Drink
>   young and cool.

Asti   Major wine-centre of PIEMONTE.

Asti Spumante   Piem. DOC w. sp.   ⟨★★★⟩   NV

>   Sweet and very fruity muscat sparkling wine. Low in alcohol.

Azienda agricola (or agraria)

>   A farm producing various crops, often incl. wine.

Azienda vitivinicola   A (specialized) wine estate.

Badia a Coltibuono   71 75 78 79 80 81 82 83 85

>   Fine Chianti-maker at Gaiole with a restaurant and remarkable
>   collection of old vintages.

Barbacarlo (Oltrepò Pavese)   Lomb. DOC r. dr. or sw. ★★→★★★ 82
83 85

>   Delicately flavoured with bitter after-taste, made in the
>   Commune of Broni in the province of Pavia.

Barbaresco   Piem. DOCG r. dr. ★★★→★★★★ 71 74 78 79 80 82 83 85

>   Neighbour of BAROLO from the same grapes but lighter, ageing
>   sooner. At best subtle and fine. At 3 yrs. becomes Riserva, 4 yrs.
>   Riserva Speciale. Best producers incl. GAJA.

Barbera

>   Dark acidic red grape, a speciality of Piemonte also used in
>   Lombardy, Emilia-Romagna and other northern provinces. Its
>   best wines are:

Barbera d'Alba   Piem. DOC r. dr. |★★| 78 79 80 82 83 85
　　Round ALBA NEBBIOLO is sometimes added. Tasty, tannic,
　　fragrant red. Superiore can age 7 years.

Barbera d'Asti   Piem. DOC r. dr. |★★| 78 79 80 82 83 85
　　To many the best of the Barberas; all Barbera grapes; grapy and
　　appetizing, young or aged up to 7 years.

Barbera del Monferrato   Piem. DOC r. dr. ★ 82 83 85
　　From a large area in the Pr. of Alessandria and ASTI. Pleasant,
　　slightly fizzy, sometimes sweetish.

Bardolino   Ven. DOC r. dr. (p.) ★★ D.Y.A.
　　Pale, light, slightly bitter red from e. shore of La Garda.
　　Bardolino Chiaretto is even paler and lighter.

Barolo   Piem. DOCG r. dr. ★★★→★★★★ 71 74 78 79 80 82 83 85
　　Small area s. of Turin with one of the highest-rated Italian red
　　wines, dark, rich, alcoholic (minimum 12°), dry but deep in
　　flavour. From NEBBIOLO grapes. Ages for up to 15 yrs, Riserva
　　after 3. Best producers incl. Vietti, Giacosa, Cogno, Conterno,
　　Pio Cesare. The coop "Terre de Barolo" is also v.g.

Bell 'Agio   Brand of sweet white MOSCATO from BANFI.

Bertani
　　Well-known producers of quality Veronese wines (VALPOLI-
　　CELLA, SOAVE, etc.), including aged AMARONE.

Bertolli, Francesco
　　Among the best-known producers of CHIANTI CLASSICO. Cellars
　　at Castellina in Chianti, n. of Siena.

Bianco   White.

Bianco d'Arquata   Umbr. w.dr. |★★★| 82 83 84 85
　　An exceptional, limpid and inspiring light and fruity white from
　　near Perugia.

Bianco di Pitigliano   Tusc. DOC w. dr. |★| D.Y.A.
　　A soft, fruity, lively wine made near Grosseto.

Bianco Vergine della Valdichiana   Tusc. DOC w. dr. ★★ D.Y.A.
　　Pale dry light wine from Arezzo. But what music in the name.

Bigi, Luigi & Figlio
　　Famous producers of ORVIETO and other wines of Umbria and
　　Tuscany.

Biondi-Santi
　　One of the leading producers of BRUNELLO with cellars in
　　Montalcino (Siena). His prices are outrageous.

Boca   Piem. DOC r. dr. |★★| 78 79 80 82 83 85
　　From same grape as BAROLO in n. of PIEMONTE, Pr. of Novara. A
　　coming name.

Bolla
　　Famous Veronese firm producing VALPOLICELLA, SOAVE, etc.
　　Top wines: Jago, Castellaro.

Bonarda
　　Minor red grape widely grown in PIEMONTE and Lombardy.

Bonarda (Oltrepò Pavese)   Lomb. DOC r. dr. ★★ 82 83 85
　　Soft, fresh, pleasant red from south of Pavia.

Bosca   Wine-producers from PIEMONTE known for their ASTI SPU-
　　MANTE and Vermouths.

Botticino   Lomb. DOC r. dr. ★★ 82 83 85
　　Strong, full-bodied rather sweet red from Brescia.

Brachetto d'Acqui   Piem. DOC r. sw. (sp.) ★ D.Y.A.
　　Sweet sparkling red with pleasant muscat aroma.

Bramaterra   Piem. DOC r. dr. |★★| 78 79 80 82 83 85
　　A substantial and stylish recent addition to Piemonte's reds.
　　Nebbiolo grapes predominate.

Breganze   Ven. DOC |★→★★| 79 80 82 83 85
　　A catch-all for many varieties around Vicenza. CABERNET and
　　PINOT BIANCO are best.

Bricco Manzoni Piem. r.   ★★★   78 79 80 82 83 85
> Excellent red of blended NEBBIOLO and BARBERA from Monforte d'Alba.

Brolio
> One of the oldest (c. 1200) and most famous CHIANTI CLASSICO estates, now owned by Seagrams. Good whites as well as red.

Brunello di Montalcino Tusc. DOCG r. dr. ★★★★ 70 71 75 77 78 79 80 81 82 83 85
> Italy's most expensive red wine. Strong, full-bodied, high-flavoured and long-lived. After 5 yrs. is called Riserva. Produced for over a century 15 miles s. of Siena.

Buttafuoco Lomb. ★★ 79 81 82 83 85
> A potent foaming red of BARBERA and other grapes, sold under the DOC OLTREPÒ PAVESE.

Ca' del Bosco
> FRANCIACORTA estate making some of Italy's v. best sparkling wine, and excellent reds ("Zanella" and FRANCIACORTA).

Cabernet
> Bordeaux grape much used in n.e. Italy and increasingly in Tuscany and the south. See place names, e.g.:

Cabernet di Pramaggiore Ven. DOC r. dr. ★★ 78 79 82 83 85
> Good, herb-scented, rather tannic, middle-weight red. Riserva after 3 yrs.

Cacchiano, Castello di
> First-rate CHIANTI CLASSICO estate at Gaiole, owned by RICASOLI.

Calcinaia, Villa
> First-class CHIANTI CLASSICO estate for centuries in the Capponi family.

Caldaro or Lago di Caldaro Tr-Aad. DOC r. dr. ★→★★ Keep 2–3yrs.
> Alias KALTERESEE. Light, soft, slightly bitter-almond red. Classico from a smaller area is better. From south of Bolzano.

Calissano
> A long-established House of PIEMONTE producing ASTI SPUMANTE, Vermouths and red wines of that region.

Caluso Passito Piem. DOC w. sw. (f.) ★★ 74 76 78 79 80 82 83 85
> Made from selected Erbaluce grapes left to partly dry; delicate scent, velvety taste. From a large area in the provinces of Turin and Vercelli.

Cannonau di Sardegna Sard. DOC r. (p.) dr. or s/sw. ★★ 83 84 85
> Cannonau is Sardinia's basic red grape; its wine often formidably strong (min. 13.5% alc.). Less potent Cannonaus without the DOC can be easier to like.

Cantina
> 1. Cellar or winery. 2. Cantina Sociale = growers' co-op.

Capena Lat. DOC w. dr. s/sw ★ D.Y.A.
> A sound wine for daily drinking from north of Rome.

Capezzana, Tenuta di
> The Tuscan estate of the ancient Bonacossi family, producers of excellent CHIANTI MONTALBANO and CARMIGNANO. Also a Bordeaux-style red, GHIAIE DELLA FURBA.

Capri
> Widely abused name of the famous island in the Bay of Naples. No guarantee of quality.

Carema Piem. DOC r. dr. ★★ 71 74 78 79 80 82 83 85
> Old speciality of northern PIEMONTE. NEBBIOLO grapes traditionally fermented Beaujolais-style before crushing. (See France: Macération carbonique.) More conventional today.

Carmignano Tusc. DOC r. dr. ★★→   ★★★   77 78 79 80 81 82 83 85
> Section of CHIANTI using 10% of CABERNET to make increasingly good, and some very fine, wine. See Capezzana.

Carso Fr.-VG. DOC r. w. dr. ★★ 85
New DOC near Trieste includes good MALVASIA.

Casa fondata nel ... Firm founded in ...

Castel del Monte Apu. DOC r. p. w. dr. ★★ 75 79 81 83 84 85
Dry, fresh, well-balanced southern wines. The red becomes
Riserva after 3 yrs. Rosé most widely known.

Castel San Michele Tr-Aad. r. dr. ☐★★☐ 79 81 82 83 85
A good red made of Cabernet and Merlot grapes by the Trentino
Agricultural College near Trento.

CAVIT
CAntina VITicultori, a co-operative of co-operatives near
Trento, producing large quantities of table wine.

Cellatica Lomb. DOC r. dr. ★★ 82 83 85
Light red with slightly bitter after-taste of Schiava grapes, from
Brescia.

Cerasuolo Abr. DOC p. dr. ★★
The rosato version of MONTEPULCIANO D'ABRUZZO.

Ceretto High-quality grower of BARBARESCO, BAROLO, etc.

Ceretto, Castello di
CHIANTI CLASSICO estate owned by Emilio Pucci.

Cerveteri Lat. DOC w. dr. s/sw. ★ 81 82 83 85
Sound wines produced n.w. of Rome between Lake Bracciano
and the Tyrrhenian Sea.

Chianti Tusc. DOCG r. dr. ☐★→★★☐ 75 77 78 79 80 81 82 83 85
The lively local wine of Florence. Fresh but warmly fruity when
young, still occasionally sold in straw-covered flasks. Variously
age-worthy. Montalbano, Rufina and Colli Fiorentini, Senesi,
Aretini, Colline Pisane are sub-districts.

Chianti Classico Tusc. DOCG r. dr. ☐★→★★★☐ 77 78 79 80 81 82 83 85
Senior Chianti from the central area. Many estates make fine
powerful slightly astringent wine. Riservas (after 3 yrs.) often
have the bouquet of age in oak. The neck-label is a black rooster.

Chianti Putto Tusc. DOC r. dr. ☐★→★★★☐
Often high-quality Chianti from a league of producers outside
the Classico zone. Neck-label is pink and white cherub.

Chiaretto
Very light reds, almost rosé (the word means "claret") produced
around Lake Garda. See Riviera del Garda.

Cinqueterre Lig. DOC w. dr. or sw. or pa. ★
Fragrant, fruity white made for centuries near La Spezia. The
PASSITO is known as Sciacchetrà.

Cinzano
Major Vermouth company also known for its ASTI SPU-
MANTE from PIEMONTE.

Cirò Cal. DOC r. (p. w.) dr. ★★ 77 78 79 81 82 83 84 85
The wine of the ancient Olympic games. Very strong red, fruity
white (to drink young).

Classico
Term for wines from a restricted, usually central, area within the
limits of a DOC. By implication, and often in practice, the best of
the region.

Clastidio Lomb. r. (p.) w. dr. ★★ 82 83 85
Pleasant, sour touch to the white. The red full, slightly tannic.

Clastidium Lomb. w. dr. ★★★ 78 82 83 85
Unique full-bodied oak-aged white of PINOTS NERO and GRIGIO.
Ages splendidly.

Col Sandago
Up-to-date estate winery near Treviso (Veneto) with good reds,
whites and sparkling Prosecco.

Collavini, Cantina
High-quality producers of GRAVE DEL FRIULI wines: PINOT
GRIGIO, RIESLING, MERLOT, PINOT NERO, etc.

Colli Means "hills" in many wine-names.

Colli Albani Lat. DOC w. dr. or s/sw. (sp.) ★→★★ D.Y.A.
Soft fruity wine of the Roman hills.

Colli Berici Ven. DOC r. w. p. dr. ★★ 79 81 82 83 85
CABERNET is the best of several promising products of these hills
south of Vicenza.

Colli Bolognesi Em-Ro. DOC r. p. w. dr. ★★ D.Y.A. (w.). 82 83 84
From the hills s.w. of Bologna. Six possible grape varieties.

Colli della Toscana Centrale
Several of the best Chianti makers are starting to use this name
for table wines.

Colli del Trasimeno Umb. DOC r. w. dr. ★★ 82 83 85
Lively wines from the province of Perugia.

Colli Euganei Ven. DOC r. w. dr. or s/sw. (sp.) ★ 82 83 85
A DOC applicable to 7 wines produced s.w. of Padua. Red is
adequate; white soft and pleasant. The table wine of Venice.

Colli Orientali del Friuli Fr-VG. DOC r. w. dr. orsw. ★★ 8283 84 85
12 different wines are produced under this DOC on the hills east
of Udine and named after their grapes, esp v.g. whites.

Collio (Goriziano) Fr-VG. DOC r. w. dr. ★★→★★★ 82 83 84 85
12 different wines named after their grapes from a small area
between Udine and Gorizia nr. the Yugoslav border. V.g. whites.

Colli Perugini Umbr. DOC r. p. w. ★ 82 83 85
New DOC for light wines in the hills of Perugia.

Coltassala Tusc. r.dr. ★★★ 80 81 82 83 85
Notable new "Bordeaux-style" red from the ancient CHIANTI
CLASSICO estate of CASTELLO DI VOLPAIA at Radda.

Conterno, Aldo
Highly regarded grower of BAROLO, etc. at Monforte d'Alba.

Contratto
Piemonte firm known for BAROLO, ASTI SPUMANTE, etc.

Copertino Apu. DOC r.dr. ★★ 82 83 84 85
Age-worthy dark red of Negroamaro grapes from the heel of
Italy.

Cora
A leading House producing ASTI SPUMANTE and Vermouth from
PIEMONTE.

Cordero, Paolo, di Montezemolo
Tiny producer of top-class Barolo.

Cori Lat DOC w. r. dr./sw. ★ 83 85
Soft and well-balanced wines made 30 miles south of Rome.

Cortese di Gavi See Gavi

Cortese (Oltrepò Pavese) Lomb. DOC w. dr. ★→★★ D.Y.A.
Delicate fresh white from western Lombardy.

Corvo Sic. r. w. dr. ★★ 77 78 79 81 83 84 85
Popular Sicilian wines. Sound dry red, pleasant soft white.

Costanti, Emilio
Tiny estate producing top-quality BRUNELLO DI MONTALCINO.

D'Ambra
Well-known producer of ISCHIA and other wines of that island.

Dolce Sweet.

Dolceacqua See Rossese di Dolceacqua

Dolcetto
Common low-acid red grape of PIEMONTE, the everyday wine of
BAROLO and BARBARESCO-producing areas, giving its name to:

Dolcetto d'Acqui Piem. DOC r. dr. ★ 83 85
Good standard table wine from s. of ASTI.

Dolcetto d'Alba Piem. DOC r. dr. ★★ 85
Among the best Dolcetti, with a trace of bitter-almond.
Superiore after 1 yr.

Dolcetto di Diano d'Alba Piem. DOC ★★ 83 85
A rival to Dolcetto d'Alba; often more potent.

Dolcetto di Ovada Piem. DOC r. dr. ★★ 79 80 82 83 85
> Reputedly the sturdiest and longest-lived of Dolcetti.

Donnaz Vd'A. DOC dr. ★★ 78 79 82 83 85
> A mountain NEBBIOLO, fragrant, pale and faintly bitter. Aged for a statutory 3 yrs.

Donnici Cal. DOC r. dr. ★
> Middle-weight southern red from Cosenza.

Elba Tusc. r. w. dr. (sp.) ★★ 82 83 85
> The island's white is admirable with fish. Good dry red.

Enfer d'Arvier Vd'A. DOC r. dr. ★★ 79 82 83 85
> An Alpine speciality: pale, pleasantly bitter, light red.

Enoteca
> Italian for "wine library", of which there are many in the country, the most comprehensive being the Enoteca Italica Permanente of Siena. Chianti has one at Greve.

THE BEST-KNOWN ITALIAN DOC WINES, REGION BY REGION, ARE:

Piemonte: Barolo, Barbaresco, Barbera, Dolcetto, Gattinara, Nebbiolo, Asti Spumante.

Liguria: Cinqueterre, Rossese di Dolceacqua.

Trentino-Alto Adige: Teroldego, Caldaro, Santa Maddalena, Merlot, Cabernet, Pinot Bianco, Gewürztraminer, etc.

Lombardy: Valtellina, Oltrepò Pavese, Franciacorta, etc.

Veneto: Soave, Valpolicella, Recioto, Bardolino, Prosecco, etc.

Friuli-Venezia-Giulia: Collio, Pinot Grigio, Merlot, Tocai, etc.

Emilia-Romagna: Albana, Lambrusco, Sangiovese.

Tuscany: Chianti, Brunello, Vino Nobile di Montepulciano.

Umbria: Orvieto, Rubesco di Torgiano.

Marches: Verdicchio, Rosso Conero, Rosso Piceno.

Latium: Frascati, Marino.

Abruzzi/Molise: Montepulciano.

Campania: Lacryma Christi, Taurasi.

Apulia: Castel del Monte, Locorotondo.

Basilicata: Aglianico del Vulture.

Calabria: Cirò.

Sicily: Marsala, Corvo, Etna, Regaleali.

Sardinia: Nuragus, Cannonau, Monica, Vermentino.

Erbaluce di Caluso Piem. DOC w. dr. ★ D.Y.A.
> Pleasant fresh hot-weather wine. See also CALUSO PASSITO.

Est! Est!! Est!!! Lat. DOC w. dr. or s/sw. ★★ D.Y.A.
> Famous soft fruity white from Montefiascone, n. of Rome. The name is more remarkable than the wine.

Etna Sic. DOC r. p. w. dr. ★★ 82 83 84 85
> Wine from the volcanic slopes. The red is warm, full, balanced and ages well; the white is distinctly grapy. See Villagrande.

Falerio dei Colli Ascolani Mar. DOC w. dr. ★ D.Y.A.
> Made in the province of Ascoli Piceno. Pleasant, fresh, fruity; a wine for the summer.

Falerno Camp. r. w. dr. ★★ 82 83 84 85
> One of the best-known wines of ancient times. Strong red, fruity white, improving in quality.

Fara Piem. DOC r. dr. ★★ 78 79 80 82 83 85
> Good NEBBIOLO wine from Novara, n. PIEMONTE. Fragrant; worth ageing. Small production.

Faro Sic. DOC r. dr. ★★ 83 84 85
> Sound strong Sicilian red, made in sight of the Straits of Messina.

Favonio Apu. r. w. dr. ★★★ **80 81 82** 83 84 85
Revolutionary estate east of Foggia using CABERNET, CHARDON-NAY and PINOT BIANCO.

Fazi-Battaglia Well-known producer of VERDICCHIO, etc.

Felluga
Brothers Livio and Marco have separate companies in the COLLIO region. Both are highly esteemed.

Ferrari
Firm making one of Italy's best dry sparkling wines by the champagne method near Trento, Trentino-Alto Adige.

Fiano di Avellino Cam. w. dr. ★★→★★★ 81 82 83 84 85
Considered the best white of Campania.

Fiorano Lat. r. w. dr. s/sw. ★★ **75 77 78 79 80 81** 82 83 85
Interesting Roman reds of Cabernet Sauvignon and Merlot.

Florio The major producer of Marsala, owning several brands, controlled by CINZANO.

Foianeghe Tr-Aad. r. ★★★
Trentino Cabernet/Merlot red to age 7–10 years.

Fontana Candida One of the biggest producers of FRASCATI.

Fontanafredda
One of the biggest producers of Piemontese wines, incl. BAROLO.

Fonterutoli
High-quality CHIANTI CLASSICO estate at Castellina.

Fracia Lomb. r. dr. ★★ **78 79 82** 83 85
Good light but fragrant red from VALTELLINA. DOC wine made by Negri.

Franciacorta Pinot Lomb. DOC w. (p.) dr. (sp.) ★★→★★★
Agreeable soft white and good sparkling wines made of PINOT BIANCO, NERO or GRIGIO. CA' DEL BOSCO is outstanding.

Franciacorta Rosso Lomb. DOC r. dr. ★★ **80 81 82 83**
Lightish red of mixed CABERNET and BARBERA from Brescia.

Franco Fiorina
Highly regarded producer of BAROLO, BARBARESCO, etc.

Frascati Lat. DOC w. dr. s/sw. sw. (sp.) ★→★★★ D.Y.A.
Best-known wine of the Roman hills: soft, ripe, golden, tasting of whole grapes. Most is pasteurized and neutral today: look for dated wines from small producers (e.g. Colli di Catone). The sweet is known as Cannellino.

Frecciarossa Lomb. r. w. dr. ★★ **82 83** 85
Sound wines from an estate nr. Casteggio in the OLTREPÒ PAVESE; the white is better known.

Freisa d'Asti Piem. DOC r. dr. s/sw. or sw. (sp.) ★★ D.Y.A.
Usually sweet, often sparkling red, said to taste of raspberries and roses. With enough acidity it can be highly appetizing.

Frescobaldi
Ancient noble family, leading pioneers of CHIANTI PUTTO at NIPOZZANO, e. of Florence. Also excellent white POMINO. See also Montesodi.

Friuli-Venezia Giulia
The north-eastern province on the Yugoslav border. Many wines, of which the DOC COLLIO includes most of the best.

Frizzante
Semi-sparkling or "pétillant", a word used to describe wines such as LAMBRUSCO.

Gaja Old family firm at BARBARESCO. Top-quality Piemonte wines. Pioneer with carbonic maceration to make VINÓT. Also an excellent new Chardonnay.

Galestro Tusc. w. dr. ★★
Name for superior light grapey white from Chianti country.

Gambellara Ven. DOC w. dr. or s/sw. (sp.) ★ D.Y.A.
Neighbour of SOAVE. Dry wine similar. Sweet (known as RECIOTO DI GAMBELLARA), agreeably fruity. Also VINSANTO.

Gancia Famous ASTI SPUMANTE house from Piemonte, also produces vermouth and OLTREPÒ PAVESE wines.

Garganega The principal white grape of SOAVE.

Gattinara Piem. DOC r. dr. ★★★ 70 74 78 79 80 82 83 85
Excellent big-scale BAROLO-type red from northern PIEMONTE. Made from NEBBIOLO, locally known as Spanna.

Gavi (or Cortese di Gavi) Piem. w. dr. ★★→ ★★★ 83 84 85 (usually D.Y.A.)
At best almost burgundian dry white. Gavi dei Gavi from Rovereto di Gavi Ligure has the highest reputation. It needs two or three years ageing.

Geografico, Chianti
Chianti Classico from a major growers' co-operative near Gaiole. Recently poor quality.

Ghemme Piem. DOC r. dr. ★★ 74 78 79 80 82 83 85
Neighbour of GATTINARA, capable of Bordeaux-style finesse.

Ghiaie della Furba Tusc. r. dr. ★★★ 78 79 80 81 82 83 85
Bordeaux-style Cabernet blend from the admirable Tenuta di CAPEZZANA, CARMIGNANO.

Giacobazzi
Well-known producers of Lambrusco wines with cellars in Nonantola and Sorbara, near Modena.

Most Italian wines have a simple name, in contrast to the combination village and vineyard names of France and Germany.

SOAVE CLASSICO

VINO A DENOMINAZIONE DI ORIGINE CONTROLLATA IMBOTTIGLIATO DAL PRODUTTORE ALL 'ORIGINE CANTINA SOCIALE DI SOAVE

Soave is the name of this wine. It is qualified only by the word Classico, a legal term for the central (normally the best) part of many long-established wine regions.
"Denominazione di Origine Controllata" is the official guarantee of authenticity.
Imbottigliato . . . all 'origine means bottled by the producer.
Cantina Sociale di Soave means the growers' co-operative of Soave.

Giacosa, Bruno
Old family business making excellent Barolo and other Piemonte wines at Neive (Cuneo).

Girò di Cagliari Sard. DOC r.dr. or sw. ★ 83 84 85
A formidably alcoholic red, most sympathetic when some of its sugar content is left unfermented.

Goldmuskateller
Aromatic grape made into wonderful dry white, esp. by TIEFENBRUNNER.

Gradi Degrees (of alcohol) i.e. percent by volume.

Grave del Friuli Fr-VG. DOC r. w. dr. ★★ 79 82 83 85
A DOC covering 14 different wines named after their grapes, from near the Yugoslav border. Good MERLOT and CABERNET.

Grechetto (or Greco)
A traditional white grape with more spirit than the ubiquitous Trebbiano, increasingly used and referred to by name in the centre and south of Italy.

Greco di Bianco (or Greco di Gerace) Cal. DOC w.sw. ★★ 75 77 78 79 81 83 85
An original smooth and fragrant dessert wine from Italy's toe. See also Mantonico.

Greco di Tufo Camp. DOC w. dr. (sp.) ★★★ 82 83 84 85
One of the best whites of the south, fruity and slightly "wild" in flavour. A character.

Grignolino d'Asti Piem. DOC r. dr. ★ 85
> Pleasant lively standard wine of PIEMONTE.

Grumello Lomb. DOC r. dr. ★★ 78 79 80 82 83 85
> NEBBIOLO wine from VALTELLINA, can be delicate and fine.

Gutturnio dei Colli Piacentini Em-Ro. DOC r. dr. (s/sw.) ★★82 83 85
> Full-bodied BARBERA/BONARDA blend from the hills of Piacenza.
> Ages admirably.

Inferno Lomb. DOC r. dr. ★★ 78 79 80 82 83 85
> Similar to GRUMELLO and like it classified as VALTELLINA
> Superiore.

Ischia Camp. DOC (r.) w. dr. ★ 84 85
> The wine of the island off Naples. The slightly sharp white
> Superiore is best; ideal with fish.

Isonzo Fr-VG. DOC r. w. dr. ★ 82 83 85
> DOC covering 10 varietal wines in the extreme north-east.

Kalterersee German name for Lago di CALDARO.

Lacryma Christi del Vesuvio Camp. r. p. w. (f.) dr. (sw.) ★82 83 84 85
> Famous but frankly ordinary wines in great variety from the
> slopes of Mount Vesuvius.

Lageder, Alois
> The senior producer of the Bolzano DOC's: STA. MADDALENA,
> etc.

Lago di Caldaro See Caldaro

Lagrein Tr-Aad. DOC r. p. dr. ★★ 76 78 79 80 81 82 83 85
> Lagrein is a Tyrolean grape with a bitter twist. Good fruity
> wine—at best very satisfying. The rosé is called Kretzer, the
> dark Dunkel.

Lamberti
> Producers of SOAVE, VALPOLICELLA and BARDOLINO at Lazise on
> the east shore of Lake Garda.

Lambrusco DOC (or not) r. p. (w.) s/sw. ⬛ D.Y.A.
> Bizarre but popular fizzy red, generally drunk secco (dry) in
> Italy but a smash hit in its sweet version in the U.S.A.

Lambrusco di Sorbara Em-Ro. DOC r. (w.) dr. or s/sw. sp. ★★★
> D.Y.A.
> The best of the Lambruscos. From near Modena.

Lambrusco Grasparossa di Castelvetro Em-Ro. DOC r. dr. or
> s/sw. sp. ★★ D.Y.A
> Similar to above. Highly scented, pleasantly acidic; often drunk
> with rich food.

Lambrusco Salamino di Santa Croce Em-Ro. DOC r. dr. or
> s/sw. sp. ★ D.Y.A
> Similar to above. Fruity smell, high acidity and a thick "head".

Langhe The hills of central PIEMONTE.

Latisana Fr-VG. DOC r. w. dr. ★★ 83 85
> DOC for 7 varietal wines from some 50 miles n.e. of Venice.
> Particularly good TOCAI FRIULANO.

Leone de Castris
> Leading producer of Apulian wines with an estate at Salice
> Salentino, near Lecce.

Lessona Piem. DOC r. d. ★★ 78 79 80 82 83 85
> Soft, dry, claret-like wine produced in the province of Vercelli
> from Nebbiolo, Vespolina and Bonarda grapes.

Liquoroso Strong and usually sweet, e.g. Tuscan VINSANTO.

Locorotondo Apu. DOC w. dr. (sp.) ★ D.Y.A.
> A pleasantly fresh southern white.

Lugana Lomb. DOC w. dr. (sp.) ★★★ D.Y.A.
> One of the best white wines of s. Lake Garda: fragrant, smooth,
> full of body and flavour. Co' de Fer is a good producer.

Lungarotti
> Leading producer of TORGIANO wine, with cellars and a Wine
> Museum near Perugia. Recently also fine CHARDONNAY.

Malfatti

Recent go-ahead estate with modern methods, near Lecce, Apulia, producing Bianco, Rosso and SALICE SALENTINO.

Malvasia

Important white or red grape for luscious wines, incl. Madeira's Malmsey. Used all over Italy for dry and sweet, still and sparkling wines.

Malvasia di Bosa   Sard. DOC w. dr. sw. ★★ 82 83 85

A wine of character. Strong and aromatic with a slightly bitter after-taste.

Malvasia di Cagliari   Sard. DOC w. dr. s/sw. or sw. (f. dr. s.) ★★ 82 83 85

Interesting strong Sardinian wine, fragrant and slightly bitter.

Malvasia di Casorzo d'Asti   Piem. DOC r. sw. sp. ★★ D.Y.A.

Fragrant grapey sweet red, sometimes sparkling.

Malvasia di Castelnuovo Don Bosco   Piem. DOC r. sw. (sp.) ★★

Peculiar method of interrupted fermentation gives very sweet aromatic red.

Malvasia delle Lipari   Sic. DOC w. sw. (pa. f.) ★★★ 84 85

Among the very best Malvasias, aromatic and rich, produced on the Lipari or Aeolian Islands n. of Sicily.

Malvoisie de Nus   Vd'A. w. dr. s/sw. ★★★

Rare Alpine white, with a deep bouquet of honey. Small production and high reputation. Can age remarkably well.

Mandrolisai   Sard. DOC r. p. dr. ⬜★ 82 83

CANNONAU at a lower strength and more approachable than the traditional style.

Manduria (Primitivo di)   Apu. DOC r. s/sw. (f. dr. or sw.) ★★ 83 84 85

Heady red, naturally strong but often fortified. From nr. Taranto. Primitivo is a southern grape.

Mantonico   Cal. w. dr. or sw. f. ★★ 78 79 81 83 85

Fruity deep amber dessert wine from Reggio Calabria. Can age remarkably well. Named from the Greek for "prophetic". See also Greco di Bianco.

Marino   Lat. DOC w. dr. or s/sw. (sp.) ⬜★ D.Y.A.

A neighbour of FRASCATI with similar wine, often a better buy.

Marsala   Sic. DOC br. dr. s/sw. or sw. f. ★★★ NV

Dark sherry-type wine invented by the Woodhouse Brothers from Liverpool in 1773; excellent apéritif or for dessert. The dry ("virgin"), sometimes made by the solera system, must be 5 years old. See also Samperi.

Marsala Speciali

These are Marsalas with added flavours of egg, almond, strawberry, etc.

Martina Franca   Apu. DOC w. dr. (sp.) ★ D.Y.A.

Agreeable but rather neutral southern white, first cousin to LOCOROTONDO.

Martini & Rossi

Well-known vermouth and sparkling wine House, also famous for its fine wine museum in Pessione, near Turin.

Marzemino (del Trentino)   Tr.-Aad. DOC r. dr. ★ 85

Pleasant local red of Trento. Fruity fragrance; slightly bitter taste. Mozart's Don Giovanni liked it.

Masi, Cantina

Well-known specialist producers of VALPOLICELLA, RECIOTO, SOAVE, etc., including fine red Campo Fiorin.

Maso Lodron   Tr-Aad. r. ★★★

One of the best Cabernet/Merlot reds, from Nogaredo.

Mastroberardino

The leading wine-producer of Campania, incl. TAURASI and LACRYMA CHRISTI DEL VESUVIO.

Melini

Long-established important producers of CHIANTI CLASSICO at Pontassieve. Inventors of the standard *fiasco*, or flask.

Melissa Cal. DOC r. w. dr. ★★ 82 83 84 85

Mostly made from Gaglioppo grapes in the province of Catanzaro. Delicate, balanced, ages rather well.

Meranese di Collina Tr-Aad. DOC r. dr. ★ 85

Light red of Merano, known in German as Meraner Hügel.

Merlot

Adaptable red Bordeaux grape widely grown in n.e. Italy and elsewhere. For example:

Merlot di Aprilia Lat. DOC r. dr. ★ 83 85

Harsh at first, softer after 2–3 yrs.

Merlot Colli Berici Ven. DOC r. dr. ★ 79 81 82 83 85

Pleasantly light and soft.

Merlot Colli Orientali del Friuli Fr-VG. DOC r.dr. ★★ 79 81 82 83 85

Pleasant herby character, best at 2–3 yrs (Riserva).

Merlot Collio Goriziano Fr-VG. DOC r. dr. ★★ 82 83 85

Grassy scent, slightly bitter taste. Best at 2–3 yrs.

Merlot Grave del Friuli Fr-VG. DOC r. dr. ★★ 82 83 85

Pleasant light wine, best at 1–2 yrs.

Merlot Isonzo Fr-VG. DOC r. dr. ★★ 82 83 84 85

A DOC in Gorizia. Dry, herby, agreeable wine.

Merlot del Piave Ven. DOC r. dr. ★★ 82 83 85

Sound tasty red, best at 2–4 yrs.

Merlot di Pramaggiore Ven. DOC r. dr. [★★] 79 82 83 84 85

A cut above most other Merlots; improves in bottle. Riserva after 2 yrs.

Merlot (del Trentino) Tr-Aad. DOC r. dr. [★] 83 85

Full flavour, slightly grassy scent, Riserva after 2 yrs.

Monica di Cagliari Sard. DOC r. dr. or sw. (f. dr. or sw.) ★★ 81 83 85

Strong spicy red, often fortified and comparable with Spanish Malaga. Monica is a Sardinian grape.

Monica di Sardegna Sard. DOC r. dr. ★ 81 83 85

Dry version of above, not fortified.

Moniga (del Garda)

Village at s.w. end of Lake Garda, known for good fresh CHIARETTO (D.Y.A.).

Montalcino

Village in the province of Siena, Tuscany, famous for its deep red BRUNELLO.

Montecarlo Tusc. DOC w. dr. r. ★★ 83 85

One of Tuscany's best whites, smooth and delicate, achieving a Graves-like style after 3–4 years. Now applies to a Chianti-style red too.

Montecompatri Colonna Lat. DOC w. dr. or s/sw. ★ D.Y.A.

A neighbour of FRASCATI. Similar wine.

Montefalco Umb. DOC r.dr. or sw. [★★] 81 82 83 85

The Sagrantino grape can give this deep red sweetness and bite.

Montepaldi

Well-known producers and merchants of CHIANTI CLASSICO at San Casciano Val di Pesa. Owned by the Corsini family.

Montepulciano, Vino Nobile di

See Vino Nobile di Montepulciano.

Montepulciano d'Abruzzo (or Molise) Abr & M. DOC r. p. dr. [★★★] 78 79 80 81 82 83 84 85

One of Italy's best reds, full of flavour and warmth, from the Adriatic coast round Pescara. See also Cerasuolo.

Monterosso (Val d'Arda) Em-Ro. DOC w. dr. or sw. (sp.) ★ D.Y.A.

Agreeable and fresh minor white from Piacenza.

Montesodi Tusc. r. ★★★

Tip-top CHIANTI riserva from FRESCOBALDI.

Moscadello Tusc. w. sw./sp. ★★ D.Y.A.

Light, fizzy, not oversweet muscat. A refreshing speciality of MONTALCINO.

Moscato Fruitily fragrant grape grown all over Italy.

Moscato d'Asti Piem. DOC w. sw. sp. ★★ NV

Low-strength sweet fruity sparkler normally made in bulk. ASTI SPUMANTE is the theoretically superior version.

Moscato dei Colli Euganei Ven. DOC w. sw. (sp.) ★★ D.Y.A.

Golden wine, fruity and smooth, from near Padua.

Moscato d'Asti Naturale Piem. DOC w. sw. ★★ D.Y.A.

The light and fruity base wine for Moscato d'Asti.

Moscato di Noto Sic. DOC w. s/sw. or sw. or sp. or f. ★ NV

Light sweet still and sparkling versions, or strong Liquoroso. Noto is near Siracusa.

Moscato (Oltrepò Pavese) Lomb. DOC w. sw. (sp.) ★★ D.Y.A.

The Lombardy equivalent of Moscato d'Asti.

Moscato di Pantelleria Sic. DOC w. sw. (sp.) (f. pa.) ★★★

Italy's best muscat, from the island of Pantelleria close to the Tunisian coast; rich, fruity and aromatic. Ages well.

Moscato di Siracusa Sic. DOC w. sw. ★★ NV

Amber dessert wine reputedly from Syracuse. Can be superb.

Moscato di Sorso Sennori Sard. DOC w. sw. (f.) ★ D.Y.A.

Strong golden dessert wine from Sassari, n. Sardinia.

Moscato di Trani Apu. DOC w. sw. or f. ★ 79 81 82 83 85

Another strong golden dessert wine, sometimes fortified, with "bouquet of faded roses".

Moscato (Trentino) Tr-Aad. DOC w. sw. ★ D.Y.A.

Typical muscat: high strength for the north.

Nasco di Cagliari Sard. DOC w. dr. sw. (f. dr. or sw.) ★ 83 84 85

Sardinian speciality, light bitter taste, high alcoholic content.

Nebbiolo The best red grape of PIEMONTE and Lombardy.

Nebbiolo d'Alba Piem. DOC r. dr. s/sw. (sp.) ★★ 79 80 82 83 85

Like light-weight BAROLO; often easier to appreciate than the more powerful classic wine.

Negroamaro

Literally "black bitter"; Apulian red grape with potential for quality. See Copertino.

Nipozzano, Castello di

The most important CHIANTI producer outside the Classico zone, to the north near Florence. Owned by FRESCOBALDI.

Nozzole Famous estate in the heart of CHIANTI CLASSICO n. of Greve.

Nuraghe Majore Sard. w. dr. ★★ D.Y.A.

Sardinian white: delicate, fresh, among the island's best.

Nuragus di Cagliari Sard. DOC w. dr. ★ D.Y.A.

Lively Sardinian white, not too strong.

Oliena Sard. r. dr. ★★

Interesting strong fragrant CANNONAU red; a touch bitter.

Oltrepò Pavese Lomb. DOC r. w. dr. sw. sp. ★→★★

DOC applicable to 7 wines produced in the province of Pavia, named after their grapes.

Orvieto Umb. DOC w. dr. or s/sw. ★★→★★★ D.Y.A.

The classical Umbrian golden-white, smooth and substantial, though the dry version is sometimes flat and rather dull. O. Classico is superior. Only the finest examples e.g. Castello della Sala, age well.

Ostuni Apu. DOC r. or w. dr. ★★ 83 85

Rather delicate, dry, balanced; produced in the Pr. of Brindisi.

Pagadebit Em-Ro. w.dr./s.sw. D.Y.A.

Pleasant traditional "payer of debts" from round Bertinoro.

Paradiso, Fattoria

Century-old family estate near Bertinoro (EM-RO). Excellent ALBANA, fine PAGADEBIT and unique red BARBAROSSA.

Parrina Tusc. r. or w. dr. **★★** 85
> Light red and fresh appetizing white from s. Tuscany.

Passito Strong sweet wine from grapes dried in the sun or indoors.

Per'e Palummo Camp. r. dr. **★★** 82 83 84 85
> Excellent red produced on the island of Ischia; delicate, slightly grassy, a bit tannic, balanced.

Petit Rouge Vd'A. ★★ 78 79 82 83 85
> Good dark lively REFOSCO-like red.

Pian d'Albola
> Renowned old CHIANTI CLASSICO estate owned by Zonin.

Piave Ven. DOC r. or w. dr. ★★ 82 83 85 (w. D.Y.A.)
> Flourishing DOC covering 8 wines, 4 red and 4 white, named after their grapes. CABERNET, MERLOT and RABOSO reds all need ageing.

Picolit (Colli Orientali del Friuli) Fr-VG. DOC w. s/sw. or sw. ★★★ 82 83 85
> Known (by its makers) as Italy's Château d'Yquem. Delicate, well balanced, high alcohol. Ages up to 6 years, but overpriced.

Piemonte
> The most important Italian region for quality wine. Turin is the capital, Asti and ALBA the wine-centres. See Barolo, Barbera, Grignolino, Moscato, etc.

Pieropan Outstanding producers of SOAVE that deserves its fame.

Pighin, Fratelli
> Top producers of COLLIO, GRAVE DEL FRIULI, etc.

Pinocchio Tusc. r. w. ★
> Long-established brand notable for its variable nose.

Pinot Bianco
> Increasingly popular in n.e., esp. good for sparkling wine.

Pinot Bianco (Alto Adige) Tr-Aad. DOC. w. dr. ★★ 82 83 84
> Italy's best and longest-lived wine of this variety.

Pinot Bianco (dei Colli Berici) Ven. DOC w. dr. ★★ D.Y.A.
> Straight satisfying dry white.

Pinot Bianco (Colli Orientali del Friuli) Fr-VG. DOC w. dr. ★★ 83 84 85
> Good white; smooth rather than showy.

Pinot Bianco (Collio Goriziano) Fr-VG. DOC w. dr. ★★ 83 84 85
> Similar to the above.

Pinot Bianco (Grave del Friuli) Fr-VG. DOC w. dr. ★★ 83 84 85
> Same again.

Pinot Grigio Tasty, low-acid white grape popular in n.e. Italy.

Pinot Grigio (Collio Goriziano) Fr-VG. DOC w. dr. ★★ 84 85
> Fruity, soft, agreeable dry white. The best age well.

Pinot Grigio (Grave del Friuli) Fr-VG. DOC w. dr. ★★ 84 85
> Hardly distinguishable from the above.

Pinot Grigio (Oltrepò Pavese) Lomb. DOC w. dr. (sp.) ★★ 85
> Lombardy's P.G. is among the best.

Pinot Nero Trentino Tr-Aad. DOC r. dr. ★★ 79 80 82 83 85
> Pinot Nero (Noir) gives lively burgundy-scented light wine in much of n.e. Italy, incl. Trentino. Riserva after 2 yrs.

Pio Cesare
> A producer of top-quality red wines of PIEMONTE, incl. BAROLO.

Poggio al Sole
> CHIANTI CLASSICO estate. Both young and Riserva wines excellent.

Pomino Tusc. DOC (r.) w. dr. (br.) ★★★
> Fine white, partly Chardonnay ("Il Benefizio" is 100%) and a Sangiovese/Cabernet blend. Also Vinsanto. From FRESCOBALDI.

Primitivo di Apulia Apu. r. dr. ★★ 81 83 84 85
> One of the best southern reds. Fruity when young, soft and full-flavoured with age (see also MANDURIA).

Prosecco di Conegliano   Ven. DOC w. dr. or s/sw. (sp.) ★★★ D.Y.A.
Popular sparkling wine of the n.e. Slight fruity bouquet, the dry pleasantly bitter, the sweet fruity; the best are known as Superiore di Cartizze. Best producer: Carpene-Malvolti.

Prunotto, Alfredo
Very serious Alba company with v.g. BAROLO, BARBARESCO, NEBBIOLO, etc.

Raboso del Piave (now DOC)   Ven. r. dr. ★★ 78 79 82 83 85
Powerful, sharp, interesting country red; needs age.

Ramandolo   See Verduzzo Colli Orientali del Friuli

Rapitalà   See Alcamo

Ravello   Camp. r. p. w. dr. ★★ 82 83 84 85
Among the best wines of Campania: full dry red, fresh clean white. Caruso is the best-known brand.

Recioto   Wine made partly of half-dried grapes. Speciality of Veneto. R. Amandorlato is ½ sweet, ½ dry.

Recioto di Gambellara   Ven. DOC w. s/sw. sp. ★ 82 83 85
Sweetish golden wine, often half-sparkling.

Recioto di Soave   Ven. DOC w. s/sw. (sp.) ★★ 81 83 85
Soave made from selected half-dried grapes; sweet, fruity, fresh, slightly almondy: high alcohol.

Recioto della Valpolicella   Ven. DOC r. s/sw. sp. ★★ 78 80 81 83 85
Strong rather sweet red, sometimes sparkling. "Amabile" is fully sweet.

Recioto Amarone della Valpolicella   Ven. DOC r. dr. ★★★★ 78 79 80 81 83 85
Dry version of the above; strong concentrated flavour, rather bitter. Impressive and expensive.

Refosco (Colli Orientali del Friuli)   Fr-VG. DOC r. dr. ★★ 80 81 82 83 85
Full-bodied dry red; Riserva after 2 yrs. Refosco is said to be the same grape as the MONDEUSE of Savoie (France).

Refosco (Grave del Friuli)   Fr-VG. DOC r. dr. ★★ 80 81 82 83 85
Similar to above but slightly lighter.

Regaleali   Sic. w. r. p.   ★★   79 80 81 82 83 84 85
Among the best Sicilian table wines, produced between Caltanissetta and Palermo.

Ribolla (Colli Orientali del Friuli)   Fr-VG. DOC w. dr. ★ D.Y.A.
Clean and fruity north-eastern white.

Ricasoli
Famous Tuscan family, "inventors" of CHIANTI, whose Chianti is named after their BROLIO estate and castle.

Riecine   Tusc.   ★★★   75 78 79 81 82 83 85
First-class CHIANTI CLASSICO estate at Gaiole started by an Englishman, John Dunkley. First wine 1975.

Riesling
Normally refers to Italian Riesling (R. Italico or "Welschriesling"). German Riesling, uncommon, is R. Renano.

Riesling Alto Adige   DOC w. dr. ★★ 83 84 85
Can often be Italy's best Riesling.

Riesling (Oltrepò Pavese)   Lomb. DOC w. dr. (sp.) ★★
The Lombardy version, quite light and fresh. Occasionally sparkling. Keeps well. Made of both types of Riesling.

Riesling (Trentino)   Tr-Aad. DOC w. dr. ★★ D.Y.A.
Delicate, slightly acid, very fruity.

Riserva   Wine aged for a statutory period in barrels.

Riunite
One of the world's largest co-operative cellars near Reggio Emilia producing huge quantities of LAMBRUSCO and other wines.

Rivera
Important and reliable winemakers at Andria, near Bari, with good red Il Falcone and CASTEL DEL MONTE rosé.

Riviera del Garda Chiaretto Ven. and Lom. DOC p. dr. ★★ D.Y.A.
Charming cherry-pink, fresh and slightly bitter, from s.w. Garda, especially round Moniga del Garda.

Riviera del Garda Rosso Ven. DOC r. dr. ★★ 81 82 83 85
Red version of the above; ages surprisingly well.

Rosa del Golfo Apu. p.dr. ★★ 85
An outstanding example of ALEZIO rosato.

Rosato Rosé.

Rosato del Salento Apu. p. dr. ★→★★ D.Y.A.
Strong but refreshing southern rosé from round Brindisi.

Rossese di Dolceacqua Lig. DOC r. dr. ★★ 82 83 85
Well-known fragrant light red of the Riviera, as clean as claret. Superiore is stronger.

Rosso Red.

Rosso Cònero Mar. DOC r. dr. ★★ 79 80 82 83 85
Substantial CHIANTI-style wine from the Adriatic coast.

Rosso delle Colline Lucchesi Tusc. DOC r. dr. ★★ 82 83 85
Produced round Lucca but not greatly different from CHIANTI.

Rosso di Assisi Umb. r.dr. ★★ 82 83
A new concept for Umbria; delicious refreshing gulpable red.

Rosso Piceno Mar. DOC r. dr. ★→ ★★ 78 79 81 82 83 85
Adriatic red with a touch of style. Can be Superiore. Best producer: Villa Pigna.

Rubesco The excellent popular red of TORGIANO.

Rubino di Cantavenna Piem. DOC r. dr. ★★ 83 85
Lively red, principally BARBERA, from a well-known co-operative s.e. of Turin.

Rufina A sub-region of CHIANTI in the hills east of Florence.

Ruffino
The biggest and best known of all CHIANTI merchants. Riserva Ducale is the top wine.

Salice Salentino Apu. DOC r. ★★ 78 79 80 81 83 84 85
Strong red from Negroamaro grapes, Riserva after 2 yrs., ages to smooth full wine. Leading maker: LEONE DE CASTRIS.

Samperi, Vecchio Sic. des. ★★★
The outstanding wine of MARSALA today, although not DOC. A dry apéritif not unlike Amontillado sherry.

Sangiovese Principal red grape of CHIANTI, used alone for:

Sangiovese d'Aprilia Lat. DOC r. or p. dr. ★ D.Y.A.
Strong dry rosé from south of Rome.

Sangiovese di Romagna Em-Ro. DOC r. dr. ★★ 80 81 82 83 85
Pleasant standard red; gains character with a little age.

Sangue di Giuda (Oltrepò Pavese) Lomb. DOC r. dr. or s/sw. ★★ 85
"Judas' blood". Strong soft red of w. Lombardy.

San Severo Apu. DOC r. p. w. dr. ★ 85
Sound neutral southern wine; not particularly strong.

Santa Maddalena Tr-Aad. DOC r. dr. ★★ 85
Perhaps the best Tyrolean red. Round and warm, slightly almondy. From Bolzano.

Sassella (Valtellina) Lomb. DOC r. dr. ★★★ 78 79 80 82 83 85
Considerable NEBBIOLO wine, tough when young. Known since Roman times, mentioned by Leonardo da Vinci.

Sassicaia Tusc. r. dr. ★★★★ 72 75 76 77 78 79 80 81 82 83 85
Perhaps Italy's best red wine, produced from CABERNET grapes in the Tenuta San Guido of the Incisa family, at Bolgheri near Livorno, since 1968 and cellared by ANTINORI. Limited production.

Sauvignon
The Sauvignon Blanc: excellent white grape used in n.e., perhaps best at TERLANO, ALTO ADIGE.

Sauvignon (Colli Berici) Ven. DOC w. dr. ★★ D.Y.A.
Delicate, slightly aromatic, fresh white from near Vicenza.

Sauvignon (Colli Orientali del Friuli) Fr-VG. DOC w. dr. ★★ 83 84 85
> Full, smooth, freshly aromatic n.e. white.

Sauvignon (Collio Goriziano) Fr-VG. DOC w. dr. ★★ 83 84 85
> Very similar to the last; slightly higher alcohol.

Savuto Cal. DOC r. p. dr. ★★ 83 85
> The ancient Savuto produced in the provinces of Cosenza and Catanzaro. Fragrant juicy wine.

Schiava
> Good red grape of TRENTINO-ALTO ADIGE with characteristic bitter after-taste, used for SANTA MADDALENA, etc.

Sciacchetrà See Cinqueterre

Secco Dry.

Seicentenario Tusc. r. ★★★★
> Perhaps ANTINORI's best-ever red, bottled (in magnums) for the firm's 600th anniversary in 1985.

Sella & Mosca
> Major Sardinian growers and merchants at Alghero.

Settesoli
> Sicilian growers' co-operative with range of adequate table wines.

Sforzato (Valtellina) Lomb. DOC r. dr. ★★★ 75 78 79 80 82 83 85
> Valtellina equivalent of RECIOTO AMARONE made with partly dried grapes. Velvety, strong, ages remarkably well. Also called Sfursat.

Sfursat See SFORZATO.

Sizzano Piem. DOC r. dr. ★★ 78 79 80 82 83 85
> Attractive full-bodied red produced at Sizzano in the Pr. of Novara, mostly from NEBBIOLO. Ages up to 10 years.

Soave Ven. DOC w. dr. ★★★ D.Y.A.
> Famous, if not very characterful, Veronese white. Fresh with attractive texture. S. Classico is more restricted and better.

Solaia Tusc. r. ★★★
> Very fine Bordeaux-style wine from ANTINORI, first made in 1978.

A new top category, DOCG, Denominazione Controllata e Garantita, is gradually being added to the Italian wine classification. It is awarded only to certain wines from top-quality zones which have been bottled and sealed with a government seal by the producer. The first five areas to be "guaranteed" are Barolo, Barbaresco, Brunello di Montalcino, Chianti and Vino Nobile di Montepulciano. But it should be remembered that several of Italy's best wines are not covered by the DOC system. Examples are Sassicaia, Tignanello, Venegazzù, Bricco Manzoni.

Solopaca Camp. DOC r. w. dr. ★ 83 85
> Comes from near Benevento, rather sharp when young, the white soft and fruity.

Sorni Tr-Aad. r. w. dr. ★★ 84 85
> Made in the Pr. of Trento. Light, fresh and soft. Drink young.

Spanna See GATTINARA.

Spumante Sparkling.

Squinzano Apu. DOC r. p. dr. ★ 79 80 81 82 83 84 85
> Strong southern red from Lecce. Riserva after 2 yrs.

Stravecchio Very old.

Sylvaner
> German white grape successful in ALTO ADIGE and elsewhere.

Sylvaner (Alto Adige) Tr-Aad. DOC w. dr. ★★ 81 82 83 84 85
> Pleasant grapy well-balanced white.

Sylvaner (Terlano) Tr-Aad. DOC w. dr. ★★ 84 85
> Attractive lively and delicate wines.

Sylvaner (Valle Isarco)   Tr-Aad. DOC w. dr. ★★ 81 82 83 84 85
Like the last. Perhaps better.

Taurasi   Camp. DOC r. dr.   ★★★   75 77 78 79 80 81 82 83 85
The best Campanian red, from Avellino. Bouquet of cherries. Harsh when young, improves with age. Riserva after 4 yrs.

Terlano   Tr-Aad. DOC w. dr.   ★★   84 85
A DOC applicable to 7 white wines from the Pr. of Bolzano, named after their grapes, esp. outstanding SAUVIGNON. Terlaner in German.

Teroldego Rotaliano   Tr-Aad. DOC r. p. dr. ★★ 81 82 83 85
The attractive local red of Trento. Blackberry-scented, slight bitter after-taste, ages moderately.

Terre Rosse
Distinguished small estate near Bologna. CABERNET, CHARDON-NAY, RIESLING ITALICO, etc., are the best of the region.

Tiefenbrunner
Distinguished grower of some of the very best ALTO ADIGE white and red wines at Schloss Turmhof, Kurtatsch (Cortaccio).

Tignanello   Tusc. r. dr.   ★★★   75 78 79 80 81 82 83 85
One of the leaders of the new style of Bordeaux-inspired Tuscan reds, made by ANTINORI. Small production.

Tocai Friulano   (Collio). ★★ 84 85
North-east Italian white grape; no relation of Hungarian or Alsace Tokay. Light dry wine. The Tocais of the Colli Orientale del Friuli and Collio Goriziano are best.

Tocai di Lison   Ven. DOC w. dr. ★★ D.Y.A.
From e. Veneto, delicate smoky/fruity scent, fruity taste. Classico is better.

Tocai (Colli Berici)   Ven. DOC w. dr. ★
Less character than the last.

Tocai (Grave del Friuli)   Fr-VG. DOC w. dr. ★★ D.Y.A.
Similar to TOCAI DI LISON, generally rather milder.

Tocai di S. Martino della Battaglia   Lomb. DOC w. dr. ★★ D.Y.A.
Small production s. of Lake Garda. Light, slightly bitter.

Torbato di Alghero   Sard. w. dr. (Pa.)   ★★   D.Y.A.
Good n. Sardinian table wine. Also PASSITO of high quality.

Torgiano, Rubesco di   Umb. DOC r. w. dr.   ★★★   77 78 79 80 81 82 83 85
Excellent red from near Perugia comparable with CHIANTI CLASSICO, the creation of the LUNGAROTTI family. RUBESCO is the standard quality. Riserva Monticchio is superb. Keep 10 years. White Torre di Giano is also good, but not as outstanding as the reds.

Torricella   Tusc. w. dr. ★★★ 81
Remarkable aged dry white from BROLIO.

Traminer Aromatico   Tr-Aad. DOC w. dr. ★★ D.Y.A.
Delicate, aromatic, rather soft Gewürztraminer.

Trebbiano
The principal white grape of Tuscany, found all over Italy. Ugni Blanc in French. Rarely remarkable unless blended.

Trebbiano d'Abruzzo   Abr & M. DOC w. dr. ★ D.Y.A.
Gentle, rather neutral, slightly tannic. From round Pescara.

Trebbiano d'Aprilia   Lat. DOC w. dr. ★ D.Y.A.
Heady, mild-flavoured, rather yellow. From south of Rome.

Trebbiano di Romagna   Em-Ro. DOC w. dr. or s/sw. (sp.) ★ D.Y.A.
Clean, pleasant white from near Bologna.

Trentino   Tr-Aad. DOC r. w. dr. or sw. ★→★★
DOC applicable to as many as 19 different wines named after their grapes.

Tunina, Vintage   Fr.-VG. w.dr. ★★★ 82 83 84 85
The trade name of a notable blended COLLIO white from the Jermann estate.

Umani Ronchi
　　A leading producer of quality wines of the Marches; notably
　　VERDICCHIO and ROSSO CÒNERO.
Uzzano, Castello di
　　Fine old estate at Greve. First-class CHIANTI CLASSICO.
Valcalepio Lomb. DOC r. w. dr. ★ 82 83 85
　　From nr. Bergamo. Pleasant red; lightly scented, fresh white.
Valdadige Tr-Aad. DOC r. w. dr. or s/sw. ★
　　Name for the ordinary table wines of the Adige valley—in
　　German Etschtal.
Val d'Arbia Tusc. DOC w. dr. ★ D.Y.A.
　　Another new DOC for a pleasant white from Chianti country.
Valgella (Valtellina) Lomb. DOC r. dr. ★★ 75 78 79 80 82 83 85
　　One of the VALTELLINA NEBBIOLOS: good dry red, growing nutty
　　with age. Riserva at 4 yrs.
Vallana, Antonio & Figlio
　　The protagonist of the "SPANNA" (Nebbiolo) near Novara,
　　Piem. Uses the DOC name Boca. Rich-flavoured reds.
Valle Isarco Tr-Aad. DOC w. dr. ★→★★ 84 85
　　A DOC applicable to 5 varietal wines made n.e. of Bolzano.
Valpolicella Ven. DOC r. dr. ★★→ ★★★ 83 84 85
　　Attractive light red from nr. Verona; most attractive when
　　young. Delicate nutty scent, slightly bitter taste. (None of this is
　　true of Valpolicella sold in litre and bigger bottles.) Classico more
　　restricted; Superiore has 12% alcohol and 1 yr. of age.
Valtellina Lomb. DOC r. dr. ★★→★★★ 79 80 82 83 85
　　A DOC applicable to wines made principally from Chiavennasca
　　(NEBBIOLO) grapes in the province of Sondrio, n. Lombardy. V.
　　Superiore is better.
Velletri Lat. DOC r. w. dr. or s/sw. ★★
　　Agreeable Roman dry red and smooth white. Drink young.
Vendemmia Harvest or vintage.
Venegazzù Ven. r. w. dr. sp. ★★★ 76 78 79 82 83 85
　　Remarkable rustic Bordeaux-style red produced from CABER-
　　NET grapes nr. Treviso. Rich bouquet, soft, warm taste, 13.5%
　　alcohol, ages well. Also sparkling white.
Verdicchio dei Castelli di Jesi Mar. DOC w. dr. (sp.) ★→★★★ D.Y.A.
　　Ancient, famous and very pleasant fresh pale white from nr.
　　Ancona. Goes back to the Etruscans. Classico is more restricted.
　　Comes in amphora-shaped bottles.
Verdicchio di Matelica Mar. DOC w. dr. (sp.) ★★ D.Y.A.
　　Similar to the last, though less well known.
Verdiso Native white grape of n.e. Italy, used with PROSECCO.
Verduzzo (Colli Orientali del Friuli) Fr-VG. DOC w. dr. s/sw. or sw.
　　★★ 84 85
　　Full-bodied white from a native grape. The best sweet is called
　　Ramandolo.
Verduzzo (Del Piave) Ven. DOC w. dr. ★★ D.Y.A.
　　Similar to the last but fresh and dry.
Vermentino Lig. w. dr. ★★ D.Y.A.
　　The best dry white of the Riviera: good clean seafood wine made
　　at Pietra Ligure and San Remo.
Vermentino di Gallura Sard. DOC w. dr. ★★ D.Y.A.
　　Soft, dry, rather strong white from northern Sardinia.
Vernaccia di Oristano Sard. DOC w. dr. (sw.) (f.) ★★★ 74 75 77 79
　　81 82 83 84 85
　　Sardinian speciality, like light sherry, a touch bitter, full-bodied
　　and interesting. Superiore with 15.5% alcohol and 3 yrs. of age.
Vernaccia di San Gimignano Tusc. DOC w. dr. (f.) ★★ 83 84 85
　　Should be a distinctive strong high-flavoured wine from near
　　Siena. Michelangelo's favourite. Much today is light and bland.
　　Try San Quirico. Riserva after 1 yr.

Vernaccia di Serrapetrona   Mar. DOC r. dr. s/sw. sw. sp. ★★D.Y.A.
Comes from the province of Macerata; aromatic bouquet, pleasantly bitter after-taste.

Vernatsch   German for Schiava.

Vicchiomaggio
Important CHIANTI CLASSICO estate near Greve.

Vietti
Excellent small producer of some of Piedmont's most character-ful wines, incl. BAROLO. At Castiglione Falletto, Prov. Cuneo.

Vignamaggio
Historic and beautiful CHIANTI CLASSICO estate near Greve.

Villa Banfi
The production department of the biggest U.S. importer of Italian wine. Huge new plantings at MONTALCINO, incl. MOS-CADELLO, CABERNET, CHARDONNAY, are part of a drive for quality plus quantity. BRUNELLO is shaping nicely. Santa Costanza is v. fruity VINO NOVELLO.

Villagrande
Imposing old estate on the slopes of Mt. Etna, Sicily, making the best wines of the ETNA DOC.

Vino da arrosto
"Wine for roast meat", i.e. good robust dry red.

Vino da pasto
"Mealtime" wine: i.e. nothing special.

Vino da tàvola
"Table wine" – but the only appellation open to many of Italy's best new-coined wines (see box on page 93).

Vino Nobile di Montepulciano   Tusc. DOCG r. dr. ★★★ 75 77 78 79 81 82 83 85
Impressive traditional Chianti-like red with bouquet and style. Aged for 3 yrs. Riserva; for 4 yrs. Riserva Speciale. Best estates incl. Boscarelli, Avignonesi, Fognano, Poliziano.

Vino novello
Italy's equivalent of France's "primeurs", (as in BEAUJOLAIS).

Vinòt   Italy's first "VINO NOVELLO", inspired by Beaujolais Nouveau. From GAJA.

V.I.D.E.
An association of better-class Italian producers for marketing their estate wines.

Vinsanto or **Vin Santo**
Term for certain strong sweet wines esp. in Tuscany: usually PASSITI.

Vinsanto di Gambellara   Ven. DOC w. sw. ★★
Powerful, velvety, golden: made near Vicenza and Verona.

Vinsanto Toscano   Tusc. w. s/sw. ★★→★★★
Aromatic bouquet, rich and smooth. Aged in very small barrels known as Carratelli. Can be astonishing.

Volpaia, Castello di
First-class CHIANTI CLASSICO estate at Radda (Siena). See also Coltassala.

VQPRD
Often found on the labels of DOC wines to signify "Vini di Qualita Prodotti in Regioni Delimitate", or quality wines from restricted areas in accordance with E.E.C. regulations.

Zagarolo   Lat. DOC w. dr. or s/sw. ★★ D.Y.A.
Neighbour of FRASCATI, similar wine.

Zonin
One of Italy's biggest privately owned estates and wineries, based at GAMBELLARA, with DOC VALPOLICELLA, etc., other large estates are at ASTI and in CHIANTI and FRIULI. Now also at Barboursville, Virginia, U.S.A.

Germany

Germany has the most complicated labelling system in the world — a fact that has put most people off tackling it seriously and driven them to settle for pleasantly innocuous blended wines: Liebfraumilch and the like. Many even in Germany would agree that it is overcomplicated, and that its complexity is not justified by strict enough enforcement of its rules. Simplification is called for — and stronger sanctions.

Yet for all that those who funk its complications will never experience the real beauty of the style of wine which is Germany's unique contribution.

The secret of the style is the balance of sweetness against fruity acidity. A great vintage in Germany is one in which the autumn weather allows the late-ripening Riesling — the grape which makes virtually all the great German wines (although it occupies only about 20% of the total vineyard) — to develop a high sugar content. What is so special about the Riesling is that as it ripens it also develops a concentration of fragrant acids and essences to balance the increasing sweetness. The resulting wine is tense and thrilling with this sugar/acid balance.

It smells and tastes vividly flowery and lively while it is young. But because of its internal equilibrium it also has the ability to mature for a remarkable length of time. As good Riesling matures subtle new scents and flavours emerge. Straight sweetness gives way to oily richness. Suggestions of countless flowers and fruits, herbs and spices develop.

These are the rewards for anyone who can be bothered to master the small print. They lead into realms of sensation where Liebfraumilch can never follow. The great German growers make wine for wine's sake. Matching it with food has only recently become a consideration. Today it is distinctly fashionable to choose drier wines and form gastronomic partnerships with them in the French manner.

The Labels and the Law

German wine law is based on the ripeness of the grapes at harvest time. Vintages vary widely, but as a general rule most German wine needs sugar added to make up for the missing warmth and sunshine of one of the world's northernmost vineyards.

The exceptional wine, from grapes ripe enough not to need sugar, is kept apart as Qualitätswein mit Prädikat or QmP. Within this top category its natural sugar-content is expressed by traditional terms — in ascending order of ripeness: Kabinett, Spätlese, Auslese, Beerenauslese, Trockenbeerenauslese.

But reasonably good wine is also made in good vineyards from grapes that fail to reach the natural sugar-content required for a QmP label. The authorities allow this, within fairly strict controls, to be called Qualitätswein as well, but with the different qualification of bestimmter Anbaugebiete (i.e. QbA) instead of mit Prädikat. QmP is therefore a vitally important ingredient of a top-quality label.

Both levels are officially checked, tested and tasted at every bottling. Each batch is given an identifying test ("prüfungs") number. No other country has quality control approaching this. It can't make dull wine exciting, but it can and does make all "quality" wine a safe bet.

The third level, Tafelwein, has no pretensions to quality and is not allowed to give itself airs beyond the name of the general region or sub-region it comes from. (But see LANDWEIN).

Though there is very much more detail in the laws this is the gist of the quality grading. Where it differs completely from the French system is in ignoring geographical difference. There are no Grands Crus, no VDQS. In theory all any German vineyard has to do to make the best wine is to grow the ripest grapes.

The law distinguishes only between degrees of geographical exactness. In labelling quality wine the grower or merchant is given a choice. He can (and always will) label the relatively small quantities of his best wine with the name of the precise vineyard or Einzellage where it was grown. Germany has about 3,000 Einzellage names. Obviously only particularly good ones are famous enough to help sell the wine. Therefore the law has created a second class of vineyard name: the Grosslage. A Grosslage is a group of neighbouring Einzellages of supposedly similar character and standing. Because there are fewer Grosslage names, and far more wine from each, Grosslagen have a better chance of building reputations, brand-name fashion.*

Thirdly the grower or merchant (more likely the latter) may choose to sell his wine under a regional name: the word is Bereich. To cope with the vast demand for "Bernkasteler" or "Niersteiner" or "Johannisberger" these world-famous names have been made legal for considerable districts. "Bereich Johannisberg" is the whole of the Rheingau; "Bereich Bernkastel" the whole of the Mittelmosel.

As with all wine names, in fact, the better the wine the more precise the labelling. The trick with German labels is to be able to recognize which is the most precise. Finally, though, and above all, it is to recognize the grower and his vineyard.

The basic German label

The order of wording on German quality wine labels follows a standard pattern.

> **MOSEL-SAAR-RUWER**
> **TRIERER**
> **ABSTBERG**
>
> **RIESLING AUSLESE**
>
> Qualitätswein mit Prädikat
> A.P. NR. 12345678
> ERZEUGERABFÜLLUNG
> WINZERVEREIN TRIER

The first mention is the Gebiet or wine region. The second is the town or parish, with the suffix -er. The third is the vineyard (either Einzellage or Grosslage—see introduction). The fourth (optional) is the grape variety. The fifth is the quality in terms of ripeness. For Qualitätswein mit Prädikat see page 110.
For A.P. Nr. see page 101.
Erzeugerabfüllung means bottled by the grower, in this case the grower's co-operative of Trier. For other words appearing on German labels see the Germany A–Z.

---

*Where the law is less than candid, however, is in pretending to believe that the general public will know a Grosslage name from an Einzellage name, when the two are indistinguishably similar (see any entry on the following pages). It is actually against the law to indicate on the label whether the name in question is that of a particular plot or a wider grouping. The names of all relevant Grosslagen are given in this book. Note that Grosslage wines are only rarely of the stature of Einzellage wines.

N.B. on the vintage notes

Vintage notes after entries in the German section are given in a different form from those elsewhere, to show the style of the vintage as well as its quality. Three styles are indicated:
The classic, super-ripe vintage with a high proportion of natural (QmP) wines, including Spätleses and Ausleses.
Example: **83**
The "normal" successful vintage with plenty of good wine but no great preponderance of sweeter wines. Example: 79
The cool vintage with generally poor ripeness but a fair proportion of reasonably successful wines, tending to be over-acid. Few or no QmP wines, but correspondingly more selection in the QbA category. Such wines sometimes mature better than expected. Example: *84*
Where no mention is made the vintage is generally not recommended, or most of its wines have passed maturity.

Recent Vintages

Mosel/Saar/Ruwer

Mosels (including Saar and Ruwer wines) are so attractive young that their keeping qualities are not often enough explored, and wines older than seven years or so are unusual. But well-made wines of Kabinett class gain from two or three years in bottle, Spätleses by a little longer, and Ausleses and Beerenausleses by anything from 10 to 20 years, depending on the vintage.

As a rule, in poor years the Saar and Ruwer fare worse than the Middle Mosel and make sharp, thin wines, but in the best years they can surpass the whole of Germany for elegance and "breed".

1985	A modest summer but beautiful autumn. 40% of the harvest is QmP. Highly promising Riesling vintage from best v'yds, incl. Eiswein.
1984	A late and rainy year. Two-thirds Tafel- or Landwein. Almost no QmP. But good acidity means some wines will keep well.
1983	The best since 1976; much good QbA, a little Kabinett, 31% Spätlese, Ausleses few but fine. For keeping.
1982	A huge ripe vintage marred by rain. Most is plain QbA but good sites made one-third Kabinett, one-third Spätlese and a little Auslese. Drink up.
1981	A wet vintage but some good middle Mosels up to Spätleses. Also Eiswein. Drink up.
1980	A terrible summer. Some pleasant wines but little more.
1979	A patchy vintage after bad winter damage. But several excellent Kabinetts and better. Light but well-balanced wines now ready.
1978	A similar vintage to '77, though very late and rather small. Very few sweet wines but many with good balance. Drink up.
1977	Big vintage of serviceable quality, mostly QbA. Drink up.
1976	Very good small vintage, with some superlative sweet wines and almost no dry. Most wines now ready; the best will keep 2–3 years.
1975	Very good; many Spätleses and Ausleses. Most now ready.
1974	Most wine needed sugaring; few Kabinetts. Drink now.
1973	Low acid and extract have meant a short life. Good Eiswein. Drink now.
1972	Should be drunk by now.
1971	Superb, with perfect balance. Some top wines will still improve.

Older fine vintages: '69, '67, '64, '59, '53, '49, '45.

Rhine/Nahe/Palatinate

Even the best wines can be drunk with pleasure after two or three years, but Kabinett, Spätlese and Auslese wines of good vintages gain enormously in character and complexity by keeping for longer. Rheingau wines tend to be longest-lived, often improving for 10 years or more, but wines from the Nahe and the Palatinate can last nearly as long. Rheinhessen wines usually mature sooner, and dry Franconian wines are best young.

The Riesling, predominant in the Rheingau, benefits most from hot summers; Palatinate wines can taste almost overripe.

1985	Frost, hail and drought led to sadly small crops, but good quality, esp. Riesling. Average 65% QmP. Comparable quality to 1983.
1984	Poor flowering and ripening. Three-quarters QbA, with QmP only in Rheinhessen, Rheinpfalz, Baden and Nahe. But flavour can be good.
1983	Very good Rieslings, esp. in the Rheingau and central Nahe. Generally about half QbA, but plenty of Spätleses.
1982	A colossal vintage gathered in torrential rain. Spätleses and even Kabinett are rare, but QbA wines are good drinking now.
1981	Poor conditions in the Rheingau but better in Nahe and Rheinhessen and very good in Palatinate.
1980	Bad weather from spring to autumn. Only passable wines.
1979	Uneven and reduced in size. Few great wines but many typical and good, esp. in Palatinate. For current drinking.
1978	Satisfactory vintage saved by late autumn. 25% QmP, but very few Spätleses. Some excellent wines in the south. Drink soon.
1977	Big and useful; few Kabinett wines or better. Not to keep.
1976	The richest vintage since 1921 in places. Very few dry wines. Balance less consistent than 1975. Generally mature.
1975	A splendid Riesling year, a high percentage of Kabinetts and Spätleses. Should be drunk fairly soon.
1974	Variable; the best fruity and good; many Kabinetts. Drink now.
1973	Very large, consistent and attractive, but not for keeping.
1972	Excess acidity was the problem. Should be drunk now.
1971	A superlative vintage. The finest are still improving.

Older fine vintages: '69, '67, '66, '64, '59, '57, '53, '49, '45.

Achkarren Bad. (r.) w. ★★
> Well-known wine village of the KAISERSTUHL, esp. for SILVANER, RULÄNDER. Best site: Schlossberg.

Adelmann, Graf
> Famous grower with 37 acres at Kleinbottwar, WÜRTTEMBERG. Uses the name Brussele. Light reds; good RIESLINGS.

Affental
> An area, not a village, just s. of Baden-Baden, producing a popular red Affentaler SPÄTBURGUNDER in a bottle moulded with a monkey ("Affe") climbing it.

Ahr Ahr r. ★→★★ 75 76 82 83 84 85
> Germany's best-known red-wine area, s. of Bonn. Very light pale SPÄTBURGUNDERS.

Amtliche Prüfungsnummer See PRÜFUNGSNUMMER

Anbaugebiet Wine-region. See QbA and WEINBAUGEBIET.

Anheuser
> Name of two distinguished growers of the NAHE.

Annaberg Rhpf. w. ★★★ 75 76 79 81 82 83 84 85
> Eighteen-acre estate at DÜRKHEIM famous for sweet and pungent wines, esp. SCHEUREBE, with prodigious keeping qualities.

A.P.Nr. Abbreviation of AMTLICHE PRÜFUNGSNUMMER.

Assmannshausen Rhg. r. ★→★★★ 71 75 76 81 82 83 84 85
> RHEINGAU village known for its pale, sometimes sweet, reds. Top v'yd.: Höllenberg. Grosslagen: Steil and Burgweg.

The German Wine Academy runs regular courses of wine-instruction at all levels for both amateurs and professionals, in German and English. The Academy is based at the glorious 12th-century Cistercian monastery of Kloster Eberbach in the Rheingau. The course normally includes tasting-tours of Germany's wine regions. Particulars can be obtained from the Academy, P. O. Box 1705, D-6500 Mainz, West Germany.

Auslese
> Specially selected wine with high natural sugar content.

Avelsbach M-S-R (Ruwer) w. ★★★ 71 75 76 79 81 82 83 84 85
> Village near TRIÉR. Supremely delicate wines. Growers: Staatliche Weinbaudomäne (see STAATSWEINGUT), BISCHÖFLICHE WEINGÜTER. Grosslage: Römerlay.

Ayl M-S-R (Saar) w. ★★★ 71 75 76 79 82 83 84 85
> One of the best villages of the SAAR. Top v'yds.: Kupp, Herrenberger. Grosslage: Scharzberg.

Bacchus Modern highly perfumed grape variety.

Bacharach (Bereich) ★→★★
> District name for the s. Mittelrhein v'yds. downstream from the RHEINGAU. Steely, racy wines, some v. pleasant. Bacharach is a romantic old town, the tourist centre of the Mittelrhein.

Baden
> Huge area of scattered wine-growing. The style is substantial, relatively low in acid, well adapted for mealtimes. Best areas are KAISERSTUHL and ORTENAU.

Badische Bergstrasse/Kraichgau (Bereich)
> Widespread district of n. BADEN. RIESLING and RULÄNDER are best.

Bad Dürkheim See DÜRKHEIM, BAD

Badisches Frankenland (Bereich)
> Minor district name of n. BADEN; Franconian-style wines.

Bad Kreuznach Na. w. ★★→★★★ 75 76 79 81 82 83 84 85
> Main town of the NAHE with some of its best wines. Many fine v'yds., incl. Brückes, Kahlenberg, Steinweg, Krötenpfuhl. Grosslage: Kronenberg.

Balbach Erben, Bürgermeister

One of the best NIERSTEIN growers. 44 acres, 80% Riesling. Best v'yds: Pettenthal, Ölberg.

Basserman-Jordan

117-acre MITTELHAARDT family estate with many of the best v'yds. in DEIDESHEIM, FORST, RUPPERTSBERG, etc.

Beerenauslese

Extremely sweet and luscious wine from exceptionally ripe selected individual bunches.

Bereich

District within an Anbaugebiet (region). See under Bereich names, e.g. Bernkastel (Bereich).

Bergweiler–Prüm Erben (Dr Pauly-Bergweiler), Zach., Weingut

Fine 24-acre estate based at BERNKASTEL. V'yds there and in WEHLEN etc. Also Nicolay wines from ÜRZIG and ERDEN.

Bergzabern, Bad Rhpf. (r.) w. *→*→** 75 76 79 81 82 83 84 85

Town of SÜDLICHE-WEINSTRASSE. Pleasant sweetish wines. Grosslage: Liebfrauenberg.

Bernkastel M-M w. **→**** 71 75 76 79 81 82 83 84 85

Top wine-town of the Mosel; the epitome of RIESLING. Best v'yds.: Doctor, Graben, Bratenhöfchen, etc. Grosslagen: Bad-stube (***) and Kurfürstlay (**).

Bernkastel (Bereich)

Wide area of mixed quality but decided flowery character. Includes all the Mittelmosel.

Bingen Rhh. w. **→***** 71 75 76 79 81 82 83 84 85

Town on Rhine and Nahe with fine v'yds., incl. Scharlachberg. Grosslage: Sankt Rochuskapelle.

Bingen (Bereich) District name for w. Rheinhessen.

Bischöfliche Weinguter Verwaltung

Outstanding M-S-R estate at TRIER, a union of the Cathedral properties with two famous charities. 230 acres of top v'yds. in AVELSBACH, WILTINGEN, SCHARZHOFBERG, AYL, KASEL, EITELS-BACH, PIESPORT, TRITTENHEIM, ÜRZIG, etc.

Blankenhornsberg

The outstanding KAISERSTUHL estate; 62 acres based at IHRIN-GEN.

Blue Nun The best-selling brand of LIEBFRAUMILCH, from SICHEL.

Bodenheim Rhh. w. ⟨**⟩

Village nr. NIERSTEIN with delicate wines, esp. from Silberberg.

Bodensee (Bereich)

Minor district of s. BADEN, on Lake Constance.

Bocksbeutel Flask-shaped bottle used for FRANKEN wines.

Brauneberg M-M w. ⟨***⟩ 71 75 76 79 81 82 83 84 85

Village near BERNKASTEL with 750 acres. Excellent full-flavoured Rieslings. Best v'yd.: Juffer. Grosslage: Kurfürstlay.

Breisach Baden

Frontier town on Rhine nr. KAISERSTUHL. Seat of the vast ZBW.

Breisgau (Bereich)

Minor district of BADEN, just n. of KAISERSTUHL. Best known for WEISSHERBST.

Brentano, von

25-acre old family estate in WINKEL, Rheingau.

Buhl, von, Geheimrat

Great RHEINPFALZ family estate. 250+ acres in DEIDESHEIM, FORST, RUPPERTSBERG, etc. In the very top class.

Bullay M-S-R *→ ⟨**⟩ 75 76 82 83 84 85

Lower Mosel village. Good light wines.

Bundesweinprämierung

The German state Wine Award: a gold, silver or bronze medal on bottles of remarkable wines.

Bürgerspital zum Heiligen Geist
    Ancient charitable estate at WÜRZBURG. 333 acres in WÜRZBURG, RANDERSACKER, etc., make rich dry wines.

Bürklin-Wolf, Dr
    Great RHEINPFALZ family estate. 247 acres in WACHENHEIM, FORST, DEIDESHEIM and RUPPERTSBERG, with rarely a dull, let alone poor, wine.

Castell'sches, Fürstlich Domänenamt
    142-acre princely estate in STEIGERWALD. Good typical FRANKEN wines: SILVANER, RIESLANER. Also SEKT.

Charta
    Organization of top RHEINGAU estates concentrating on TROCKEN and HALBTROCKEN RIESLINGS. Members must observe higher standards then the legal minima.

Crown of Crowns
    Popular brand of LIEBFRAUMILCH from LANGENBACH & CO.

Crusius
    30-acre family estate at TRAISEN, Na. Excellently-made, fresh RIESLINGS from Bastei and Rotenfels v'yds age v. well. Also SEKT of high quality.

Deidesheim Rhpf. w. (r.) ★★→★★★★ 71 75 76 79 81 82 83 84 85
    Biggest top-quality wine-village of RHEINPFALZ with 1,000 acres. Rich, high-flavoured, lively wines. V'yds. incl. Grainhübel, Herrgottsacker, Leinhöhle, Hohenmorgen, Kieselberg, Paradiesgarten, etc. Grosslagen: Hofstück (★★), Mariengarten (★★★).

Deinhard
    Famous old Koblenz merchants and growers of top-quality wines in RHEINGAU, MITTELMOSEL and RHEINPFALZ (see WEGELER-DEINHARD), also makers of v.g. SEKT.

Deinhard, Dr
    62-acre family estate in DEIDESHEIM with many of the best v'yds.

Deutscher Tafelwein
    TAFELWEIN from Germany (only). See Tafelwein.

Deutsches Weinsiegel
    A quality "seal" (i.e. neck label) for wines which have passed a stiff tasting test.

DLG (Deutsche Landwirtschaft Gesellschaft)
    The German Agricultural Society. The body that awards national medals for quality.

Dhron See Neumagen-Dhron

Diabetiker Wein
    Wine with minimal residual sugar (less than 4gms/litre); thus suitable for diabetics—or those who like very dry wine.

Dienheim Rhh. w. ★★ 76 79 81 82 83 84 85
    Southern neighbour of OPPENHEIM. Mainly run-of-the-mill wines. Best v'yds.: Kreuz, Herrenberg, Schloss. Grosslagen: Güldenmorgen, Krötenbrunnen.

Dom German for Cathedral. Wines from the famous TRIER Cathedral properties have "Dom" before the v'yd. name.

Domäne
    German for "domain" or "estate". Sometimes used alone to mean the "State domain" (Staatliche Weinbaudomäne).

Durbach Baden w. (r.) ★★→ ★★★ 76 79 81 82 83 84 85
    775 acres of the best v'yds. of BADEN. Top growers: Schloss Staufenberg, Wolf-Metternich, von Neveu. Choose their KLINGELBERGERS and KLEVNERS. Grosslage: Fürsteneck.

Dürkheim, Bad Rhpf. w. or (r.) ★★→★★★ 76 79 80 81 82 83 84 85
    Main town of the MITTELHAARDT. Top v'yds.: Hochbenn, Michelsberg. Grosslagen: Feuerberg, Schenkenböhl.

Edel Means "noble". Edelfäule means "noble rot": the condition which gives the greatest sweet wines (see p. 46).

Edenkoben Rhpf. w.(r.) ★→ ★★ 76 79 81 82 83 84 85

Important village of n. SÜDLICHE WEINSTRASSE. Grosslage: Ludwigshöhe. The best wines have plenty of flavour.

Egon Müller zu Scharzhof

Top Saar estate of 32 acres at WILTINGEN. His delicate, racy SCHARZHOFBERGER Rieslings are supreme in top years.

Eiswein

Wine made from frozen grapes with the ice (e.g. water content) rejected, thus very concentrated in flavour and sugar, of Beerenauslese ripeness or more. Rare and expensive. Sometimes produced as late as the January or February following the vintage. Alcohol content can be as low as 5.5 percent.

Eitelsbach Ruwer w. ★★→★★★ 71 75 76 79 81 82 83 84 85

RUWER village now part of TRIER, incl. superb Karthäuserhofberg estate. Grosslage: Römerlay.

Elbling

Inferior grape widely grown on upper Mosel.

Eltville Rhg. w. ★★ →★★★ 71 75 76 79 81 82 83 84 85

Major wine-town with cellars of the Rheingau State domain, FISCHER and VON SIMMERN estates. Excellent wines. Top v'yds.: Sonnenberg, Taubenberg. Grosslage: Steinmäcker.

Eltz, Schloss

Former Rheingau estate now divided. The name and a small portion are connected with PIEROTH.

Enkirch M-M w. ★★→ ★★★ 71 75 76 79 81 82 83 84 85

Minor middle-Mosel village, often overlooked but with lovely light tasty wine. Grosslage: Schwarzlay.

Erbach Rhg. w. ★★★→★★★★ 71 76 79 81 82 83 84 85

One of the best parts of the Rheingau with powerful, perfumed wines, incl. the great MARCOBRUNN; other top v'yds.: Schlossberg, Siegelsberg, Honigberg, Michelmark. Grosslage: Deutelsberg. Major estates: SCHLOSS REINHARTSHAUSEN, von SCHÖNBORN.

Erden M-M w. ★★→★★★ 71 75 76 79 81 82 83 84 85

Village between Urzig and Kröv with full-flavoured vigorous wine. Top v'yds.: Prälat, Treppchen. Leading grower: BISCHÖFLICHE WEINGÜTER, BERGWEILER-PRÜM, Nicolay. Grosslage: Schwarzlay.

Erzeugerabfüllung

Estate-bottled; bottled by the grower.

Escherndorf Franc. w. ★★→★★★ 75 76 81 82 83 84

Important wine-town near WÜRZBURG. Similar tasty dry wine. Top v'yds.: Lump, Berg. Grosslage: Kirchberg.

Remember that vintage information about German wines is given in a different form from the ready/not ready distinction applying to other countries. Read the explanation on page 97.

Feine, feinste, hochfeinste

Terms formerly used to distinguish a good grower's best barrels. Now, unfortunately, illegal.

Forst Rhpf. w. ★★→★★★★ 71 75 76 78 79 81 82 83 84 85

MITTELHAARDT village with 500 acres of Germany's best v'yds. Ripe, richly fragrant but subtle wines. Top v'yds.: Kirchenstück, Jesuitengarten, Ungeheuer, etc. Grosslagen: Mariengarten, Schnepfenflüg.

Franken

Franconia: region of excellent distinctive dry wines, esp. SILVANER. The centre is WÜRZBURG. BEREICH names: MAINVIERECK, MAINDREIECK, STEIGERWALD.

Freiburg Baden w. (r.) ★→★★ D.Y.A.

Centre of MARKGRÄFLERLAND. Good GUTEDEL. Look for NOBLING.

Friedrich Wilhelm Gymnasium

Superb 111-acre charitable estate based in TRIER with v'yds. in BERNKASTEL, ZELTINGEN, GRAACH, TRITTENHEIM, OCKFEN, etc., all M-S-R.

Geisenheim Rhg. w. ★★→★★★ 71 75 76 79 81 82 83 84 85

Village famous for Germany's leading wine-school. Best v'yds. incl. Rothenberg, Kläuserweg. Grosslagen: Burgweg and Erntebringer.

Gemeinde A commune or parish.

Gewürztraminer

Spicy grape, speciality of Alsace, used a little in s. Germany, esp. RHEINPFALZ and BADEN. See Traminer.

Gimmeldingen Rhpf. w. ★→★★ 76 81 82 83 84 85

Village just s. of MITTELHAARDT. At their best, similar wines. Grosslage: Meerspinne.

Goldener Oktober

Popular brand of Rhine and Mosel blends from ST. URSULA.

Graach M-M w. ★★→ ★★★ 71 75 76 79 81 82 83 84 85

Small village between BERNKASTEL and WEHLEN. Top v'yds.: Himmelreich, Domprobst, Abstberg, Josephshöfer. Grosslage: Münzlay.

Green Label

Germany's best-selling MOSEL (BEREICH BERNKASTEL). Brand-name of DEINHARD.

Grosslage See Introduction, p. 99

Guntersblum Rhh. w. ★→★★ 76 79 81 82 83 84 85

Big wine-town s. of OPPENHEIM. Grosslagen: Krötenbrunnen, Vogelsgarten.

Guntrum, Louis

Fine 164-acre family estate in NIERSTEIN, OPPENHEIM, etc., and merchant house with high and reliable standards.

Gutedel German for the Chasselas grape, used in s. BADEN.

Gutsverwaltung Estate administration.

Halbtrocken

"Semi-dry". Containing less than 18 but more than 9 grams per litre unfermented sugar. An increasingly popular category of wine intended for meal-times, often better-balanced than TROCKEN.

Hallgarten Rhg. w. ★★→★★★ 71 75 76 79 81 82 83 84 85

Important little wine-town behind HATTENHEIM. Robust full-bodied wines. Top v'yds. incl. Schönhell, Jungfer. Grosslage: Mehrhölzchen.

Hallgarten, House of Well-known London-based wine-merchant.

Hanns Christof

Estimable Rhine-wine brand from DEINHARD'S.

Hattenheim Rhg. w. ★★→★★★★ 71 75 76 79 81 82 83 84 85

Superlative 500-acre wine-town. V'yds. incl. STEINBERG, NÜSSBRUNNEN, MANNBERG, HASSEL ETC. GROSSLAGE: Deutelsberg. MARCOBRUNN lies on the ERBACH boundary.

Heilbronn Württ. w. r. ★→★★ 76 81 82 83 84 85

Wine-town with many small growers and a big coop. Seat of DLG competition.

Hessische Bergstrasse w. ★★→★★★ 76 81 82 83 84 85

Germany's smallest wine-region (1000 acres) n. of Heidelberg. Pleasant Riesling from State domain v'yds. in Heppenheim and Bensheim.

Hessische Forschungsanstalt für Wein-Obst-& Gartenbau.....

Germany's top wine-school and research establishment, at GEISENHEIM, Rheingau.

Heyl zu Herrnsheim

Fine 72-acre estate at NIERSTEIN, 55% Riesling.

Hochfeinste

"Very finest." Traditional label-term, illegal since 1971.

Hochheim Rhg. w. ★★→★★★71 75 76 79 81 82 83 84 85

600-acre wine-town 15 miles e. of RHEINGAU. Similar fine wines. Top v'yds.: Domdechaney, Kirchenstück, Hölle, Königin Viktoria Berg. Grosslage: Daubhaus.

Hock English term for Rhine-wine, derived from HOCHHEIM.

Huesgen, Adolph Important merchant house at TRABEN-TRARBACH.

Huxelrebe

Modern very aromatic grape variety, linked in some minds to cats.

Ihringen Bad. r. w. ★→★★★81 82 83 84 85

One of the best villages of the KAISERSTUHL, BADEN. Proud of its SPÄTBURGUNDER red, WEISSHERBST and v.g. SILVANER.

Ilbesheim Rhpf. w. ★→★★81 82 83 84 85

Base of important growers' cooperative of SÜDLICHE WEIN-STRASSE. See also SCHWEIGEN.

Ingelheim Rhh. r. or w. ★76 81 82 83 84 85

Town opposite the Rheingau historically known for red wine.

Iphofen Franc. w. ★★→★★★ 75 76 81 82 83 84 85

Village e. of WÜRZBURG. Superb top v'yd.: Julius-Echter-Berg. Grosslage: Burgweg.

Jesuitengarten

15-acre vineyard in FORST. One of Germany's best.

Johannisberg Rhg. w. ★★→★★★★71 75 76 79 81 82 83 84 85

260-acre village with superlative subtle RIESLINGS. Top v'yds. incl. SCHLOSS JOHANNISBERG, Hölle, Klaus, etc. Grosslage: Erntebringer.

Johannisberg (Bereich) District name of the entire RHEINGAU.

Josephshöfer

Fine v'yd. at GRAACH, the property of von KESSELSTATT.

Juliusspital

Ancient charity at WÜRZBURG with 374 acres of top FRANKEN v'yds. Look for SILVANERS.

Kabinett

The term for the lightest category of natural unsugared (QmP) wines. Low in alcohol (average 7–9%).

Kaiserstuhl-Tuniberg (Bereich)

Best v'yd. area of BADEN. Villages incl. IHRINGEN, ACHKARREN.

Kallstadt Rhpf. w. (r.) ★★→★★★ 75 76 79 81 82 83 84 85

Village of n. MITTELHAARDT. Fine rich wines. Top v'yd.: ANNABERG. Grosslagen: Saumagen (★★★), Kobnert (★★).

Kammerspreismünze See Landespreismünze.

Kanzem M-S-R (Saar) w. ★★→★★★71 75 76 79 81 82 83 84 85

Small but excellent neighbour of WILTINGEN. Top v'yds.: Sonnenberg, Altenberg. Grosslage: Scharzberg.

Kasel M-S-R (Ruwer) w. ★★→★★★ 71 75 76 81 82 83 84 85

Village with wonderfully attractive light wines. Best v'yd.: Nies'chen. Grosslage: Römerlay.

Keller Wine-cellar. Kellerei: winery.

Kerner Modern very flowery grape variety, esp. in PALATINATE.

Kesselstatt, von

The biggest private Mosel estate, 600 years old. Over 200 acres in GRAACH (Josephshöfer), PIESPORT, KASEL, MENNIG, WILTINGEN, etc., plus substantial rented or managed estates, making light and fruity typical Mosels. Now belongs to Gunther Reh of Leiwen.

Kesten M-M w. ★→★★★71 75 76 79 81 82 83 84 85

Neighbour of BRAUNEBERG. Best wines (from Paulinshofberg v'yd.) similar. Grosslage: Kurfürstlay.

Kiedrich Rhg. w. ★★→★★★★ 71 75 76 79 81 82 83 84 85
> Neighbour of RAUENTHAL; almost as splendid and high-flavoured. Top v'yds.: Gräfenberg, Wasseros, Sandgrub. Grosslage: Heiligenstock.

Klevner (or Clevner)
> Red Klevner (synonym, Blauer Frühburgunder) is supposedly Italian Chiavenna, an early-ripening black Pinot. Also the ORTENAU (BADEN) name for TRAMINER.

Klingelberger
> BADEN term for the RIESLING, esp. at DURBACH.

Kloster Eberbach
> Glorious 12th-century Abbey at HATTENHEIM, Rheingau, now State domain property and H.Q. of the German Wine Academy. See panel, p. 101.

Klüsserath M-M w. ★★→ ★★★ 71 76 79 81 83 84 85
> Minor Mosel village worth trying in good vintages. Best v'yds.: Brudeschaft, Königsberg. Grosslage: St. Michael.

Kraichgau
> Small BADEN region s. of Heidelberg. Best-known wines are from Neckarzimmern and Wiesloch.

Kreuznach (Bereich)
> District name for the entire northern NAHE. See also BAD KREUZNACH.

Kröv M-M w. ★→★★★ 75 76 81 83 84 85
> Popular tourist resort famous for its Grosslage name: Nacktarsch, meaning "bare bottom".

Landespreismünze
> Prizes for quality at state, rather than national, level. Considered by some more discriminating than DLG medals.

Landgräflich Hessisches Weingut
> Wide-ranging 75-acre estate in JOHANNISBERG, WINKEL, KIEDRICH and ELTVILLE.

Landwein
> A new (1982) category of theoretically better quality TAFELWEIN from 15 designated regions. It must be TROCKEN or HALBTROCKEN. Similar in intention to France's *vins de pays*.

Langenbach & Co.
> Well-known wine merchants of London and WORMS.

Lauerburg
> One of the four owners of the famous Doctor v'yd. in BERNKASTEL, with THANISCH, DEINHARD and Heilig-Geist-Armenspende.

Liebfrauenstift
> 26-acre v'yd. in the city of WORMS, said to be the origin of the name LIEBFRAUMILCH.

Liebfraumilch
> Legally defined as a QbA "of pleasant character" from RHEINHESSEN, RHEINPFALZ, NAHE or RHEINGAU, of a blend dominated by RIESLING, SILVANER or MÜLLER-THURGAU. Most is mild semisweet wine from RHEINHESSEN and RHEINPFALZ. The rules now say it must have more than 18 gms. per litre unfermented sugar. Nowadays sometimes very cheap and of inferior quality, depending on brand/shipper.

Lieser M-M w. ★→ ★★ 71 75 76 79 81 82 83 84 85
> Little-known neighbour of BERNKASTEL. Grosslage: Beerenlay, Kurfürstlay.

Lorch Rhg. w. (r.) ★→★★ 71 76 79 81 83 84 85
> At extreme w. end of Rheingau. Some fine light RIESLINGS more like MITTELRHEIN wines. Best grower: von Kanitz.

Löwenstein, Fürst
> 66-acre FRANKEN estate: classic dry powerful wines.

Maikammer Rhpf. w. (r.) ★→ ★★ 76 81 82 83 84 85
  Village of n. SÜDLICHE WEINSTRASSE. Very pleasant wines incl.
  those from coop at Rietburg. Grosslage: Mandelhöhe.

Maindreieck (Bereich)
  District name for central part of FRANKEN, incl. WÜRZBURG.

Marcobrunn
  Historic RHEINGAU vineyard; one of Germany's best. See
  ERBACH.

Markgräflerland (Bereich)
  Minor districts. of Freiburg (BADEN). GUTEDEL wine is delicious
  refreshment when drunk very young.

Martinsthal Rhg. w. ★★→ ★★★ 71 75 76 79 81 82 83 84 85
  Little-known neighbour of RAUENTHAL. Top v'yds.: Langen-
  berg, Wildsau. Grosslage: Steinmächer.

Matuschka-Greiffenclau, Graf Erwein
  Owner of the ancient SCHLOSS VOLLRADS estate. President of the
  VdP and CHARTA associations.

Maximin Grünhaus M-S-R (Ruwer) w. ★★★★ 71 75 76 79 81 82 83 84
  Supreme RUWER estate of 80 acres at Mertesdorf.

Mennig M-S-R (Saar) w. ★★ 71 75 76 79 81 82 83 84
  Village between TRIER and the SAAR. Its Falkensteiner v'yd. is
  more famous than the village (Nieder-Obermennig).

Mertesdorf See MAXIMIN GRÜNHAUS

Mittelheim Rhg. w. ★★→ ★★★ 71 75 76 79 81 82 83 84 85
  Minor village between WINKEL and OESTRICH. Top grower:
  WEGELER-DEINHARD. Grosslage: Honigberg.

Mittelhaardt
  The north-central and best part of RHEINPFALZ, incl. FORST,
  DEIDESHEIM RUPPERTSBERG, WACHENHEIM, etc., largely plan-
  ted with RIESLING.

Mittelmosel
  The central and best part of the Mosel, incl. BERNKASTEL,
  PIESPORT, etc. Its best sites are entirely RIESLING.

Mittelrhein
  Northern Rhine area of secondary importance, incl.
  BACHARACH. Some attractive RIESLINGS, esp. in 1983, 1985.

Morio Muskat
  Stridently aromatic grape variety popular in RHEINPFALZ.

Moselblümchen
  The "LIEBFRAUMILCH" of the Mosel, but on a lower quality
  level: mostly TAFELWEIN, seldom QbA.

Mosel-Saar-Ruwer
  31,000-acre region between TRIER and KOBLENZ. Includes
  MITTELMOSEL, SAAR, RUWER and lesser areas.

Müller, Felix
  Fine small SAAR estate with delicate SCHARZHOFBERGER, now
  run by VON KESSELSTATT.

Müller zu Scharzhof, Egon See Egon Müller

Müller-Thurgau
  Fruity, usually low-acid grape variety; the commonest in
  RHEINPFALZ and RHEINHESSEN, but increasingly planted in all
  areas, including the Mosel; there generally to the detriment of
  quality.

Mumm, von
  173-acre estate in JOHANNISBERG, RUDESHEIM, etc. Under the
  same control as SCHLOSS JOHANNISBERG.

Munster Nahe w. ★→★★★ 71 75 76 79 81 82 83 84 85
  Best village of northern NAHE, with fine delicate wines. Top
  grower: State Domain. Grosslage: Schlosskapelle.

Nackenheim Rhh. w. ★→ ★★★ 75 76 79 81 82 83 85
  Neighbour of NIERSTEIN; best wines (Engelsberg, Rothenberg)
  similar. Grosslagen: Spiegelberg (★★★), Gutes Domtal (★).

Nahe

Tributary of the Rhine and high quality wine region. Balanced, fresh and clean but full-flavoured wines, the best are RIESLING. Two Bereiche: KREUZNACH and SCHLOSS BÖCKELHEIM.

Neef M-S-R w. ↦→ ★★ 71 75 76 *81 83 84 85*

Village of lower Mosel with one fine v'yd.: Frauenberg.

Neipperg, Graf

71-acre top WÜRTTEMBERG estate at Schwaigern, esp. known for red wines and TRAMINER.

Nell, von (Weingut Thiergarten).

40-acre family estate at TRIER and AYL, etc.

Neumagen-Dhron M-M w. ★★→★★★ 71 75 76 79 81 82 83 84 85

Neighbours of PIESPORT. Top v'yd.: Hofberger. Grosslage: Michelsberg.

Neustadt

Central city of RHEINPFALZ, with a famous wine school.

Niederhausen Na. w. ★★→★★★★ 71 75 76 79 81 82 83 84 85

Neighbour of SCHLOSS BÖCKELHEIM and H.Q. of the Nahe State Domain. Wines of grace and power. Top v'yds. incl. Hermannshöhle, Steinberg. Grosslage: Burgweg.

Niedermennig See MENNIG

Niederwalluf See WALLUF

Nierstein (Bereich)

Large e. RHEINHESSEN district of very mixed quality.

Nierstein Rhh. w. ★→★★★ 71 75 76 79 81 82 83 84 85

Famous but treacherous name. 1,300 acres incl. superb v'yds.: Hipping, Ölberg, Pettenthal, etc., and their Grosslagen Rehbach, Spiegelberg, Auflangen: ripe, racy wines. But beware Grosslage Gutes Domtal: no guarantee of anything.

GERMANY'S QUALITY LEVELS

The range of qualities in ascending order is

1) Deutscher Tafelwein; sweetish light wine of no special character.
2) Landwein: dryish Tafelwein with some regional style.
3) Qualitätswein: dry or sweetish wine with sugar added to increase the strength but tested for quality and with distinct local and grape character.
4) Kabinettwein: dry or dryish natural (unsugared wine) of distinct personality and distinguishing lightness – can be very fine.
5) Spätlese: stronger, often sweeter than Kabinett. Full bodied.
6) Auslese: sweeter, sometimes stronger than Spätlese, often with honey-like flavours, intense and long.
7) Beerenauslese: very sweet and usually strong, intense, can be superb.
8) Trockenbeerenauslese: intensely sweet and aromatic.
9) Eiswein: (Beeren- or Trockenbeerenauslese) concentrated, sharpish and very sweet. Extraordinary and everlasting.

Nobling

New grape variety giving light fresh wine in BADEN, esp. Markgräflerland.

Norheim Nahe w. ★→★★★ 71 75 76 79 81 82 83 84 85

Neighbour of NIEDERHAUSEN. Top v'yds.: Klosterberg, Kafels, Kirschheck. Grosslage: Burgweg.

Oberemmel M-S-R (Saar) w. ★★→★★★ 71 75 76 79 81 82 83 84 85

Next village to WILTINGEN. Very fine wines from Rosenberg, Hütte, etc. Grosslage: Scharzberg.

Obermosel (Bereich)

District name for the upper Mosel above TRIER. Generally uninspiring wines from the Elbling grape.

Ockfen M-S-R (Saar) w. ★★→★★★ 71 75 76 79 81 82 83 84 85

200-acre village with superb fragrant austere wines. Top v'yds.: Bockstein, Herrenberg. Grosslage: Scharzberg.

Oechsle

Scale for sugar-content of grape-juice (see page 19).

Oestrich Rhg. w. ★★→★★★ 71 75 76 *81* 82 83 *84* 85

Big village; variable but capable of splendid Riesling Ausleses. V'yds. incl. Doosberg, Lenchen, Klosterberg. Grosslage: Gottesthal.

Oppenheim Rhh. w. ★→★★★★ 71 75 76 79 81 82 83 *84* 85

Town s. of NIERSTEIN with a 13th-century cathedral. Best wines (Kreuz, Sackträger) similar. Grosslagen: Guldenmorgen (★★★) Krötenbrunnen (★).

Ortenau (Bereich)

District just s. of Baden-Baden. Good KLINGELBERGER and RULÄNDER. SPÄTBURGUNDER (not so good) is a speciality. Best village DURBACH.

Palatinate English for RHEINPFALZ.

Perlwein Semi-sparkling wine.

Pfalz See RHEINPFALZ

Pieroth

Major wine-sales company; also has vineyard holdings.

Piesport M-M w. ★★→★★★★ 71 75 76 79 81 82 83 *84* 85

Tiny village with famous amphitheatre of vines giving (at best) glorious gentle fruity RIESLINGS. Top v'yds.: Goldtröpfchen, Falkenberg. Treppchen is on flatter land and inferior. Grosslage: Michelsberg (much planted with MÜLLER-THURGAU).

Plettenberg, von

Fine 100-acre Nahe estate at BAD KREUZNACH.

Pokalwein Wine by the glass. A pokal is a big glass.

Portugieser

Second-rate red-wine grape now often used for WEISSHERBST.

Prädikat

Special attributes or qualities. See QmP.

Prüfungsnummer

The official identifying test-number of a quality wine.

Prüm, J. J.

Superlative 34-acre Mosel estate in WEHLEN, GRAACH, BERNKASTEL. Delicate, long-lived wines, esp. in W. Sonnenuhr.

Prüm, S. A., Erben

Small separate part of the Prüm family estate making fine Wehleners, etc.

Qualitätswein bestimmter Anbaugebiete (QbA)

The middle quality of German wine, with added sugar but strictly controlled as to grape areas, etc.

Qualitätswein mit Prädikat (QmP)

Top category, incl. all wines ripe enough to be unsugared, from KABINETT to TROCKENBEERENAUSLESE.

Randersacker Franc. w. ★★→★★★ 76 79 81 82 *83 84*

Leading village for distinctive dry wine. Top v'yds. incl. Teufelskeller. Grosslage: Ewig Leben.

Rauenthal Rhg. w. |★★★| →★★★★ 71 75 76 79 81 82 83 *84* 85

Supreme village for spicy complex wine. Top v'yds. incl. Baiken, Gehrn, Wulfen. Grosslage: Steinmacher. The State Domain is an important grower.

Rautenstrauch Erben

Owners of the Karthäuserhof, EITELSBACH.

Reh, Franz & Sohn

Thriving wine-merchant at Leiwen (Mosel) with two small estates.

Ress, Balthasar

RHEINGAU grower with 50 acres of good land, cellars in HATTENHEIM. Also runs SCHLOSS REICHARTSHAUSEN. Fine fresh wines; highly original artists' labels.

Rheinart Erben

26-acre SAAR estate known for its OCKFENER BOCKSTEIN. Owned by H. SCHMITT SÖHNE.

Rheinburgengau (Bereich)

District name for the v'yds. of the MITTELRHEIN round the famous Rhine gorge. Moderate quality only.

Rheingau

The best v'yd. region of the Rhine, near Wiesbaden. 7,000 acres. Classic, substantial but subtle RIESLING. Bereich name, for the whole region, JOHANNISBERG.

Rheinhessen

Vast region (62,000 acres of v'yds.) between Mainz and Worms, bordered by the river NAHE, most second-rate, but incl. top wines from NIERSTEIN, OPPENHEIM, etc.

Rheinpfalz

Almost as vast 56,000-acre v'yd. region s. of Rheinhessen. (See MITTELHAARDT and SÜDLICHE WEINSTRASSE.) This and the last are the chief sources of LIEBFRAUMILCH. Grapes ripen to relatively high degrees. The great classics are rich wines but TROCKEN and HALBTROCKEN are increasingly fashionable.

Rhodt

Village of SÜDLICHE WEINSTRASSE with well-known co-operative. Agreeable fruity wines. Grosslage: Ordensgut.

Richter, Max Ferd, Weingut

37-acre MITTELMOSEL family estate based at Müllheim. Fine barrel-aged RIESLINGS from WEHLEN, GRAACH, BRAUNEBERG (Juffer), Mülheim (Helenenkloster).

Rieslaner

Cross between SILVANER and RIESLING; has made fine Auslesen in FRANKEN.

Riesling

The best German grape: fine, fragrant, fruity, long-lived.

Roseewein

Rosé wine made of red grapes fermentated without their skins.

Rotenfelser See TRAISEN.

Rotwein Red wine.

Rüdesheim Rhg. w. ★★→★★★★ 71 75 76 79 81 82 83 84 85

Rhine resort with 650 acres of excellent v'yds.; the three best called Berg. ... Full-bodied wines, fine-flavoured. Grosslage: Burgweg.

Rüdesheimer Rosengarten

Rüdesheim is also the name of a NAHE village near BAD KREUZNACH. Do not be misled by the ubiquitous blend going by this name. It has nothing to do with Rheingau RÜDESHEIM.

Ruländer

The PINOT GRIS: grape giving soft, full-bodied wine, alias Grauburgunder. Best in BADEN.

Ruppertsberg Rhpf. w. ★★→★★★ 75 76 79 81 82 83 84 85

Southern village of MITTELHAARDT. Top v'yds. incl. Hoheburg. Reiterpfad, Linsenbüsch. Grosslage: Hofstück.

Ruwer

Tributary of Mosel near TRIER. Very fine delicate wines. Villages incl. EITELSBACH, MERTESDORF, KASEL.

Saar Tributary of Mosel s. of RUWER. Brilliant austere "steely" RIESLINGS. Villages incl. WILTINGEN (SCHARZHOFBERG) AYL, OCKFEN, SERRIG. Grosslage: Scharzberg.

Saar-Ruwer (Bereich)

District incl. the two above.

Salem, Schloss

190-acre estate of Margrave of Baden on L. Constance in s. Germany. MÜLLER-THURGAU and WEISSHERBST.

St. Ursula

Well-known merchants at BINGEN; owners of VILLA SACHSEN.

Scharzberg

Grosslage name of WILTINGEN and neighbours.

Scharzhofberg Saar w. **★★★★** 71 75 76 79 *81* 82 83 *84* 85

Superlative 30-acre SAAR v'yd.: austerely beautiful wines, the perfection of RIESLING. Do not confuse with the last entry. Top estate: EGON MÜLLER.

Schaumwein Sparkling wine.

Scheurebe

Fruity aromatic grape of good quality used in RHEINHESSEN and RHEINPFALZ.

Schillerwein

Light red or rosé QbA, speciality of WÜRTTEMBERG (only).

Schlossböckelheim Nahe w. **★★→★★★★** 71 75 76 79 81 82 83 *84* 85

Village with the best NAHE v'yds., incl. Kupfergrübe, Felsenberg. Firm yet delicate wine. Grosslage: Burgweg.

Schloss Böckelheim (Bereich)

District name for the whole southern NAHE.

Schloss Groenesteyn

Fine Rheingau estate (80 acres) in Kiedrich and Rüdesheim, owned by Baron von Ritter zu Groenesteyn.

Schloss Johannisberg Rhg. w. **★★★→★★★★** 76 79 *81* 82 83 *84* 85

Famous RHEINGAU estate of 86 acres belonging to the Oetke family and now run in conjunction with VON MUMM. Polished, elegant wine.

Schloss Reichartshausen

10-acre formerly Cistercian estate at HATTENHEIM run by RESS.

Schloss Reinhartshausen

Fine 165-acre estate in ERBACH, HATTENHEIM, etc. much improved since 1976.

Schloss Vollrads Rhg. w. **★★★→★★★★** 71 75 76 79 *81* 82 83 85

Great estate at WINKEL, since 1300. 116 acres producing classical RHEINGAU RIESLING, esp. since 1977. TROCKEN and HALB-TROCKEN wines a speciality. The owner, Graf Matuschka-Greiffenclau, leads the "German wine with food" campaign.

Schmitt, Gustav Adolf

Merchant house with fine old 250-acre family estate at NIER-STEIN.

Schmitt, Franz Karl Even older 74-acre ditto.

Schmitt H., Söhne

One of the largest merchant-houses of the Mosel, at LONGUICH, also with three small estates.

Schönborn, Schloss

One of the biggest and best Rheingau estates, based at HATTENHEIM. Full-flavoured wines, at best excellent. Also very good SEKT.

Schoppenwein Café wine: i.e. wine by the glass.

Schorlemer, Freiherr von

Important MOSEL estate of 116 acres in 5 parts, based at LIESER, known for crisp, delicate wines.

Schubert, von Owner of MAXIMIN GRÜNHAUS.

Schweigen Rhpf. w. **★→** **★★** 76 81 82 83 *84* 85

Southernmost Rheinpfalz village with important cooperative, Deutsches WEINTOR. Grosslage: Guttenberg.

Sekt

German (QbA) sparkling wine, best when RIESLING is on the label.

Senfter, Reinhold

One of the best growers in NIERSTEIN, with 32 acres. Best v'yds: Niersteiner Hipping and Oppenheimer Sackträger.

Serrig M-S-R (Saar) w. **★★→★★★** 71 75 76 79 *81* 82 83 *84* 85

Village known for "steely" wine, excellent in hot years. Top growers: VEREINIGTE HOSPITIEN and State Domain. Grosslage: Scharzberg.

Sichel H., Söhne

Famous wine-merchants of London and Mainz with new KELLEREI in Alzey, Rhh.

Silvaner

The third most-planted German white grape, best in FRANKEN and the KAISERSTUHL.

Simmern, Langwerth von

Top 120-acre family estate at ELTVILLE. Famous v'yds: Mannberg, MARCOBRUNN, Baiken etc. Some of the very best, most typical RHEINGAU RIESLINGS.

Sonnenuhr

"Sun-dial." Name of several v'yds., esp. the famous one at WEHLEN.

Spätburgunder

PINOT NOIR: the best red-wine grape in Germany esp. in BADEN and WÜRTEMBERG.

Spätlese

"Late gathered." One better (stronger/sweeter) than KABINETT. Wines to age *at least* three years. Dry spätleses can be v. fine.

Spindler, Wilhelm

Fine 33-acre family estate at FORST, Rheinpfalz.

Staatliche Hofkeller

The Bavarian State Domain. 287 acres of finest FRANKEN v'yds with spectacular cellars under the great baroque Residenz at WÜRZBURG.

Staatsweingut (or Staatliche Weinbaudomäne)

The State wine estate or domain.

Staufenberg, Schloss

69-acre DURBACH estate of the Margrave of Baden. Fine "Klingelberger" (RIESLING).

Steigerwald (Bereich)

District name for eastern part of FRANKEN.

Steinberg Rhg. w. ★★★→★★★★ 71 75 76 79 81 82 83 84 85

Famous 79-acre v'yd. at HATTENHEIM walled by Cistercians 700 yrs. ago. Now property of the State Domain, ELTVILLE.

Steinwein

Wine from WÜRZBURG's best v'yd., Stein. In the past the term was loosely used for all Franconian wine.

Stuttgart

Chief city of WÜRTTEMBERG, producer of some pleasant wines (esp. Riesling), recently beginning to be exported.

Südliche Weinstrasse (Bereich)

District name for the s. RHEINPFALZ. Quality has improved tremendously in the last 20 years.

Tafelwein

"Table wine." The vin ordinaire of Germany. Mostly blended with other EEC wines. But DEUTSCHER TAFELWEIN must come from Germany alone. (See also LANDWEIN.)

Thanisch, Weingut Wwe. Dr. H

32-acre BERNKASTEL family estate of top quality, incl. part of Doctor v'yd.

Traben-Trarbach M M w. ★★ 76 79 81 82 83 84 85

Secondary wine-town, some good light wines. Top v'yds. incl. Würzgarten, Schlossberg. Grosslage: Schwarzlay.

Traisen Na. w. ★★★ 71 75 76 79 81 82 83 84 85

Small village incl. superlative Bastei and Rotenfels v'yds, making RIESLINGS of great concentration and class.

Traminer See GEWÜRZTRAMINER

Trier M-S-R w. ★★→★★★

Important wine city of Roman origin, on the Mosel, adjacent to RUWER, now incl. AVELSBACH and EITELSBACH. Grosslage: Römerlay.

Trittenheim M-M w. ★★ →★★★   71 75 76 79 81 82 83 84 85
    Attractive light wines. Top v'yds. Apotheke, Altärchen, Gross-
    lage: Michelsberg.

Trocken
    Dry. On labels Trocken *alone* means with a statutory maximum
    of unfermented sugar (9 grams per litre). But see next entry. See
    also HALBTROCKEN.

Trockenbeerenauslese
    The sweetest and most expensive category of wine, extremely
    rare, made from selected withered grapes. See also EDELFÄULE.

Trollinger
    Common red grape of WÜRTTEMBERG: locally very popular.

Ungstein Rhpf. w. ★★→ ★★★   71 75 76 79 81 82 83 84 85
    MITTELHAARDT village with fine harmonious wines. Top v'yd.
    Herrenberg. Top growers Fuhrmann (Weingut Pfeffingen),
    Fitz-Ritter, BASSERMANN-JORDAN. Grosslage: Honigsäckel.

Urzig M-M w. ★★★   71 75 76 79 81 82 83 84
    Village famous for lively spicy wine. Top v'yd.: Würzgarten.
    Grosslage: Schwarzlay.

VdP
    The Deutscher Prädikats – und Qualitätsweinguter, an associa-
    tion of premium growers.

Vereinigte Hospitien
    "United Hospitals." Ancient charity at Trier with large holdings
    in SERRIG, WILTINGEN, TRIER, PIESPORT, etc.

Verwaltung Administration (of property/estate etc).

Villa Sachsen
    67-acre BINGEN estate belonging to ST. URSULA Weingut.

Wachenheim Rhpf. w. ★★★ →★★★★ 71 75 76 79 81 82 83 84 85
    840 acres, incl. exceptionally fine Rieslings. V'yds. incl. Gerüm-
    pel, Böhlig, Rechbächel. Top grower: BÜRKLIN-WOLF. Gros-
    slagen: Schenkenbohl, Schnepfenflug, Mariengarten.

Waldrach M-S-R (Ruwer) w. ★★ 75 76 79 81 82 83 84 85
    Some charming light wines. Grosslage: Römerlay.

Walluf Rhg. w. ★★ 75 76 79 81 82 83 84 85
    Neighbour of ELTVILLE; formerly Nieder- and Ober-Walluf.
    Good but not top wines. Grosslage: Steinmächer.

Walporzheim Ahrtal (Bereich)
    District name for the whole AHR valley.

Wawern M-S-R (Saar) w. ★★→★★★ 71 75 76 79 81 82 83 84 85
    Small village with fine RIESLINGS. Grosslage: Scharzberg.

Wegeler-Deinhard
    136-acre RHEINGAU estate. V'yds. in OESTRICH, MITTELHEIM,
    WINKEL, GEISENHEIM, RÜDESHEIM, etc. Consistent quality;
    classic AUSLESES, finest EISWEIN. Also 67 acres in MITTELMOSEL,
    incl. major part of BERNKASTELER DOCTOR (GRAACH, WEHLEN
    etc.) and 46 acres in MITTELHAARDT (FORST, DEIDESHEIM,
    RUPPERTSBERG).

Wehlen M-M w. ★★★ →★★★★ 71 75 76 79 81 82 83 84 85
    Neighbour of BERNKASTEL with equally fine, somewhat richer,
    wine. Best v'yd.: Sonnenuhr. Top growers: Prüm family.
    Grosslage: Münzlay.

Weil, Dr.
    Fine 46-acre private estate at KIEDRICH. Currently below top
    form.

Weinbaugebiet A named TAFELWEIN area, e.g. Rhein, Mosel.

Weingut
    Wine estate. Can only be used on the label by estates that grow all
    their own grapes.

Weinkellerei
    Wine cellars or winery. See Keller.

Weinstrasse

"Wine road." Scenic route through v'yds. Germany has several, the most famous the Deutsche Weinstrasse in RHEINPFALZ.

Weintor, Deutsches   See SCHWEIGEN

Weissherbst

Rosé of QbA standard or above, even occasionally BEEREN-AUSLESE, the speciality of BADEN, WÜRTTEMBERG, and RHEIN-PFALZ. Currently v. popular in Germany.

Werner, Domdechant

Fine 33-acre family estate on the best slopes of HOCHHEIM.

Wiltingen   Saar w. **→**** 71 75 76 79 81 82 83 85

The centre of the Saar. 790 acres. Beautiful subtle austere wine. Top v'yds. incl. SCHARZHOFBERG, Braune Kupp, Braunfels, Klosterberg. Grosslage (for the whole Saar): Scharzberg.

Winkel   Rhg. w. ***→**** 71 75 76 79 81 82 83 84 85

Village famous for fragrant wine, incl. SCH. VOLLRADS. V'yds. incl. Hasensprung, Jesuitengarten. Grosslagen: Honigberg and Erntebringer.

Winningen   M-S-R. w. **

Village of lower Mosel near Koblenz with some fine delicate RIESLING. Best v'yds: Uhlen, Röttgen.

Wintrich   M-M w. **→*** 71 75 76 79 81 82 83 84 85

Neighbour of PIESPORT; similar wines. Top v'yds.: Grosser Herrgott, Ohligsberg, Sonnenseite. Grosslage: Kurfürstlay.

Winzergenossenschaft

Wine-growers' cooperative, usually making good and reasonably priced wine.

Winzerverein   The same as the last.

Wirsching, Hans

Well-known estate in IPHOFEN, FRANKEN. Robust, full-bodied wines. 100 acres in top v'yds: Julius-Echter-Berg, Kalb etc.

Wonnegau (Bereich)   District name for s. RHEINHESSEN.

Worms   Rhh. w. **

City with the famous LIEBFRAUENSTIFT v'yd.

Württemberg

Vast s. area little known for wine outside Germany. Some good RIESLINGS, esp. from Neckar valley. Also TROLLINGER.

Würzburg   Frank. **→**** 71 75 76 79 81 82 83 84 85

Great baroque city on the Main, centre of Franconian (FRAN-KEN) wine: fine, full-bodied and dry. Top v'yds.: Stein, Leiste, Schlossberg. No Grosslage. See also MAINDREIECK.

ZBW (Zentralkellerei Badischer Winzergenossenschaften)

Germany's (and Europe's) biggest ultra-modern co-operative, at Breisach, BADEN, with 25,000 grower-members with 12,000 acres, producing 80 percent of Baden's wine at all quality levels.

Zell   M-S-R w. *→** 75 76 79 81 82 83 84 85

The best-known lower Mosel village, esp. for its Grosslage name Schwarze Katz ("Black Cat"). RIESLING on steep slate gives aromatic light wines.

Zell (Bereich)

District name for the whole lower Mosel from Zell to Koblenz.

Zeltingen-Rachtig   M-M w. ** →**** 71 75 76 79 81 83 84 85

Important Mosel village next to WEHLEN. Typically lively crisp RIESLING. Top v'yds.: Sonnenuhr, Schlossberg. Grosslage: Münzlay.

Zentralkellerei Mosel-Saar-Ruwer

The biggest coop of the MOSEL, incl. Saar-Winzer-Verein at Wiltingen. Its 5,200 members produces 25% of all M-S-R wines.

Zwierlein, Freiherr von

55-acre family estate in Giesenheim. 100% Riesling. Best v'yds: Rothenberg, Kläuserweg.

Spain & Portugal

Map of Spain & Portugal showing regions: Galicia (Gal), Asturias, Basque Provinces, Guipúzcoa (Gui), Navarra (Nav), Catalonia (Ca), Santiago de Compostela, León, Burgos, Old Castile (O. Cas), Rioja, Aragon (Ara), Barcelona, Minho (M'o), Douro, Tras-os-Montes (Tras-os-m), SPAIN, Tarragona, Porto (Port), Beira Littoral (Bei. Lit), Beira Alta (B'a al), Madrid, R. Tagus, Estremadura (Est'a), Extremadura (Ext), New Castile (N.Cas), Valencia, PORTUGAL, Lisbon, Alto Alentejo (Alen), Valdepeñas, Levante (Lev), Alicante, Algarve (Alg), Cordoba, Seville, R. Guadalquivir, Sherry, Granada, Jerez, Andalucia (And), Cadiz, Malaga, Bilbao, R. Ebro

Abbreviations of regional names shown in bold type are used in the text.

The following addition abbreviations are used in the Spanish section (see box p. 122):
R'a.A.   Rioja Alta
R'a.Al. Rioja Alavesa
Res.   Reserva
g.   see Vino generoso

With the rarest exceptions the very finest wines of Spain and Portugal are respectively sherry and port and Maderia, which have a section to themselves on pages 128–133.

Spain's table wines have hitherto fallen into two distinct quality ranges; the fair to fine wines of Rioja, Catalonia and scattered northern regions, and the very middling bulk wines of the centre, south and east. Both categories are becoming steadily more interesting. Technical improvements, including earlier picking, are raising standards in former backwaters.

Rainy north-west Spain and northern Portugal make similar fresh and slightly fizzy wines. Central Portugal has an excellent climate for wines like full-bodied Bordeaux.

The old and outdated Portuguese system of controlled appellation is being progressively overhauled. Small areas of dwindling interest are being supplemented with promising new "determinate areas". The Spanish system dates from the post-war era and, although much amended in recent years, is still for the moment over-optimistic, delimiting some areas of purely domestic interest.

The listing here includes the best and most interesting types and regions of each country, whether legally delimited or not. Geographical references (see map) are to the traditional division of Spain into the old kingdoms, and the major provinces of Portugal.

Spain

A.G.E., Bodegas Unidas R'a.A. r. (p.) w. dr. or sw. res. ★→★★ 73 74 75 78 80 81 82

Large bodega making a wide range of wines, of which the best are the red Siglo Saco and Marqués de Romeral.

Agronavarra S.A. Nav. r. w. dr. ★★

A marketing organization shipping a range of Navarra wines, inc. a flowery new-style white and a fruity red "Agramont".

Alavesas, Bodegas R'a. Al. r. (w. dr.) res. ★★→★★★ 68 70 73 74 75 76 78 80 82

The pale orange-red SOLAR DE SAMANIEGO is one of the most delicate of the soft, fast-maturing Alavesa wines.

Albariño del Palacio Gal. w. dr. ★★

Flowery and pétillant young wine from FEFIÑANES near Cambados, made with the Albariño grape, the best of the region.

Alella Cat. r. (p.) w. dr. or sw. ★★

Small demarcated region just n. of Barcelona. Makes pleasantly fresh and fruity wines. (See MARFIL and MARQUÉS DE ALELLA.)

Alicante Lev. r. (w.) ★

Demarcated region. Its wines tend to be "earthy", high in alcohol and heavy.

Almansa Lev. r. ★

Demarcated region w. of ALICANTE, with similar wines.

Aloque N. Cas. r. ★ D.Y.A.

A light (though not in alcohol) variety of VALDEPEÑAS, made by fermenting together red and white grapes.

Almendralejo Ext. r. w. ★

Commercial wine centre of the Extremadura. Much of its produce is distilled to make the spirit for fortifying sherry.

Alvear, S.A. And. g. ★★★

The largest producer of excellent sherry-like apéritif and dessert wines from MONTILLA-MORILES.

Ampurdán See PERELADA

Año 4° Año (or Años) means 4 years old when bottled.

Banda Azul R'a.A. r. ★★ 75 76 80 81

Big-selling wine from BODEGAS PATERNINA, S.A..

Barceló S.A. And. br. ★★→★★★

One of the best-known makers of dessert Málaga.

Berberana, Bodegas R'a.A. r. (w. dr.) res. ★→★★★ 73 74 75 76 78 80 82

Best are the fruity, full-bodied reds: the 3° año Carta de Plata, the 5° año Carta de Oro and the smooth velvety reservas.

Beronia, Bodegas R'a.A. r. w. dr. res. ★★→★★★ 73 75 77 78 80 81 82 83

A small new bodega making excellent reds in the traditional oaky style. Their unaged "Beron" is very attractive.

Bilbainas, Bodegas R'a.A. r. (p.) w. dr. sw. or sp. res. ★★ →★★★ 66 69 70 72 73 75 76 78

Large bodega in HARO, making a wide range of reliable wines, including Viña Pomal, Pomal Junior, Viña Zaco, Vendimia Especial Reserves and "Royal Carlton" by the champagne method.

Blanco White.

Bodega

1. a wineshop: 2. a concern occupied in the making, blending and/or shipping of wine.

Campanas, Las See VINICOLA NAVARRA.

Campo Neuvo Nav. r. p. w. dr. ★

Worthwhile bodega for NAVARRA wines.

Campo Viejo, Bodegas R'a.A. r. (w. dr.) res. ★ →★★★ 64 70 71 73 76 78 79 81 82

Branch of Savin S.A., one of Spain's largest wine companies. Makes the popular 2° año San Asensio and some big, fruity red reservas esp. Marqués de Villamagna.

Cañamero Ext. w. ★
> Remote village near Guadalupe whose wines grow FLOR and acquire a sherry-like taste.

Caralt, Cavas Conde de Cat. sp. r. w. res. ★★ 78 80 81 82
> "CAVA" sparkling wines from SAN SADURNÍ DE NOYA; also pleasant still wines.

Cariñena Ara. r. (p.w.) ★
> Demarcated region and large-scale supplier of strong wine for everyday drinking, now being invigorated (and enlightened) by modern technology.

Casar de Valdaigo O.Cas. r. w. dr. ★★
> Producer in El Bierzo, n. of LEÓN, with a light, very dry clarete of fair quality.

Castillo Ygay See MARQUÉS DE MURRIETA.

Cava
> 1. an establishment making sparkling wines by the champagne method; 2. a Spanish name for such wines.

Cenicero Wine township in the RIOJA ALTA.

Cepa Wine or grape variety.

Chacolí Gui. (r.) w. ★
> Alarmingly sharp pétillant young wine from the Basque coast, containing only 9% to 11% alcohol.

Chaves, Bodegas Gal. w. dr. ★★→★★★ 81 82 84 (D.Y.A.)
> Small family firm making a good and fragrant, though slightly acidic, ALBARIÑO; perhaps the best Galician wine exported.

Chivite, Bodegas Julián Nav. r. (p.) w. dr. or sw. res. ★★ 82 83
> Largest of the firms in Navarra, producing full-bodied, fruity red wines and a flowery, well-balanced white.

Clarete
> Term frowned upon by the EEC describing light red wine (occasionally dark rosé).

Codorníu, S.A. Cat. sp. ★★★
> One of the two largest and best known of the firms in SAN SADURNÍ DE NOYA making good wines by the champagne method. Non Plus Ultra is matured, Ana de Codorníu a fresher style.

Compañía Vinícola del Norte de España (C.V.N.E.) R'a.A. r. (p.) w. dr. or sw. res. ★★→★★★ 66 70 73 74 75 76 78 80 81 82
> The 3° año is among the best of young red Riojas and Monopole one of the best slightly oaky whites. Excellent red Imperial and Viña Real reservas. C.V.N.E. is pronounced "Coonay."

Consejo Regulador
> Official organization for the defence, control and promotion of a DENOMINACIÓN DE ORIGEN.

Contino R'a. Al. r. res. ★★★ 74 75 76 78
> Superior single-vineyard red wine made by a subsidiary of COMPAÑIA VINICOLA DEL NORTE DE ESPAÑA.

Cosecha Crop or vintage.

Criado y embotellado por . . .
> Grown and bottled by . . .

Crianza
> Literally, "nursing", the ageing of wine. New or unaged wine is "sin crianza". Crianza wines are at least 2 years old, with one year in oak.

Cumbrero See MONTECILLO, BODEGAS

Domecq, S.A. R'a. Al. r. (w. dr.) res. ★★→★★★ 73 74 76 78 79 80
> Best of the wines from this Riojan outpost of Pedro Domecq is the fruity red Domecq Domain, exceptional in '76.

Denominación de origen
> Officially regulated wine region. (See introduction, p. 116.)

Dulce Sweet.

Elaborado y añejado por . . . Made and aged by . . .

El Coto, Bodegas   R'a. Al. r. (w. dr.) res. ★★→★★★ **73 76 78** 80 82

    Best-known for light, soft red wines labelled as El Coto and Coto de Imaz.

Espumoso   Sparkling.

Faustino Martinez, S.A.   R'a. Al. r. w. dr. (p.) res.   **★★**   →★★★ **64 70 73 74 75 76 78**

    Good red wines and the dry, light, fruity new-style white Faustino V. Gran Reserva is Faustino I. Do not be put off by the repellent bottles.

Ferrer, José L.   Mallorca r. res. ★★

    His wines, made in Binisalem, are the only ones of any distinction from Mallorca.

Flor

    A wine yeast peculiar to sherry and certain other wines that oxidize slowly and tastily under its influence.

Franco–Españolas, Bodegas   R'a.A. r. w. dr. or sw. res. ★→★★ **64 68 70 73 74 75 76 78 79** 82 83

    Reliable wines from LOGROÑO. Bordón is a fruity red. The semi-sweet white Diamante is a favourite in Spain.

Freixenet, S.A., Cavas   Cat. sp.   **★★→★★★**

    Cava, rivalling Codorníu in size through new acquisitions, making a range of good sparkling wines by the champagne method. Paul Cheneau is a low-price brand.

Gaseoso

    A cheap sparkler made by pumping carbon dioxide into wine.

Gonzalez y Dubosc, S.A., Cavas   Cat. sp.   **★★**

    A branch of the sherry giant Gonzales Byass. Pleasant sparkling wines exported as "Jean Perico".

Gran Vas

    Pressurized tanks (*cuves closes*) for making inexpensive sparkling wines; also used to describe this type of wine.

Green Wines

    There are objections from the EEC and the Portuguese to the use of this harmless English translation of VINHOS VERDES.

Gurpegui, Bodegas   R'a. B. r. (p. w. dr.) res. ★→★★ **70 73 75 78** 80 81

    Large family firm making some of the best wines from the RIOJA BAJA, labelled as Berceo. They incl. a fresh rosé.

Haro   The wine centre of the RIOJA ALTA.

Huelva   And. r. w. br. ★→★★

    Demarcated region w. of Cadiz. White table wines and sherry-like *generosos*, formerly sent to JEREZ for blending.

Irache, S.L.   Nav. r. p. (w. dr.) res. ★★ **64 70 73 78** 81 82

    Well-known bodega with substantial exports.

Jean Perico   See GONZALEZ Y DUBOSC

Jerez de la Frontera

    The capital city of sherry. (See p. 128).

Jumilla   Lev. r. ★ (w. dr. p.) ★

    Demarcated region in the mountains north of MURCIA. Its full-bodied wines (sometimes approaching 18% of alcohol) are now being lightened by earlier harvesting and better wine-making.

Labastida, Cooperativa Vinícola de   R'a.Al. r. res. ★★→   **★★★**   **66 70 75 78** 82

    Very drinkable Manuel Quintano, fruity, well-balanced Montebuena, Gastrijo and Castillo Labastida reservas and gran reservas, and a fresh dry white of real character.

La Granja Remelluri   R'a. Al. r. res. ★★★ **74 76 79** 80

    Since it was founded in 1970 this small firm has been making good red Riojas by traditional methods.

Laguardia

    Picturesque walled town at the centre of the wine-growing district of LA RIOJA ALAVESA.

Lagunilla, Bodegas   R'a.A. r. ★★ 73 75 78 81

Modern firm owned by the British Grand Met. Co. Easy oaky light reds incl. Viña Herminia and Gran Reserva.

Lan, Bodegas   R'a.A.r. (p.w.) res. ★★→★★★ 73 75 78 82

A huge new bodega, lavishly equipped and making aromatic red Riojas, including the good Lancorta and fresh white Lan Blanco.

La Rioja Alta, Bodegas   R'a.A. r. (p.) w. dr. (or sw.) res. ★★→★★★ 64 68 70 73 76 78 80

Excellent wines, esp. the red 3° año Viña Alberdi, the velvety 5° año Ardanza, the lighter 6° año Araña, the splendid Reserva 904 and dry white Metropol Extra (*not* D.Y.A.).

León   O.Cas. r. p. w. ★→★★ 78

Northern region becoming better known. Its wines, particularly those from the unfortunately named V.I.L.E. (e.g. the young Coyanza and Don Suero reserva), are fruity, dry and refreshing.

León, S.A., Jean   Cat. r. w. dr. res ★★★ 77 78 79 80

Tiny firm owned by a Los Angeles restaurateur and making a good white CHARDONNAY and deep, full-bodied CABERNET SAUVIGNON wines that repay long bottle-ageing.

Logroño   Principal town of the RIOJA region.

López de Heredia, S.A.   R'a.A. r. (p.) w. dr. or sw. res. ★★→ ★★★★ 68 70 73 75 76 77 78 79

Old established bodega in HARO with typical and good dry red Viña Tondonia of 6° año or more. Its wines are exceptionally long-lasting, and the Tondonia whites are also impressive.

Los Llanos   N.Cas, r. (p. w. dr.) res. ★★ 75 78

One of the few VALDEPEÑAS bodegas to age wine in oak. Señorio de Los Llanos Gran Reserva is remarkably scented and silky.

Majorca   No wine of interest except from José FERRER.

Málaga   And. br. sw. ★★→★★★

Demarcated region around the city of Málaga. At their best, its dessert wines yield nothing to tawny port.

Mancha   N.Cas. r. w. ★

Large demarcated region n. and n.e. of VALDEPEÑAS. Mainly white wines, lacking the lively freshness of the best Valdepeñas, but showing signs of improvement.

RIOJA VINTAGES

Thanks to a more consistent climate and the blending of a proportion of wine from better vintages in poor years, Riojas do not vary to the same extent as the red wines from Bordeaux and Burgundy. With few exceptions the '72 and '77 vintages were a disaster, owing to high rainfall and the onset of rot and oidium. Of other recent years, the best were: 52 55 58 64 66 68 70 73 76 78 80 81 82 and 83. (Those in bold type were outstanding.)

Riojas are put on the market when they are ready to drink. The best reservas of the best vintages, however, have very long lives and improve with more bottle age. Certain '64s, for example, are still improving.

Marfil   Cat. r. (p.) w. ★★

Brand name of Alella Vinicola (Bodegas Cooperativas), best known of the producers in ALELLA. Means "ivory".

Marqués de Alella   Cat. w. dr. (sp.) ★★→★★★ 83 84 (D.Y.A.)

Small bodega making light and fragrant white Alella wines by modern methods. Also a little CAVA by the champagne method.

Marqués de Cáceres, Bodegas   R'a.A. r. p. w. dr. res. ★★→★★★ 70 71 73 75 76 78 80 81

Good red Riojas of various ages made by French methods of Cenicero (R'a.A.) grapes and also a surprisingly light and fragrant white (D.Y.A.).

Marqués de Griñon O. Cas. (r.) w. dr. ★★ 82

The Marqués has recently begun making refreshing white wine in Rueda from the Verdejo grape. Also a very promising Cabernet Sauvignon from nr. Toledo.

Marqués de Monistrol, Bodegas Cat. w. r. (dr. or sw.) sp. res. ★★→★★★ 75 77

A family firm recently taken over by Martini & Rossi. Refreshing whites, esp. the Vin Nature, a good red reserva and an odd sweet red wine.

Marqués de Murrieta, S.A. R'a.A. r. p. w. dr. res. ★★→ ★★★★ 34 42 60 64 68 70 74 75 76 78 79 80 81

Highly reputed bodega near LOGROÑO making some of the best of all Riojas. Makes 4° año Etiqueta Blanca, superb red Castillo Ygay and an "old-style" oaky white, dry, fruity, and worth bottle-ageing.

Marqués de Riscal, S.A. R'a.Al. r. (p. and w. dr.) res. ★★→★★★★ 64 65 68 71 73 75 76 78 80 81 82

The best-known bodega of the RIOJA ALAVESA. Its red wines are relatively light and dry. Old vintages are very fine.

Marqués de Romeral R'a.A. r. w. dr. ★★ 76

Everyday Romeral and Gran Reserva are both v.g. values.

Martinez-Bujanda R'a.Al. r. w. dr. res ★★★ 73 75 80 83

Refounded (1985) family-run Rioja bodega, remarkably equipped. Excellent wines, incl. fruity SIN CRIANZA as well as reservas.

Mascaró, Cavas Cat. sp. (w. dr. r.) ★★→ ★★★

Maker of some of the best Spanish brandy, good sparkling wine and a refreshing dry white Viña Franca.

Masía Bach Cat. r. p. w. dr. or sw. res. ★★ →★★★ 70 74 78

Extrísimo Bach from near SANSADURNÍDE NOYA is a luscious and oaky sweet white wine. Also good full-bodied red reserva.

Méntrida N.Cas. r. w. ★

Demarcated region w. of Madrid, supplying everyday red wine.

Monopole

See COMPANIA VINICOLA DEL NORTE DE ESPAÑA.

Montánchez Ext. r. g. ★

Village near Mérida, interesting because its red wines grow FLOR yeast like FINO sherry.

Montecillo, Bodegas R'a.A. r. w. (p.) res. ★★ 73 75 76 78 80 81

"State of the art" Rioja bodega owned by Osborne (see Sherry). Red and fresh, dry white Cumbrero are currently among the best of the 3° año wines. Viña Monty is the worthy Reserva.

Montecristo, Bodegas ★★

Well-known brand of MONTILLA-MORILES wines.

Monterrey Gal. r. ★

Region near the n. border of Portugal, making strong wines like those of VERIN.

Montilla-Moriles And. g. ★★★

Demarcated region near Cordoba. Its crisp, sherry-like FINO and AMONTILLADO contain 14% to 17.5% natural alcohol and remain unfortified and singularly toothsome.

Morenito, Bodegas N.Cas. r. (p. w. dr.) res. ★★ 78 79

Old Valdepeñas bodega ageing its best reds in oak.

Muga, Bodegas R'a.A. r. (w.) res. (sp.) ★★★ 70 73 75 76 78 80

Small family firm in HARO, making some of the best red Rioja now available by strictly traditional methods in oak. Its wines are light but intensely aromatic, with long complex finish. The best is Prado Enea. Whites not so good.

Navarra Nav. r. p. (w.) ★→ ★★

Demarcated region; mainly fresh and fruity rosés and sturdy red wines, but some reservas up to Rioja standards. See AGRO-NAVARRA, CHIVITE, etc.

Olarra, Bodegas R'a.A.r. (w. p.) res. ★★→★★★ 73 75 76 78 80 81

A new and vast bodega near LOGROÑO, one of the show-pieces of RIOJA, making good red and white wines and excellent Cerro Añon reservas. Since '81, Añares is the top reserva.

Palacio de Arganza O. Cas. r. p. w. dr. res. ★★→★★★ 65 70 74 76 79

Best-known bodega in El Bierzo between LEÓN and GALICIA. White Vega Burbia; red Almeña del Bierzo.

Palacio de Fefiñanes Gal. w. res. ★★★

Best of all the ALBARIÑO wines, though without pétillance, since it is aged in oak for 2–6 yrs.

Paternina, S.A., Bodegas R'a.A.r. (p.) w.dr.orsw.res. ★→★★★ 28 59 67 68 71 73 75 76 78 79 80 81

Bodega at Ollauri and a household name esp. for Banda Azul red (currently 81) and Banda Dorada white. Its best wines are the red Viña Vial (now 80) and the magnificent older reservas.

Pazo Gal. r. p. w. dr. ★ D.Y.A.

Brand name of the co-operative at RIBEIRO, making wines akin to Portuguese VINHOS VERDES. The rasping red is the local favourite. The pleasant slightly fizzy white is safer.

Peñafiel O.Cas. r. and w. dr. res. ★★ 76

Village on the R. Duero near Valladolid. Best wines are fruity reds from the Cooperativa de Ribero del Duero, including the outstanding 5° año PROTOS.

RIOJA'S CHARACTERISTIC STYLE

To the Spanish palate the taste of luxury in wine is essentially the taste of oak. Oak contains vanillin, the taste of vanilla. Hence the characteristic vanilla flavour of all mature Spanish table wines of high quality — exemplified by the reservas of Rioja (red and white).

Historically the reason for long oak-ageing was to stabilize the best wines while their simple fruity flavours developed into something more complex and characteristically winey. Fashion has swung (perhaps too far) against the oaky flavour of old Rioja whites. But the marriage of ripe fruit and oak in red Rioja is still highly appreciated.

Penedès Cat. r. w. dr. sp. ★→★★★

Demarcated region including Vilafranca del Penedès, SAN SADURNÍ DE NOYA and SITGES. See also TORRES.

Perelada Cat. (r. p.) w. sp. ★★

In the demarcated region of Ampurdán on the Costa Brava. Best known for sparkling wines made both by the champagne and tank or *cuve close* system.

Priorato Cat. br. dr. r. ★★

Demarcated region, an enclave in that of TARRAGONA, known for its alcoholic "rancio" wines and also for almost black full-bodied reds, often used for blending. Lighter blended Priorato is a good carafe wine in Barcelona restaurants.

Protos See PEÑAFIEL

Raimat Cat. r. w. p. ★→★★

Intriguing, well-made wines from old v'yds. near Lérida, recently replanted by CODORNÍU with Cabernet, Chardonnay and other foreign vines.

René Barbier Cat. r. w. dr. res. ★★ 73 80

Part of the FREXINET group known for fresh white Kraliner and red R.B. Reservas.

Reserva

Good-quality wine matured for long periods. Red reservas must spend at least 1 year in cask and 2 in bottle; Gran Reservas 2 in cask and 3 in bottle.

Ribeiro Gal. r. (p.) w. dr. ★→★★

> Demarcated region on the n. border of Portugal making wines
> similar to Portuguese VINHO VERDE – and others.

Rioja O.Cas. r. p. w. sp. esp. **64 66 68 70 73 75 76 78** 80 81 82 83

This upland region along the R. Ebro in the n. of Spain
produces most of the country's best table wines in some 50
BODEGAS DE EXPORTACIÓN. It is sub-divided into:

Rioja Alavesa

North of the R. Ebro, the R'a.Al. produces fine red wines,
mostly light in body and colour.

Rioja Alta

South of the R. Ebro and w. of LOGROÑO, the R'a.A. grows
most of the finest red and white wines; also some rosé.

Rioja Baja

Stretching e. from LOGROÑO, the Rioja Baja makes coarser
red wines, high in alcohol and often used for blending.

Riojanas, Bodegas R'a.A r. (w. p.) res. ★★→★★★ **34 42 56 64 66 68
70 73 74 75 76** 78 81 82

> One of the older bodegas, making a good traditional Viña Albina.
> Monte Real reservas are big, mellow, above average.

Rioja Santiago, S.A. R'a.A. r. (w. dr. or sw. p.) res. ★→★★★ 78

> Bodega at HARO with well-known wines. The flavour sometimes
> suffers from pasteurization, and appropriately, as it now belongs
> to Pepsi-Cola, it makes the biggest-selling bottled SANGRÍA. Top
> reds: Condal and Gran Enologica.

Rosado Rosé.

Rueda O.Cas. br. w. dr. ★→★★

> Small demarcated area w. of Valladolid. Traditional producer of
> flor-growing sherry-like wines up to 17° of alcohol, now making
> fresh young whites including that of the MARQUÉS DE RISCAL.

Salceda, S.A., Bodegas Viña R'a.Al. r. res. ★★→★★★ **73 75 78** 80 81

> Makes fruity, well-balanced red wines.

Sangre de Toro

> Brand name for a rich-flavoured red wine from TORRES S.A.

Sangría

> Cold red wine cup with citrus fruit, water, ice and brandy.

Sanlúcar de Barrameda

> Centre of the Manzanilla district. (See Sherry p. 128.)

San Sadurní de Noya Cat. sp. ★★→★★★

> Town s. of Barcelona, hollow with cellars where dozens of firms
> produce sparkling wine ("Cava") by the champagne method.
> Standards are high, even if the ultimate finesse is lacking.

Sarría, Señorío de Nav. r. (p. w. dr.) res. ★★→★★★ **74 75 76 78** 82 84

> The vineyards and model winery near Pamplona produces wines
> up to (high) RIOJA standards.

Scholtz, Hermanos, S.A. And. br. ★★→ ★★★

> Makers of the best MÁLAGA, including a good, dry 10-year-old
> amontillado. Best is the dessert Solera Scholtz 1885.

Seco Dry.

Segura Viudas, Cavas Cat. sp. ★★→ ★★★

> Producers of some of the best CAVA of PENEDÈS.

Siglo Popular sack-wrapped RIOJA brand of Bodegas A.G.E.

Sin Crianza See Crianza.

Sitges Cat. w. sw. ★★

> Coastal resort s. of Barcelona noted formerly for sweet dessert
> wine made from Moscatel and MALVASIA grapes.

Tarragona Cat. r. w. dr. or sw. br. ★→★★★

> 1. Table wines from the demarcated region; of little note. 2.
> Dessert wines from the firm of de Muller, comparable with good
> cream sherries or Málaga. 3. The town makes vermouth and
> Chartreuse and exports cheap blended wine.

Tierra de Medina O.Cas. w. ★→★★

Area w. of Valladolid. Includes La Nava and RUEDA.

Tinto Red.

Toro O.Cas. r. ★→★★

Town, 150 miles n.w. of Madrid, and its powerful (to 16°) wine. Leading producer Bodegas Mateos. His 3° año is good.

Torremilanos O. Cas. r. res. ★★ 76 79 81 82 83

Label of Bodegas López Peñalba, a small family firm near Aranda de Duero making good red wines from the Tinta Fina grape.

Torres, Bodegas Cat. r. w. dr. or semi-sw. p. res. ★★→★★★★ 76 71 73 74 75 76 77 78 79 80 81 82

Distinguished family firm making the best wines of PENEDÈS, esp. flowery white Viña Sol and Gran Viña Sol, semi-dry aromatic Esmeralda, Waltraud RIESLING, red Tres Torres and Gran Sangredetoro, beautiful Gran Coronas (Cabernet) reservas, and Santa Digna (alias Viña Magdala) from Pinot Noir. The family now also has vineyards in Chile.

Utiel-Requeña Lev. r. (w.) p.

Demarcated region w. of Valencia. Apart from sturdy reds and chewy vino de doble pasta for blending, it makes some deliciously light and fragrant rosé.

Valbuena O.Cas. r. ★★★ 75 76 77 78 79 80

Made with the same grapes as VEGA SICILIA but sold as 3° año or 5° año. Some prefer it to its elder brother.

Valdeorras Gal. r. w. dr. ★→★★

Demarcated region e. of Orense. Dry and refreshing wines.

Valdepeñas N.Cas. r. (w.) ★→ ★★

Demarcated region near the border of Andalucia. Its mainly red wines, though high in alcohol, are sometimes surprisingly light in flavour. Some superior wine is now being matured in oak.

Valencia Lev. r. w. ★

Demarcated region producing earthy high-strength wine.

Vega Sicilia O.Cas. r. res. ★★★★ 41 48 53 59 61 64 66 67 69 72 73

One of the very best Spanish wines, full-bodied, fruity and almost impossible to find. Contains up to 16% alcohol. VALBUENA is the same wine with less time in oak (78 80).

Vendimia Vintage.

Verín Gal. r. ★

Town near n. border of Portugal. Its wines are the strongest from Galicia, without a bubble, and up to 14% alcohol.

Vicente, Suso y Pérez, S.A. Ara. r. ★★

A bodega s. of Sarragossa producing superior CARIÑENA.

Viña

Literally, a vineyard. But wines such as Tondonia (LOPEZ DE HEREDIA) or Zaco (BILBAINAS) are not necessarily made with grapes exclusively from the vineyard named.

Vinícola de Castilla N.Cas. r. p. w. dr. ★

One of the largest firms in LA MANCHA, marketing its wines under the labels of "Castillo de Manza" and Gran Verdad.

Vino Blanco

White wine.

Vino comun/corriente Ordinary wine.

clarete Light red wine.

dulce Sweet wine.

espumoso Sparkling wine.

generoso Apéritif or dessert wine rich in alcohol.

rancio Maderized (brown) white wine.

rosado Rosé wine.

seco Dry wine.

tinto Red wine.

verde Wine akin to Portuguese VINHO VERDE.

Yecla Lev. r. w. ★

Demarcated region n. of Murcia. Its cooperative, "La Purisima", is said to be Spain's biggest. Its wines, once heavy-weight bruisers, have been lightened for export.

Ygay See MARQUÉS DE MURRIETA

Portugal

For Port and Madeira see pages 128 to 133.

Adega A cellar or winery.

Alentejo Alen. r. ★→★★

Vast and long-neglected area s. of the R. Tagus, now being developed as a wine region, chiefly for red wine.

Algarve Alg. r. w. ★

Newly demarcated region in the holiday area. It wines are nothing to write home about.

Aliança, Caves r. w. dr. sp. res. ★★→★★★

Large Bairrada-based firm, making sparkling wine by the champagne method and a variety of reds and whites, including good Bairrada wines and mature DÃOS. Tinta Velha is the largest-selling red in Portugal.

Amarante

Sub-region in the VINHOS VERDES area. Rather heavier and stronger wines than those from farther n.

Aveleda Douro dr. ★★ D.Y.A.

A first-class "GREEN WINE" made on the Aveleda estate of the Guedes family. Sold dry in Portugal but a little sweetened for export.

Bacalhoa, Quinta de Est'a. r. res. ★★★ 81 82

American-owned estate near Setúbal, whose excellent Cabernet Sauvignon wine is vinified by J. M. DA FONSECA.

Bairrada Bei. Lit. r. w. dr. and sp. ★→ ★★

Newly demarcated region supplying much of Oporto's (often good) carafe wine and some excellent red GARRAFEIRAS. Also good-quality sparkling wines by the champagne method.

Barca Velha ("Ferreirinha") Trás-os-m. r. res. ★★★★ 57 64 65 66 78

Perhaps Portugal's best red, made in very limited quantity by the port firm of Ferreira. Powerful and fine with deep bouquet.

Barrocão, Cavas do Bei. Lit. r. w. dr. res. ★→ ★★★

Based in the BAIRRADA, the firm blends good red DÃOS and makes first-rate old Bairrada garrafeiras, such as 60 and 64.

Basto A sub-region of the VINHOS VERDES area on the R. Tamego, producing more astringent red wine than white.

Borba Alen. r. ★

Small "determinate area" near Evora, making some of the best wine from the ALENTEJO.

Braga Sub-region of the VINHOS VERDES area, good for both red and white wines.

Buçaco B'a.Al. r. (p.) w. res. ★★★★ r. 51 53 57 58 60 63 67 70 72 75 77; w. 56 65 66 70 72 75

The legendary speciality of the luxury Buçaco hotel near Coimbra, not seen elsewhere. Incredible quality.

Bucelas Est'a. w. dr. ★★★ 79

Tiny demarcated region just n. of Lisbon. Caves Velhas make delicate, perfumed wines with 11% to 12% alcohol.

Camarate Est'a. r. ★★ 74 78 80

Reliable CLARETE from FONSECA at Azeitão, s. of Lisbon.

Carcavelos Est'a. br. sw. ★★★

Minute demarcated region w. of Lisbon. Its excellent sweet wines average 19% alcohol and are drunk cold as an apéritif or with dessert.

Cartaxo   Ribatejo r. w. ★
　　　A district in the Ribatejo n. of Lisbon, now a "determinate area" making everyday wines popular in the capital.

Casal García   Douro w. dr. ★★ D.Y.A.
　　　One of the biggest-selling "GREEN WINES" in Portugal, made by SOGRAPE.

Casal Mendes   M'o. w. dr. ★★ D.Y.A.
　　　The "GREEN WINE" from CAVES ALIANÇA.

Casaleiro
　　　Trade mark of Caves Dom Teodosio—João T. Barbosa, who make a variety of reliable wines: DÃO, VINHOS VERDES, etc.

Cepa Velha   M'o. (r.) w. dr.   ★★★
　　　Brand name of Vinhos de Monção, Lda. Their Alvarinho, from the grape of that name, is one of the best "GREEN WINES".

Clarete
　　　Light red wine.

Colares   Est'a. r. ★★★
　　　Small demarcated region on the coast w. of Lisbon. Its classical dark red wines, rich in tannin, are from vines which survived the phylloxera epidemic. Drink the oldest available.

Conde de Santar   B'a.al. r. (w. dr.) res.   ★★→★★★   70 73 78
　　　The only estate-grown DÃO, later matured and sold by Carvalho, Ribeiro & Ferreira. The reservas are fruity, full-bodied and exceptionally smooth.

Dão   B'a.al. r. w. res. ★→   ★★★
　　　Demarcated region round Viseu on the R. Mondego. Produces some of Portugal's best table wines: solid reds of some subtlety with age: substantial dry whites. All are sold under brand names.

Douro
　　　The northern river whose valley produces port and more than adequate (though undemarcated) table wines.

Evel   Trás-os-m. r.   ★→★★
　　　Reliable middle-weight red made near VILA REAL by Real Companhia Vinícola do Norte de Portugal. Ages well in bottle.

Faisca   Est'a. p. ★
　　　Sweet carbonated rosé from FONSECA INTERNACIONAL.

Fonseca, J. M. da   Est'a. r. w. dr. br. res.   ★→★★★
　　　Large, old-established family firm in Azeitão making a wide range of good wines, incl. the red Periquita, Pasmados and Camarate (formerly known as Palmela) and Terras Altas Dão, as well as the famous Moscatel de Setúbal.

Fonseca Internacional J.M. da   Est'a p. ★
　　　Formerly part of the last, now owned by Heublein Inc. Produces LANCERS rosé and FAISCA for the mass market.

Gaeiras   Est'a. r. ★★
　　　Dry, full-bodied and well-balanced red made in the neighbourhood of Óbidos.

Garrafeira
　　　The "private reserve" aged wine of a merchant; usually his best, though often of indeterminate origin.

Gatão   M'o. w. dr. ★★ D.Y.A.
　　　Reliable "GREEN WINE" from the firm of Borges & Irmão, fragrant but sometimes a little sweetened.

Gazala   M'o. w. dr. ★★ D.Y.A.
　　　A new VINHO VERDE made at Barcelos by Sogrape since the AVELEDA estate went to a different branch of the Guedes family.

Grão Vasco   B'a.al. r. w. res.   ★★→★★★   70 73 75 78 80
　　　One of the best brands of DÃO, blended and matured at Viseu by SOGRAPE. Fine red reservas; fresh young white (D.Y.A.).

Green Wine (Vinho verde)
>Wine made from barely ripe grapes and undergoing a special secondary fermentation, which leaves it with a slight sparkle. Ready for drinking in the spring after the harvest. It may be white or red. "Green wine" is not an official term.

Lagoa See ALGARVE.

Lagosta M'o. w. dr. ★★ D.Y.A.
>Well-known "GREEN WINE" from the Real Companhia Vinícola do Norte de Portugal.

Lancers Est'a. p. ★
>Sweet carbonated rosé extensively shipped to the USA by FONSECA INTERNACIONAL.

Lima Sub-region in the n. of the VINHOS VERDES area making mainly astringent red wines.

Madeira Island br. dr./sw. ★★→★★★★
>Producer of the famous apéritif and dessert wines. See pages 128 to 132.

Magrico M'o. w. dr. ★★ D.Y.A.
>At a time when many VINHOS VERDES are being slightly sweetened for export, this is a genuinely dry "GREEN WINE".

Mateus Rosé Trás-os-m. p. (w.) ★
>World's biggest-selling medium-sweet carbonated rosé, made by SOGRAPE at VILA REAL and Anadia in the BAIRRADA.

Monção
>Sub-region of the VINHOS VERDES area on R. Minho, producing the best of "GREEN WINES" from the ALVARINHO grape.

Moscatel de Setúbal Est'a. br. ★★★
>Small demarcated region s. of the R. Tagus, where J. M. DA FONSECA make an aromatic dessert muscat, 6 and 25 years old.

Palacio de Brejoeira M'o. (r.) w. dr. ★★★
>Outstanding estate-made "GREEN WINE" from MONÇÃO, with astonishing fragrant nose and full, fruity flavour.

Penafiel Sub-region in the s. of the VINHOS VERDES area.

Periquita Est'a. r. ★★ 71 74 77 78 80
>One of Portugal's more robust reds, made by J. M. DA FONSECA at Azeitão s. of Lisbon from a grape of that name.

Pinhel B'a.al. (r.). w. sp. ★
>Undemarcated region e. of the DÃO, making similar white wine, mostly processed into sparkling.

Ponte de Lima, cooperativa de M'o. r. ★★
>Maker of one of the best bone dry red VINHOS VERDES.

Quinta de S. Claudio M'o. w. dr. ★★★ D.Y.A.
>Estate at Esposende and maker of the best "GREEN WINE" outside MONÇÃO.

Quinta do Corval Trás-os-m. r. ★★
>Estate near Pinhão making good light CLARETES.

Raposeira B'a.al. sp. ★★
>One of the best-known Portuguese sparkling wines, made by the champagne method at Lamego. Ask for the *Bruto*.

Ribalonga, Vinícola B'a.al. r. res. ★★ 71 74 76 78
>Makers of a sound and very reasonably priced red Dão.

Rosado Fernandes, Viuva Alen. r. res. ★★ 71 75
>Small private firm, producing the most sophisticated of the full-bodied wines from the Alentejo and ageing them in oak.

Santola B'a.al. w. dr. ★★ D.Y.A.
>A refreshing dry "GREEN WINE" from Vinhos Messias.

São João, Caves Bei. Lit. r. w. dr. sp. res. ★★→★★★ 70 75 76
>One of the best firms in the BAIRRADA, known for its fruity and full-bodied red wines and Porto dos Cavaleiros DÃOS.

Serradayres Est'a. r. (w.) res. ★★ 78
>Blended Ribatejo table wines from Carvalho, Ribeiro & Ferreira, Lda. Sound and very drinkable.

Setúbal   See MOSCATEL.
Sogrape
> Sociedad Comercial dos Vinhos de Mesa de Portugal. Largest wine concern in the country, making VINHOS VERDES, DÃO, MATEUS ROSÉ, VILA REAL red, etc.

Terras Altas   B'a.al. r. w. res. ★★ 75 76 78 79 80 81
> Good DÃO wines made by J. M. DA FONSECA.

Vila Real   Trás-os-m. r. ★→ ★★
> Town in a new "determinate area" of the upper DOURO, now making some good red table wine.

Vinho branco   White wine.
> **consumo**   Ordinary wine.
>
> **doce**   Sweet wine.
>
> **espumante**   Sparkling wine.
>
> **garrafeira**   A reserve with long bottle age.
>
> **generoso**   Apéritif or dessert wine rich in alcohol.
>
> **maduro**   A normal, mature table wine — as opposed to a VINHO VERDE.
>
> **rosado**   Rosé wine.
>
> **seco**   Dry wine.
>
> **tinto**   Red wine.
>
> **verde**   See under Green Wines.

Vinhos Verdes   M'o. and Douro. r. ★ w. dr. ★→★★★
> Demarcated region between R. Douro and n. frontier with Spain, producing "GREEN WINES".

Sherry, Port & Madeira

The original, classical sherries of Spain, ports of Portugal and madeiras of Madeira are listed in the A–Z below. Their many imitators in South Africa, California, Australia, Cyprus, Argentina are not. References to them will be found under their respective countries.

The map on page 116 locates the port and sherry districts. Madeira is an island 400 miles out in the Atlantic from the coast of Morocco, a port of call for west-bound ships: hence its historical market in North America.

In this section most of the entries are shippers' names followed by a brief account of their wines. The names of wine-types are included in the alphabetical listing.

Almacenista
> Individual old unblended sherry; high-quality, usually dark dry wines for connoisseurs. Often superb quality and value.

Amontillado
> In general use means medium sherry; technically means a FINO which has been aged to become more powerful and pungent.

Amoroso
> Type of sw. sherry, not much different from a sweet OLOROSO.

Barbadillo, Antonio
> The largest SANLUCAR firm, with a range of 50-odd MANZANILLAS and sherries, incl. Sanlucar Fina, Solera Manzanilla Pasada, Eva Cream, etc. Also fresh young Castillo de San Diego table wines.

Barbeito
> Shippers of good-quality Madeira, including the driest and best apéritif Madeira, "Island Dry".

Bertola
> Sherry shippers best known for their Bertola Cream Sherry.

Blandy

Old family firm of Madeira shippers. Duke of Clarence Malmsey is their most famous wine. 10-y-o Malmsey v. popular.

Blazquez

Sherry bodega at JEREZ with outstanding FINO, "Carta Blanca", and "Carta Oro" amontillado "al natural" (unsweetened).

Brown sherry

British term for a style of dark sweet sherry.

Bual   One of the grapes of Madeira, making a soft smoky sweet wine, not as sweet as Malmsey.

Caballero

Sherry shippers best known for Gran Señor Choice Old Cream. Their best FINO is Don Guisa.

Calem   Old Portuguese house with a good reputation, owning the excellent Quinta da Foz. Vintages: **50 54 58 60 63** 70 **75** 77 78.

Cockburn

British-owned port shippers with a range of good wines incl. 20-y-o "Directors' Reserve". Fine vintage port from very high v'yds. can look deceptively light when young, but has great lasting power. Vintages: **55 60 63 67** 70 **75** 83.

Cossart Gordon

Leading firm of Madeira shippers founded 1745, best known for their "Good Company" range of wines but also producing old vintages and soleras (esp. Sercial Duo Centenary).

Cream sherry

A style of amber sweet sherry made by sweetening a blend of well-aged OLOROSOS.

Crofts   One of the oldest firms shipping vintage port: 300 years old in 1978. Bought early this century by Gilbey's. Well-balanced vintage wines last as long as any. Vintages: **55 60 63 66** 70 **75** 77, and lighter vintage wines under the name of their Quinta da Roeda in several other years ('80). Also now in the sherry business with Croft Original (PALE CREAM), Delicado (FINO).

Crusted

Term for a vintage-style port, but blended from several vintages not one, bottled young and aged in bottle, so forming a "crust" in the bottle. Needs decanting.

Cuvillo

Sherry bodega at Puerto de Santa Maria best known for their Cream, dry Oloroso Sangre y Trabajadero and Fino "C" and a fine Palo Cortado.

Delaforce

Port shippers owned by International Distillers and Vintners, particularly well known in Germany. "His Eminence" is an excellent tawny. "Vintage Character" is also good. Vintage wines are very fine, among the lighter kind: **55 58 60 63 66** 70 **75** 77. "Quinta da Corte" in 1980.

Diez-Merito S.A.

Fast-growing JEREZ firm specializing in "own-brand" sherries. Latest acquisition is Zoilo Ruiz Mateus, formerly part of the ill-fated Rumasa empire. Its own Fino Imperial and Olorose Victoria Regina are excellent. DON ZOILO wines are outstanding.

Domecq

Giant family-owned sherry bodegas at JEREZ. Double Century Original Oloroso is their biggest brand, La Ina their excellent FINO, Guitar a new pale cream. Other famous wines incl. Celebration Cream, Botaina (old amontillado) and Rio Viejo (dry oloroso). Now also in Rioja (p. 123).

Don Zoilo

Luxury sherry brand, incl. deep velvety FINO, sold by DIEZ-MERITO.

Dow

Old name used on the British market by the port shippers Silva & Cosens, well known for their relatively dry vintage wines, said to have a faint "cedarwood" character. Also v.g. "Vintage Character". Vintages: **55 57 58 60 63 66** 70 **75** 77 80.

Dry Sack   See Williams & Humbert

Duff Gordon

Sherry shippers best known for their El Cid AMONTILLADO. Owned by the big Spanish firm Bodegas Osborne.

Duke of Wellington

Luxury range of sherries from Bodegas Internacionales.

Eira Velha, Quinta da

Small port estate with old-style vintage wines shipped by HARVEY's of Bristol. Vintages: **72** 78 80.

Ferreira

The biggest Portuguese-owned port growers and shippers (since 1751); well-known for old tawnies and good, relatively light, vintages: **60 63 66** 70 **75** 77 80. Also Special Reserve, Donna Antonia and sublime tawny Duque de Braganza.

Findlater's

Old established London wine merchant shipping his own very successful brand of medium sherry: Dry Fly amontillado.

Fino

Term for the lightest and finest of sherries, completely dry, very pale and with great delicacy. Fino should always be drunk cool and fresh: it deteriorates rapidly once opened. TIO PEPE is the classic example.

Flor   The characteristic natural yeast which gives FINO sherry its unique flavour.

Fonseca

British-owned port shipper of high reputation. Robust, deeply coloured vintage wine, sometimes said to have a slight "burnt" flavour. Vintages: **55 60 63 66** 70 75 77. Also popular Vintage Character "Bin 27".

Garvey's

Famous old sherry shippers at JEREZ. Their finest wines are Fino San Patricio, Tio Guillermo Dry Amontillado and Ochavico Dry Oloroso. San Angelo Medium Amontillado is their most popular. Also Bicentenary Pale Cream.

Gonzalez Byass

Enormous concern shipping the world's most famous and one of the best sherries: Tio Pepe. Other brands incl. La Concha Medium Amontillado, Elegante Dry Fino, San Domingo Pale Cream, Nectar Cream and Alfonso Dry Oloroso.

Gould Campbell   See Smith Woodhouse.

Graham

Port shippers famous for one of the richest and sweetest of vintage ports, largely from their own Quinta Malvedos, also excellent brands, incl. Ruby, Late Bottled 10- and 20-year-old Tawny. Vintages: **55 58 60 63 66** 70 **75** 77 80.

Harvey's

World-famous Bristol shippers of Bristol Cream and Bristol Milk sweet sherries, Club Amontillado and Bristol Dry, which are medium. Luncheon Dry and Bristol Fino, which are dry, and excellent Palo Cortado.

Henriques & Henriques

Well-known Madeira shippers of Funchal. Their wide range includes a good dry apéritif wine: Ribeiro Seco.

Jerez de la Frontera

Centre of the sherry industry, between Cadiz and Seville in s. Spain. The word sherry is a corruption of the name, pronounced in Spanish "Hereth". In French, Xérès.

Late-bottled vintage

Port of a single good vintage kept in wood for twice as long as vintage port (about 5 years). Therefore lighter when bottled and ageing quicker. A real "L.B.V." will "throw a crust" like vintage port.

Leacock One of the oldest firms of Madeira shippers. Most famous wine is "Penny Black" Malmsey. 10-y-o Malmsey and 13-y-o Bual are excellent.

Lustau

The largest independent family-owned sherry bodega in JEREZ, making many wines for other shippers, but with a very good "Dry Lustau" range (particularly the OLOROSO) and "Jerez Lustau" PALO CORTADO.

Macharnudo

One of the best parts of the sherry v'yds., n. of Jerez, famous for wines of the highest quality, both FINO and OLOROSO.

Malmsey

The sweetest form of Madeira; dark amber, rich and honeyed yet with Madeira's unique sharp tang.

Manzanilla

Sherry, normally FINO, which has acquired a peculiar bracing salty character from being kept in bodegas at Sanlucar de Barrameda, on the Guadalquivir estuary near JEREZ.

Morgan A subsidiary of Croft port, best known in France.

Offley Forester

Port shippers and owners of the famous Quinta Boa Vista. Their vintage wines tend to be round, "fat" and sweet, good for relatively early drinking. Vintages: **55 60 62 63 66 67** 70 **72 75** 77 (an exception to the "early-drinking" rule).

Oloroso

Style of sherry, heavier and less brilliant than FINO when young, but maturing to greater richness and roundness. Naturally dry, but generally sweetened for sale, as CREAM.

Osborne

Brandy well known, but good sherries include Fino Quinta, Coquinero, dry AMONTILLADO, 10 R.S. Oloroso.

Pale Cream

Increasingly popular style of sherry made by sweetening FINO, pioneered by CROFTS.

Palo Cortado

A style of sherry close to OLOROSO but with some of the character of an AMONTILLADO. Dry but rich and soft. Not often seen.

Palomino & Vergara

Sherry shippers of JEREZ, best known for Palomino Cream, Medium and Dry. Best FINO: Tio Mateo.

Puerto de Santa Maria

The second city of the sherry area with a number of important bodegas.

P.X.

Short for Pedro Ximenez, the grape part-dried in the sun used in JEREZ for sweetening blends.

Quarles Harris

One of the oldest port houses, since 1680, now owned by the Symingtons (see WARRE). Vintages: **60** 63 66 70 **75** 77 80.

Quinta Portuguese for "estate".

Quinta do Noval

Great Portuguese port house making splendidly dark, rich and full-bodied vintage port; a few pre-phylloxera vines still at the Quinta make a small quantity of "Nacional"—very dark, full and slow-maturing wine. Vintages: **55 58 60 63 66** 70 **75** 78 82.

Rainwater A fairly light, not very sweet blend of Madeira—in fact of VERDELHO wine—traditionally popular in the USA and Canada.

Real Tesoro, Marques de
>One of the smaller family firms of JEREZ, with excellent MANZANILLA La Bailadora and a range of good sherries, esp. their AMONTILLADO.

Rebello Valente
>Name used for the vintage port of ROBERTSON. Their vintage wines are light but elegant and well-balanced, maturing rather early. Vintages: **55 60 63 66 67** 70 **75** 77.

La Riva
>Distinguished firm of sherry shippers making one of the best FINOS, Tres Palmas, among many good wines.

Robertson
>Subsidiary of SANDEMAN'S, shipping REBELLO VALENTE vintage port and Gamebird Tawny and Ruby.

Rozes Port shippers controlled by Moët-Hennessy. Tawny very popular in France; also Ruby and 77.

Ruby The youngest (and cheapest) style of port: very sweet and red. The best are vigorous and full of flavour. Others can be merely strong and rather thin.

Rutherford & Miles
>Madeira shippers with one of the best known of all Bual wines: Old Trinity House.

Saccone & Speed
>British sherry shippers owned by Courage's the Brewers. Popular Troubador and Cuesta ranges and a good Fino.

Sanchez Romate
>Family company founded in 1781. Best known in Spanish-speaking world esp. for their brandy, Cardinal Mendoza. Makes good sherry—Fino Cristal, Oloroso Dona Juana, Amontillado N.P.U.

Sandeman
>Giant of the port trade and a major figure in the sherry one owned by Seagrams. Founder's Reserve is their best-known tawny port; their vintage wines are robust—some of the old vintages were superlative [**55 58 60 63 66 67** 70 **75** 77 80 82]. Of the sherries, Medium Dry Amontillado is the best-seller, Don Fino is particularly good and a new range of wonderful old luxury sherries incl. Royal Ambrosante, Imperial Corregidor, Character Amoroso, etc.

Sanlucar Seaside sherry-town (see MANZANILLA).

Sercial Grape (reputedly a RIESLING) grown in Madeira to make the driest of the island's wines—a good apéritif.

Smith Woodhouse
>Port firm founded in 1784, now owned by the Symington family (see WARRE). GOULD CAMPBELL is a subsidiary. Wines incl. Old Priory Vintage Character, Old Lodge Tawny, 70 **75** 77 80 83.

Solera System used in making both sherry and Madeira, also some port. It consists of topping up progressively more mature barrels with slightly younger wine of the same sort: the object to attain continuity in the final wine. Most commercial sherries are blends of several solera wines.

Tarquinio Lomelino
>Madeira shippers famous for their collection of antique wines. Standard range is Dom Henriques; top range, "Lomelino".

Tawny A style of port aged for many years in wood (in contrast to vintage port, which is aged in bottle) until tawny in colour.

Taylor Perhaps the best port shippers, particularly for their full, rich, long-lived vintage wine and tawnies of stated age (40-year-old, 20-year-old, etc.). Their Quinta de Vargellas is said to give Taylor's its distinctive scent of violets. Vintages: **55 60** 63 **66** 70 75 77 80. Vargellas is shipped unblended in certain (lesser) vintages (**67 72**). Their L.B.V. is also better than most.

De Terry, Carlos y Javier
    Family-owned bodega at PUERTO DE SANTA MARIA with a good range of sherries.

Tio Pepe   The most famous of FINO sherries (see GONZALEZ BYASS).

Valdespino
    Famous family-owned bodega at JEREZ, owner of the Inocente v'yd., making the excellent FINO of the same name. Tio Diego is their splendid dry AMONTILLADO, Solera 1842 a ditto oloroso, Matador the name of their popular range.

Varela   Sherry shippers best known for their Varela Medium and Cream.

Verdelho   Madeira grape making fairly dry wine without the distinction of SERCIAL. A pleasant apéritif.

Vintage Port
    The best port of exceptional vintages is bottled after only 2 years in wood and matures very slowly, for up to 20 years or even more, in its bottle. It always leaves a heavy deposit and therefore needs decanting.

Vintage Character
    Somewhat misleading term used for a good-quality full and meaty port like a first-class RUBY made by the solera system. Lacks the splendid "nose" of vintage port.

Warre   Probably the oldest of all port shippers (since 1670), now owned by the Symington family. Fine long-maturing vintage wines, a good TAWNY, Nimrod and Vintage Character Warrior. Vintages: **55 58 60** 63 **66** 70 75 77 80.

White Port
    Port made of white grapes, golden in colour. Formerly made sweet, now more often dry: a good apéritif but a heavy one.

Williams & Humbert
    Famous and first-class sherry bodega. Dry Sack (medium AMONTILLADO) is their best-selling wine. Pando is an excellent FINO. Canasta Cream and Walnut Brown are good in their class. Dos Cortados is their famous PALO CORTADO.

THE STRENGTH OF WINE *The alcoholic strength of wine varies considerably. Alcohol provides much of the feeling of "body" in strong wines, but needs to be balanced by the flavouring elements: sugar, acidity, tannin and assorted "extract". Without this richness of flavour it would be fierce and unpleasant.*

Typical alcoholic strengths (% by volume), as found in a laboratory analysing commercial samples, are:

German Tafelwein 8–11   *German Kabinett* 8–9
German Auslese 10–10.5   *German Beerenauslese* 12.8–14
French vin de table 9–12   *Red Bordeaux* 10.5–13
Bordeaux cru class 1e 11–12   *Beaujolais-Villages* 10–10.5
Muscadet 12   *Alsace Riesling* 10.5–11.5
Chablis Premier Cru 10.5–12.7   *Beaune* 11–14   *Chambertin* 12.4
Châteauneuf-du-Pape 12.6 +   *Montrachet* 12.6
California Zinfandel 12–16   *California Chardonnay* 10.5–13.5
California Cabernet 11.44   *Australian Cabernet/Shiraz* 13.8
Barolo 12–14   *Chianti* 12–13   *Valpolicella* 11.7
Rioja reserva 12.5   *Sauternes* 12–15   *Château Yquem* 13.5–16
Fino sherry 18–20   *Oloroso sherry* 18–20   *Vintage port* 19–20

Central & South-east Europe

Weinviertel
Langenlois
Wachau • Vienna

Mátraal

Somló
Sopron • Budap

AUSTRIA
Burgenland
Graz •

HUNGARY

Styria
Balaton

Lutomer

Vilanyi-Pecs

Ljubljana •
Slovenia
Slavonia
Trieste
Zagreb •

Voivodin

Croatia

Bosnia-Herzegovina
YUGOSLAVIA

Dalmatia • Sarajevo
Split •

Montene

Dubrovnik •

Corf

The huge range of wines from the countries covered by this map offers some very good value for money, complete with off-the-beaten track characters which true wine-lovers will enjoy exploring. Quality is moderate to high, tending to improve, and reliability on the whole is excellent.

The references are arranged country by country, with all geographical references back to the map on this page.

Labelling in all the countries involved except Greece is based on the German, now international, pattern of place-name plus grape-variety. The main grape-varieties are therefore included alongside areas and other terms in the alphabetical listings. Quality ratings in this section are given where there is enough information to warrant it.

Austria

In 1985 the Austrian wine industry was crippled by a serious scandal, when diethylene glycol was found in wines claiming high natural sweetness, particularly from the Burgenland. Although nobody was poisoned, enormous damage was done to many innocent and well-run businesses. New legislation should now ensure that nothing of the kind happens again. Meanwhile, Austria offers (as it did before) very good value in fresh, fruity dry wines and succulent sweet ones.

Recent vintages:

1985	A small but excellent-quality harvest.
1984	Good wines for early drinking.
1983	Outstandingly ripe; many sweet wines though some are low in acidity.
1982	Early harvest of record size, fewer sweet wines.
1981	Small crop, quality high, esp. sweet wines.
1980	A difficult vintage, as in most of Europe.
1979	Reduced crop; excellent quality.

Apetlon Burgenland w. s./sw. or sw. ∗ → ⭐ **∗∗**
Village of the SEEWINKEL making tasty whites on sandy soil, incl. very good sweet wines.

Ausbruch
Term used for very sweet wines between Beerenauslese and Trockenbeerenauslese (see Germany) in richness.

Baden Vienna (r.) w. dr. or sw. ∗ → ∗∗∗
Town and area s. of VIENNA incl. GUMPOLDSKIRCHEN. Good lively high-flavoured wines, best from ROTGIPFLER and ZIERFÄNDLER grapes.

Blaufränkisch
The GAMAY grape.

Blue Danube
Popular GEWÜRZ/WÄLSCHRIESLING blend from LENZ MOSER.

Bouvier
Native Austrian grape giving soft but aromatic wine.

Burgenland Burgenland r. w. dr. sw. ∗ → ⭐ **∗∗∗**
Region on the Hungarian border with ideal conditions for sweet wines. "Noble rot" occurs regularly and Ausleses, Beerenausleses, etc., are abundant. (See Rust, etc.)

Dürnstein w. dr. sw. ∗∗ → ∗∗∗
Wine centre of the WACHAU with a famous ruined castle and important WINZERGENOSSENSCHAFT. Some of Austria's best whites, esp. Rheinriesling and GRÜNER VELTLINER.

Eisenstadt Burgenland (r.) w. dr. or sw. ∗∗ → ∗∗∗
Town in BURGENLAND and historic seat of the ESTERHAZYS.

Esterhazy
Noble and historic family whose AUSBRUCH and other BURGENLAND wines are of superlative quality.

Falkenstein See Weinviertel.

Grinzing Vienna w. ∗∗ D.Y.A.
Suburb of VIENNA with delicious lively HEURIGE wines.

Grüner Veltliner
Austria's most characteristic white grape (31% of her white v'yds.) making short-lived but marvellously spicy and flowery, racy and vital wine.

Gumpoldskirchen Vienna (r.) w. dr. or sw. ∗∗ → ∗∗∗
Pretty resort s. of VIENNA with wines of great character.

Heiligenkreuz, Stift

Cistercian Monastery at THALLERN making some of Austria's best wine, particularly from a fine steep v'yd.: Wiege.

Heurige

Means both new wine and the tavern where it is drunk.

Kahlenberg Vienna w. ★★

Village and v'yd. hill n. of VIENNA, famous for HEURIGEN.

Kamp Langenlois (r.) w. dr. or sw. ★→★★

Tributary of the Danube (Donau) giving its name to wines from its valley, n. and e. of the WACHAU, incl. pleasant Veltliner (see Grüner Veltliner) and RIESLING.

Klöch Steiermark (r.) p. w. ★→★★

The chief wine town of Styria, the s.e. province. No famous wines, but agreeable ones, esp. Traminer.

Klosterneuberg Danube r. w. ★→★★★

District just n. of VIENNA, with a famous monastery, which is a major producer, a wine college and a research station.

Krems Danube w. ★→★★★

Town and district just e. of the WACHAU with good GRÜNER VELTLINER and Rheinriesling (see Riesling) esp. from Austria's biggest WINZERGENOSSENSCHAFT.

Langenlois Langenlois r. w. ★→★★

Chief town of the KAMP valley with many modest and some good wines, esp. peppery GRÜNER VELTLINER and Rheinriesling (see Riesling). Reds less interesting.

Lenz Moser

Austria's best known and most progressive grower, invented a high vine system and makes good to excellent wine at Röhrendorf near KREMS, APETLON, MAILBERG and elsewhere.

Mailberg Weinviertel w. ★

Town of the WEINVIERTEL known for lively light wine, esp. LENZ MOSER's Malteser.

Morandell, Alois

Big-scale Viennese wine-merchant.

Mörbisch Burgenland r. w. dr. or sw. ★→★★★

Leading wine-village of BURGENLAND. Good sweet wines. Reds and dry whites not inspiring.

Müller-Thurgau

9% of all Austria's white grapes are Müller-Thurgau.

Muskat-Ottonel

The strain of muscat grape grown in e. Europe, incl. Austria.

Niederösterreich

Lower Austria: i.e. all the n.e. corner of the country.

Neuberger

Popular white grape: pleasant wine in KREMS/LANGENLOIS but soft and coarse in BURGENLAND.

Neusiedlersee

Shallow lake in sandy country on the Hungarian border, creating autumn mists and giving character to the sweet wines of BURGENLAND.

Nussdorf Vienna w. ★★

Suburb of VIENNA with well-known HEURIGEN.

Oggau Burgenland (r.) w. sw. ★★→★★★

One of the wine-centres of BURGENLAND, famous for Beerenausleses (see Germany) and AUSBRUCH.

Portugieser

With BLAUFRÄNKISCH, one of the two main red-wine grapes of Austria, giving dark but rather characterless wine.

Retz Weinviertel w. ★

Leading wine-centre of the WEINVIERTEL, known for pleasant GRÜNER VELTLINER, etc.

Ried Vineyard: when named it is usually a good one.

Riesling

German Riesling is always called Rheinriesling. "Riesling" is Wälschriesling.

Rotgipfler

Good and high-flavoured grape peculiar to BADEN and GUMPOLDSKIRCHEN. Used with ZIERFÄNDLER to make lively whites. Very heavy/sweet on its own.

Ruländer

The PINOT GRIS grape.

Rust Burgenland (r.) w. dr. or sw. ★→★★★

Most famous wine centre of BURGENLAND, long and justly famous for its AUSBRUCH, often made of mixed grapes.

St. Laurent

Traditional Austrian red grape, faintly muscat-flavoured.

Schilcher

Pleasant sharp rosé, speciality of STYRIA.

Schloss Grafenegg

Famous castle and estate of the Metternich family near KREMS. Good standard whites and excellent Ausleses.

Schluck

Name for the common white wine of the WACHAU, good when drunk very young. Also a good brand of GRÜNER VELTLINER from LENZ MOSER.

Seewinkel

"Sea corner": the sandy district around the NEUSIEDLERSEE.

Sepp Hold

Well-known BURGENLAND grower and merchant.

Siegendorf, Klosterkeller

First-class private BURGENLAND wine estate.

Sievering Vienna w. ★★

Suburb of VIENNA with notable HEURIGEN.

Spätrot Another name for ZIERFÄNDLER.

Spitzenwein

Top wines—as opposed to TISCHWEIN: ordinary table wines.

Steiermark (Styria)

Province in the s.e., not remarkable for wine but well-supplied with it.

Stift

The word for a monastery. Monasteries have been, and still are, very important in Austria's wine-making, combining tradition and high standards with modern resources.

Thallern Vienna (r.) w. dr. or sw. ★★→★★★

Village near GUMPOLDSKIRCHEN and trade-name of wines from Stift HEILIGENKREUZ.

Tischwein

Everyday wine, as opposed to SPITZENWEIN.

Traiskirchen Vienna (r.) w. ★★

Village near GUMPOLDSKIRCHEN with similar wine.

Veltliner

See Grüner Veltliner

Vöslau Baden r. (w.) ★

Spa town s. of BADEN (and WIEN) known for its reds made of PORTUGIESER and BLAUFRÄNKISCH: refreshing but no more.

Wachau

District on the n. bank of the Danube round DÜRNSTEIN with cliff-like slopes giving some of Austria's best whites, esp. Rheinriesling (see Riesling) and GRÜNER VELTLINER.

Weinviertel

"The wine quarter": name given to the huge and productive district between VIENNA and the Czech border. Mainly light white wines. Now officially divided into Falkenstein – Matzen (east) and Retz (west).

Wien (Vienna)
>The capital city, with 1,800 acres of v'yds. in its suburbs to supply its cafés and HEURIGEN.

Winzergenossenschaft Growers' cooperative.

Zierfändler
>White grape of high flavour peculiar to the BADEN area. Used in a blend with ROTGIPFLER.

Hungary

The traditional and characteristic firmness and strength of character which can make Hungarian wine the most exciting of Eastern Europe are being modified by modern ideas. Average quality is still high; whites are lively and reds made to last, but much of the drama has gone—at least from the standard exported lines. Foreign buyers seem frightened of real character. Visitors to the country will find plenty of excellent wines in the old style. They are distinguished by numbered bottles – and higher prices.

Alföld
>Hungary's Great Plain, producer of much everyday wine. See also HAJÓS.

Aszu Word meaning "syrupy" applied to very sweet wines, esp. Tokay (TOKAJI), where the "aszu" is late-picked and "nobly rotten" as in Sauternes. (See p. 46.)

Aszu Eszencia Tokaji br. sw. ★★★★
>The lightest quality of Tokay commercially available: superb amber wine of Yquem-like quality.

Badacsony Balaton w. dr. sw. `★★→★★★`
>Famous 1,400 ft. hill on the n. shore of L. BALATON whose basalt soil can give rich high-flavoured wines, among Hungary's best.

Balatonfüred Balaton (r.) w. dr. sw. ★★
>Town on the n. shore of L. BALATON centre of the Balatonfüred-Csopak district. Good but softer, less fiery wines.

Balaton Balaton r. w. dr. sw. `★` →★★★
>Hungary's inland sea and Europe's largest lake. Many wines take its name and most are good. The ending "i" (e.g. Balatoni, Egri) is the equivalent of -er in Londoner.

Bikavér
>"Bull's Blood"—or words to that effect. The historic name of the best-selling red wine of EGER: full-bodied and well-balanced, but much less impressive than formerly.

Chardonnay
>Experiments with Chardonnay at BALATON show promise.

Csopak Village next to BALATONFÜRED, with similar wines.

Debrö Mátraalja w. sw. ★★★
>Important centre of the MÁTRAALYA famous for its pale, aromatic and sweet HÁRSLEVELÜ.

Eger Eger district r. w. dr. sw. ★→ `★★`
>Best-known red wine centre of n. Hungary; fine baroque city of cellars full of BIKAVÉR. Also delicate white LEANYKA and dark sweetish MÉDOC NOIR.

Eszencia
>The fabulous quintessence of Tokay (TOKAJI): intensely sweet grape-juice of very low, if any, alcoholic strength, reputed to have miraculous properties. Now almost unobtainable.

Ezerjó The grape grown at MÖR to make one of Hungary's best dry white wines: potentially distinguished, fragrant and fine.

Furmint

The classic grape of Tokay (TOKAJI), with great flavour and fire, also grown for table wine on L. BALATON, sometimes with excellent results.

Hajós   Alföld r.   ⭐

Village in s. Hungary becoming known as a centre for good CABERNET SAUVIGNON reds.

Hárslevelü

The "lime-leaved" grape used at DEBRÖ and as the second main grape of TOKAJI. Gentle sweet wine.

Kadarka

The commonest red grape of Hungary, grown in vast quantities for everyday wine on the plains in the s.; also used at EGER; capable of ample flavour and interesting maturity.

Kékfrankos

Hungarian for GAMAY, literally "blue French". Makes good light red at SOPRON on the Austrian border.

Kéknyelü

High-flavoured white grape making the best and "stiffest" wine of Mt. BADACSONY. It should be fiery and spicy stuff.

Leanyka

Old Hungarian white grape also grown in Transylvania. Makes admirable pale soft wine at EGER.

Mátraalya

Wine-district in the foothills of the Matra range in n. Hungary, incl. DEBRÖ, GYÖNGYÖS and NAGYREDE.

Mecsekalja

District in the foothills of the Mecsek range in s. Hungary, known for the good whites of PÉCS.

Médoc Noir

Grape apparently similar to MERLOT, used to make sweet red and in BIKAVER, at EGER.

Monimpex

The main Hungarian export company, with great cellars at Budafok, near Budapest.

Mór   North Hungary w. dr.   ★★★

Town in n. Hungary famous for its fresh dry EZERJÓ.

Muskotály

Hungarian muscat, used to add aroma to Tokay (TOKAJI) and occasionally alone at EGER, where its wine is long-lived and worth tasting.

Nagyburgundi

Literally "black burgundy" — the PINOT NOIR makes admirable wine in s. Hungary, esp. round VILÁNY.

Olaszriesling

The Hungarian name for the Italian, or Wälschriesling.

Pécs   Mecsek (r.) w. dr.   ⭐ → ★★

Town in the Mecsek hills known in the West for its agreeable well-balanced (if rather sweet) Riesling.

Puttonyos

The measure of sweetness in Tokay (TOKAJI). A 7-gal. container from which ASZU is added to SZAMORODNI. One "putt" makes it sweetish; 6 (the maximum) very sweet indeed.

Sauvignon Blanc

Recent results at BALATON have been impressive—with plenty of Hungarian vigour.

Siklos

Southern district known for its white wines.

Siller   Pale red or rosé. Usually made from KADARKA grapes.

Somló   North Hungary w. dr.   ★★★

Isolated small v'yd. district n. of BALATON making intense white wines of high repute from FURMINT and RIESLING.

Sopron West Hungary r. ★★

Little Hungarian enclave in Burgenland s. of the Neusiedlersee (see Austria) specializing in KÉKFRANKOS (Gamay) red.

Szamorodni

Word meaning "as it comes"; used to describe (TOKAJI) without ASZU grapes. Can be dry or (fairly) sweet.

Szürkebarát

Literally means "grey friar": Hungarian for PINOT GRIS, which makes rich heavy wine in the BALATON v'yds.

Szekszárdi Mecsek r. ★★

District in south-central Hungary. Dark strong red wine which needs age.

Tokaji (Tokay) Tokaji w. dr. sw. ★★ →★★★★

Hungary's famous strong sweet wine, comparable to an oxidized Sauternes, from hills in the n.e. close to the Soviet Union. See Aszu, Eszencia, Furmint, Puttonyos, Szamorodni.

Tramini The TRAMINER grape; increasingly grown in Hungary.

Vilány Siklos r. p. (w.) ★★

Southernmost town of Hungary and well-known centre of red wine production. Vilányi Burgundi is largely KÉKFRANKOS and rather good.

Wälschriesling

Austrian name sometimes used for Olasz (Italian) Riesling.

Zöldszilváni

"Green Sylvaner"—i.e. Sylvaner. Grown round L. BALATON.

Romania

The wine industry is orientated towards Russia as its biggest customer, and consequently specializes in the sweet wines that Russians like. Recent Soviet moves to discourage drinking threaten this trade. The need for foreign currency makes export to the West highly desirable, so the best qualities are available at subsidized prices. They include sound and good-value reds and whites, including dry ones, but at present nothing memorable.

Alba Iulia

Town in the TIRNAVE area in Transylvania, known for off-dry whites blended from Italian Riesling, FETEASCA and MUSKAT-OTTONEL.

Aligoté The junior white burgundy grape makes pleasantly fresh white wine in Romania.

Babeasca

Traditional red grape of the FOCSANI area: agreeably sharp wine tasting slightly of cloves.

Banat The plain on the border with Serbia. Workaday Riesling and light red CADARCA.

Cabernet

Increasingly grown in Romania, particularly at DEALUL MARE, to make dark intense wines, though locally sometimes too sweet for French-trained palates.

Cadarca

Romanian spelling of the Hungarian Kadarka.

Chardonnay

The great white burgundy grape is used at MURFATLAR to make honey-sweet dessert wine.

Cotesti

Part of the FOCSANI area making reds of PINOT NOIR, MERLOT, etc., and dry whites said to resemble Alsace wines.

Cotnari

Romania's most famous historical wine: light dessert wine from MOLDAVIA. Like very delicate Tokay.

Dealul Mare

Important up-to-date v'yd. area in the s.e. Carpathian foothills. Red wines from CABERNET, MERLOT, PINOT NOIR, etc.

Dobruja

Black Sea region round the port of Constanta. MURFATLAR is the main v'yd. area.

Dragaşani

Region on the River Olt south of the Carpathians, growing both traditional and "modern" grapes. Good MUSKAT-OTTONEL.

Feteasca

Romanian white grape of mild character, the same as Hungary's Leanyka (and some say Switzerland's Chasselas).

Focsani

Important eastern wine region including those of COTESTI, ODOBESTI and NICORESTI.

Grasa

A form of the Hungarian Furmint grape grown in Romania and used in, among other wines, COTNARI.

Mehana

Branded wines shipped to Britain, tending to sweetness.

Moldavia

The n.e. province, now largely within the USSR.

Murfatlar

Big modern v'yds. near the Black Sea specializing in sweet wines, incl. CHARDONNAY. Now also dry reds and whites.

Muskat-Ottonel

The e. European muscat, at its best in Romania.

Nicoresti

Eastern area of FOCSANI best known for its red BABEASCA.

Odobesti

The central part of FOCSANI; mainly white wines of FETEASCA, RIESLING, etc.

Perla The speciality of TÎRNAVE: a pleasant blended semi-sweet white of RIESLING, FETEASCA and MUSKAT-OTTONEL.

Pitesti

Principal town of the Arges region south of the Carpathians. Traditionally whites from FETEASCA, TAMIÎOASA, RIESLING.

Premiat

Reliable range of higher-quality wines for export.

Riesling

Italian Riesling. Very widely planted. No exceptional wines.

Sadova

Town in the SEGARCEA area exporting a rosé.

Segarcea

Southern wine area near the Danube. Exports rather sweet CABERNET.

Tamiîoasa A traditional white-wine grape variety of no very distinct character.

Tîrnave

Important Transylvanian wine region, known for its PERLA and MUSKAT-OTTONEL.

Trakia

Branded wines that are shipped to U.S.A. Well-balanced and successful.

Valea Calugareasca

"The Valley of the Monks", part of the DEALUL MARE v'yd. with a well-known research station. CABERNET, MERLOT and PINOT NOIR are generally made into heavy sweetish wines.

Yugoslavia

A well-established supplier of wines of international calibre if not generally exciting quality. Yugoslav "Riesling" was the pioneer, now followed by Cabernet, Pinot Blanc and Traminer, as well as such worthwhile specialities as Zilavka and Prokupac. All parts of the country except the central highlands make wine, almost entirely in giant cooperatives. Tourists on the Dalmatian coast will find more original products—all well worth trying. 1985 was a very good vintage.

Amselfelder
> German marketing name for the Red Burgundac (Spätburgunder or PINOT NOIR) wine of KOSOVO.

Babic Agreeable standard red of the Dalmatian coast, ages better than ordinary PLAVAČ.

Banat Sandy north-eastern area, partly in Romania, with up-to-date wineries making adequate RIESLING.

Beli Pinot The PINOT BLANC, a popular grape in SLOVENIA.

Bijelo White.

Blatina
> The red grape and wine of MOSTAR. Not in the same class as the white ZILAVKA.

Bogdanuşa
> Local white grape of the Dalmatian islands, esp. Hvar and Brac. Pleasant refreshing faintly fragrant wine.

Burgundac Bijeli
> The CHARDONNAY, grown a little in SLAVONIA and VOJVODINA.

Cabernet
> See Grapes for red wine. Now introduced in many places with usually pleasant, occasionally exciting, results. See KOSOVO.

Crno Black—i.e. red wine.

Cviček
> Traditional pale red or dark rosé of the Sava valley, SLOVENIA.

Dalmaciajavino
> Important co-operative based at Split and selling a full range of Dalmation coastal and island wines.

Dalmatia
> The middle coast of Yugoslavia from Rijeka to Dubrovnik. Has a remarkable variety of wines of character.

Dingac
> Heavy sweetish red from the local PLAVAC grape, speciality of the mid-Dalmatian coast.

Faros Smooth and substantial age-worthy red from the island of Hvar.

Fruska Gora
> Hills in VOJVODINA, on the Danube n.w. of Belgrade, with a growing modern v'yd. and a wide range of wines, incl. good Traminer and Sauvignon Blanc.

Graşevina
> Slovenian for Italian Riesling (also called Wälschriesling, LASKI RIZLING, etc.). The normal Riesling of Yugoslavia.

Grk
> Strong almost sherry-like white from the Grk grape. Speciality of the island of Korcula.

Istria Peninsula in the n. Adriatic, Porec its centre, with a variety of pleasant wines, the MERLOT as good as any.

Jerusalem
> Yugoslavia's most famous v'yd., at LJUTOMER. Its best wines are late-picked RAJNSKI RIZLING, LASKI RIZLING and more aromatic whites.

Kadarka
> The major red grape of Hungary, widely grown in SERBIA.

Kosovo (or Kosmet)

Region in the s., between SERBIA and Macedonia, with modern v'yds. The source of AMSELFELDER and some well-balanced, lively CABERNET.

Kraski

Grown on the coastal limestone "karst" of SLOVENIA.

Laski Rizling

Yet another name for Italian Riesling.

Ljutomer (or Lutomer)-Ormoz

Yugoslavia's best known and probably best wine district, in n.e. SLOVENIA, famous for its Wälschriesling: full-flavoured, full-strength and at its best rich and satisfying wine.

Malvasia

White grape giving luscious heavy wine, used in w. SLOVENIA.

Maraština

Strong dry white of the Dalmatian islands.

Maribor

Important wine-centre of n. SLOVENIA. White wines, mainly from VINAG, incl. LASKI RIZLING, RIESLING, SAUV BLANC, PINOT BLANC, TRAMINER.

Merlot

The Bordeaux red grape, grown in SLOVENIA and ISTRIA with reasonable results.

Mostar

Islamic-looking little city inland from DALMATIA, making admirable dry white from the ZILAVKA grape. Also BLATINA.

Muskat-Ottonel

The East European muscat, grown in VOJVODINA.

Navip

The big growers' co-operative of SERBIA, with its headquarters at Belgrade.

Opol

Pleasantly light pale red made of PLAVAČ grapes round Split and Sibenik in DALMATIA.

Plavać Mali

Native red grape of SLOVENIA and DALMATIA: makes DINGAC, POSTUP, OPOL, etc. Ordinary reds are often called "Plavać".

Plavina

Light red of the DALMATIAN coast round Zadar.

Plovdina

Native red grape of Macedonia in the s., giving mild wine. Grown and generally blended with PROKUPAC.

Portugizac   Austria's Portugieser: plain red wine.

Pošip

Pleasant, not-too-heavy white wine of the Dalmatian islands, notably Korcula.

Postup

Sweet and heavy DALMATIAN red from the Peljesać peninsula near Korcula. Highly esteemed locally.

Prokupać

Principal native red grape of s. SERBIA and Macedonia: 85% of the production. Makes good dark rosé (RUZIĆA) and full-bodied red of character. Some of the best comes from ZUPA. PLOVDINA is often added for smoothness.

Prošek

The dessert wine of DALMATIA, of stupefying natural strength and variable quality. The best is excellent, but hard to find.

Radgonska Ranina

Ranina is Austria's BOUVIER grape (see Austria). Radgona is near MARIBOR. The wine is sweet and carries the trade name TIGROVO MLJEKO (Tiger's Milk).

Rajnski Rizling

The Rhine Riesling, rare in Yugoslavia but grown a little in LJUTOMER-ORMOZ.

Refosco
> Italian grape grown in e. SLOVENIA and ISTRIA under the name TERAN.

Renski Rizling Alternative spelling for Rhine Riesling.

Riesling Without qualification used to mean Italian Riesling. Now limited to real Rhine Riesling.

Ruzića
> Rosé, usually from PROKUPAĆ. Darker than most; and better.

Serbia
> The e. state of Yugoslavia, with nearly half the country's v'yds., stretching from VOJVODINA to Macedonia.

Sipon Yugoslav name for the FURMINT grape of Hungary, also grown in SLOVENIA.

Slamnak A good late-harvest LJUTOMER estate Riesling.

Slavonia
> Northern Croatia, on the Hungarian border between SLOVENIA and SERBIA. A big producer of standard wines, mainly white, including most "Yugoslav Riesling".

Slovenia
> The n.w. state, incl. Yugoslavia's most European-style v'yds. and wines: LJUTOMER, etc. Slovenija-vino, the sales organization, is Yugoslavia's biggest.

Teran Stout dark red of ISTRIA. See REFOSCO.

Tigrovo Mljeko
> See Radgonska Ranina

Tocai The PINOT GRIS, making rather heavy white wine in SLOVENIA.

Traminać
> The TRAMINER. Grown in SLOVENIA and VOJVODINA. Particularly successful in the latter.

Vinag Huge production cellars at MARIBOR.

Vojvodina
> An autonomous province of n. SERBIA with substantial, growing and improving v'yds. Wide range of grapes, both European and Balkan.

Vranać
> Red grape making attractive vigorous wine in Montenegro.

Zilavka
> The white wine of MOSTAR in Hercegovina. Can be one of Yugoslavia's best: dry, pungent and memorably fruity, with a faint flavour of apricots. Exported samples are disappointing.

Zupa Central SERBIAN district giving its name to above-average red and rosé (or dark and light red) of PROKUPAC and PLOVDINA: respectively Zupsko Crno and Zupsko Ruzića.

Bulgaria

A dramatic entry into the world's wine-diet in the late 1970s. State-run and state-subsidized wineries have learned a great deal from the New World and offer Cabernet and Chardonnay at bargain prices and in rapidly improving quality and variety. Controlled appellation ("Controliran") wines, recently introduced, have marked an important new step in quality.

Asenovgrad
> Main MAVRUD-producing cellar on the outskirts of Plovdiv, Bulgaria's second city.

Cabernet
> The Bordeaux grape is highly successful in n. Bulgaria. Dark, vigorous, fruity and well-balanced wine, needs ageing.

Chardonnay

> The white burgundy grape is scarcely less successful. Very dry but full-flavoured wine improves with a year in bottle.

Controliran See introductory note.

Dimiat

> The common native white grape, grown in the east towards the coast. Agreeable dry white without memorable character.

Euxinograd (Chateau)

> Ageing cellar on the coast, part of the ex-King's palace. Wines reserved for State functions and top restaurants.

Fetiaska

> The same grape as Romania's Feteasca and Hungary's Leanyka. Rather neutral but pleasant pale wine, best a trifle sweet, sold as Donau Perle.

Gamza

> Good red grape, possibly related to Hungary's Kadarka.

Han Krum

> Bulgaria's most modern white-wine plant, near Varna in the east.

Iskra

> The national brand of sparkling wine, normally sweet but of fair quality. Red, white or rosé.

Kadarka Popular brand of GAMZA red from n. Bulgaria.

Karlovo

> Town in central Bulgaria famous for the "Valley of Roses" and its very pleasant white MISKET.

Lositza

> "Controliran" CABERNET from the north; perhaps Bulgaria's most elegant yet.

Mavrud

> Darkly plummy red from s. Bulgaria. Improves with age. Traditionally considered the country's best.

Melnik

> City of the extreme south-east. Such concentrated red wine that the locals say it can be carried in a handkerchief.

Merlot

> Soft red grape variety grown mainly in Haskovo district of southern Bulgaria.

Misket

> Muscat-flavoured local grape used for sweet whites.

Muscat Ottonel

> Normal muscat grape, grown in eastern Bulgaria for medium-sweet, fruity whites.

Novi Pazar

> Controlled appellation CHARDONNAY winery near VARNA. Finer wines than VARNA.

Novo Selo

> "Controliran" red MISKET from the north.

Orjahoviza

> Major s. area for "Controliran" CABERNET/MERLOT. Rich savoury red best at 4–5 years.

Pamid

> The light, soft, everyday red of south-west and north-west Bulgaria.

Pavlikeni

> Northern wine town with an estate specializing in GAMZA and CABERNET.

Pleven

> Northern cellar important for PAMID, GAMZA and CABERNET. Also Bulgaria's wine research station.

Provadya

> East of SHUMEN, near the coast, another centre for good white wines, especially dry CHARDONNAY.

Rcatzitelli

> One of Russia's favourite white grapes for strong, sweet wine. Grown in north-east Bulgaria to produce bulk dry or medium white wines.

Riesling

> Normally refers to Italian Riesling. Some Rhine Riesling is grown and is now made into Germanic-style whites.

Sauvignon Blanc

> Grown in eastern Bulgaria, just being released as dry white wine on export markets.

Shumen

> Eastern Bulgaria's largest white wine-producing cellar specializing in dry wines. Also makes good brandy.

Sonnenkuste

> Brand of medium-sweet white sold in Germany.

Suhindol

> Pavlikeni's neighbour, site of Bulgaria's first cooperative (1909). Good cellar for GAMZA, CABERNET and PAMID.

Sungarlare

> Eastern town giving its name to a dry "controliran" MISKET.

Svishtov

> CABERNET-producing winery by the Danube in the n. The front-runner in Bulgaria's controlled appellation wines.

Sylvaner

> Some pleasant dry Sylvaner is exported as "Klosterkeller".

Tamianka Sweet white; sweeter than HEMUS.

Targovichte

> Independent (non-VINPROM) white wine cellar near SHUMEN that concentrates on medium and sweet wines.

Tirnovo Strong sweet dessert red wine.

Trakia "Thrace". Brand name of a good export range.

Varna

> Major coastal appellation for CHARDONNAY.

Vinimpex

> The "State Commercial Enterprise for Export and Import of Wines and Spirits".

Vinprom

> State body controlling all 145 cooperative cellars responsible for dramatic quality improvements over last 7 years. Owns 10% of country's vineyards and 3 research institutes.

Greece

Entry into the EEC gives Greece the challenge of modernizing and internationalizing a wine industry that has been up a backwater for two thousand years, concentrating on resin-flavoured white Retsina. (The resin is that of the Aleppo pine.) A new EEC-style system of 29 appellations is now in place and much is spoken of the hopeful future for Greek wines.

Achaia-Clauss

> The best-known Greek wine-merchant, with cellars at Patras, n. PELOPONNESE, makers of DEMESTICA, etc.

Agioritikos

> Mount Athos, the monastic peninsula in Chalkidiki. Source of CABERNET and other grapes for TSANTALI wines. Brand name of a good dry rosé.

Aminteion (Appellation)

> Crisp red or rosé from the mountains of Macedonia.

Attica Region round Athens, the chief source of RETSINA.

Boutari

> Merchants and makers with high standards in Macedonian and other wines, esp. good NAOUSSA. Grand Réserve is the best wine.

Cambas, Andrew

> Important Athenian wine-growers and merchants.

Carras, John

> Hotelier at Sithonia, Chalkidiki, n. Greece, producing interesting new red and white wines under the names Château Carras, Porto Carras and CÔTES DU MELITON. Ch. Carras is a Bordeaux-style barrel-aged red, particularly good in **79 80** 81 82.

Castel Danielis

> One of the best brands of dry red wine, from ACHAIA-CLAUSS.

Corfu Adriatic island with wines scarcely worthy of it. Ropa is the traditional red.

Côtes du Meliton (Appellation)

> Thracian red, white and rosé of fair quality, made by CARRAS.

Courtakis, D.

> Athenian merchant with good dark NEMEAN red.

Crete Island with the name for some of Greece's better (red) wine. Appellations are: Archanes, Daphnes, Peza and Sitia.

Demestica

> A reliable standard brand of dry red and white from ACHAIA-CLAUSS.

Gentilini New up-market white from KEPHALONIA.

Goumenissa (Appellation)

> Good-quality, oak-aged mid-weight red from BOUTARI.

Hymettus

> Standard brand of red and dry white without resin.

Kalligas

> The leading merchant of KEPHALONIA. Good red Monte Nero and dry white ROBOLA.

Kephalonia

> Ionian (western) island with good white ROBOLA. Also MAVRODA-PHNE. See also GENTILINI.

Kokkineli

> The rosé version of RETSINA: like the white. Drink very cold.

Lac des Roches

> Sound, blended Dodecanese white from BOUTARI.

Lindos

> Name for the higher quality of RHODES wine, whether from Lindos itself or not. Acceptable; no more.

Malvasia

> The famous grape is said to originate from Monemvasia in the s. PELOPONNESE.

Mantinia (Appellation)

> A fresh white from the PELOPONNESE, offered by CAMBAS.

Mavro

> "Black"—the word for dark red wine.

Mavrodaphne (Appellation)

> Literally "black laurel": dark sweet concentrated red; a speciality of the Patras region, n. PELOPONNESE.

Mavroudi (Appellation)

> The red wine of Delphi and the n. shore of the Gulf of Corinth: dark and plummy.

Metsovo (Appellation)

> Cabernet red from Epirus in the north.

Minos Popular Cretan brand; the Castello red is best.

Naoussa (Appellation)

> Above-average strong dry red from Macedonia in the n. esp. from BOUTARI and TSANTALI.

Nemea (Appellation)

> Town in the e. PELOPONNESE famous for its lion (a victim of Hercules) and its fittingly forceful MAVRO.

Patras (Appellation)

> Important wine town at the mouth of the Gulf of Corinth.

Peloponnese

> The s. landmass of mainland Greece, with a half of the whole country's v'yds.

Pendeli

> Reliable brand of dry red from ATTICA, grown and bottled by Andrew CAMBAS.

Retsina

> White wine with pine resin added, tasting of turpentine and oddly appropriate with Greek food. The speciality of ATTICA. Drink it very cold.

Rhodes

> Easternmost Greek island. Its sweet MALVASIAS are its best wines. LINDOS is the brand name for tolerable table wines.

Rombola (or Robola) (Appellation)

> The dry white of Cephalonia; island off the Gulf of Corinth.

Samos (Appellation)

> Island off the Turkish coast with a reputation for its sweet pale-golden muscat. The normal commercial quality is nothing much.

Santorin

> Island north of Crete, making sweet Vinsanto from sun-dried grapes, and dry white Thira.

Tsantali

> Producers at Agios Pavlos with a wide range of table wines, including Macedonian Cabernet, wine from the monks of Mt. Athos, NAOUSSA and Muscat from PATRAS. "Cava" is a good blend.

Verdea The dry white of Zakinthos, the island just w. of the PELOPONNESE. The red is Byzantis.

Cyprus

A well-established exporter of strong wines of reasonable quality, best known for very passable Cyprus sherry, though old Commandaria, a treacly dessert wine, is the island's finest product. Until recently only traditional grape varieties of limited potential were available; now better kinds are beginning to improve standards, but regrettably slowly.

Afames

> Village at the foot of Mt. Olympus, giving its name to one of the better red (MAVRON) wines from SODAP.

Aphrodite

> Full-bodied medium-dry white from KEO, named after the Greek goddess of love.

Arsinöe

> Dry white wine from SODAP, named after an unfortunate female whom Aphrodite turned to stone.

Bellapais

> Fizzy medium-sweet white from KEO named after the famous abbey near Kyrenia. Essential refreshment for holidaymakers in Cyprus.

Commandaria

> Good-quality br. dessert wine made since ancient times in the hills n. of LIMASSOL, named after a crusading order of knights. The best (sold as "100 yrs old") is superb, of incredible sweetness.

Domaine d'Ahera
> Modern-style lighter red from KEO.

Emva Cream
> Best-selling sw. sherry from Etko, a HAGGIPAVLU subsidiary.

Etko See Haggipavlu

Haggipavlu
> Well-known wine-merchant at LIMASSOL. Trades as Etko.

Hirondelle
> The sweet white and some of the other wines of this popular brand are produced by Etko (see Emva).

Keo
> One of the biggest and most go-ahead firms in the wine trade at LIMASSOL.

Khalokhorio
> Principal COMMANDARIA village, growing only XYNISTERI.

Kokkineli
> Rosé: the name is related to "cochineal".

Kolossi
> Red and white table wines from SODAP.

Limassol
> "The Bordeaux of Cyprus". The wine-port in the south.

Loel
> Major producer. Amathus and Kykko brands, Command Cyprus sherry and fine Negro red.

Mavron
> The black grape of Cyprus (and Greece) and its dark wine.

Mosaic
> The brand-name of KEO's Cyprus sherries includes a fine dry wine.

Othello
> A good standard dry red: solid, satisfying wine from KEO.

Palomino
> Very drinkable soft dry white made of this (sherry) grape by LOEL.

Pitsilia
> Region south of Mt. Olympus producing the best white and COMMANDARIA wines.

Rosella
> Brand of strong medium-sweet rosé.

St Panteleimon
> Brand of strong sweet white from Keo.

Semeli
> Good traditional red from HAGGIPAVLU.

Sherry
> Cyprus makes a full range of sherry-style wines, the best (particularly the dry) of very good quality.

SODAP
> Major wine cooperative at LIMASSOL.

Xynisteri
> The native white grape of Cyprus.

Zoopiyi
> Principal COMMANDARIA village, growing MAVRON grapes.

North Africa & Asia

Algeria

The massive v'yds. of Algeria have dwindled in the last ten years from 860,000 acres to under 500,000. Red, rosé and white wines of some quality are made in the coastal hills of Tlemcen, Mascara, Haut-Dahra, Zaccar and Ain-Bessem. Most goes for blending.

India

In 1985 a Franco-Indian firm launched a sparkling wine, Royal Mousseux, made at Narayangaon, s.e. of Bombay. Plans are to export up to 2m. bottles.

Israel

Israeli wine, since the industry was re-established by a Rothschild in the 1880s, has been primarily of Kosher interest until recently, when CABERNET, SAUVIGNON BLANC, SEMILLON, PETITE SIRAH and GRENACHE of fair quality have been introduced. Carmel is the principal brand. Galilee and Samson are two areas producing superior reds.

Japan

Japan has a small wine industry in Yamanashi Prefecture, w. of Tokyo. Wines are here blended with imports from Argentina, E. Europe, etc. Premium wines of Semillon, Cabernet and the local white grape, Koshu, are light but can be good, though expensive. The main producers are Suntory, Mercian, Mann's. In 1985 tainted Austrian wine was discovered being sold as Japanese by a major company.

Lebanon

The small Lebanese wine industry, based on Ksara in the Bekaa valley n.e. of Beirut, has made red wine of real vigour and quality. Château Musar (**★★★**) produces splendid matured reds, largely of CABERNET SAUVIGNON.

Morocco

Morocco today makes North Africa's best wine from v'yds. along the Atlantic coast and round Meknes. In ten years the v'yds. have declined from 190,000 to 54,000 acres. Chante Bled and Tarik are the best reds, Gris de Guerrouane a very pale dry rosé. In Morocco they sell as Les Trois Domaines.

Tunisia

Tunisia now has 75,000 acres compared with 120,000 ten years ago. Her speciality is sweet muscat, but reasonable reds and rosés come from Carthage, Mornag and Cap Bon.

Turkey

Most of Turkey's huge v'yds. produce table grapes. But her wines, from Thrace, Anatolia and the Aegean, are remarkably good. Trakya (Thrace) white and Buzbag (Anatolian) red are the well-known standards of the State wineries. Doluca and Kavaklidere are private firms of good quality. Villa Doluca red from Thrace is very well made. Buzbag is a bargain.

USSR

With over 3 million acres of v'yds. the USSR is the world's fourth-biggest wine-producer — but almost entirely for home consumption. Ukraine (incl. the Crimea) is the biggest v'yd. republic, followed by Moldavia, the Russian Republic and Georgia. The Soviet consumer has a sweet tooth, for both table and dessert wines. Of the latter the best come from the Crimea (esp. Massandra). Moldavia and Ukraine use the same grapes as Romania, plus Cabernet, Riesling, Pinot Gris, etc. The Russian Republic makes the best Rieslings (Arbau, Beshtau, Anapa) and sweet sparkling Tsimlanskoye "Champanski". Georgia uses mainly traditional grapes (esp. white Tsinandali and red Mukuzani) for the best table wines of the USSR.

Soviet wines are classified as ordinary (unmatured), "named" (matured in cask or vat) or "kollektsionye" (which are matured both in cask and bottle).

California

California has been making wine for 150 years, but her modern wine industry has grown from scratch in scarcely more than 25. Today it leads the world in good-quality cheap wines and startles it with a handful of luxury wines of brilliant quality. In the last decade the industry has expanded and altered at a frenzied pace. The majority of the wineries listed here have a history shorter than ten years. Quality-ratings must therefore be tentative.

Grape-varieties (combined with brand-names) are the key to California wine. Since grapes in California play many new roles they are separately listed on pages 154 to 155.

Vineyard areas

Amador
County in the Sierra foothills e. of Sacramento. Grows fine Zinfandel, esp. in Shenandoah Valley.

Central Coast
A long sweep of coast with scattered wine activity, from San Francisco Bay s. to Santa Barbara.

Central Coast/Santa Barbara
Some of the most promising recent planting in the state is in the Santa Ynez Valley n. of Santa Barbara, where coastal fog gives particularly cool conditions.

Central Coast/Santa Cruz Mts.
Wineries are scattered round the Santa Cruz Mts. s. of San Francisco Bay, from Saratoga down to the HECKER PASS.

Central Coast/Hecker Pass
Pass through the Santa Cruz Mts. s. of San Francisco Bay with a cluster of small old-style wineries.

Central Coast/Salinas Valley/Monterey
The main concentration of new planting in the Central Coast: the Salinas Valley runs inland s.e. from Monterey.

Central Coast/San Luis Obispo
Edna Valley just s. of San Luis Obispo and new more scattered v'yds. nr. Paso Robles.

Livermore
Valley e. of San Francisco Bay long famous for white wines but now largely built over.

Lodi Town and district at the n. end of the San Joaquin Valley, its hot climate modified by a westerly air-stream.

Mendocino
Northernmost coastal wine country; a varied climate coolest in Anderson Valley nr. the coast, warm around Ukiah inland.

Napa The Napa Valley, n. of San Francisco Bay, well established as the top-quality wine area. Coolest at southern end (Carneros).

San Joaquin Valley
The great central valley of California, fertile and hot, the source of most of the jug wines and dessert wines in the State.

Sonoma
County n. of San Francisco Bay, between Napa and the sea. Most v'yds. are in the north (see below). A few, historically important, are in the Valley of the Moon in the south. Vineyards extend south into Los Carneros.

Sonoma/Alexander Valley/Russian River
High-quality area from Alexander Valley (n. of Napa Valley) towards the sea (Russian River). Incl. Dry Creek Valley.

Temecula (Rancho California)
Very new small area in s. California, 25 miles inland halfway between San Diego and Riverside.

Recent Vintages

The Californian climate is far from being as consistent as its reputation. Although on the whole the grapes ripen regularly, they are subject to severe spring frosts in many areas, sometimes a wet harvest-time, and such occasional calamities as the two-year drought of 1975–7.

Wines from the San Joaquin Valley tend to be most consistent year by year. The vintage data on these, where there is one, is more important for telling the age of the wine than its character.

Vineyards in the Central Coast are mainly so new that no pattern of vintage qualities has yet emerged.

The Napa Valley is the one area where comment can be made on the last dozen vintages of the top varietal wines: Cabernet Sauvignon and Chardonnay.

	Chardonnay	Cabernet Sauvignon
1985	Big crop, good acidity, should last.	Coolish ripening season, elegant wines
1984	Wonderfully perfumed when young.	Very promising, very ripe and fragrant.
1983	Very good; finesse.	Similar to '80 but will mature faster.
1982	Sound, agreeable; drink soon	Many outstanding.
1981	Very early vintage; good if not too strong.	Promising.
1980	Small crop; high alcohol. The best well-balanced.	Outstanding; begin to drink.
1979	Excellent; drink up.	Rain; generally light.
1978	Very good if not too heady.	Excellent.
1977	Generally excellent.	Attractive: ageing well.
1976	Difficult: variable.	Small crop but splendid.
1975	Very good; drink up.	Delicate: charming; drink soon.
1974	Good: ready.	Difficult: but many superb.
1973	Very good, but drink up.	Big and good; drink up.
1972	The best wines of a cool year.	Uneven: rain: many poor wines.
1971	Good balance: long lived.	Average; drink up.
1970	Good all round: not great: mature.	Best ever.

California: grape varieties

Barbera
Darkly plummy variety from Piemonte (see Italy). Gives full-blooded and astringent wine in cool areas, good but softer wine in hot ones. Most of 17,000 acres is in San Joaquin Valley.

Cabernet Sauvignon
The best red-wine grape in California with a wide range of styles from delicately woody to overpoweringly fruity. The classic Napa grape. 22,000 + acres, mainly in n. coast countries.

Carignane   Bulk-producing red grape rarely used as a "varietal".

Charbono
Rare red grape of Italian origin. Only in NAPA. Nothing special.

Chardonnay
The best white-wine grape—indeed the best wine-grape—in California. Styles of making vary from merely clean and grapy to rich and complex like the best white burgundies. 22,000 + acres.

Chenin Blanc
A work-horse white grape with a surprising turn of speed when made dry and in limited, concentrated quantities. But usually made soft and sweet. 43,000 + acres, mainly in San Joaquin Valley.

Emerald Riesling
A Californian original in the German manner. Clean, flowery/fruity and a touch tart.

Flora   California-bred white. Mildly flowery; best made sweet and/or sparkling (e.g. by SCHRAMSBERG).

French Colombard
High-acid white coming into favour for clean semi-dry wines made more German-style than French. Best from north coast.

Fumé Blanc   See Sauvignon Blanc.

Gamay (or Napa Gamay)
The red grape of Beaujolais. Not remarkable in California.

Gamay Beaujolais
Not the red grape of Beaujolais, but a selection of Pinot Noir capable of good Beaujolais-style reds in California.

Gewürztraminer
Generally softer and less aromatically thrilling in California than in France, but at best (esp. in SONOMA) one of the real successes.

Gray Riesling
Not a Riesling. Full-bodied but scarcely notable white.

Green Hungarian
A minority interest: rather tasteless white. Can be lively.

Grenache   Used mainly for sweetish rosés in California.

Grignolino
Highly seasoned grape good for young reds and rosés.

Johannisberg Riesling
Real Rhine Riesling (also known as White Riesling). Often rather strong and bland in California, but at its best (esp. in Auslese-style wines) gloriously complex and satisfying.

Merlot   The Pomerol grape now has 2,000 + acres in California. Very good smooth and aromatic reds have been made.

Muscat   Light sweet pale gold muscat is one of California's treats.

Petite Sirah and Syrah
The name of the Rhône's and Australia's great red grape has been wrongly applied to a poor one. Generally used in Burgundy blends. But the real one (Syrah) is present in small quantities, and has great promise. See PHELPS, ESTRELLA RIVER.

Pinot Blanc   Much in the shade of the better Chardonnay.

Pinot Noir
Has yet to reach consummation in California. Most wine with the name is disappointing; a minute proportion thrilling. 9,000-odd acres. Much used in the best sparkling wines.

Riesling See Johannisberg Riesling. Also Sylvaner.

Ruby Cabernet

A California-bred cross between Carignan and Cabernet Sauvignon with enough of the character of the latter to be interesting. Good in hot conditions. 13,000 + acres.

Sauvignon Blanc

Excellent white grape used either Sancerre style (fresh, aromatic, effervescent) or Graves style (fat, chewable). N. Coast, Livermore, Central Coast. 12,000 acres.

Semillon

High-flavoured whites from the cooler areas; bland ones from hotter places. The most memorable are sweet.

Zinfandel

California's own red grape, open to many interpretations from light-weight fruity to galumphing. The current fad is for white or "blush" ZIN. The red is capable of ageing to great quality.

California wineries

Acacia Napa. ★★★★ CH 80 81′ 82 83 84 PN 79′ 80 81 82 83

Carneros winery (first wine 1979) specializing in CHARDONNAY and PINOT NOIR. Both are fulfilling marvellous promise.

Alderbrook Sonoma ★★

New ('82) winery using owner-grown and other grapes to make full-flavoured whites. CHARD, SAUVIGNON BLANC and SEMILLON all good.

Alexander Valley Vineyards Alexander Valley. ★★→★★★ CH 80 81 82 83 CS 81 82

Small winery best known for well-balanced CHARD., and J.R.

Almaden Central Coast. ★→★★ CS 79 80 81 82

Big winery famous for pioneer varietal labelling and planting in Central Coast. Now owned by National Distillers. Best regular wines incl. GEWÜRZTRAMINER, CABERNET and (sparkling) Eye of the Partridge. Charles le Franc label for top wines.

S. Anderson Vineyard Napa ★★★ CH 80 81 82 83

New winery with extensive caves. Good CHARDONNAY and recently good sparkling wine.

Balverne Sonoma/Russian River ★★ CH 80′

New mid-sized winery near Windsor, started in '80 with fine CHARDONNAY, SAUVIGNON BLANC, and blended "Healdsburger". C.S. and ZIN are above average.

Beaulieu Napa. ★★★ CS 74 76 77 78 79 80 81 82 83

Rightly famous medium-size growers and makers of esp. CABERNET. Top wine: De Latour Private Reserve Cabernet. Crackerjack SAUV. BLANC. Now owned by Heublein Corp.

Bel Arbres A second label of FETZER.

Beringer Napa. ★★→★★★★ CH 80 81 82 83 84 CS 79 80 81 82

Century-old winery recently restored to the front rank. Increasingly fine wines incl. esp. CHARD (excellent Private Reserve), CABERNET (ditto) and "Nightingale", the eponymous winemaker's induced-botrytis dessert wine.

Boeger Amador. ★→★★ CS 79 80

Small winery in Sierra foothills. Good ZIN.

Brander Central Coast/Santa Barbara ★★★

Small new winery specializes in excellent SAUVIGNON BLANC of the Santa Ynez valley grapes.

Bruce, David Central Coast. ★★★ CH 80 81 82 83 84

Small luxury winery with heavy-weight old-style wines.

Buena Vista Sonoma. ★★→★★★ CH 80 81 82 83 CS 79 80 81 82

Historic pioneer winery with new owners and much improved recent record esp. in whites (RIESLING, FUMÉ BLANC).

Burgess Cellars Napa. ★★★ CH 79 80 81 82 83 CS 78 79 80 82 Z 81 82
Small hillside winery, originally called Souverain, making good
CHARDONNAY, CABERNET, and very good ZIN.

Bynum, Davis Sonoma. ★→★★
Well-established maker of standard varieties, w. of Healdsburg.

B.V.
Abbreviation of BEAULIEU VINEYARDS used on their labels.

Cakebread Napa. ★★→★★★ CH 80 81 82 83 CS 79 80 81 82
Started 1973. Increasing reputation, esp. for SAUVIGNON BLANC
and CABERNET (79 esp.); also CHARDONNAY.

Calera Monterey-San Benito. ★★★ PN 79 80 81 82
1975 winery ambitious with PINOT NOIR; also high-alcohol ZIN.

Callaway S. California. ★★ CH 83
Small new winery in new territory at TEMECULA. Sound whites;
no more reds.

Carneros Creek Napa. ★★★ CH 80 81 82 83 CS 74 75 77 78 79 80 81
The first winery in the cool Carneros area between Napa and San
Francisco Bay. First PINOT NOIR ('77) was sensational. Good
CHARDONNAY and CABERNET.

Cassayre-Forni Napa. ★★→★★★ CS 79' 80 81 CH 81 82 83
Small new Rutherford winery. Good CABERNET, ZIN, dry
CHENIN BLANC and CHARDONNAY.

Caymus Napa. │★★★│ CS 74' 75' 76 77 78' 79' 80' 81 82
Outwardly modest small winery at Rutherford with v. high
standards, esp. for notably complex CAB; also white P.NOIR,
CHARDS, SAUV. BLANC. Second label: Liberty School.

Chalone Central Coast/Salinas. │★★★★│ CH 78 79 80 81 82 83 PN 78 79
80 81
Unique small hilltop v'yd./winery at the Pinnacles. French-style
CHARDONNAY and PINOT NOIR of superb quality. Also excellent
PINOT BLANC.

Chappellet Napa. ★★★★ CH 80 81 82 CS 74 75' 76 78 79' 80 81
Luxury winery and beautiful amphitheatrical hillside v'yd.
Excellent long-lived CABERNET, CHARDONNAY and RIESLING:
very good dry CHENIN BLANC.

Château Bouchaine Napa/Carneros. ★★★ (?)
New firm in old Carneros barn started with Acacia-style oaky
PINOT NOIR. Now similar CHARDONNAY and SAUV. BLANC.

Château Montelena Napa. ★★★ CH 79 80 81 82 83 CS 75 77 78 79 80 81
Small 1969 winery making very good distinctive CHARDONNAY
and CABERNET SAUVIGNON.

Château St Jean Sonoma. ★★★★ CH 78 79 80 81' 82 83 84
Impressive winery specializing in lively, long-lived whites from
individual v'yds., incl. CHARDONNAY, PINOT BLANC and esp. late
harvest RIESLING. Now also fine sparkling wine and bargain "Vin
Blanc".

Christian Brothers Napa and San Joaquin. │★→★★│
The biggest Napa winery, run by a religious order, shifting from
blends to named vintages, incl. sound CABERNET, useful FUMÉ
BLANC, sweet white Ch. La Salle, very good brandy and ZIN
"port". '84 NAPA CHARD is v. fine.

Clos du Bois Sonoma. ★★→★★★ CH 79 80 81 82 83 CS 78 79 80 81 82
Healdsburg winery of big grower in Dry Creek and Alexander
Valleys. Good GEWÜRZ, P.NOIR, MERLOT, CHARD, SAUV. BLANC.

Clos du Val Napa. ★★★→★★★★ CH 80 81 82 83 CS 77 78' 79' 80' 81 82
French-owned. Bold ZIN, fine delicate CAB, CHARD and SEM.

Concannon Livermore. Table. ★★→★★★ CH 83
Substantial winery first famous for whites, reds now prominent.
Now owned by Distillers' Company. To watch.

Congress Springs Santa Clara/Santa Cruz. ★★
Tiny winery above Saratoga. Well-made whites, esp. SAUVIGNON
BLANC, SEMILLON.

Conn Creek Napa. ★★→★★★ CH 79 80 81 82 83 CS 78 79 80 81 82
New winery built on Silverado Trail in 1979 has a growing reputation. Best known for CABERNET.

Corbett Canyon Central Coast/San Luis Obispo ★★
New ('83) Edna Valley winery to make sizeable amounts of varietal and generic ("Coastal Classic") wines. Also Shadow Creek sparkling with SONOMA grapes.

Cresta Blanca Mendocino. ★★
Old name from Livermore revived on the n. coast by new owners, GUILD. Husky ZIN and PETITE SYRAH. Mild whites.

Cuvaison Napa. ★★→★★★ CH 80 81 82 83 CS 78 79 80 81
Small winery with expert new direction. Austere CABERNET and CHARDONNAY may become more approachable.

Culbertson San Diego. ★★★ (?)
New sparkling-wine specialist using local grapes of an improbable region with gold-medal results.

Dehlinger Sonoma. ★★→ ★★★ CS 76 78 80 CH 77 79 80' 81 82
Small winery and v'yd. w. of Santa Rosa. Since 1976 CHARDONNAY, CABERNET and ZIN all extremely well made.

DeLoach Vineyards Sonoma. ★★★ CH 80' 81' 82 83' PN 80 81' 82 83
Russian River winery founded 1975 for CHARDONNAY, GEWÜRZ, P. NOIR. Also good ZIN. (v.g. white ZIN) C.S. and SAUV. BLANC.

Diamond Creek Napa. ★★★ CS 74 75 76 77 78 79 80 81 82
Small winery since the 60s with austere, long-ageing CABERNET from hills w. of Calistoga.

Domaine Chandon Napa. ★★★
Californian outpost of Moët & Chandon Champagne. Launched 1976. Promise is being fulfilled. First Reserve wine (released in 1985) is a showstopper.

Domaine Laurier Sonoma. ★★★ CH 80 81' 82 83' 84 CS 78 79 80 81
Small new winery with beautifully structured wines, esp. CABERNET and SAUVIGNON BLANC, using the new appellation Green Valley. A classic in the making.

Dominus Napa ★★★★ 83
First fruits (1983 vintage released '86) of partnership ("John Daniel Society") between inheritor of ex-Inglenook v'yd. n. of Yountville and Christian Moueix of Pomerol. B'x-style Cabernets-Merlot blend shows immense promise.

Donna Maria Sonoma/Russian River. ★★ (?)
Considerable vineyards in Chalk Hills near Windsor. Encouraging early wines.

Dry Creek Sonoma. ★★★ CH 78 79 80' 81 82 83 CS 79 80 81 82
Small winery with high ideals, making old-fashioned dry wines, esp. whites, incl. CHARDONNAY, CHENIN BLANC and FUMÉ BLANC and outstanding CAB. SAUV. (best California Wine award 1985).

Duckhorn Vineyards Napa. ★★★ MERLOT 79 80 81 82 CS 79 80 81 82
Small winery on Silverado Trail best known for reds, esp. MERLOT. Also SAUVIGNON BLANC and now "Robert Hunter" Sparkling Brut de Noirs from Sonoma grapes (first, 1980).

Durney Vineyard Central Coast/Monterey. ★★→★★★ CS 79 80 81 82
Good CABERNET from Carmel Valley, riper than most in Monterey. Also CHENIN BLANC. Since '76.

Edmeades Mendocino. ★★ CH 78 79 80 81 CH 81' 82
Tiny winery in Anderson Valley near Pacific. CABERNET and now good CHARD and ZIN.

Edna Valley Vineyard Cen. Coast/San Luis Obispo. ★★→★★★
Joint venture of grape-grower with CHALONE winemakers. Fat, stylish CHARDONNAY, and PINOT NOIR to keep.

Estrella River San Luis Obispo/Santa Barbara. ★★ CH 79 80 81
Impressive new winery with 700 acres. CHARDONNAY, RIESLING, MUSCAT, SYRAH are promising.

Far Niente Napa. ★★★ CH 79 80 81' 82 83
    Founded 1885; reactivated in 1979. CHARDONNAY first, now promising CABERNET.

Felton-Empire Vineyards Cent. Coast/Santa Cruz Mts. ★★★
    The old Hallcrest property revived. Excellent RIESLING; good GEWÜRZ. Reds rather shaky.

Fetzer Mendocino. ★★ CH 81 82 83 84 CS 79 80 81 82
    Rapidly expanding winery with interesting reliable wines, esp. CHARD and CAB. Also SAUV. BLANC, RIES and strong dark ZIN..

Ficklin San Joaquin. ★★★
    Family firm making California's best "port" and minute quantities of table wine.

Field Stone Sonoma (Alexander Valley). ★★
    Small winery founded by mechanical harvester maker. Makes a delicious CABERNET rosé.

Firestone Central Coast/Santa Barbara. ★★★ CH 79 80 81 82 83 CS 81 82
    Ambitious 1973 winery in a new area n. of Santa Barbara. Cool conditions are producing unusual wines, incl. PINOT NOIR, RIESLING, GEWÜRZ and esp. CHARDONNAY.

Flora Springs Wine Co. Napa. ★★★ CH 79 80 81 82 83 CS 80 81 82
    Old stone cellar in St. Helena reopened 1979. CHARDONNAY and SAUV. BLANC are v. successful; CABERNET less certain.

Foppiano Sonoma. ★★
    Old winery at Healdsburg refurbished with estate varieties incl. CHENIN BLANC, FUMÉ BLANC, CAB, ZIN, PETITE SYRAH.

Franciscan Vineyard Napa. ★★ CH 81 82 83 84 CS 79 80 81 82
    Rapidly growing enterprise with a meet-the-folks approach. Good ZIN., CAB., CHARD. and RIES.; also "Harvest Nouveau".

Franzia San Joaquin. ★
    Large old winery with well-distributed brands. Various labels, but all say "made and bottled in Ripon".

Freemark Abbey Napa. ★★★★ CH 76 77 78 79 80' 81' 82 83 CS 74' 75 76 77 78' 79 80' 81 82
    Small connoisseur's winery with high reputation for CABERNET, CHARDONNAY and RIESLING (esp. late-harvest "Edelwein").

Gallo, E. & J. San Joaquin ★→★★ CS 78
    The worlds biggest winery, pioneer in both quantity and quality. Family owned. Hearty Burgundy and Chablis Blanc set national standards. Varietals incl. SAUV. BLANC, GEWÜRZ, RIES., CHARD, CABERNET. Vintage-dated CAB. SAUV. has won wide approval.

Gemello Santa Clara/Santa Cruz. ★★
    Old winery with reputation for reds, esp. PETITE SYRAH, ZIN.

Geyser Peak Sonoma. ★★
    Old winery revived by Schlitz Brewery sold recently to local grower Henry Trione. Best wines bear his name.

Giumarra San Joaquin. ★★
    Modern installation making attractive RUBY CAB., CHENIN BLANC from family v'yds. in hottest part of valley.

Glen Ellen Sonoma ★★★
    Father-and-son team making restrained elegant wines from own-grown and other Sonoma grapes. SAUV. BLANC, CHARD and CABERNET.

Grand Cru Sonoma. ★★→★★★ CS 78 79 80 81 82
    Small 1971 winery making good GEWÜRZ and increasingly CABERNET, CHENIN and SAUVIGNON BLANC.

Grgich-Hills Cellars Napa. ★★★★ CH 80' 81 82 83 Z 77 78' 79 80 81
    Grgich (formerly of Ch. Montelena) is winemaker, Hills grows the grapes—esp. CHARDONNAY and RIESLING. Delicate, lively wines include ZINFANDEL and now CABERNET.

Guenoc Vineyards Lake County. ★★
    Ambitious new vineyard/winery venture just beyond the Napa county line. CHENIN BLANC and PETITE SIRAH are esp. appealing.

Guild San Joaquin. ★
Big growers' cooperative famous for Vino da Tavola semi-sweet red and B. Cribari label.

Gundlach-Bundschu Sonoma. |★★★| CH 81 82 83 CS 79′ 80 81 82
Very old small family winery revived by the new generation. Excellent CABERNET, MERLOT, ZIN and good whites: CHARDONNAY, GEWÜRZ, RIESLING.

Hacienda Sonoma. ★★→★★★ CH 81 82 83 CS 79 80 81
Small winery at Sonoma specializing in high-quality CHARDONNAY and GEWÜRZ. Recently good CABERNET.

Hanzell Sonoma. ★★★ CH 77 78 79 80 81 82 83 PN 77 78 79 80 81
Small winery whose (late) founder revolutionized Californian CHARDONNAYS in the '50s. CHARD and P. NOIR are both huge wines. CABERNET first released in 1986.

Haywood Vineyard Sonoma. ★★→★★★ CH 81 83
Small new estate on hills above Sebastiani. First wines were lovely fruity CHARDONNAY and RIESLING. Now CABERNET.

Heitz Napa. ★★★★ CH 76 78 80 81 82 83 CS 75 76 77′ 78 79 80 81
An inspired individual winemaker who has set standards for the whole industry. His CABERNETS (esp. "Martha's Vineyard") are dark, deep and emphatic, his best CHARDONNAYS peers of Montrachet. Other wines can be eccentric. Added substantial new v'yds. in 1984.

Hill, William Winery Napa. ★★→★★★ CH 82 83 CS 80 81 82
Huge new plantings in the Mayacamas mts. and a new winery have yielded very emphatic (but well-received) early wines.

H.M.R. (formerly Hoffmann Mtn. Ranch) Cen. Coast/San Luis Obispo. ★★
Small winery in new area near Paso Robles. New owners after financial difficulties. To watch.

Hop Kiln Sonoma/Russian River. ★★ CS 81
Small winery. Individual, tasty PETITE SYRAH, ZIN, GEWÜRZ.

Inglenook Napa and San Joaquin. |★| →★★★ CS 76 77′ 78 79 80′ 81 82
One of the great old Napa wineries much changed by current owners: Heublein Corp. Inglenook Napa Valley is Napa label, with three qualities: Reserve, Estate, Cabinet. Reserve CAB is best wine. CHARD and S. BLANC much improved. Inglenook Navalle are good-value Central Valley wines.

Iron Horse Vineyards Sonoma. ★★★ CH 80 81 82 83 CS 79 80 81 82
Stylish Russian River property with CHARDONNAY, CABERNET, P. NOIR and SAUV. BLANC of vivid flavours. Sparkling wines are new and extremely good. Tin Pony is second label.

(Italian Swiss) Colony San Joaquin and Sonoma. ★→★★
Honourable old name from Sonoma recently re-acquired by Allied Growers. Policy steering upwards.

Jekel Vineyards Central Coast/Monterey. ★★→★★★ CH 80 81 82 83 CS 78 79 80 81
Well-made RIESLING and CHARDONNAY. CABERNET caused a stir when released. Wines (esp. whites) mature fast but tastily.

J. Lohr Central Coast. ★★
Small winery in San José with its own v'yds. in SALINAS. Reliable RIESLING and CABERNET rosé.

Johnson-Turnbull Napa. ★★→★★★ CS 80 81
Very small new estate producing balanced and distinguished, not overweight, CABERNETS from next-door to Mondavi.

Johnsons of Alexander Valley Sonoma. ★★ 79 80
Small winery with good v'yd. land. CABERNET best.

Jordan Sonoma. ★★★★ CH 79 80 81 82 83 CS 76 77 78 79 80′ 81 82
Extravagant winery, CABERNET modelled on Bordeaux, smooth Chardonnay. Polished wines have matured well.

Keenan, Robert Napa. ★★★ CH 77 78 79 80 81 82
V'yds. on Spring Mountain giving over-strong and tannic wines.

Kendall–Jackson Lake County. ★★→★★★

New (1980) and growing maker of good uncomplicated CHARD. RIES. SAUV. BLANC. CABERNET and ZIN show real promise. White House favourites.

Kenwood Vineyards Sonoma. ★★→★★★ CH 79 80 81 82 83 84 CS 78 79 80 81 82

Steady small producer of increasingly stylish reds, esp. CABERNET and ZIN., v.g. SAUV. BLANC, good CHARD and CHENIN.

Kistler Vineyards Sonoma. ★★ CH 79 80 81 82 83 CS 80 81 82

New small winery in hills. First CHARDONNAY (79) was overwhelming; 82 shows more restraint. Now also CAB and P. NOIR.

Korbel Sonoma. ★★

Long-established sparkling wine specialists. "Natural" and "Brut" are among California's best standard "champagnes".

Kornell, Hanns Napa. ★★

Fine sparkling wine house making full-flavoured dry wines: Brut and Sehr Trocken.

Krug, Charles Napa. ★→★★ CS 72 73 74 77 78 79 80 81 82

Historic old winery with generally sound range, incl. good CABERNET SAUVIGNON, sweet CHENIN BLANC and very sweet Muscat Canelli. C.K. is the jug-wine brand.

La Crema Vinera Sonoma. ★★→ ★★★ CH 80 81 82 83 PN 79 80 81 82

Founded 1979 at Petaluma. CHARD. is huge; P. NOIR impressive.

Lambert Bridge Sonoma. ★★ CS 80 81

Small 1975 winery nr. Healdsburg. CHARD less oaky in '82, '83 than formerly; CABERNET austere, needs ageing.

Landmark Sonoma. ★★ CH 80 81 82 83 84 CS 78 79 80 81

New winery nr. Windsor; sound CHARD. and CAB. Signs of class.

Laurel Glen Sonoma. ★★(?)

Splendid '81 CABERNET is first wine of tiny Glen Ellen winery.

Laurent Perrier Central Coast/San Jose. ★★★ CH 81 82

Almaden-linked branch of the French Champagne firm started 1981 with excellent dry still CHARDONNAY.

Leeward Winery Central Coast/Ventura. ★★★ CH 80 81 82 83 CS 80 81

CHARDONNAY from Monterey and San Luis Obispo grapes started this new venture near Santa Barbara well in 1980.

Long Vineyards Napa. ★★→★★★ CH 78 79 80 81 82 83 CS 79 80 81

Small winery in eastern hills nr. CHAPPELLET. First good CHARDONNAY and late-harvest RIESLING, now CABERNET.

Lytton Springs Sonoma. ★★

Small specialist in Russian River ZIN; thick, heady, tannic.

Mark West Sonoma ★★→★★★ CH 80 81' 82 PN 79' 80 81 82 83

New winery in cool sub-region. Very satisfactory GEWÜRZ, CHARDONNAY. Now P. NOIR and sparkling Blanc de Noirs.

Markham Napa. ★★★ CS 78 79 80 81

1979 winery with 300 acres. Cabernet very sound, not thrilling. Good bone dry CHENIN BLANC.

Martin Ray Central Coast/S. Cruz Mts. ★★★ CH 81 82 83 CS 81

Eccentric small winery long famous for high prices; winemaker has changed, so may philosophy.

Martini, Louis Napa. ★★→ ★★★ CS 74 75 76 77 78 79 80 81 82 Z 77 78 79 80 81 82

Large but individual winery with very high standards, from standard "Mountain" wines up. CABERNET SAUVIGNON "Vineyard Selection" one of California's best. BARBERA, MERLOT, P.NOIR, ZIN, GEWÜRZ, FOLLE BLANCHE and Moscato Amabile are all well made. Sauvignon/Semillon white introduced in '83.

Masson, Paul Central Coast. ★→★★

Big, lively and reliable middle-quality winery with reliable "carafes" and good-value varietals, incl. CHARDONNAY, ZINFANDEL. Also Emerald Dry. Rubion (RUBY), good cheap sparkling and very good Souzão port-type.

Matanzas Creek Sonoma. *** CH 78 79 80 81 82 83 CS 79 80 81
First wines were GEWÜRZ and very good P. BLANC. CHARD even better, with '84 better balanced, less strong than forerunners.

Mayacamas Napa. **** CH 77 78 79 80 81 82 83 CS 76 77 78 79 80 81
First-rate very small v'yd. and winery offering CABERNET, CHARDONNAY, SAUV. BLANC and ZINFANDEL (sometimes).

McDowell Valley Vineyards Mendocino. ** CS 80 81 82
Big new development using old-established v'yd. to make wide range. To watch, esp. for ZIN and real SYRAH.

Milano Winery Mendocino ** CH 79 80 81 82 82 83 CS 79 80 81
Very small winery worth noting for CHARD. CAB is overweight.

Mill Creek Sonoma. **
1974 winery near Healdsburg with pleasant, easy-going CHARDONNAY, MERLOT, CABERNET.

Mirassou Central Coast. **→***
Dynamic mid-sized growers and makers, the fifth generation of the family. Pioneers in SALINAS v'yds. Notable GAMAY BEAUJOLAIS, GEWÜRZ and very pleasant sparkling.

Mondavi, Robert Napa. **→**** CH 76 77 78' 79 80' 81 82 83 CS 74' 75 76 77 78' 79' 80 81 82
Twenty-year-old winery with a brilliant record of innovation in styles, equipment and technique. Solid successes incl. CABERNET SAUVIGNON, SAUVIGNON BLANC (sold as Fumé Blanc), CHARDONNAY, PINOT NOIR. "Reserves" are marvellous. Also useful table wines. See also Opus One.

Monterey Peninsula Central Coast/Salinas. **→*** CH 78 79 80 81 82 83 CS 78 80 81
Very small winery near Carmel making chunky chewable ZINFANDEL and CABERNET from SALINAS and other grapes.

Monterey Vineyard Central Coast/Salinas. **
The first big modern winery of SALINAS, opened 1974. Now owned by Seagrams. Good ZINFANDEL, GEWÜRZ and SYLVANER and fruity feather-weight GAMAY BEAUJOLAIS.

Monteviña Amador. ** CS 79 80 81 Z 75 76 77 78 79 80 81 82
Pioneer small winery in revitalized area: the Shenandoah Valley, Amador County, in the Sierra foothills. ZINFANDEL, BARBERA and SAUVIGNON BLANC are achieving balance.

Monticello Cellars Napa. *** CH 81 82 83 CS 80 81 82
Ultra-modern new winery near Trefethen. Outstanding GEWÜRZ and SAUVIGNON BLANC first caught the eye. Now very good CHARDONNAY and CABERNET.

De Moor Napa. ** CH 80 81 82 83 CS 80 81 82
Small Yountville winery (formerly Napa Cellars) with steady record, esp. for CABERNET and ZINFANDEL. New (European) owners.

J. W. Morris Sonoma. ***
Small former specialist in high-quality port-types from SONOMA grapes. Just changed hands, moved to Healdsburg and started table wines.

Mount Eden Vineyards Central Coast. *** CH 78 79 80 81 82 83
Company owning a major share of what were MARTIN RAY Vineyards. Expensive wines. M.E.V. is a second-line label.

Mount Veeder Napa. *** CS 74 75 77 78 79 80 81
Ambitious little 1973 winery. High prices but good CABERNET.

Navarro Vineyards Mendocino. ** '
Grower of sound CHARD, P.NOIR, GEWÜRZ in cool Anderson Valley.

Opus One Napa. **** 79 80 81
Not a winery but a wine; the joint venture of Robert Mondavi and Baron Philippe de Rothschild. So far, in effect, a Mondavi Reserve of Reserves at a far-fetched price, however good.

Papagni, Angelo   San Joaquin.   ★★
  Grower of an old family with a technically outstanding modern winery at Madera. Dry coastal-style varietals incl. ZIN, CHARDONNAY, light "Moscato d'Angelo" and enjoyable Alicante Bouschet.

Parducci   Mendocino.   ⸢★★→★★★⸥   CH **80 81 83 84** CS **78 79 80 81 82**
  Well-established mid-sized winery with v'yds. in several locations. Good sturdy reds: CABERNET (and an excellent Cab./Merlot blend), PETITE SYRAH, ZINFANDEL, Burgundy. Also pleasant CHENIN BLANC and FRENCH COLOMBARD.

Pecota, Robert   Napa.   ⸢★★⸥   CH **82 83**
  Small cellar of ex-BERINGER man with high standards. Wines are CABERNET, SAUV. BLANC, CHARD, good light GAMAY.

Pedroncelli   Sonoma/Russian River.   ⸢★★→★★★⸥   CH **80 81** CS **78 79 80**
  Long-established family business with recent reputation for well-above-average ZINFANDEL, GEWÜRZTRAMINER and CHARDONNAY growing more stylish with practice.

Pepi, Robert   Napa ★★
  New stone hilltop winery between Oakville and Yountville has launched well as a SAUVIGNON BLANC specialist.

Phelps, Joseph   Napa.   ⸢★★★→★★★★⸥   CH **77 78 79 80' 81 82 83** CS **74 75 76 77 78 79 80 81 82**
  De luxe mid-size winery and v'yd. Late harvest RIESLING exceptional. Very good CHARDONNAY, CABERNET, SYRAH. The "Reserve" wine, "Insignia", is monstrously tannic.

Pine Ridge   Napa.   ★★→★★★   CH **80 81' 82 83** CS **79' 80 81 82**
  Small winery near Stag's Leap has made constantly stylish CHARDONNAY, MERLOT and CABERNET. Also mild but fresh off-dry CHENIN BLANC.

Piper–Sonoma   Sonoma.   ★★★
  A joint venture between Piper-Heidsieck of Champagne and Sonoma Vineyards released its first (very good) sparkling cuvée in 1980. The '81 needed until '85 to round out.

Preston   Sonoma.   ★★★
  Tiny winery with very high standards in Dry Creek Valley, Healdsburg, esp. for SAUV. BLANC, and ZIN.

Quail Ridge   Napa.   ★★
  Small specialist in barrel-fermented CHARDONNAY. Good wines, if pricey.

Rafanelli, J.   Sonoma.   ⸢★★⸥
  Tiny cellar specializing in outstanding ZIN; also Gamay.

Raymond Vineyards   Napa.   ⸢★★★→★★★★⸥   CH **77 79 80' 81' 82 83 84** CS **77 78 79 80' 81**
  Small 1974 winery near St. Helena with experienced owners. CHARD, RIESLING and CABERNET all excellent.

Ridge   Central Coast S. CRUZ.   ★★★★ CS **77 78 79** 80 81 82 Z **79 80 81 82**
  Small winery of high repute among connoisseurs for powerful concentrated reds needing long maturing in bottle. Notable CAB and strong ZIN from named v'yds; esp. Montebello.

River Oaks   Sonoma.   ★→★★
  Sound commercial wines from same winery as CLOS DU BOIS, but different vineyards.

Rombauer Vineyards   Napa ★★ (?)
  New ('80) small winery buying Napa grapes for impressive CHARD and CAB. SAUV.

Roudon–Smith   Santa Clara/Santa Cruz. ★★→   ⸢★★★⸥   CH **79 80 81 82 83 84** CS **78 79 81 82**
  Small winery offering really stylish CHARDONNAY.

Round Hill   Napa.   ⸢★★⸥   CH **80 81 82** CS **79 80 81**
  Consistent good value, esp. GEWÜRZ and FUMÉ BLANC, from St. Helena. Second label: Rutherford Ranch.

Rutherford Hill   Napa.   `***`   CH **77 78 79 80 81 82** 83 CS **76 77 78 79** 80 81 82

Larger stable-mate of FREEMARK ABBEY. Good GEWÜRZ. Excellent CHARD, MERLOT and CABERNET.

Rutherford Vintners, Inc.   Napa.   `**→***`   CH **80 81 82 83** CS **77 78 79** 80 81

Small winery started in 1977 by Bernard Skoda. "Chateau Rutherford" is "Reserve" label.

St. Andrews   Napa.   `***` **81 82** 83

Small CHARDONNAY estate on Silverado Trail near Napa city. Steadily excellent wine.

St. Clement   Napa.   `***` CH **79 80 81 82 83** CS **77 78 79 80** 81

Small production. Good CABERNET, powerful CHARD and delicious SAUVIGNON BLANC.

St. Francis   Sonoma.   `**` CH **80 81 82** 83

New small winery is using excellent CHARD, CABERNET, GEWÜRZ grapes from older v'yd. Wines have been disappointing.

Saintsbury   Napa.   `***` CH **81 82 83** PN 81 82 83

New winery with encouraging first wines.

Sanford   Santa Barbara.   `***`

New winery started with striking 1982 SAUV. BLANC and CHARDONNAY in the toast and oak school. '83 P. NOIR is much praised; also P. NOIR Blanc.

San Martin   Central Coast.   `**` CS **78 80** 81

Restructured old company using SALINAS and SAN LUIS OBISPO grapes to make clean, correct varietals. "Select Vintage" is top label. Also pioneers in "soft" (low-alcohol) wines.

Santa Cruz Mountain V'yd.   C. Coast.   `**→***` CS **78 79 80** 81 PN **79** 80 81

Small winery in the hills with hopes for fine PINOT NOIR, but problems with high alcohol. Now CABERNET, too.

Santa Ynez Valley Winery   Santa Barbara.   `***` CH **79 80 81** 82

Established producer of very good SAUV. BLANC and CHARD.

Sausal   Sonoma.   `**`

Small specialist in stylish ZIN, etc.

Schramsberg   Napa.   `****`

A dedicated specialist using historic old cellars to make California's best "champagne", incl. splendid "Reserves". "Blanc de Noirs" is outstanding.

Schug Winery   Napa.   `***` CH **82** PN **80** 81

New (1982) enterprise of PHELPS' ex-winemaker. Very tough PINOT NOIR.

Sebastiani   Sonoma.   `*→***` CS **78 79** 80 81

Substantial and distinguished old family firm with robust appetizing wines, incl. BARBERA. Top wines have SONOMA appellation. New "Eagle" Cabernets (80, 81) are remarkable.

Sequoia Grove   Napa `**→***`

Small winery nr. Oakville. CHARD since '79 has been well-balanced. CAB.SAUV. (Napa and Alexander Valleys) is tannic and meant to age.

Shafer Vineyards   Napa.   `**→***` CH **80** 81' **82** CS **80** 81 82 83

New winery and vineyard near Stag's Leap have made polished CHARDONNAY and very stylish CABERNET.

Shaw, Charles F., Vineyards and Winery   Napa.   `**` CH 83

St. Helena specialist in GAMAY light red, has added CHARD, CABERNET, SAUVIGNON BLANC (N.B. 83).

Silver Oak   Napa.   `**→***` CS **78 79 80** 81

Small 1972 winery succeeding with oaky CABERNET.

Silverado Cellars   Napa.   `***`

A showy new winery east of Yountville. Early CHARDONNAY and SAUVIGNON BLANC have been excellent. Now CABERNET too. The owner is Mrs. Walt Disney, which suggests adequate capital.

Simi   Alexander Valley.   `**→***`   CH 80 81 82 83 CS 78 79 80 81
Restored old winery with expert direction of Zelma Long. Lovely
CHARDONNAY, delicate CABERNET and (since '82) splendid
SAUV. BLANC.

Smith-Madrone   Napa. `**→***` CH 81 82 83 CS **79 80** 81 82
New v'yd. high on Spring Mountain made first good RIESLING in
'77. PINOT NOIR and CABERNET are catching up.

Smothers   Santa Clara/Santa Cruz. `***`
Tiny winery owned by T.V. comic made promising first wines,
esp. late-harvest GEWÜRZ. Still more smoke than fire.

Sonoma-Cutrer Vineyards, Inc.   Sonoma. `***→****` CH 82 83 84
Perhaps the ultimate (so far) in specialist estates, using new
techniques to display the characters individual v'yds give to
CHARDS (as in Burgundy). So far Les Pierres v'yd has made the
best.

Souverain   Alexander Valley.   `**` CH81 82 83 CS 78' 79 80' 81
Luxurious mid-sized winery with a record of competent wines,
bought by BERINGER in 1986.

Spring Mountain   Napa. `***` CH 79 80 81 82 83 CS 75 77 78 79 80 81
Renovated small 19th-century property with winery noted for
good CHARDONNAY, SAUVIGNON BLANC and CABERNET.

Stag's Leap Wine Cellars   Napa. `***→****` CH 77 78 79 80 81' 82 83
CS 74' 75 76 77 78' 79' 80 81 82
Celebrated small v'yd. and cellar with the highest standards.
Excellent CABERNET and MERLOT, fresh GAMAY, fine CHARD.

Sterling   Napa. `***` CH 77 78 79 80 81 82 83
Spectacular mid-sized winery, now owned by Seagrams. Strong,
tart SAUVIGNON BLANC and CHARDONNAY; fruity CABERNET and
MERLOT. New joint venture with Mumm launched Domaine
Mumm sparkling in 1986.

Stonegate   Napa. `**→***` CH 79 80 81 82 83 CS 78 79 80 83
Small privately owned winery and v'yd. making CABERNET,
CHARDONNAY and better and better SAUV. BLANC.

Stony Hill   Napa. `****` CH 74 75 76 77 78 79 80 81 82 83
Many of California's very best whites have come from this
minute winery over 30 years. Owner Fred McCrea died in 1977;
his widow Eleanor carries on. Stony Hill CHARDONNAY, GEWÜRZ
and RIESLING are all delicate and fine.

Stratford   Napa. `**` (?)
First wine ('82) was an impressive blended CHARD. New winery
nr. Rutherford will provide more.

Strong, Rodney, Vineyards   Sonoma/Russian River.   `**` →`***`
CS 78 79 80
Quick-growing business formerly called Sonoma Vineyards.
Well regarded, esp. for CHARD. Range includes single-v'yd.
wines, esp. Alexander's Crown CABERNET. See also Piper-
Sonoma.

Sutter Home   Napa.   `**` Z 77 78 79 80 81 82 83
Small winery revived and greatly expanded on the success of its
invention: white ZINFANDEL.

Swan, J.   Sonoma. `**` Z 74 76 77 78 80 81
Young one-man winery with a name for rich ZINFANDEL.

Trefethen   Napa. `**→****` CH 77 78' 79 80' 81 82 83 CS 74' 75 76 77
78 79 80 81 82
Growing family-owned winery in Napa's finest old wooden
building. Very good dry RIESLING, CABERNET, P.NOIR. Brilliant
CHARDONNAY and a notable low-price blend, Eshcol.

Tulocay   Napa. `**` CS 80
Tiny new winery at Napa City. First wines are good PINOT NOIR
and CABERNET.

Ventana   Central Coast/Monterey. `**` CH 78 79 80 81 82
New in '78 with flavoury PINOT BLANC and CHARDONNAY.

Vichon Winery   Napa. ★→★→★★★ CH **80 81' 82 83** CS 81 82
Founded 1980; original and ambitious. Fine CHARDONNAY and blended (50/50) SAUVIGNON/SEMILLON "Chevrignon Blanc". Now promising CABERNETS. Bought (1985) by ROBERT MONDAVI.

Villa Mount Eden   Napa. ★★★ CH **78 80 81 82 83** CS **77 78 79** 80 81
Small Oakville estate with excellent dry CHENIN BLANC, good CHARDONNAY, and outstanding CABERNET.

Weibel   Central Coast and Mendocino.   ★→★★
Veteran mid-sized winery giving value in its class. Specialist in own-label sparkling wines.

Wente   Livermore and Central Coast. ★→★★★
Important and historic specialists in Bordeaux-style whites. Fourth-generation Wentes are as dynamic as ever. CHARDONNAY, SAUVIGNON BLANC and RIESLING are all successful commercial wines. Now also sparkling.

Zaca Mesa   Central Coast/Santa Barbera.   ★★   CH **78 79 81** CS **79** 80
Santa Ynez Valley pioneer with good CHARD. and RIESLING.

Z-D Wines   Napa. ★★ CH **80 81 82** CS **79** 80 81
Very small winery (moved from Sonoma to Rutherford) with a name for powerful PINOT NOIR and CHARDONNAY.

The Pacific North-West

There are now 15,000 acres of vines, and over 100 wineries in the States of Washington, Oregon and Idaho.

Oregon's vines lie mainly in the cool-temperate Willamette and warmer Umpqua valleys between the Coast and Cascades ranges. Those of Washington and Idaho are mainly east of the Cascades in the semi-arid Yakima Valley and Columbia basin areas, with very hot days and cold nights. Most Oregon-grown wines are consequently more delicate, Washington's more intensive in flavour. Some wineries use both. Whites are in the majority, though Oregon does very well with Pinot Noir and Washington with Merlot.

The principal current producers are:

Adelsheim Vineyard   Willamette, Oregon
Small winery: promising P. NOIR, oaky CHARDONNAY.

Amity Vineyards   Willamette, Oregon
1976 70-acre winery; variable quality: PINOT NOIR best.

Arbor Crest   Spokane, Washington
Expanding and encouraging newcomer. Early CHARD and SAUV. BLANC v.g. Reds also promising. To watch.

Champs de Brionne   George, Washington
New winery. Fast start in whites.

Château Ste. Michelle   Seattle, Columbia and Yakima valleys, Washington
The leading north-west winery, with some 5,000 acres, ultra-modern equipment and a wide range of labels. Best wines are CABERNET, SEMILLON, CHARDONNAY, MERLOT. Sparkling wines also good. Jug wines: Farron Ridge.

Columbia (formerly Associated Vintners)   Washington
A Washington pioneer at Redmond, nr. Seattle. CABERNET, RIESLING, dry spicy GEWÜRZ and esp. SEMILLON have all been successful. Good value. Now good Chardonnay.

Covey Run (formerly Quail Run)   Yakima, Washington
Admirable whites incl. ALIGOTÉ; reds esp. MERLOT.

Elk Cove Vineyards   Willamette, Oregon
Very small 1977 winery. Good CHARDONNAY and esp. RIESLING from named v'yds. PINOT NOIR probably best.

The Eyrie Vineyards   Willamette, Oregon
>   Early (1965) winery with Burgundian ideas. Oregon's most consistently good P. NOIR, and v. oaky CHARD. Also Pinots Gris, Meunier and dry Muscat.

Hillcrest Vineyard   Umpqua Valley, Oregon
>   Early (1961) winery in warmer area. Inconsistent; CAB best.

Hogue Cellars   Yakima, Washington
>   Big new winery outstanding for off-dry whites, esp. RIESLING, CHENIN BLANC, SAUV. BLANC. And bold CHARD.

Knudsen Erath   Willamette, Oregon
>   Oregon's second-biggest winery with reliable good-value PINOT NOIR, esp. Vintage Select. Austere CHARDONNAY.

F. W. Langguth Winery   Yakima, Washington
>   German Mosel-maker succeeding with German-style RIESLINGS, esp. late harvest. Second label: Saddle Mountain.

Oak Knoll   Willamette, Oregon
>   Fruit-winemaker also making good-value red wines, esp. P. NOIR (red and white).

Preston Wine Cellars   Yakima Valley, Washington
>   Small winery acclaimed especially for RIES, CHARD, GEWÜRZ.

Château Ste. Chapelle   Caldwell, Idaho
>   The first Idaho winery, near Boise. CHARDONNAY and RIESLING with exceptionally intense flavours but beautiful balance.

Shafer Vineyard Cellars   Willamette, Oregon
>   Small meticulous P. NOIR specialist. White P. NOIR may be Oregon's best.

Sokol Blosser Vineyards   Willamette, Oregon
>   Largest Oregon winery with wide range, incl. CHARD (esp. "Yamhill County"), SAUV. BLANC, MERLOT and (slightly sweet) RIESLING. P. NOIR is best regular effort.

Tualatin Vineyards   Willamette, Oregon
>   Third-largest Oregon winery. Mainly whites with emphasis on CHARD, P. NOIR (red and white). Both Washington and home-grown grapes. Mixed reports.

The North and East

New York State and its neighbours Ohio and Ontario make their own style of wine from grapes of native American ancestry, rather than the European vines of California. American grapes have a flavour known as "foxy"; a taste acquired by many easterners. Fashion is moving in favour of hybrids between these and European grapes with less, or no, foxiness, and increasingly towards true European varieties. Greatly improved quality, however, has coincided with high costs and intense competition to put the industry in a delicate situation. The entries below include both wineries and grape varieties.

Andres
> Canada's second-largest wine-producer, with wineries in Ontario and British Columbia.

Aurora
> One of the best white French-American hybrid grapes, the most widely planted in New York. Formerly known as Seibel 5279. Good for sparkling wine.

Baco Noir
> One of the better red French-American hybrid grapes. High acidity but good clean dark wine.

Benmarl
> Highly regarded and expanding v'yd. and winery at Marlboro on the Hudson River. Wines are mainly from French-American hybrids, but CHARD can be splendid.

Brights
> Canada's biggest winery, in Ontario, now tending towards French-American hybrids and experiments with European vines. Their BACO NOIR is a sound red, CHARDONNAY is steely, ALIGOTÉ pleasant. Now also in British Columbia..

Bully Hill
> New (since 1970) FINGER LAKES winery using both American and hybrid grapes to make varietal wines.

Château des Charmes
> Smaller Ontario winery, doing well with CHARD, P. NOIR, GAMAY, RIESLING.

Château Gai
> Big Canadian (Ontario) winery making European and hybrid wines, incl. v. light CHARD, GAMAY, MERLOT.

Catawba
> One of the first American wine-grapes, still the second most widely grown. Pale red and foxy flavoured.

Chautauqua
> The biggest grape-growing district in the east, along the s. shore of Lake Erie from New York to Ohio.

Chelois
> Popular red French-American hybrid, formerly called Seibel 10878. Dry red wine with some richness, slightly foxy.

Concord
> The archetypal American grape, dark red, strongly foxy, making good grape jelly but dreadful wine.

Delaware
> Old American white-wine grape making pleasant, slightly foxy dry wines. Used in "Champagne" and for still wine.

De Chaunac
> A good red French-American hybrid grape, popular in Canada as well as New York. Full-bodied dark wine.

Finger Lakes
> Century-old wine district in upper New York State, best-known for its "Champagne". The centre is Hammondsport.

Fournier, Charles

> The top quality of "Champagne" made by the GOLD SEAL company, named for a former pioneering winemaker.

Glenora Wine Cellars

> Recent FINGER LAKES winery. Successful RIES and CHARD.

Gold Seal

> One of New York's biggest wineries, makers of Charles FOURNIER "Champagne" and the HENRI MARCHANT range. Known for high quality and readiness to experiment. Recent Chardonnay has been excellent, winning significant prizes.

Great Western

> The brand name of the PLEASANT VALLEY WINE CO'S "Champagne", one of New York's sound traditional wines.

Hargrave Vineyard

> Trend-setting winery planting extensively on North Fork of Long Island, N.Y. Very promising CHARDONNAY, PINOT NOIR.

Henri Marchant

> GOLD SEAL'S range of mainly traditional American wines.

Inniskillin

> Small 1974 Canadian winery at Niagara. European and hybrid wines, incl. good MARÉCHAL FOCH, also CHARDONNAY.

Phylloxera is an insect that lives on the roots of the vine. Its arrival in Europe from North America in the 1860s was an international catastrophe. It destroyed almost every vineyard on the continent before it was discovered that the native American vine is immune to its attacks. The remedy was (and still is) to graft European vines on to American rootstocks. Virtually all Europe's vineyards are so grafted today. Whether their produce is just as good as the wine of pre-phylloxera days is a favourite debate among old-school wine-lovers.

Maréchal Foch

> Promising red French hybrid between PINOT NOIR and GAMAY. Makes good burgundy-style wine in Ontario.

Niagara

> Old American white grape used for sweet wine. Very foxy.

Pleasant Valley Wine Co.

> Winery at Hammondsport, FINGER LAKES, owned by TAYLOR'S, producing GREAT WESTERN wines.

Seibel   One of the most famous French grape hybridists, responsible for many successful French-American crosses originally known by numbers, since christened with such names as AURORA, DE CHAUNAC, CHELOIS.

Seyve-Villard

> Another well-known French hybridist. His best-known cross, no. 5276, is known as Seyval Blanc.

Taylor's

> The biggest wine-company of the Eastern States, based at Hammondsport in the FINGER LAKES. Brands incl. GREAT WESTERN and LAKE COUNTRY. Most vines are American.

Vinifera Wines

> Small but influential winery of Dr Konstantin Frank, pioneer in growing European vines, incl. RIESLING, CHARDONNAY and PINOT NOIR, in the FINGER LAKES area. Some excellent wines.

Widmers

> Major FINGER LAKES winery selling native American varietal wines: DELAWARE, NIAGARA, etc.

Wiemer, Herman J.

> Creative and daring German FINGER LAKES winemaker. Fine RIESLINGS; ferments CHARDONNAY in oak.

South America

The flourishing vineyards of Argentina (the world's fifth largest) and Chile are known to the world chiefly as a source of cheap wine of sometimes remarkable quality. Most of it is drunk within South America. Brazil also has an expanding wine industry in the Rio Grande do Sul area, but as yet no exports.

ARGENTINA

The quality vineyards are concentrated in Mendoza province in the Andean foothills at about 2,000 feet. They are all irrigated. San Raphael, 140 miles s. of Mendoza city, is centre of a slightly cooler area. San Juan, to the north, is hotter and specializes in sherry and brandy. Salta, in the north, also produces interesting wines.

Bianchi, Bodegas
Well-known premium wine producer at San Rafael owned by Seagrams. "Don Valentin" CABERNET and Bianchi Borgoña are best-sellers. "Particular" is their top CABERNET.

Crillon, Bodegas
1972-built winery owned by Seagram's, principally for tank-method sparkling wines.

Esmeralda Producers of a good CABERNET, St Felician, at Cordoba.

Flichman, Bodegas
Old Mendoza firm now owned by a bank. Top "Caballero de la Cepa" white and red, plus SYRAH, MERLOT and sparkling.

Giol The enormous State cooperative of Maipu province. Mainly bulk wines. Premium range called "Canciller" is good.

Gonzales Videla, Bodegas
Old-established family firm re-equipped for modern methods. Brands include "Tromel" and "Panquehua".

Goyenechea, Bodegas
Basque family firm in San Rafael making old-style wines, including Aberdeen Angus red.

La Rural, Bodegas ("San Filipe")
Family-run winery at Coquimbito (Mendoza) making some of Argentina's best RIESLING and GEWÜRZ whites and some good reds. Also a charming wine museum.

Lopez, Bodegas
Family firm best known for their "Château Montchenot" red and white and "Château Vieux" CABERNET.

Norton, Bodegas
Old firm, originally English. Reds (esp. Malbec) are best. "Perdriel" is their premium brand. Also good sparkling wines.

Orfila, José
Long-established bodega at St. Martin, Mendoza. Top wines are Cautivo CABERNET and white Extra Dry (PINOT BLANC).

Peñaflor
Argentina's biggest wine company, reputedly the world's third-largest. Bulk wines, but also some of Argentina's finest premium wines incl. Trapiche (esp. "Medalla"), Andean Vineyards and Fond de Cave CHARDONNAY and CABERNET. A respectable sherry, Tio Quinto, is exported.

Proviar, Bodega Producers of "Baron B" and "M. Chandon" sparkling wine under MOËT ET CHANDON supervision. Also still reds and whites including v.g. Castel Chandon, less exciting Kleinburg, Wunderwein (whites), smooth easy Comte de Valmont, Beltour and Clos du Moulin reds.

Santa Ana, Bodegas
Small, old-established family firm at Guaymallen, Mendoza. Wide range of wines include good Syrah Val Semina.

San Telmo
Modern winery with an almost Californian air and outstanding fresh, full-flavoured CHARD, MERLOT, CAB and esp. MALBEC.

Suter, Bodegas
Swiss-founded firm owned by Seagram's, making best-selling "Etiquetta Marron" white and good "Etiquetta Blanca" red.

Toso, Pascual
Old Mendoza winery at San José, making one of Argentina's best reds, Cabernet Toso. Also RIESLING and sparkling wines.

Trapiche
See PEÑAFLOR

Weinert, Bodegas
Small winery. Tough old-fashioned reds and over-dry whites.

CHILE

Natural conditions are ideal for wine-growing in central Chile, just south of Santiago. But political conditions have been very difficult, and the country's full potential still has to be explored. The Cabernets are best. The principal bodegas exporting wine from Chile are:

Canepa, José
Chile's most modern big bodega, handling wine from several areas. Very good frank and fruity CABERNET from Lontüé, Talca, 100 miles south; dry SAUV and SEMILLON, sweet Moscatel.

Concha y Toro
The biggest and most outward-looking wine firm, with several bodegas and 2,500 acres in the Maipo valley. Remarkable dark and deep CABERNET, MERLOT, Verdot. Brands are St. Emiliana, Marques de Casa Concha, Cassillero del Diablo. 300 acres of new white varieties have recently been planted.

Cousiño Macul
Distinguished estate near Santiago. Very dry "green" SEMILLON and CHARDONNAY. Don Luis light red, Don Matias dark and tannic, are good CABERNETS. Some old vintages are notable.

Los Vascos
New family estate in Colchagua Prov. 400 acres starting to make really stylish SAUV/SEM "Chevrier" and perhaps Chile's best CABERNET (84) influenced by B'x and California.

Santa Carolina
Splendid old Santiago bodega with old-style "Reserva de Familia" and better "Ochagavia" wines.

San Pedro
Long established at Lontüé, Talca. Range of good wines sold all over S. America, esp. Bordeaux-like CABERNET Llave de Oro.

Santa Rita
Bodega in the Maipo valley s. of Santiago. Pleasant soft wines including the "120" brand. Casa Real CAB is the best wine.

Torres, Miguel
New enterprise of Catalan family firm (see Spain) at Lontüé. Good SAUV ("Bellaterra" is oak-aged) and CHARD, v.g. RIESLING. CAB still rather lightweight.

Undurraga
Famous family business; one of the first to export to the U.S.A. Wines in both old and modern styles: good clean SAUVIGNON BLANC and oaky yellow "Viejo Roble". "Gran Vino Tinto" is one of the best buys in Chile.

Viña Linderos
Small family winery in the Maipo valley exports good full-bodied CABERNET which gains from bottle-age.

PERU

Tacama, Viña
Amazing SAUV. BLANC and sparkling from Ica Prov. Also CAB.

England

The English wine industry started again in earnest in the late 1960s after a pause of some 400 years. More than a million bottles a year are now being made from over 1,000 acres; almost all white and generally Germanic in style, many from new German and French grape varieties designed to ripen well in cool weather. The annual Gore-Brown Trophy is awarded for the best English wine. N.B. Beware "British Wine", which is neither British nor wine, and has nothing to do with the following

Adgestone nr. Sandown, Isle of Wight. K. C. Barlow
Prize-winning 9½-acre v'yd. on chalky hill site. Vines are MÜLLER-THURGAU, Reichensteiner, SEYVAL BLANC. First vintage 1970. Light, fragrant, dryish wines age surprisingly well.

Barton Manor East Cowes, Isle of Wight. A. Goddard
5½-acre v'yd producing an aromatic medium dry blend, winner of the '84 Gore-Brown Trophy. Consistently good.

Beaulieu nr. Lymington, Hampshire. The Hon. Ralph Montagu
6-acre v'yd, principally of MÜLLER-THURGAU, established in 1960 by the Gore-Brown family on an old monastic site.

Biddenden nr. Tenterden, Kent. R. A. Barnes
18-acre mixed v'yd. planted in 1970, making crisp medium-dry white of MÜLLER-THURGAU and Ortega; also a rosé with PINOT NOIR. First vintage 1973. Also makes wine for other growers. Gold medal winner in 1983.

Bosmere nr. Chippenham, Wiltshire. G. H. Walton
16 acres of MÜLLER-THURGAU and SEYVAL BLANC; some GAMAY and PINOT NOIR.

Breaky Bottom nr. Lewes, Sussex P. Hall
Good dry wines from 4-acre vineyard.

Bruisyard nr. Saxmundham, Suffolk. I. H. Berwick
10 acres of MÜLLER-THURGAU making medium-dry wines since 1976. Well distributed..

Carr Taylor Vineyards nr. Hastings, Sussex. D. Carr-Taylor
21 acres, planted 1974. Gutenborner, Huxelrebe, KERNER and Reichensteiner. Exports to France.

Cavendish Manor nr. Sudbury, Suffolk. B. T. Ambrose
10½-acre v'yd. of MÜLLER-THURGAU planted on a farm. Fruity dry wine has won several awards at home and abroad since 1974.

Chilford Hundred Linton, nr. Cambridge. S. Alper
20 acres of MÜLLER-THURGAU, Schönburger, Huxelrebe, Siegerrebe and Ortega making fairly dry wines since 1974.

Chilsdown nr. Chichester, Sussex. Paget Brothers
10 acres of MÜLLER-THURGAU, Reichensteiner and SEYVAL BLANC making full dry French-style white since 1974.

Ditchling nr. Hassocks, Sussex. D. & A. Mills
5-acres v'yd well-reputed for consistency.

Elmham Park nr. East Dereham, Norfolk. R. Don
7½-acre v'yd. of a wine-merchant/fruit farmer, planted with MÜLLER-THURGAU, Madeleine-Angevine, etc. "Mosel-style" light dry flowery wines. First vintage 1974. Also a fine dry cider.

Gamlingay nr. Sandy, Bedfordshire. G. P. and N. Reece
8½ acres of MÜLLER-THURGAU, Reichensteiner and SCHEUREBE making wine since 1970.

Hambledon nr. Petersfield, Hampshire. Hambledon Vineyards Ltd
The first modern English v'yd., planted in 1951 on a chalk slope with advice from Champagne. Grapes are CHARDONNAY, PINOT NOIR and SEYVAL BLANC. Now 7½ acres. Fairly dry wines.

Hascombe Godalming, Surrey. Lt. Cdr. T. P. Baillie-Grohman
5½-acre v'yd., principally MÜLLER-THURGAU, making dry delicate wines since 1971.

Highwaymans nr. Bury St. Edmunds, Suffolk. Macrae Farms
25 acres, planted 1974. MÜLLER-THURGAU and PINOT NOIR.

Lamberhurst Priory nr. Tunbridge Wells, Kent. K. McAlpine
England's biggest v'yd. with 48 acres, planted 1972. Largely
MÜLLER-THURGAU, SEYVAL BLANC, also Reichensteiner, Schön-
burger. Production capacity approx. half a million bottles a year
including winemaking for other small v'yds. Also makes Horam
Manor, 8 acres at Heathfield, Sussex. A regular prize-winner.

Lexham Hall nr. King's Lynn, Norfolk. N. W. D. Foster
8 acres, planted 1975. MÜLLER-THURGAU, SCHEUREBE, Reichensteiner and Madeleine-Angevine.

New Hall nr. Maldon, Essex. S. W. Greenwood
24 acres of a mixed farm planted with Huxelrebe, MÜLLER-
THURGAU and PINOT NOIR. Makes award-winning whites.
Experimental reds.

Penshurst nr. Tunbridge Wells, Kent. D. E. Westphal
12 acres of the usual varieties in production since 1976.

Pilton Manor nr. Shepton Mallet, Somerset. N. Godden
6½-acre hillside v'yd., chiefly MÜLLER-THURGAU and SEYVAL
BLANC, planted 1966. Also a méthode champenoise sparkling
wine.

Pulham nr. Norwich, Norfolk. P. W. Cook
6-acre v'yd. planted 1973; principally MÜLLER-THURGAU,
Auxerrois and experimental Bacchus.

Rock Lodge nr. Haywards Heath, Sussex. N. D. Cowderoy
3½-acre v'yd. of MÜLLER-THURGAU and Reichensteiner making
dry white since 1970.

St. Etheldreda nr. Ely, Cambridgeshire. N. Sneesby
2-acre mixed v'yd. making a MÜLLER-THURGAU and a CHAR-
DONNAY since 1974.

St. George's Waldron, Heathfield, E. Sussex. P. & G. Biddlecombe
5 acres planted 1979. MÜLLER-THURGAU etc. and some GEWÜRZ.
Well-publicized young venture has sold wine to Japan.

Spots Farm nr. Tenterden, Kent. S. Skelton.
10 acres; MÜLLER-THURGAU, Gutenborner, Reichensteiner, etc.
Has won several awards.

Staple nr. Canterbury, Kent. W. T. Ash
7 acres, mainly MÜLLER-THURGAU. Some Huxelrebe and
Reichensteiner. Dry and fruity wines.

Stocks nr. Suckley, Worcestershire. R. M. O. Capper
Successful 11-acre v'yd. All MÜLLER-THURGAU.

Tenterden nr. Tenterden, Kent. S. P. Skelton
12 acres of a 100-acre fruit farm. Planted 1977. Six wines from
very dry to sweet, incl. MÜLLER-THURGAU, Gutenborner, SEYVAL
BLANC and rosé, silver medal in '84 Gore-Brown Trophy.

Three Choirs nr. Newent, Gloucestershire. T. W. Day.
17½ acres of MÜLLER-THURGAU and Reichensteiner.

Westbury nr. Reading, Berkshire. B. H. Theobald
12½ acres of a mixed farm. 11 varieties in commercial quantities
since 1975, incl. PINOT NOIR red.

Wootton nr. Wells, Somerset. Major C. L. B. Gillespie
6-acre v'yd. of Schönburger, MÜLLER-THURGAU, SEYVAL BLANC,
etc., making award-winning fresh and fruity wines since 1973.

Wraxall nr. Shepton Mallet, Somerset. A. S. Holmes
6 acres of MÜLLER-THURGAU and SEYVAL BLANC. Planted 1974.

Australia

S.A.

Hunter Valley

Clare/ Watervale

Murray Valley

N.S.W.

Barossa

Riverina

●Adelaide

Canberra ●

outhern Vales

Langhorne Creek

Rutherglen

N.E. VIC.

Coonawarra

CENTRAL VIC.
Great Western

● Melbourne

It is only 20 years since modern wine technology revolutionized Australia's 150-year-old wine industry, ending the dominance of fortified wines and making table wines of top quality possible. Traditional-style Australian wines were thick-set and burly Shiraz reds or Semillon or Riesling whites grown in warm to hot regions. A progressive shift to cooler areas, to new wood fermentation and maturation, to noble varieties (with Cabernet, Merlot, Pinot Noir, Chardonnay and Sauvignon Blanc at the forefront) has seen a radical change in style which has by no means run its course. Nonetheless, extract and alcohol levels continue to be high and the best wines still have great character and the ability to age splendidly.

The parallels with California abound. The most obvious is a suddenly-developed need to find new markets. For the first time, Australia's best wines are to be found in New York and London. But it is not easy to keep tabs on them. New wineries multiply at an alarming rate: there are now almost 500 wineries in commercial production. Labels are becoming less garrulous (and less informative) as Australian consumers become more sophisticated. The information they give can be relied on, while prizes in shows (which are highly competitive) mean a great deal. In a country without any sort of established grades of quality the buyer needs all the help he can get.

Wine areas

The vintages mentioned here are those rated as good or excellent for the reds of the areas in question. Excellent recent vintages are marked with an accent, e.g. 82'.

Adelaide Hills (Sth Aust)   84' 85' 86'
Spearheaded by PETALUMA: numerous new v'yds at very cool 1500' sites in Mt Lofty ranges coming into production.

Adelaide Plains (Sth Aust) 79 80 82 84' 86'
Small area immediately n. of Adelaide formerly known as Angle Vale. Anglesey, Normans and PRIMO ESTATE best known wineries.

Barossa (Sth Aust) 66 73 75 76 79 80 81 82' 84' 85 86'

> Australia's most important winery (though not v'yd) area, processing grapes from diverse sources (local, to MURRAY VALLEY, through to high quality cool regions from adjacent hills to far-distant COONAWARRA) to make equally diverse styles.

Bendigo/Ballarat (Vic) 73 75 76 78 79 80' 82 84' 85

> Widespread small v'yds some of extreme quality, re-creating the glories of the last century. 14 wineries incl. Ch. le Amon, Heathcote Winery and Passing Clouds.

Canberra District (ACT)

> 10 wineries now sell cellar door to local and tourist trade. Quality is variable, as is style.

Clare Watervale (Sth Aust) 66' 70' 71' 73' 76' 79' **80' 82'** 84' **85'** 86'

> Small high-quality area 90 miles n. of Adelaide best known for RIESLING; also planted with SHIRAZ and CABERNET. 17 wineries spill over into new adjacent sub-district of Polish Hill River.

Coonawarra (Sth Aust) 66 70 71 72 73 76 77 79 80' 82' 84 85 86'

> Southernmost and greatest v'yd. of state, long famous for well-balanced reds, recently successful with RIESLING, CHARDONNAY. Numerous recent arrivals incl. Hollicks, Haselgrove, Koppamurra, Ladbroke Grove, Zema Estates.

Geelong (Vic) 78 80' 82 84' 85

> Once famous area destroyed by phylloxera, re-established mid 60s. Very cool, dry climate produces firm table wines from premium varieties. Names incl. IDYLL.

Goulburn Valley (Vic) 68 71 76 79 80' 82 84'

> A mixture of old (e.g. CH. TAHBILK) and new (e.g. MITCHELTON) wineries in temperate region; full flavoured table wines.

Great Western/Avoca (Vic) 78 80' 82' 84 85

> Adjacent cool to temperate regions in central w. of state; Avoca also known as Pyrenees area. High quality table and sparkling wines. Now 8 wineries, 6 of recent origin.

Hunter Valley (N.S.W.) 66 67 70 72 73 75 76 77 79 80' 82 84 85' 86

> The great name in N.S.W. Broad soft earthy SHIRAZ reds and SEMILLON whites with a style of their own. Now also CABERNET and CHARDONNAY. Many changes in identity.

Keppoch/Padthaway (Sth Aust) 75 76 79 80 81 82' 84 85

> Large new v'yd. area (no wineries) developed by big companies as an overspill of adjacent COONAWARRA. Cool climate; good commercial reds and whites and CHARD/PINOT NOIR sp. wines.

N.E. Victoria 66' 70' 71' 73' 75' 76' **80' 82' 84'** 86'

> Historic area incl. Rutherglen, Corowa, Wangaratta. Heavy reds and magnificent sweet dessert wines.

Margaret River (W. Aust) 75' 76' 79' **81'** 82' 83' **85**

> New cool coastal area producing superbly elegant wines, 280 kms s. of Perth. 15 operating wineries; others planned.

Mornington Peninsula (Vic.) 84' 86'

> Five commercial wineries on dolls-house scale making exciting wines in new cool coastal area 40km s. of Melbourne. 20 growers, wineries incl. Elgee Park.

Mount Barker/Franklin River (W. Aust) 76 80 81' 82 83

> Promising new far-flung cool area in extreme south of state.

Mudgee (N.S.W.) 72 74 75 78 79 80 82' 84'

> Small isolated area 270 kms n.w. of Sydney. Big r. of colour and flavour and full coarse w., recently being refined.

Murray Valley (Sth Aust, Vic & N.S.W.) NV

> Important irrigated v'yds. near Swan Hill, Mildura (N.S.W. and Vic), Renmark, Berri, Loxton, Waikerie and Morgan (S.A.). Principally "cask" table wines. 40% of total wine production.

Pyrenees (Vic) **82'** 84' 85'

> Central Vic. region with seven wineries producing rich minty reds and one or two interesting whites esp. FUMÉ BLANC.

Riverina   (N.S.W.) NV
> Large volume producer centred around Griffith; good quality cask wines esp. whites.

Southern Vales   (Sth Aust) 67' 71' 75' 76' 80' 81' 82' 84' 85' **86'**
> Covers energetic McLaren Vale/Reynella regions on s. outskirts of Adelaide. Big styles now being rapidly refined and improved; promising CHARDONNAY.

Swan Valley   (W. Aust) 75' 78' 81' **82' 84'** 85'
> The birthplace of wine in the west, on the n. outskirts of Perth. Hot climate makes strong low-acid table, good dessert wines. Declining in importance viticulturally.

Tasmania   82' 84' **85'**
> 13 vineyards now offer wine for commercial sale, producing over 200,000 litres in all. Has great potential particularly for CHARDONNAY and P. NOIR.

Upper Hunter   (N.S.W.) 75' 79' 80' 81' 83' 85' 86'
> Est. early 60s; with irrigated vines produce mainly w. wines, lighter and quicker-developing than Hunter w. Often good value.

Yarra Valley ("Lilydale")   76' 78' **80'** 81' 82' **84'** 85' 86'
> Historic wine area near Melbourne fallen into disuse, now being redeveloped by enthusiasts with small wineries. A superb viticultural area with noble varieties only.

Wineries

Allandale   Hunter Valley. Table ★→★★★
> Small winery without v'yds. buying selected local grapes. Quality variable; can be outstanding: esp. CHARD.

All Saints   N.E. Vic. Full range ★
> Famous old family winery with faltering quality.

Angove's   Riverland. Table and dessert ⎡★⎤ →★★
> Family business in Adelaide and Renmark in the Murray Valley. Some interesting fresh white wines recently.

Arrowfield   Upper Hunter. Table ⎡★★⎤
> Substantial vineyard, on irrigated land. Light CABERNET and succulent CHARDONNAY; also "wooded" SEMILLON.

Bailey's   N.E. Vic. Table and dessert ★★→★★★★
> Rich old-fashioned reds of great character, esp. Bundarra Hermitage and magnificent dessert MUSCAT and TOKAY.

Balgownie   Bendigo/Ballarat. Table ⎡★★★★⎤
> Specialist in fine reds, particularly straight CABERNET and P. NOIR. Also exceptional CHARDONNAY. Now owned by MILDARA.

Basedow   Barossa Valley. Table ★★
> Small winery buying grapes for good SHIRAZ, etc.

Berri-Renmano Coop.   Riverland. Full range ★→★★
> By far Aust's largest winery following recent merger with Renmano, selling mostly to other companies. Now developing own brands on local and export markets.

Best's   Great Western. Full range ★→★★
> Conservative old family winery at Great Western with good strong old-style claret, hock and sparkling wines.

Blass, Wolf (Bilyara)   Barossa V. Table and sp. ★★★
> Wolf Blass is the ebullient German winemaker. Dazzling labels and extraordinary wine-show successes, with mastery of blending varieties, areas and lashings of new oak.

Bowen Estate   Coonawarra. Table ⎡★★★⎤
> Small Coonawarra winery; intense CABERNET SAUVIGNON, good RIESLING. Sparkling CHARDONNAY on the way.

Brand   Coonawarra. Table ★★→★★★
> Family estate. Fine, bold and stylish CABERNET and SHIRAZ under the Laira label. A few quality blemishes in late 70's/early 80's, now rectified.

Brokenwood   Hunter Valley. Table ★★★
>Exciting quality of CABERNET SAUVIGNON and SHIRAZ since 1973; new winery 1983 adds high quality CHARD and SEM.

Brown Brothers   Milawa. Full range ★→★★★
>Old family firm with new ideas, wide range of rather delicate varietal wines, many from cool mountain districts. CHARD and dry white MUSCAT outstanding.

Buring, Leo   Barossa. Full range ★★→ ★★★
>"Château Leonay", old white-wine specialists, now owned by LINDEMAN. Outstanding "Reserve Bin" Rhine Riesling.

Campbells of Rutherglen   N.E. Vic. Full range ★★
>Impressive new whites and reds plus good dessert wines.

Cape Mentelle   Margaret River. Table ★★→★★★★
>Idiosyncratic robust CABERNET departs from district style and can be magnificent; also ZINFANDEL.

Capel Vale   S.W. Western Aust. ★★
>Very good CABERNET.

Chambers' Rosewood   N.E. Vic. Full range ★★→ ★★★
>Good cheap table and great dessert wines, esp. TOKAY.

Chateau Le Amon   Bendigo. Table ★★★
>Very stylish minty CAB and peppery SHIRAZ reaffirm this district's suitability for red wine.

Château Hornsby   Alice Springs, N. Territory. ★→★★
>A charming aberration. Full-flavoured clean reds from the Bush.

Château Remy   Great Western/Avoca. Sparkling and Table ★★
>Owned by Remy Martin, run by French-trained champagne maker Christian Morlaes and winemaker wife. Trebbiano surprisingly successful; CHARDONNAY will boost things.

Château Tahbilk   Goulburn Valley. Table ★★ →★★★
>Family-owned wine-estate making CABERNET, SHIRAZ, Rhine Riesling and Marsanne. "Special Bins" are outstanding.

Conti, Paul, Wines   Swan Valley. Table ★★
>Elegant Swan Valley Hermitage, also newly introduced CHARD.

Craigmoor   Mudgee. Table and Port ★★→★★★
>Oldest district winery now part of MONTROSE group with radical lift in quality.

Cullens Willyabrup   Margaret River. Table ★★★
>Brilliant austere CABERNET/MERLOT, pungent SAUV. BLANC and "wooded" CHARDONNAY are typical of the new wave.

d'Arenberg   Southern Vales. Table and dessert ★→★★
>Old-style family outfit with strapping rustic reds.

De Bortoli   Griffith, N.S.W. ★→★★★
>Irrigation-area winery. Standard reds but magnificent sweet "Sauternes".

Drayton   Hunter Valley, N.S.W. Table ★
>Traditional Hermitage and SEMILLON; occasionally good CHARD; recent quality disappointing.

Enterprise Wines   Clare Valley. Table ★★★
>Tim Knappstein, an exceptionally gifted winemaker, produces Rhine Riesling, FUMÉ BLANC and CABERNET SAUVIGNON.

Evans and Tate   Swan Valley. Table ★★→★★★
>Fine and elegant reds principally from the Margaret River Redbrook v'yd. Good SEMILLON too.

Evans Family   Hunter Valley N.S.W. ★★★
>Good CHARD, fermented in new oak, from small v'yd. owned by family of Len Evans.

Hardy's   Southern Vales, Barossa, Keppoch, etc. Full range ★→★★★
>Famous family-run company using and blending wines from several areas, reliable light St. Thomas Burgundy, good Old Castle Riesling and Australia's greatest vintage Ports. Hardy's recently bought HOUGHTON and Reynella; the latter's beautifully restored buildings are now group headquarters.

Heemskerk Tasmania. Table ★★★
> Most successful commercial operation in Tasmania. Herbaceous CAB; promising CHARD. Also P.N. Recent partnership with Louis Roederer plans high class sp. wine in years to come.

Henschke Barossa. Table ★★★
> Family business known for sterling SHIRAZ and good CAB. New high-country v'yds on Adelaide Hills add excitement and variety.

Hickinbotham Winemakers Geelong. Table ★★→★★★
> Innovative winemaking by Hickinbotham family (since 1980) has produced some fascinating styles incl. carbonic maceration, dry ausleses, etc.

Hollick Coonawarra. Table ★★★
> Ian and Wendy Hollick have won instant stardom with trophy and winning CAB; also v.g. CHARD and RIES from small winery.

Houghton Swan Valley, W.A. Full range. ★→ ★★
> The most famous old winery of W.A. Soft, ripe "White Burgundy" is top wine; also excellent CAB. See Hardy's.

Hungerford Hill Hunter Valley and Coonawarra. Table ★→★★★
> Medium-sized winery producing high class varietals esp. RIESLING and CABERNET from COONAWARRA.

Huntington Estate Mudgee. Table ★★→★★★
> New small winery; the best in Mudgee. Fine CABERNETS and clean SEMILLON and CHARDONNAY. Invariably under-priced.

Idyll Geelong. Vic. ★★★
> Small winery with CABERNET of low strength but highest quality.

Jeffrey Grosset Clare. Table ★★→★★★
> Exceedingly elegant w. and r. table wines made in consistent style by fastidious young winemaker Jeffrey Grosset.

Kaiser Stuhl Barossa. Full range ★→★★★
> Now part of Penfolds; a huge winery processes fruit from diverse sources. "Individual v'yd." RIESLINGS are excellent. So are Red Ribbon reds.

Katnook Estate Coonawarra. Table ★★★
> Excellent pricey CAB and CHARD.

Lillydale Vineyards Yarra Valley. Table ★★★
> Foremost producer of CHARD using sophisticated techniques; also scented Gewürztraminer.

Krondorf Wines Barossa Valley. Table ★★→★★★
> Acquired by MILDARA in 1986, but quality and brand image will be preserved.

Lake's Folly Hunter Valley. Table ★★★★
> The work of an inspired surgeon from Sydney. CABERNET and new barrels make fine complex reds. Also excl. CHARDONNAY.

Leeuwin Estate Margaret River. Table ★★→★★★★
> New lavishly equipped estate leading Australia with superb (and very expensive) CHARD; developing P.N., RIES., and CAB.

Lehmann Wines, Peter Barossa. Table ★★
> Defender of the Barossa faith, Lehmann makes vast quantities of wine, mostly sold in bulk and special cuvees under his own label.

Leconfield Coonawarra. Table ★→★★★
> Coonawarra CABERNET of great style. RIESLING less successful.

Lindeman Orig. Hunter, now everywhere. Full range ★→★★★
> One of the oldest firms, now a giant owned by Phillip Morris Corp. Its Ben Ean "Moselle" is a market leader. Owns BURINGS in Barossa and Rouge Homme in COONAWARRA, and most important v'yds at Padthaway producing outstanding CHARD. Many inter-state blends. Pioneers in modernizing wine styles.

McWilliams Hunter Valley and Riverina. Full range ★→★★
> Famous family of Hunter winemakers at Mount Pleasant (HERMITAGE and SEMILLON). Pioneers in RIVERINA with noble varieties, incl. CABERNET and sweet white "Lexia".

Mildara Coonawarra. Murray Valley. Full range ★→★★★
Sherry and brandy specialists at Mildura on the Murray river also making fine CABERNET and RIESLING at COONAWARRA. Now own BALGOWNIE and YELLOWGLEN.

Mitchells Clare Valley. Table ★★★
Small family winery, excellent RIESLING and CABERNET.

Mitchelton Goulburn Valley. Table ★★★
Big modern winery. A wide range incl. v.g. wood-matured Marsanne, CAB and botrytised RIESLING from COONAWARRA.

Montrose Mudgee. Table ★★→★★★
Recent winemaking and marketing initiatives have had much success; superb CHARD, interesting Barbera and Nebbiolo.

Moorilla Estate Tasmania. Table ★★★
Senior winery on outskirts of Hobart on Derwent River producing superb P.N., v.g. CHARD and CAB in tiny quantities.

Morris N.E. Vic. Table and dessert ★★ →★★★★
Old winery at Rutherglen making Aust's greatest dessert muscats and tokays; recently v.g. cheap table wines.

Moss Wood Margaret River. Table ★★★★
Best Margaret River winery (with only 29 acres). CABERNET SAUVIGNON, PINOT NOIR, CHARDONNAY all with rich fruit flavours not unlike the best Californians.

Mount Mary Yarra Valley. Table ★★★★
Dr. John Middleton is a perfectionist boutique maker with CHARD. P. NOIR and CABERNET/CABERNET FRANC/MERLOT.

Orlando (Gramp's) Barossa Valley. Full range ★★→★★★
Great pioneering company, now owned by Reckitt & Colman. Full range from good standard Jacob's Creek Claret to excellent COONAWARRA CABERNET; CHARDONNAY and great Steingarten RIESLING. William Jacob is a low-price line.

Penfold's Orig. Adelaide, now everywhere. Full range ★→★★★★
Ubiquitous and excellent company: in BAROSSA, RIVERINA, COONAWARRA, CLARE VALLEY, etc. Grange Hermitage is ★★★★, St. Henri Claret not far behind. Bin-numbered wines are usually outstanding. "Grandfather Port" is sensational.

Petaluma Adelaide Hills. ★★★★
A recent rocket-like success with CAB, CHARD and RIESLING, now centred around new winery in ADELAIDE HILLS using COONAWARRA and CLARE grapes. Bollinger now part owner, with ambitious sparkling wine v'yds and facilities in ADELAIDE HILLS.

Piper's Brook Tasmania. Table ★★★
Cool-area pioneer with very good RIESLING, P. NOIR, steely CHARD from Tamar Valley near Launceston. Lovely labels.

Plantaganet Mt. Barker. Full range ★★→★★★
The region's largest producer with a wide range of varieties esp. rich CHARD, SHIRAZ and vibrant, potent CAB.

Quelltaler Clare Watervale. Full range ★→★★★
Old winery known for good "Granfiesta" sherry. Recently good Rhine Riesling and SEMILLON. Owned by Remy Martin.

Redman Coonawarra. Red Table ★→★★
The most famous old name in COONAWARRA makes two wines (Claret, CABERNET) in family winery est. 1966. Recent quality disappointing.

Reynella S. Vales. S.A. Full range ★★→★★★
Historic red wine specialists s. of Adelaide. Rich CABERNET, Claret and "port". See Hardy's.

The Robson Vineyard Hunter Valley. Table ★★→★★★
Fastidious winery. Wide range of varietals; CHARDONNAY CABERNET and Hermitage consistently show winners.

Rosemount Upper Hunter and Coonawarra. Table ★→★★★
Bustling newcomer; rich, unctuous HUNTER CHARDONNAY and COONAWARRA CABERNET lead the wide range.

Rothbury Estate   Hunter Valley. Table ★★→ ★★★

Important syndicate-owned wine estate concentrating on traditional HUNTER wines: "Hermitage" and long-lived SEMILLON. New CHARD (from Cowra) and P. NOIR are promising.

St. Huberts   Yarra Valley. Vic. Table ★★→★★★

Small and sometimes fine—much sought-after CABERNET.

St. Leonards   N.E. Vic. Full range ★★

Excellent varieties sold only at cellar door and mailing list, incl. exotics e.g. Fetyaska and Orange Muscat.

Saltram   Barossa. Full range ★→★★★

Seagram-owned winery making wines of variable quality. "Pinnacle Selection" best wines; also Mamre Brook.

Sandalford   Swan Valley. Table ★→★★

Fine old winery with contrasting styles of red and white varietals from Swan and Margaret rivers.

Saxonvale   Hunter Valley. Table ★★

Medium-sized operation now making good early-maturing SEMILLON and CHARDONNAY. Also good soft CABERNET, SHIRAZ. Acquired by WYNDHAM ESTATE, early 1986.

Seppelt   Barossa, Great Western, Keppoch, etc. Full range ★→★★★

Far-flung producers of Australia's most popular "champagne" (Gt. Western Brut), good dessert wines, the reliable Moyston claret and some very good private bin wines from Gt. Western and Drumborg in Victoria, and Keppoch and Barossa in S.A.

Seville Estate   Yarra Valley. Table ★★→★★★

Tiny Yarra Valley winery with well-made CHARDONNAY, very late-picked RIESLING, SHIRAZ, PINOT NOIR, etc.

Stanley   Clare Valley. Full range ★→★★★

Important medium-size quality winery owned by Heinz. Good Rhine Riesling and CABERNET and complex Cabernet-Shiraz-Malbec blends under Leasingham label.

Stanton & Killeen   N.E. Vic. Table and dessert ★★

Small old family firm with rich muscats.

Taltarni   Great Western/Avoca. Table ★★★

Dominique Portet, brother of Bernard (Clos du Val, Napa), son of André (Ch Lafite), produces huge reds, good SAUV. BLANC and fine sparkling wines.

Taylors Wines   Clare Valley. Table ★→★★

Large new red wine-producing unit (CABERNET and HERMITAGE) turning to whites (RHINE RIESLING, generics).

Tisdall Wines   Goulburn Valley. Table ★★→★★★

Exciting young winery in the Echuca river area, making local wines plus finer material from central ranges (Mount Helen CABERNET SAUVIGNON, CHARDONNAY, RHINE RIESLING).

Tollana   Barossa, S.A. Full range ★→★★

Old company famous for brandy, has latterly made some quite fine CABERNET and RHINE RIESLING.

Tulloch   Hunter Valley, N.S.W. Table ★

An old name at Pokolbin, with good dry reds and "RIESLING", now part of PENFOLD's group.

Tyrrell   Hunter Valley, N.S.W. Table ★★→ ★★★

Some of the best traditional Hunter wines, Hermitage and SEMILLON, are "Vat 47". Also big rich CHARDONNAY and delicate PINOT NOIR becoming known in Europe.

Vasse Felix   Margaret River. Table ★★→★★★

The pioneer of the Margaret River. Elegant CABERNETS that have been compared to St. Julien.

Virgin Hills   Bendigo/Ballarat. Table ★★★★

Former Tom Lazar claimed to make the greatest Aust. wine, equal to Bordeaux's best. Since '76 this claim has had substance, notwithstanding subsequent change in ownership and winemaker.

Westfield   Swan Valley. Table ★
> John Kosovich's CABERNETS and Verdelhos show particular finesse in a hot climate.

Wirra Wirra   Southern Vales. Table ★★→★★★
> Under Petaluma influence high quality, beautifully packaged whites and reds have made a big impact recently.

Woodleys   Adel, S.A. Table ★
> Well-known for Queen Adelaide label claret and RIESLING, acquired by SEPPELT's in late 1985.

Wyndham Estate   Branxton, N.S.W. Full range ⬚★⬚ →★★
> Aggressive, large new Hunter group with Richmond Grove, Hunter Estate, Hollydene and Saxonvale as rating divisions.

Wynns   Coonawarra, Southern Vales. Table ⬚★⬚ →★★★
> Large inter-state company, originators of flagon wines, with largest winery and vineyards at COONAWARRA, making good CAB. Together with Seaview, acquired by PENFOLD's in 1985.

Yalumba (S. Smith & Sons)   Barossa. Full range ★→★★★
> Big old family firm with considerable verve, using computers, juice evaluation, etc., to produce full spectrum of high quality wines.

Yarra Yering   Yarra Valley. Table ⬚★★★⬚
> The largest (30 acre) Lilydale boutique winery and one of the best. Esp. racy powerful PINOT and deep CABERNET.

Yellowglen   Bendigo/Ballarat. Sparkling ★★→★★★
> High-flying sparkling winemaker acquired by MILDARA but run autonomously by French-trained Dominique Landragin.

New Zealand

An infant wine industry already making an international impact with fruity and well-balanced table wines from the classic grape varieties. Progress has accelerated since new vineyard areas were planted in the early '70s on both North and South Islands. There are now well over 10,000 acres. White grapes predominate. Müller-Thurgau is the most planted variety.

The general style of wine is relatively light with fairly high acidity. The distinctive flavours of grape varieties are well marked and critical opinion sees a very bright future for the industry. The principal producers are:

Babic
> Old Dalmatian family firm nr. Auckland. Standard "Riesling-Sylvaner"; good GEWÜRZ, CHARD and reds.

Cooks
> Progressive company at Te Kauwhata nr. Auckland. 1,000 acres+ produce fine light CABERNET, CHARDONNAY and GEWÜRZ: also late-picked MÜLLER-THURGAU.

Corbans
> Old-established firm at Henderson, nr. Auckland, now owned by Rothman's. Emphasis on whites. New v'yds at MARLBOROUGH.

Delegat's   Impressive Gisborne whites, esp. CHARD and M-T Auslese.

Gisborne   Major white-grape district in n.e. of North Island.

Glenvale
> Old-established fruit company with 250 acres of vines at Napier, HAWKES BAY. Table wines (esp. "Esk Valley") improving.

Hawkes Bay
> The biggest vineyard area on the east coast of North Island.

Hunter Estate

New producer at MARLBOROUGH and Christchurch. Stunning early CHARD and SAUV. BLANC.

Marlborough

Recently developed vineyard area at north end of South Island, now with over 2,000 acres mostly in white grapes.

Matawhero

Small GISBORNE producer with high-quality GEWÜRZTRAMINER, CHARDONNAY, SAUV and CHENIN BLANC.

McWilliams

Older winery at HAWKES BAY. Related to the Australian company. Some famous old CABERNETS, but current wines led by CHARD.

Montana

The largest winery, originally at GISBORNE, pioneer with fine wines and in planting at MARLBOROUGH. "Blenheimer" MÜLLER-THURGAU is best seller. Marlborough CAB is light; CHARDONNAY and (Gisborne) SAUV are much better.

Nobilo's

Yugoslav family firm, making deep-flavoured, ageable reds at Huapai, n. of Auckland.

Penfolds

Founded 1963 by the Australian company. Grapes from GISBORNE, HAWKES BAY, MARLBOROUGH. Good whites (esp. GEWÜRZ) and CAB.

Te Mata Estate

Old HAWKES BAY property restored, making excellent CABERNET/MERLOT. Also CHARDONNAY, FURMINT.

Vidal's

Highly proficient and atmospheric Hawkes Bay winery. Fine CABERNET, sparkling wine and popular St. Aubyn's Claret.

Villa Maria

Yugoslav family winery nr. Auckland. HAWKES BAY Riesling-Sylvaner is popular. GEWÜRZ, CHARD, SAUV. BLANC, CAB all well made.

South Africa

South Africa has made excellent sherry and port for many years, but has taken table wine seriously only in the past 15 years. Since 1972 a new system of Wines of Origin and registered "estates" has started a new era of competitive modern wine-making. Cabernet Sauvignon reds of high quality are already well established; the signs are that Chardonnay, Sauvignon Blanc and other superior grapes now being introduced will be similarly successful.

Allesverloren ★★

Estate in MALMESBURY with 395 acres of v'yds., well known for "port", and now also specializing in powerful, almost roasted, reds, incl. ripe, soft CABERNET, and Tinta Barocca. Distributed by BERGKELDER.

Alphen ★

Winery originally at Constantia, now at Somerset West. Name is used as a brand by Gilbeys.

Alto ★★

STELLENBOSCH estate of 247 acres high on a hill, best known for massive-bodied CABERNET and a good SHIRAZ-based blend: Alto Rouge. Distributed by BERGKELDER.

Backsberg ★★ → ★★★

A prize-winning 395-acre estate at PAARL with notably good white wines (incl. CHARD.) and med. body CABERNET and SHIRAZ.

Bellingham ★→★★★

Top brand name of UNION WINE. Reliable reds and whites, esp. CABERNET. The GRAND CRU is well known.

Bergkelder

Big wine concern at STELLENBOSCH, member of the OUDE MEESTER group, making and distributing many brands (FLEUR DU CAP, GRÜNBERGER) and estate wines. Now combined with STELLENBOSCH FARMERS' WINERY. See CAPE WINE AND DISTILLERS LTD.

Bertrams ★★

Gilbeys' brand with a wide range of varietals, good CABERNET and SHIRAZ.

Blaauwklippen ★★→★★★

Estate s. of STELLENBOSCH producing top reds, CAB, P. NOIR and ZIN, and good RHINE RIES, and SAUV BLANC.

Boberg Controlled region of origin for fortified wines consisting of the districts of PAARL and TULBAGH.

Bonfoi ★★

Estate in STELLENBOSCH district. CHENIN BLANC (demi-sec) and Cuvée Agée (dry) are marketed through the BERGKELDER.

Boschendal ★★

Vast (617 acre) estate in PAARL area on an old fruit farm. Emphasis on white wines and sparkling "Brut", but CABERNET improving. Also a charming restaurant.

Breede River Valley

Fortified wine region east of Drakenstein Mtns.; hotter than coastal area.

Buitenverwachting

Part of original 17thC Constantia estate, redeveloped with best of vines cellar equipment available. First vintages creditable.

Bukettraube

White-wine grape with high acidity and muscat aroma, most popular as a blend component.

Cabernet

The great Bordeaux grape particularly successful in the COASTAL REGION. Sturdy, long-ageing wines.

Cape Wine and Distillers Ltd.

> The holding company for the reconstructed liquor interests of Oudemeester, STELLENBOSCH FARMERS' WINERY, etc.

Carlonet

> See UITKYK

Cavendish Cape ★★

> Range of remarkably good sherries from the K.W.V.

Chardonnay

> Classic white variety, very rare in S.A. due to official restrictions. Most S.A. bottles carrying Chardonnay labels, vintaged 1985 and earlier, contain Auxerrois, a minor white var., due to widespread smuggling by growers and subsequent confusion.

Chenin Blanc

> Workhorse grape of the Cape; one vine in four. Adaptable and sometimes very good. Alias STEEN. K.W.V. makes a very good example at a bargain price.

Cinsaut

> The principal bulk-producing French red grape in S. Africa; formerly known as Hermitage. Often blended with CABERNET, but can make reasonable wine on its own.

Coastal Region

> Demarcated wine region, includes PAARL, STELLENBOSCH, Durbanville, SWARTLAND, TULBAGH.

Colombard

> The "FRENCH COLOMBARD" of California. Prized in S. Africa for its high acidity and fruity flavour.

Constantia

> Once the world's most famous muscat wine, from the Cape. Now the southernmost district of origin.

Delheim ★★→★★★

> Winery at Driesprong in one of the highest areas of STELLENBOSCH, known for delicate STEEN and GEWÜRZ whites and also light reds: PINOTAGE, SHIRAZ. The CABERNET is more gripping. Grande Reserve (presently pure CAB.) is top class.

Drostdy ★★

> Range of sherries from BERGKELDER.

Edelkeur ★★★★

> Excellent intensely sweet white made with nobly rotten (p. 46) grapes by NEDERBURG.

Estate wine

> A strictly controlled term applying only to registered estates making wines of grapes grown on the same property.

Fleur du Cap ★★

> Popular and well-made range of wines from the BERGKELDER, STELLENBOSCH. Particularly good CABERNET; interesting SAUVIGNON BLANC.

Gewürztraminer

> The famous spicy grape of Alsace, best at Simonsig. Naturally low acidity makes wine-making difficult at the Cape.

Grand Cru (or Premier Grand Cru)

> Term for a totally dry white, with no quality implications. Generally to be avoided.

Goede Hoop ★

> Estate in STELLENBOSCH district. Pleasant blended red bottled and sold by BERGKELDER.

Groot Constantia ★★

> Historic estate, now government-owned, near Cape Town. Source of superlative muscat wine in the early 19th century. Now making wide range of wines, especially good RHINE RIESLING.

Grünberger ★

> Brand of not-quite-dry STEEN white from the BERGKELDER.

Hamilton–Russell ★★
> New estate in cool coastal valley. Very promising PINOT NOIR, also Bordeaux-style red, CHARDONNAY and SAUVIGNON BLANC.

Hanepoot
> Local name for Muscat of Alexandria, widely grown for sweet dessert wines.

Hartenberg ★★
> Previously known as Montagne, this Stel. estate still produces fine CABERNET and SHIRAZ. Whites less good.

Hazendal ★★
> Family estate in w. STELLENBOSCH specializing in semi-sweet STEEN, marketed by the BERGKELDER.

Jacobsdal ★
> Estate in STELLENBOSCH district, overlooking False Bay. PINOTAGE bottled and sold by BERGKELDER.

Kanonkop ★★★
> Outstanding estate in n. STELLENBOSCH, specializing in high-quality and particularly full-bodied CABERNET, and PINOTAGE. Paul Sauer Fleur is a Bordeaux-style blend.

Klein Constantia
> Sophisticated new estate. No expense spared in plan to create wines of equivalent quality to original Constantia muscats.

Koopmanskloof ★
> STELLENBOSCH estate making good dry Chenin Blanc-based blend "Blanc de Marbonne".

K.W.V.
> The Kooperatieve Wijnbouwers Vereniging, S. Africa's national wine co-operative originally organized by the State to absorb embarrassing surpluses, at vast and splendidly equipped premises in PAARL making a range of good wines, particularly sherries.

Laborie ★
> New K.W.V.-owned showpiece estate on Paarl Mtn. CABERNET and PINOTAGE-based Blanc de Noirs sparkling.

Landgoed
> South African for Estate; a word which appears on all estate-wine labels and official seals.

Landskroon ★
> Family estate owned by Paul and Hugo de Villiers. Mainly port-type wines for K.W.V. but recently some good dry reds – PINOT NOIR, TINTA BAROCCA and CABERNETS Sauv. and Franc.

Late Harvest Term for a mildly sweet wine. "Special Late Harvest" must be naturally sweet. "Noble Late Harvest" is the highest quality level of all.

Le Bonheur ★★★
> Stellenbosch estate producing Cape's finest white, Blanc Fumé, a non-wooded SAUVIGNON BLANC.

J.C. Le Roux ★
> Old Cape brand revived as BERGKELDER'S sparkling wine house. Currently a SAUVIGNON BLANC (Charmat) and PINOT NOIR (Méthode Champenoise).

Malmesbury
> Centre of the SWARTLAND wine district, on the w. coast n. of Cape Town, specializing in dry whites and distilling wine.

Meerendal ★★
> Estate near Durbanville producing robust reds (esp. SHIRAZ and PINOTAGE) marketed by the BERGKELDER.

Meerlust ★★★
> Beautiful old family estate s. of STELLENBOSCH making outstanding CABERNET and Rubicon (Médoc-style blend) marketed by the BERGKELDER. They age faster than some S.A. reds.

Monis ★→★★
> Well-known wine concern of PAARL, with fine "Vintage Port".

Montpellier ★
> Pioneering TULBAGH estate with 370 acres of v'yds. specializing in white wine. Recent wines have been distinctly dull.

Muratie ★
> Ancient estate in STELLENBOSCH, best known for its port and PINOT NOIR. 110 acres of v'yds. also grow CABERNET, RIESLING, STEEN and CINSAUT.

Nederburg ★★→★★★★
> The most famous wine farm in modern S. Africa, operated by the STELLENBOSCH FARMERS' WINERY. Its annual auction is a major event. Pioneer in modern cellar practice and with fine CABERNET, "Private Bin" blends, EDELKEUR and GEWÜRZ. Also good sparkling wines and Paarl RIESLINGS.

Neethlingshof ★
> New management have started an ambitious planting programme to lift quality. Full-bodied Colombard and CABERNET best.

Overberg
> Demarcated wine district in the Caledon area, COASTAL REGION, with some of the coolest Cape vineyards.

Overgaauw ★→★★★
> Estate w. of STELLENBOSCH making good STEEN, very good CABERNET, and Tria Corda, a CABERNET/MERLOT blend.

Paarl
> South Africa's wine capital, 30 miles n.e. of Cape Town, and the surrounding demarcated district, among the best in the country, particularly for white wine and sherry. Most of its wine is made by co-operatives. See also BOBERG.

Paarlsack ★
> Well-known range of sherries made at PAARL by the K.W.V.

Pinot Noir
> Like counterparts in California and Australia, Cape producers struggle to get complexity of flavour. Best are HAMILTON RUSSELL, BLAAUWKLIPPEN, MEERLUST.

Pinotage
> South African red grape, a cross between PINOT NOIR and CINSAUT, useful for high yields and hardiness. Its wine is lush and fruity but never first-class.

Premier Grand Cru See GRAND CRU

Rhine Riesling
> Produces full-flavoured dry and off-dry wines. Generally needs two years or more of bottle age. See WEISSER RIESLING.

Riesling
> South African Riesling (actually Crouchen Blanc) is very different to RHINE RIESLING, which has only recently been planted in any quantity in S. Africa.

Rietvallei ★★
> New ROBERTSON estate. Excellent fortified Muscadel.

Robertson
> Small demarcated district e. of the Cape and inland. Mainly dessert wines (notably Muscat), but red and white table wines are on the increase. Includes Bonnievale. Irrigated vineyards.

Roodeberg ★★
> High-quality brand of blended red wine from the K.W.V. Has good colour, body and flavour and ages well in bottle.

Rustenberg ★★★
> Effectively, if not officially, an estate red wine from just n.e. of STELLENBOSCH. Rustenberg Dry Red is a good CABERNET/CINSAUT blend. The straight CABERNET is outstanding. Also promising PINOT NOIR.

Sauvignon Blanc

Adapting well to warm conditions. Widely grown and marketed in both "wooded" and "unwooded" styles.

Schoongezicht ★

Partner of RUSTENBERG, one of S. Africa's most beautiful old farms and producer of agreeable white wine from STEEN, RIESLING and Clairette Blanche. Now registered as an estate.

Shiraz

The red Rhône grape, recently gaining in popularity in S. Africa for rich deep-coloured wine.

Simonsig ★★

Estate owned by F.J. Malan, pioneering estate producer. Produces a wide range, incl. GEWÜRZ, Vin Fumé, wood-matured dry white and a "Méthode Champenoise".

Simonsvlei

One of S. Africa's best-known co-operative cellars, just outside PAARL. A prize-winner with PINOTAGE.

Spier ★→★★

Estate of five farms w. of STELLENBOSCH producing reds and whites. COLOMBARD and PINOTAGE are best.

Steen South Africa's commonest white grape, said to be a clone of the CHENIN BLANC. It gives strong, tasty and lively wine, sweet or dry, normally better than S. African RIESLING.

Stein

Name used for any medium dry white wine.

Stellenbosch

Town and demarcated district 30 miles e. of Cape Town, extending to the ocean at False Bay. Most of the best estates, esp. for red wine, are in the mountain foothills of the region.

Stellenbosch Farmers' Winery (S.F.W.)

South Africa's biggest winery (after the K.W.V.) with several ranges of wines, incl. NEDERBURG and ZONNEBLOEM. Wide range of med.- and low-priced wines. See CAPE WINE AND DISTILLERS.

Stellenryck ★★★

Top-quality BERGKELDER range, RHINE RIESLING, Fumé Blanc and CABERNET.

Superior

An official designation of quality for WINES OF ORIGIN. The wine must meet standards set by the Wine & Spirit Board.

Swartland

Demarcated district around MALMESBURY. ALLESVERLOREN is the best estate.

Tassenberg ★

Popular and good-value red table wine known to thousands as Tassie.

Theuniskraal ★★

Well-known TULBAGH estate specializing in white wines, esp. RIESLING, GEWÜRZTRAMINER and Sémillon. Distributed by the BERGKELDER.

Tulbagh

Demarcated district n. of PAARL best known for the white wines of MONTPELLIER, THEUNISKRAAL and TWEE JONGEGEZELLEN, and the dessert wines from Drostdy. See also BOBERG.

Twee Jongegezellen ★★

Estate at TULBAGH. One of the great pioneers which revolutionized S. African wine in the 1950s, still in the family of its 18th-century founder. Mainly white wine, incl. RIESLING, STEEN and SAUVIGNON BLANC. Best wines: "Schanderl" and "T.J.39". The name means "two young friends". Exports via GILBEYS.

Uiterwyk ★★

Old estate w. of STELLENBOSCH making a very good CABERNET SAUVIGNON and pleasant whites.

Uitkyk ★★

Old estate at STELLENBOSCH famous for Carlonet (big gutsy CABERNET) and Carlsheim (chiefly SAUV BLANC) white. Now 400 acres. Distribution by BERGKELDER.

Union Wine

Company with HQ in Wellington, near PAARL. Brand names Culemborg and BELLINGHAM.

Van Loveren ★

Robertson producer of full-flavoured whites from irrigated vineyards.

Van Riebeck

Co-operative at Riebeck Kasteel, MALMESBURY, known for pioneering work in white wine technology.

Vergenoegd ★★→★★★

Old family estate in s. STELLENBOSCH supplying high-quality sherry to the K.W.V. but recently offering deeply flavoured CABERNET and excellent SHIRAZ under an estate label.

Villiera ★★→★★★

Paarl estate with Tradition top class Méthode Champenoise, good SAUVIGNON BLANC and RHINE RIESLING.

Vriesenhof ★★★

Small-scale winery with vines high on Stellenbosch mountain slope where Jan Boland Coetzee is making highly rated CABERNET.

Weisser Riesling

Alias Rhine Riesling. Considerably finer than the S.A. RIESLING, which it is gradually replacing.

Welgemeend ★★★

Boutique PAARL estate producing delicate and complex Bordeaux blend, fine CABERNET and Amadé, a Grenache, SHIRAZ and Pinotage blend.

Weltevrede ★→★★

Progressive ROBERTSON estate. Colombard and blended whites and fortified wines.

De Wetshof ★★

Pioneering estate in ROBERTSON district marketed by BERGKELDER. CHARDONNAY, SAUVIGNON BLANC and a sweet noble-rot white, Edeloes.

Wine of Origin

The S. African equivalent of Appellation Contrôlée. Demarcated regions are described on these pages.

Worcester

Demarcated wine district round the Breede and Hex river valleys, e. of PAARL. Many co-operative cellars make mainly dessert wines, brandy and dry whites.

Zandvliet ★★

Estate in the ROBERTSON area marketing a light SHIRAZ through the BERGKELDER.

Zonnebloem ★★

Good-quality brand of CABERNET, RIESLING, PINOTAGE and SHIRAZ from the STELLENBOSCH FARMERS' WINERY.

A few words about words

In the shorthand essential for this little book (and sometimes in bigger books as well) wines are often described by adjectives that can seem irrelevant, inane – or just silly. What do "fat", "round", "full", "lean" and so on mean, when used about wine? Some of the more irritatingly vague are expanded in this list:

Attack
The first impression of the wine in your mouth. It should "strike" positively, if not necessarily with force. Without attack it is feeble.

Attractive
Means "I like it, anyway". A slight put-down for expensive wines; encouragement for juniors. At least a refreshing drink.

Big
Concerns the whole flavour, including the alcohol content. Sometimes implies clumsiness, the opposite of elegance. Generally positive, but big is easy in California and less usual in, say, Bordeaux. So the context matters.

Charming
Rather patronizing when said of wines that should have more impressive qualities. Implies lightness, possibly slight sweetness. A standard comment on Loire wines.

Deep/ depth
This wine is worth tasting with attention. There is more to it than the first impression; it fills your mouth with developing flavours as though it had an extra dimension. (Deep colour simply means hard to see through.) All really fine wines have depth.

Easy
Used in the sense of "easy come, easy go". An easy wine makes no demand on your palate (or intellect). The implication is that it drinks smoothly, doesn't need maturing, and all you will remember was a pleasant drink.

Elegant
A professional taster's favourite term when he is stuck to describe a wine whose proportions (of strength, flavour, aroma), whose attack, middle and finish, whose texture and all its qualities call for comparison with other forms of natural beauty, as in the movement of horses, the forms and attitudes of women . . . .

Fat
With flavour and texture that fills your mouth, but without aggression. Obviously inappropriate in e.g. a light Moselle, but what you pay your money for in Sauternes.

Finish
See Length

Firm
Flavour that strikes the palate fairly hard, with fairly high acidity or tannic astringency giving the impression that the wine is in youthful vigour and will age to gentler things. An excellent quality with high-flavoured foods, and almost always positive.

Flesh
Refers to both substance and texture. A fleshy wine is fatter than a "meaty" wine, more unctuous if less vigorous. The term is often used of good Pomerols, whose texture is notably smooth.

Fresh	Implies a good degree of fruity acidity, even a little nip of sharpness, as well as the zip and zing of youth. All young whites should be fresh: the alternative is flatness, staleness . . . ugh.
Fruity	Used for almost any quality, but really refers to the body and richness of wine made from good ripe grapes. A fruity aroma is not the same as a flavoury one. Fruitiness usually implies at least a slight degree of sweetness.
Full	Interchangeable with full-bodied. Lots of "vinosity" or wineyness: the mouth-filling flavours of alcohol and "extract" (all the flavouring components) combined.
Hollow	Lacking a satisfying middle flavour. Something seems to be missing between first flavour and last. A characteristic of wines from greedy proprietors who let their vines produce too many grapes. An extremely hollow wine is "empty".
Lean	A bit more flesh would be an improvement. Lack of mouth-filling flavours: often astringent as well. But occasionally a term of appreciation of a distinct and enjoyable style.
Length	The flavours and aromas that linger after swallowing. In principle the greater the length the better the wine. One second of flavour after swallowing = one "caudalie". Ten caudalies is good; 20 terrific.
Light	With relatively little alcohol and body, as in most German wines. A very desirable quality in the right wines.
Meaty	Savoury in effect with enough substance to chew. The inference is lean meat; leaner than in "fleshy".
Oaky	Smelling or tasting (or both) of fresh-sawn oak; e.g. a new barrel.
Plump	The diminutive of fat, implying a degree of charm as well.
Rich	Not necessarily sweet, but giving an opulent impression.
Robust	In good heart, vigorous, and on a fairly big scale.
Rough	Flavour and texture give no pleasure. Acidity and/or tannin are dominant and coarse.
Round	Almost the same as fat, but with more approval.
Stylish	Style is bold and definite; wears its cap on its ear.
Supple	Often used of young red wines which might be expected to be more aggressive. More lively than an "easy" wine, with implications of good quality.
Well-balanced	Contains all the desirable elements (acid, alcohol, flavours, etc) in appropriate and pleasing proportions.

What to drink in an ideal world

Wines at their peak in 1987

Red Bordeaux:
Top growths of 1980, 1976, 1973, 1971, 1966, 1964, 1961 . . .
Other Crus Classés of 1980, 1979, 1976, 1975, 1973, 1971, 1970, 1966 . . .
Petits châteaux of 1982, 1981, 1979, 1978, 1976, 1975, 1970

Red Burgundy
Top growths of 1982, 1980, 1979, 1973, 1971, 1969, 1966, 1964 . . .
Premiers Crus of 1984, 1982, 1980, 1979, 1978, 1976, 1971
Village wines of 1984, 1982, 1980, 1979, 1978, 1976

White Burgundy
Top growths of 1982, 1981, 1979, 1978, 1973, 1971, 1969 . . .
Premiers Crus of 1983, 1982, 1981, 1979, 1978, 1973 . . .
Village wines of 1984, 1983, 1981

Sauternes
Top growths of 1981, 1980, 1979, 1978, 1976, 1975, 1971, 1970, 1967 . . .
Other wines of 1983, 1982, 1980, 1979, 1978, 1976, 1975 . . .

Sweet Loire wines
Top growths of (Anjou/Vouvray) 1981, 1979, 1978, 1976, 1975, 1973, 1971, 1969, 1964, 1961 . . .

Alsace
Grands Crus and late-harvest wines of 1983, 1981, 1979, 1978, 1976 . . .
Standard wines of 1985, 1984, 1983

Rhône
Hermitage/top Northern Rhône reds of 1980, 1979, 1978, 1976, 1973, 1971, 1969
Châteauneuf-du-Pape of 1981, 1979, 1978, 1976 . . .

German wines
Great sweet wines of 1976, 1975, 1971 . . .
Ausleses of 1983, 1981, 1979, 1976 . . .
Spätleses of 1983, 1981, 1979, 1976 . . .
Kabinett and QbA wines of 1985, 1984, 1983, 1982, 1981, 1979

Californian
Top Cabernets, Pinot Noirs, Zinfandels of 1979, 1978, 1977, 1976, 1975, 1974 . . .
Most Cabernets etc. of 1982, 1981, 1980, 1979, 1978 . . .
Top Chardonnays of 1982, 1981, 1979 . . .
Most Chardonnays of 1984, 1983 . . .

Vintage Port 1975, 1970, 1967, 1966, 1963, 1960 . . .

The 1985 vintage

Anyone who experienced the heatwave of vintage time in northern Europe in 1985 will have no problem notching it up as an all-round success—a rare year (although '83 was one as well) when most growers were happy about the quality of their wine if not always the quantity. Heatwaves at vintage time bring risks as well. It takes proficiency to pick at the right moment and not to let the fermenting vat overheat.

Bordeaux and Burgundy are both very pleased with their splendid ripe red wines (the whites have low acidity). Pomerol and St-Emilion are ecstatic. Champagne, Alsace and the Loire made very good wines. Germany had a very useful, if not outstanding harvest. Italy reports a very good vintage indeed in most regions. Nor was there anything to complain about in California or Australia, where we can expect excellent wines in most categories.

Quick reference vintage charts for France and Germany

These charts give a picture of the range of qualities made in the principal areas (every year has its relative successes and failures) and a guide to whether the wine is ready to drink or should be kept.

drink now   ▬ needs keeping   ✓ can be drunk with pleasure now, but the better wines will continue to improve

▮ no good   10 the best

(There are often wines in several categories.)

FRANCE

	Red Bordeaux		White Bordeaux	
	Médoc/Graves	Pom/St-Em.	Sauternes & sw.	Graves & dry
85	6–9	7–10	6–8	5–7
84	4–7	2–5	4–7	6–8
83	6–8	6–9	6–10	7–9
82	7–10	7–9	3–7	7–9
81	5–8	6–9	5–8	7–8
80	4–6	3–5	5–9	5–7
79	5–8	5–9	6–8	4–6
78	6–9	6–8	4–6	7–9
77	3–5	2–5	2–4	6–7
76	6–8	7–8	7–9	4–8
75	9–10	8–10	8–10	8–10
74	4–6	3–5	0	4–6
73	5–6	5–7	2–4	7–8
72	2–5	2–4	2–4	4–5
71	5–8	6–8	8–9	8–9
70	9–10	9–10	9–10	9–10
67	5–7	6–8	7–10	8–10

	Red Burgundy	White Burgundy		
	Côte d'Or	Côte d'Or	Chablis	Alsace
85	7–10	5–8	5–8	7–10
84	3–6	4–7	4–7	4–6
83	5–9	6–9	7–9	8–10
82	4–7	4–8	6–7	6–8
81	3–6	4–8	6–9	7–8
80	4–7	4–6	5–7	3–5
79	5–6	6–8	6–8	7–8
78	8–10	7–9	7–10	6–8
77	2–4	4–6	5	3–5
76	7–10	7–8	8	10
75	0–5	4–8	8–10	9
74	2–5	5–8	6–8	6–7
73	4–7	8	7–8	7–8

Beaujolais: 85 is the vintage to buy and drink. Mâcon-Villages (white): 85, 84, 83 are good now. **Loire:** Sweet Anjou and Touraine. Best recent vintages: 85, 84, 83, 82, 79, 78, 76. **Upper Loire:** Sancerre and Pouilly-Fumé 85, 84 are good now. **Muscadet:** D.Y.A.

GERMANY

	Rhône			Rhine	Moselle
85	6–8		85	6–8	6–9
84	5–7		84	4–6	4–6
83	6–9		83	6–9	7–10
82	5–8		82	4–6	4–7
81	5–7		81	5–8	4–8
80	6–8		80	4–7	3–7
79	6–9		79	8–10	6–8
78	8–10		78	5–7	4–7
77	4–6		77	5–7	4–6
76	6–9		76	9–10	9–10
75	0–5		75	7–9	8–10
74	4–7		74	3–6	2–4
73	5–8		73	6–7	6–8
72	6–9		72	2–5	1–4
71	7–9		71	9–10	10

N.B. Detailed charts will be found on pages 22, 23 (France), 100 (Germany).

Notes